John Rogers, Edward Rogers

Some Account of the Life and Opinions of a Fifth-Monarchy-Man

John Rogers, Edward Rogers

Some Account of the Life and Opinions of a Fifth-Monarchy-Man

ISBN/EAN: 9783744622257

Printed in Europe, USA, Canada, Australia, Japan

Cover: Foto ©Thomas Meinert / pixelio.de

More available books at **www.hansebooks.com**

SOME ACCOUNT OF

THE LIFE AND OPINIONS OF A

Fifth-Monarchy-Man.

CHIEFLY EXTRACTED FROM THE WRITINGS

of JOHN ROGERS, Preacher,

by THE REV. EDWARD ROGERS, M.A.

Student of Chrift Church, Oxford.

" *The chief of thefe, among the Laiety, were Major-General Harrifon, Mr. John Carew, Colonel Rich ; among the Clergy, Mr. Rogers, Mr. Feak, Mr. Sympfon.*"--OLDMIXON's Hiftory of the Stuarts.

LONDON:

LONGMANS, GREEN, READER AND DYER.

1867.

G

PREFACE.

HE following account can claim no attention on the ground of the merits and
importance of a Fifth-Monarchy-Man,
whofe name has been forgotten for
nearly two hundred years. If it fhould
prove interefting, it muft be becaufe it
prefents the " vera effigies," the life-like and authentic por-
trait of one who, with much perfonal fingularity, is no
unfair reprefentative of a faction which by its turbulent
fanaticifm earned for itfelf a momentary influence on politics, the hearty abhorrence of its opponents, and a certain
place in hiftory.

In the endeavour to conftruct a likenefs of fuch a man
as *John Rogers* appeared to his contemporaries and to himfelf, I have ftudioufly availed myfelf of his own words,
for in truth it is fcarcely fo much what he thought, did,
and fuffered, as the manner in which he himfelf defcribed
what he thought, did and fuffered, which will enable the
reader to underftand him.

In thus compiling his life, chiefly from his own writings,
my great difficulty has arifen from his exceeding volubility.
"You will talk, I fee," *Oliver Cromwell* faid to him,

"although it be nothing to the purpofe." As he talked
fo he wrote; mixing with much that is terfe and graphic a
far greater quantity of what is tedious and irrelevant. I
have been forced, therefore, to include in my extracts only
fo much as anfwered fome purpofe, omitting without fcruple
what I did not want, whether a word, a phrafe, or a paragraph. By thefe excifions the continuity of my extracts
has been fo often interrupted that I have found it impoffible,
without perplexing the reader and disfiguring my book,
even to mark their places by afterifks; I have printed,
therefore, as confecutive what in ftrictnefs fhould have been
printed as a feries of fragments.

This acknowledgment applies chiefly to the hiftory of
Rogers' early life and of his prifon fufferings, to the Epiftle
to Purleigh, and to the five Epiftles to *Cromwell.* In fome
of thefe, too, I have occafionally interpolated a word
(within brackets) for the fake of grammar, or fubftituted a
fynonym for an expreffion which might unduly offend our
modern fenfe of decorum.

In the Narrative of his interview with *Oliver Cromwell*
I have indicated the omiffions by the ufual figns.

In dealing with his controverfial works, " Bethfhemefh "
and " Sagrir," and with *Crofton's* " Bethfhemefh Clouded,"
I have only aimed at giving a general and juft idea of their
ftyle and the more characteriftic parts of their contents; I
have therefore not fcrupled to extract, to re-arrange, or to
condenfe, and that either in my own words, or in thofe of the
refpective authors, according to my judgment and conve-
nience.

In extracts from books of the feventeenth century, the
fpelling and dates have been modernifed except in a few in-

ſtances, where either inadvertently, or for ſome expreſs purpoſe, the old form of ſpelling has been retained.   Some of the more evident miſprints, with which books of that period abounded, have been corrected.

I have only further to expreſs my cordial acknowledgments to *Colonel J. L. Cheſter,* of the United States of America, the author of " The Life of John Rogers, the Marian Protomartyr," whoſe biographical ſketch of the Fifth-Monarchy-Man in that book furniſhed me with authorities from which I commenced my own inquiries, and who has given me much friendly and valuable aſſiſtance in the courſe of them.

CONTENTS.

CHAPTER I.

Contents.

Contents.

Contents.

Contents.

Contents.

Contents.

LIFE AND OPINIONS OF A

Fifth-Monarchy-Man.

CHAPTER I.

OHN ROGERS, the Fifth-Monarchy-Man, was the fon of *Nehemiah Rogers*, Preben- dary of Ely in the reign of Charles I, and the grandfon of *Vincent Rogers*, minifter of Stratford-le-Bow, in the reign of Elizabeth. Family tradition affigns to him and them a defcent from *John Rogers*, the firft fufferer for religion in the reign of Mary.

The life and charaéter of Nehemiah are only remarkable for the contraft they afford to the life and charaéter of his fon. He was born in 1594, loft his father, Vincent, when he was eight years old, and was educated at Merchant Tailors' School and at Cambridge, where he became fellow of Jefus. Afterwards, as a clergyman of the Church of England, he held the curacy of St. Margaret's, Fifh Street, London, from which he was transferred to the vicarage of Meffing in Effex. In 1632 he publifhed a fermon which he had preached at Kelvedon, on the occafion of Laud's fecond triennial vifitation. In 1635 Laud announced to the prefident of St. John's, Oxford, that he had procured for the college the perpetual inheritance of the Reétory of Gatton, adding, "He that gives it to the college for my fake is *Mr. Nehemiah Rogers*, now a minifter in Effex, and a man of good note. . . To whom and in what order this benefice upon

B

Laud's Works,
Ang. Cath.
Lib. vol. vii. p.
242.

Newcourt's
Repertorium,
vol. i. p. 313.

Walker's
Sufferings of
Clergy, part ii.
p. 22.

every avoidance fhall be given, *Mr. Rogers* hath left wholly to my care." In 1636 he was preferred to a prebend at Ely, and in 1642 to the Rectory of St. Botolph's, Bifhopfgate, London. In 1642 and 1643 the Puritans caft out from their parfonages all the clergy of the Church of England who remained conftant to Church and King. *Nehemiah Rogers* fhared the fate of his brethren, and was thrown forth deftitute on the world.

Like many others of the loyal clergy, when he loft his own home he found another in the homes of the country gentry. In procefs of time, but with great difficulty, he procured liberty to exercife his miniftry, and during the later years of his life he officiated in various parifhes in Effex. He died in 1660, a few days before Charles II. was publicly proclaimed in London.

He was a diligent writer while he could fafely publifh— that is to fay, before 1640 and after 1658. His works, which were chiefly in expofition of the Parables, appear to have been popular in their day, but have not obtained any lafting reputation. One merit, however, they poffefs, for which they are here referred to ; they reflect very clearly the character of the author, and it is in them that the contraft between father and fon ftands out moft diftinctly. Unlike his fon, *Nehemiah Rogers* was of a gentle and peaceful difpofition, and of moderate opinions ; unlike his fon, he had the art of conciliating thofe with whom he was brought in contact ; and unlike his fon, he loved to dwell not on political, but on practical religion, not on the iniquity of his adverfaries, but on the kindnefs of his friends. Thefe characteriftics are moft vifible in his dedications, and efpecially in the earlieft and the lateft of them. Two or three extracts from thefe compofitions, which are devoted, as he tells us, " to the teftification of a thankful heart to thofe from whom he had received undeferved kindnefs," feem to illuftrate his temper, and to a certain extent that of the times in which he lived. His firft dedications are to the London citizens, of whofe hofpitality he had partaken in the good old times of King James I. " While I live," he fays, " I fhall confefs your love, and the encouragement I had amongft you. What Candala, Queen of Pannonia, fometimes faid to the Venetians for her royal entertainment, that fhe never knew herfelf to be queen till fhe came to their territories, I think the preachers of the Gofpel may

Parable of
Prodigal Son,
2nd Ed. 1632,

fay, hardly can they know themfelves, by their entertainment in the world, to be minifters of Jefus Chrift, till they come to Londoners' houfes and tables."

His lateſt dedications are to his pariſhioners in Eſſex, or to
thoſe friends and patrons among the country gentry who had
befriended him in his adverſity and old age. He thus writes to
the worſhipful and religious gentleman, *Mr. Thomas Roberts*, of
Little Braxted in Eſſex ; and to the pious and religious gentlewoman, *Mrs. Dorothy Roberts*, his virtuous and worthy wife :—
" Good Sir . . . . To you I am many ways obliged for
your abundant favours and fruits of love really expreſſed even
then when it pleaſed God moſt to darken my outward eſtate.
For three years' ſpace I moſt comfortably enjoyed my miniſtry
through God's goodneſs and yours in that pariſh where you now
dwell, all which time I found your houſe to be both to me and
mine, as the houſe of Oneſiphorus was to Paul, a houſe of
great refreſhment. . . . . Good *Mrs. Roberts* . . . .
To myſelf you have been like that godly Shunamite to Eliſha ;
you have joined as a partner to your huſband in his love and
bounty, providing light and lodging, houſe room and firing, and
other neceſſaries fitting for an Eliſha ; and therefore I make
bold to join you with him in this dedication, craving the like
acceptance from you as from him." . . . .

    Thus, too, he commemorates the kindneſs of another of his
lay patrons, *Mr. Edward Herrys*, of Much Badow :—" Worthy
Sir . . . . Your friendly favours I may not bury in a
kind of tacit acknowledgment, but I muſt needs acquaint the
world with part of them. Under God, you were the principal
means of my obtaining my liberty for the exerciſing of my
miniſterial funćtions, and that in ſuch a time when it was
thought ſcarce feaſible. You engaged your friends in it and
were at coſt about it, and at length effećted it, to my great
comfort and content, who, having ſerved my Lord and Maſter
ſix full 'prenticeſhips in the works of the Goſpel, could not be
but much troubled now in my old age, to be turned out of my
ſervice, and have my indenture torn before death brought me
my freedom, which I daily expećt, wanting but few of thoſe
years which David allows in common account to the days of
man. This being done, yet you had not done, but were pleaſed,
having the power in your hand, to remove me from that place
where I was, from which I muſt confeſs I was drawn with much
unwillingneſs, and preſent me to a living then vacant and in
your power to diſpoſe of, where, with the general deſire and

Figleſs fig-tree,
1659.
Epiſtle
dedicatory.

2 Tim. i. 16.

" The Faſt
Friend," 1658.
Epiſtle
dedicatory.

Ps. xc. 10.

good liking of the people as yet I am . . . . I have not been altogether idle in my younger time, no, not in a tempeftuous feafon (to the glory of God who hath enabled me I fpeak it); albeit I fee great caufe, now that my almond tree doth bloom, and the weather ferves, to double my diligence that my laft works may be more than my firft."

Eccles. xii. 5.

Rev. ii. 19.

The following is part of his farewell to the parifhioners from whom he had been drawn with fo much reluctance, and affords a curious contraft to a farewell addrefs from his fon John, which will appear hereafter:—

Infra, p. 34.

Infra, p. 34.

" Faft Friend."
Epift. to the
Reader.
Galat. iv. 19.
2 Cor. xii. 15.

" Friendly Reader,— . . . . Whilft God was pleafed to caft out my lot amongft you at St. Ofyth* for the fpace of fix years and upwards, I can comfortably ufe the Apoftle's words —I travailed with pain, that Chrift might be found in you. . . . . St. Paul goes further, and tells the Corinthians, notwithftanding this, yet the more abundantly he loved, the lefs he was beloved of them; but that was not my cafe, and it was a great part of my happinefs that it was fo, for it is many a good minifter's cafe. I found you for the generality at my firft coming amongft you to be a moft loving and willing people, and fo you continued (fo many as God continued life unto), even unto the time of my departing from you; you prevented me with your abundant courtefies, nor could I modeftly defire anything of you that was not readily granted. To which, if I fhould add the great encouragement I had from thofe honourable perfons now refiding amongft you, both in countenancing my miniftry and other great favours received, it may raife a wonder how it came about that I deferted you. . . . And now that I am removed from you, I cannot forget you, and my defire is that I may not be forgotten by you. That I remember you thefe few lines may let you underftand, and that I may not be forgotten of you my hearty defire is that my labours amongft you may live in your hearts and lives. . . . . And fo, brethren, I com-

---

* From a manufcript lift of the livings in Effex about the year 1653, it appears that St. Ofyth had then " neither parfonage nor vicarage," and that Mr. Nehemiah Rogers, the Incumbent, was " maintained by the Countefs of Rivers."—*Lanfdowne MSS.* 459.

mend you to God and to the word of his grace, which is able to build you up and to give you an inheritance amongſt all them which are ſanctified (Acts xx. 32), being the laſt text that was preached among you by him who is

A ſervant to you all
for the furtherance of
your ſouls' ſalvation,

Doddinghurſt,   NEHEMIAH ROGERS.
July 22, 1658."

St. Oſyth, the pariſh which Nehemiah left, muſt have been a remarkable pariſh in thoſe days, but Doddinghurſt, to which he was transferred, muſt have been even more ſo. He tells the inhabitants that God had ſo bleſſed the labours of his predeceſſors " that there is not for anything that yet I perceive at preſent any faction or fraction amongſt you, no Papiſt, Anabaptiſt, Quaker, or any ſuch like ſchiſmatic ; you live in amity and peace one with another (generally), which is not ordinary, and in theſe times a ſingular mercy."

The feelings with which he regarded the civil war and its conſequences are ſufficiently indicated in the following paſſage from a ſermon, which he publiſhed about ſix weeks before the death of *Oliver Cromwell :*—" Let us look backward, and then take forward. How can we, in the firſt place, but lament and bewail our horrible ingratitude and unkind dealing with ſo bountiful and liberal a maſter. Marvellous hath been God's dealings towards this land and nation. Never any nation under Heaven that taſted more of the riches of God's bounty, nor ſtood more bound to God than this for his liberality. What peace ! what plenty ! what deliverances ! What brightneſs of heavenly light for fourſcore years did we enjoy ! Whilſt our neighbour nations were wearied with bloody wars, and ſcarce received any other dew than the blood of the inhabitants, we ſat under our own vines and fig-trees, having peace within our walls and plenteouſneſs within our palaces. We ſlept when they bled, we abounded when they wanted, we ſurfeited when they ſtarved. Our ſun did ſhine out glorioufly whilſt theirs was ſet. We had magiſtrates, miniſters, ſchools, churches, laws, trade, all of the beſt, whilſt they would have been glad of the worſt, being deprived of them all. Aſk Bohemia, aſk Germany, what they thought of us. Would they not ſay, Happy

Deut. xxxiii. 29.

Deut. iv. 7.

art thou, O England! who is like unto thee, O people faved
by the Lord? That which Mofes faid to Ifrael might be made
ours (Deut. iv. 7): 'What nation is there fo great, who hath
God fo nigh to them as the Lord our God is in all things we call
unto him for?' But what ufe made we of this our Mafter's
liberality? Surely whilft we fhould have been recounting mer-
cies we were finding faults and fpying flaws in our ftate and
government. The civil was tyrannical, the ecclefiaftical papifti-

Ifai. v. 4, 7.

cal, &c. Nothing pleafed, not the hedge, not the wine-prefs,
not the watch-tower, not the watchmen. Thefe we trample
down with our own feet, pluck down with our own hands.
When God looked for grapes, behold wild grapes; for judgment
and righteoufnefs, fin and wickednefs, hellifh atheifm and pro-
fanenefs, horrid oaths and blafphemies, contempt of God's word
and ordinances, violation of God's fabbaths, rebellion againft governors, murder, theft, lying, and what not. . . . This was
that which caufed God to pull up the hedge, &c. to lay us even
with other diftreffed churches, and make us know what we had

" Faft Friend,"
p. 449.

by what we have loft. Thank we unthankfulnefs for what we
have loft, for God takes no forfeiture but what unthankfulnefs
makes."

    Nehemiah Rogers married Margaret, fifter of *William Col-
lingwood*, a loyal clergyman of Effex, who was ejeƈted from his
preferments in the Rebellion, and was one of the firft Preben-
daries of St. Paul's after the Reftoration. With fuch relations it
is not furprifing that *John Rogers*, the Fifth-Monarchy-Man,
found but little fympathy in his own family when he broke away
from them, and held communion with Puritans and Roundheads.

    This John was the fecond fon of Nehemiah, and was born in
1627. The following account of his early life is extraƈted from the
hiftory of his religious experiences, which he narrated by word of
mouth before a congregation at Dublin. It was one of his tenets
that every candidate for church-memberfhip fhould deliver in
according to his ability fome fuch account of the previous works
of grace upon his heart.

Ohel or
Bethfhemefh,
p. 419.

    To give a formal account from year to year of my life
would make me too tedious to you and myfelf. I hope
we fhall have opportunities hereafter to open ourfelves in
this kind one to another; in the mean time I fhall cite

fome of the moft remarkable paffages which to my prefent remembrance I have met with in former years to this day to do their duty and homage before you.

And firft, when I was a fchoolboy at Maldon, in Effex, I began to be roufed up by two men, viz. *Mr. Fenner* and *Mr. Marfhall.** ɪ The firft of thefe about the tenth year of mine age, as I take it (for what I was before I know not, a mere—I know not what, although I was kept continually in good order, as to read every day and be catechized and the like), yet then hearing *Mr. William Fenner* full of zeal, ftirring about, and thundering, and beating the pulpit, I was amazed and thought he was mad,— I wondered what he meant, and whilft I was gazing upon him I was ftruck, and faw that it was we that were mad, which made him fo. " Oh," fays he, " you knotty! rugged! proud piece of flefh! you ftony, rocky, flinty, hard heart, what wilt thou do when thou art roaring in hell amongft the damned!" &c. This made me at firft amazed, which run often in my mind after, and I began now to be troubled, being fcared and frighted, and out of fear of hell I fell to duties, hear fermons, read the fcriptures, (though I knew not what I read, but only thought the bare reading was enough, morning and

Margin notes:
1. Call to awaken him by the Word.

Scared at the thoughts of hell.

Very formal and ftrict in it.

---

* Dr. William Fenner was born in 1600; was prefented by the Earl of Warwick to the Rectory of Rochford, in Effex, in 1629, and died in 1640. Anthony à Wood fays that he " was much admired and frequented by the Puritanical party."—Brook's *Lives of the Puritans,* ii. 451; Anthony a Wood's *Faft. Oxon.* i. 223.

Stephen Marfhall, the Prefbyterian, was minifter fucceffively of Weathersfield and Finchingfield, in Effex, and lecturer at St. Margaret's, Weftminfter. He was a conftant preacher before the Long Parliament, by which he was confulted in all matters of importance relating to religion. Without doubt," fays Clarendon, "the Archbifhop of Canterbury had never fo great an influence upon the counfels at Court as Dr. Burgefs and Mr. Marfhall had then upon the Houfes " of Parliament.—Brook's *Lives of the Puritans,* iii. 241, and *Clarendon,* ii. 25.

evening), and learned to pray, at firſt out of books, and all the graces, ſo called, that I could get. And beſides family prayers I was afraid every night left the devil ſhould carry me away to Hell, if I did not firſt to myſelf, whilſt my brother, my bedfellow, was faſt aſleep, ſay my prayers and my " Our Father," and " I believe in God," &c. and the Ten Commandments, and my little catechiſm (Dr. Hall's), which I had learned, and this I did every night duly before I durſt ſleep, and I made as much of them as of a charm to keep me well that night, which elſe I conceited the devils would tear me to pieces. And yet ſometimes, when I was ſleepy, to make the more haſte I ſhould

Right formality.

ſay ſome of them at leaſt, to be in a forwardneſs, in the chimney corner, whilſt I was unbuttoning me, or untying my hoſe, or the like, preparing to go to bed, thinking all was well enough, ſo 'twas but done, only ſometimes, though I was unwilling to it, yet out of fear I remember of the Devil, or ſome miſchief, being ready to fancy anything to be the Devil, I ſhould ſay my prayers, or commandments,

Under great bondage of works.

or catechiſm, or all, twice over, ſuſpecting I ſaid them not well enough before. Thus, as the Apoſtle ſays, when I was a child I did childiſh things, and I thought this was very well, and very oftentimes would I be talking with ſome boy or other, getting him from all the reſt to walk with me, and I would tell him of Hell and ſin, and ſuch like things, for it ran always in my mind, and I lived under a deſperate fear. But for all this, *Mr. Marſhall*, a while after in the ſame pulpit, took me napping, whiles I

2. Call to awaken by the Word.

was, I know not how, bewitched to nod, and began to ſleep ; but his powerful voice * thundering againſt ſuch as are drowſy, and ſleep and ſlumber away their ſalvation, was at that time picked out for me, and very prevalent. I

---

* " Roar like Marſhall, that Geneva Bull,
Hell and Damnation a pulpit-full."
—*Cleveland's Rebel Scot.*

ſtarted up with an aching heart, and was frighted at his words, which he yet purſued, and wounded me to the heart, when he told us how that when time was loſt we could not call it again. O, I was ſufficiently wounded, and fell a weeping. I could not hold, and after ſermon I went home where I boarded, and ſat alone crying and complaining that I had loſt my time: and at that time I took up a purpoſe never to ſleep at church more, and made a covenant with it, which I think to this day I obſerved ever ſince; and when I began (as at firſt I was often tempted) to be drowſy, I would always ſtand and hold on nothing, and caſt my eyes about to open them more. ⟩But after this I reſolved to write down as well as I could every ſermon I heard, and to get them by heart, and to ſay every night one ſermon; and this courſe which I took made me more ready at night, when my father repeated the ſermons, or the landlord where I boarded—for they both did it, being very godly,—this made me readier to anſwer when we were aſked what we could remember. And this courſe I took cuſtomarily for nine or ten years together, long after I came from Cambridge; and hereby I was not only able to tell many men's ſermons together, but alſo able (though chiefly by higher means) to preach at eighteen or nineteen years of age, as I did in Huntingdonſhire, if not ſooner, to the amazement of many, but to the table-talk of more.

But not long after this that I heard *Mr. Marſhall* as before, I was further awakened by my father, who, preaching upon the Good Samaritan, and ſhewing his compaſſion, &c. preached and preſſed ſo powerfully, that I was thrown into a trembling as lying under the guilt of Chriſt's blood, and was long perplexed about it.

But after all this there is another remarkable paſſage that I muſt never forget, which I met with, or rather met with me, to the purpoſe. About 1637, as I take it, at

How to keep from ſleeping in the church.

More formal.

How to keep Sermons many years.

Nehemiah Rogers, that writ on the Parables.

3. Call to awaken by the Word.

Meffing, in Effex, I was playing with children, my fitteft companions then, and running round about the houfe we lived in through two or three little gates, in fport and idlenefs as I was running with the reft, I know not how or upon what occafion, I threw out vain words, and crying, "O Lord" (which we were not fuffered to do), my heart was fuddenly fmitten upon it, and I was fuddenly fet a running as if I had been poffeffed by I know not what power or fpirit, not having any ftrength to ftay myfelf, were it upon my life, until I was headlong carried through a little gateway, where as plainly to my thinking and in my appearance as ever I faw anything by the funfhine, there was fet a naked fword gliftering with a fearful edge, I thought, and which took up the whole fpace of the gate from one poft to another, with a broad blade moft keen and cruel, at which fad fight fo fraught with frights I ghaftly fcreeched, and yet had not the leaft power to ftay or ftop my precipitant courfe, but I was quickly carried quite unto it, fo as that the edge of the cruel blade meeting with my body, it feemed to me impoffible I fhould efcape death, and I made no other account but to be quite cut off and parted afunder; but afterward being hurried through with that headlong and furious force, I had ftrength to ftay a little beyond it, and to perpend the perplexible peril which I was in. I ftood as one amazed, or rather as one that knew not whether he were alive or dead; I knew not how to believe myfelf lefs than a dead man, and afterward at leaft mortally and deadly wounded, if not defperately and deplorably cut in twain. Oh! how I ftood trembling and tumbling in my thoughts, until the vital blood, which was fled for the heart's defence, began to difperfe again and to go quietly to their own homes, and then I looked about and turned me to the gateway, but the appearance was paffed away, the fword gone and vanifhed, whilft I was left alone, the reft running away, in a labyrinth of fears, with-

4. Call to
awaken by a
ftrange vifion.

A warning to
fuch as take
God's name in
vain.

out any wound without, but deeply and woefully wounded within, and never fince (to the praife of God's grace), as I know of, have I had fuch extravagant, prepofterous expreffions pafs from me.

But, good God, what was thy will herein? Thou who art not tied to means or order, beft ordereft and difpofeft of all things for thine own defign and glory, and fo this was, I am fure; but what it was I know not, yet it left a lafting impreffion upon me, and the fcar is yet to be feen in my heart, though the wound be healed. But, alas! how long and lamentably I lay afflicted and in continual fears after this! Every thunder and lightning I looked upon as my fate and fent for me, and then I would fall to my prayers, and faying my Creed and Commandments, and to my fermons, as faft as might be, that I might be found well-doing at leaft, if not as a charm to defend me, or a challenge to God by virtue of them to keep and blefs me. But all this while like an Ifraelite in Egypt I worked for life, and my fervices were my saviours, and I would to my brothers, fifters, and fchoolfellows and companions, take occafion to talk of Heaven and Hell, and what a hard thing it was to be faved.

Some time after this in Maldon, where I was boarded, and put to the Free-fchool, I had a certain dream, which by the confequence proved a previfion of what is now come to pafs. It was on a night about the time when the Spaniards and Hollanders had a fcuffling and a kind of naumachie* upon the Downs, for then fome talking of that fight filled me full of fears, and in the night my dream was that fire rained (as I may fay), or rather poured down round about, and looking where I was, I thought it to be without the coach-yard gate of my father's houfe, and I

A previfion in a dream at Maldon, in Effex.

---

* " 1639, Sept. 7, Fight in the Downs between the Spanifh and Dutch fleets."—*Hiftorian's Guide.*

was frighted to fee nothing but fire, looking upward and
round about, praying for deliverance.   None came nigh
me round about by a good fpace, but flaming elfe I thought
in all places, and I could fee none exempted ; wherefore
being afflicted for my father and our family, I fell on my
knees for them, and I thought I continued fo, long ere I
could be heard, but was at laft bid to arife and look, and
then I thought the fire fell not fo faft on my father's houfe
as it did before, but by little and little abated till I awaked.
Now, although this dream had feized much upon my
fpirits, yet I made no other account of it than of a fancy
till five or fix years after, in the Ifle of Ely, meeting with

Interpreted by
Dr. Drayton.

Dr. Drayton, D.D. he declared to me for feveral reafons
that this muft be more than a mere dream, and that he
was confident it did fhew fome fiery and angry difpenfation
upon all our family, and my father and the reft fhould lie
under fome trouble by the times or otherwife, and myfelf
fhould be fet free, and at this liberty to pray for them, and
that by degrees they fhould be recovered and brought out,
and the fire abate.   Which interpretation (more fully by
far from his own mouth) is for the moft part verified at

Came to pafs.

this day.   But all this while I was labouring for life, exceedingly formal, and I did much covet to know the things
of God, and therefore wifhed oft I were but a minifter,

Refting in
doings.

fuch a one as *Mr. Fenner* is, or *Mr. Marfhall*, or *Mr.
Hooker*, or my father, or fome other that was eminent, that
I might attain to their knowledge, and then I thought I
fhould do abundance more for God (as if God were beholding to me for my obedience), and I would then, I
thought, be fure to get falvation (as if I could then eafily
do it).

Thus, a poor creature, I continued for feveral years
together, and if you knew but half what I met with in that
time you would fay I was a poor creature indeed as any
alive, for I kept to myfelf many faft-days, and would eat

nothing ; heard, read, fang pfalms ; meditated, ufed foliloquies, and prayed many times a day, and what not ; and yet at laft defpaired even to the depth. What by often thoughts of Hell, reading Drexellius upon eternity, and then thinking of endlefs, endlefs and remedilefs torments, and what by frequent frights as before, and what by my father once preaching on the fool in the Gofpel (Luke xii. 20), "Thou fool, this night will I take away thy foul ; then whofe fhall thofe things be that thou haft provided ?" —whence he handled a point of the folly of men to lay up here and forget Heaven, and fhewing that Heaven came not with eafe on a down bed, but many fhall ftrive hard to enter and fhall not be able, and that except you exceed the righteoufnefs of the Scribes and Pharifees (Matt. v. 20), you fhall in no cafe enter into the kingdom of Heaven,— what with thefe and other things I was almoft in the bottomlefs abyfmes of torments. I took the Bible to look thefe Scriptures, read them over and over and over again, but the more I read the more I roared in the black gulf of defpair, where I was caft fo deep as to me and others I feemed fometimes paft all recovery. I prayed, fafted, mourned, got into corners, yea many times, being I was afhamed to make my cafe known, I have ran into barns, ftables, anywhere, pretending as if I had bufinefs, on purpofe to pray, figh, weep, knocking my breaft, curfe that ever I was born, wifhing I were a ftone, anything but what I was, for fear of Hell and the devils, whom I thought I faw every foot in feveral ugly fhapes and forms, according to my fancies, and fometimes with great rolling flaming eyes like faucers, having fparkling firebrands in the one of their hands, and with the other reaching at me to tear me away to torments. O the leaps that I have made ! the frights that I have had ! the fears that I was in ! which continued off and on to the beginning of thefe times. Befides, great outward afflictions that I met with were of

Defpaired.

5. Knock, awakened by the Word.

Fearful afflictions and tears.

Temptations.

much force to bring me into this condition, being often (and doubtlefs I might deferve it too, too much) beaten, bruifed, turned out of doors, whirled and kicked about, hardly and unkindly ufed, at which times I fhould fometimes be tempted to murder myfelf, fometimes think I could not belong to God, for then he could not endure to fee me thus ufed and afflicted ; and yet I fly to Him and pray, and pray, and pray, but as good fpeak to a poft, for I am not relieved. Sometimes I fhould read and weep, and, as my ufual manner was in the time of my great defpair, fall flat all along with my face on the ground, and cry, and call, and figh, and weep, and call for help ; but the Lord's time was not yet come to anfwer, and I was wont to weep half the night together, if not all fometimes, and to water my bed with my tears, for fear of Hell and the Devil, and therefore for fins or rebellious difobedience, and ever flept with my hands clafped clofe together in a praying pofture, that if I did die, or that the devils did prey upon me, they might find me in a praying pofture, fleeping as well as waking. I never durft go to fleep otherwife to my knowledge for five or fix years together.

The greateft blow.

But the greateft blow I had was from the fentence of the aforefaid Scripture in *Matt.* v. 20. Surely, thought I, I but ftrive againft the ftream and feek out impoffibilities, if I muft exceed the righteoufnefs of the Scribes and Pharifees ; I had often read of their ftrictnefs in their Houfes and Synhedriums and Schools, &c. [and] thefe confiderations and fuch like made me think it in vain to feek to be faved.

Defpair.

In a word, to fuch a height was I grown up unto, that I did not only defpair, but began to be diftracted and out of my wits, as we ufe to fay. I thought trees fometimes good Angels, fometimes bad, and looked upon bufhes as the Dens of Devils. I fhould fit up whole nights fometimes in a little turret we had, in an orchard, from the houfe, ftudying, finging, whiftling, whooping, or drawing figures, or one thing or other, or elfe be walking in the fields, woods, or fome other places, talking to myfelf, fpeaking to trees as to men, or as to angels or God, and thinking the leaft whiftling of the wind, or chirping of a bird, or lowing of a beaft, to be fome anfwer fent to me, as I would fancy it. But as thefe diftracted diftempers grew higher, I could not avoid the forcible temptations of a furious Devil, making me fometimes whet a knife, fometimes take a billet, fometimes one thing, fometimes another, to murder myfelf and fome- times others, and fometimes all—for I would have had all to have gone my way, methought. Many ways I tried, but was always prevented, till at laft I was taken and bound hand and foot, and held or tied faft in a bed till the raging fits were over; and then, when I was fpent and patient, if let go, yet without a watchful eye, though it may be I faid nothing, yet the firft thing I went about, it may be, would be to feek a knife, or to get to the window to caft myfelf down headlong; but I have been ftrangely and almoft miraculoufly kept, even in the very act and inftant of time, when a few minutes longer had been too late to fave my life.

Miraculoufly faved from felf-murder.

I dare boldly fay, few that faw me in thofe headlong diftempers did think me at the beft fit for any place but Bedlam, and that I fhould ever be reftored to what I am, which was alfo as ftrangely; for, as the diftracted fits did much abate me, they did turn more to inward malady and melancholy, my continual cry being, " I am damned! I am damned! I am fure I can't be faved—it is impoffible. Oh, Hell! Hell! fire about me! the devils are at me!" and I thought I heard the damned roaring and raving, and faw them as 'twere roafting, and their frifking and frying in everlafting torments. My mind and all was taken up with their howlings and fcreechings. This fad condition, day and night, lafted upon me until I was perfuaded that there was a God, and that this God was righteous, and that he

Inward melancholy and defpairs.

A word to the wicked.

would hear prayers if I continued but knocking with importunity and gave not over ; then I refolved with myfelf, (and gathered together here and there thofe fcattered reliques of reafon which were left me), that I would continue prayer, and fo I did (though by fits I was froward and mute, and wild and I know not how), yet off and on, five days together, fcarce eating a bit of bread in all that time, and was after that in another form and frame of fpirit, though by fits full of diftraction and defperate thoughts, yet more ferious and fet to weigh things as in a balance, and to expoftulate with the Lord, and to pray by fits moft furioufly, and now and then tears began again, which were all dried up before, to trickle and come tumbling down my face like fwollen drops of blood, and I continued thus three or four days ; till one afternoon, coming into a chamber, my heart being as big as it could hold, I threw myfelf flat on my face as I ufed to do, knocking the boards and calling and crying to the Lord for deliverance, and ufing fuch exorcifing expreffions as might difcover me in defpair ; and ftarting up, I walked a turn or two, faying, " Is there not a God ? Is he gracious ? Are the Scriptures falfe ? Canft thou take delight to fee a poor foul thus fet on the rack, fighing and roaring in torment ? Rife up and appear for thyfelf, thou great God, fhow thyfelf gracious in one act of mercy, maugre all the devils in Hell !" And with knocking my breaft and tearing my hair, I threw myfelf upon the bed, whilft my eyes were glazed with tears, and there I

Reftored
extraordinarily
by a dream.

lay in a fudden fleep which feized upon me, and I dreamed of the fame Scripture (the letter, which killed me), and yet of Chrift (the Spirit which quickened me), and that his righteoufnefs, by faith made mine, did exceed the righteoufnefs of the Scribes and Pharifees, and except I, in and by the righteoufnefs of Chrift made mine, did excel the righteoufnefs of the Scribes and Pharifees, I could not be faved—that is, not without the righteoufnefs of Chrift.

When I awaked, I was fo much changed that I was amazed
at myfelf at the fuddennefs of it; for I dreamed I was
comforted and my heart filled with joy, and when I awaked
it was fo indeed. I ftarted up and rebuked myfelf, faying,
" Why, I am not damned! What's the matter? am I fo
filled with a fancy? with a fudden hope of I know not
what nor whence?" At which time I fell to pray, and
whilft I was praying I faid, " Lord, is this true? fay, is it
true? if it be fo, let it be fhown me that it is fo." So I
was perfuaded that the righteoufnefs of Chrift was mine,
and thus I had the firft affurance of falvation, for that very
fame Scripture that before condemned me did now juftify
me, that is, in Chrift. Well, with this joy I continued to
this hour, holding and keeping ground againft all temptations (which are infinite) that I have met with ever fince.
Yet Satan, my continual and never-ceafing enemy, now
began to mufter up afrefh more troubles againft me, and to
follow me with an hoft of afflictions and temptations, as
Pharaoh followed Ifrael with a purpofe to deftroy him.
And fee how a bird that is efcaped out of the hand is
hunted up and down by the boys; the doors are fhut, the
windows and holes ftopped to hinder her efcape, and fee
how they hunt her, throw their hats at her, fcare her up and
down till they think to tire her and make her fall into their
fingers again. So did Satan fet upon me, I may fay a thoufand ways, by himfelf and his agents, to hunt me up and down,
and to tire me out and to make me if he could fall into his
fingers again, but that my God whom I unfeignedly ferve
from my foul did deliver me, does deliver me, and I truft
will deliver me, as the Apoftle fays. For though the
Devil did ufe many fnares, and befet me fo about, as you
will hear, that it feemed fcarce poffible I fhould efcape, yet
the Lord fet me at liberty from the fnares of the fowler,
though fometimes fo fubtlely laid that I could not difcern
them; and what he could not do by his fair infinuations

Evangelical.

Confirmed and feconded by prayer and the Word.

And got into an affurance of falvation, and how.

Satan's frefh bouts.

2 Cor. i. 10.

and fubtleties and inward motions and temptations, he tried to do by violence in tormenting me and making me the moft objeét of afflidtion and mifery all about. For, to proceed, my friends became mine enemies, and my precife-nefs was an eyefore to many; near relations caft me off, and I was looked upon as difobedient for keeping company with fuch as were godly Puritans and accounted then Roundheads, and for praying and holding communion with them (though commanded to the contrary). At length I found fo little love and fo much malice from fome, that I was turned out of doors,* and forced, as men fay, to feek my fortune—to fly with my own feathers, with three fhil-lings and fixpence or thereabouts, as I take it—to travel up and down in ftrange countries, and that in the coldeft winter time of the year; in fnowy weather up to the knees very often, and whilft the very icicles hung on my hair and cheeks a conflux of tears that came hot would thaw them, which fell abundantly from me in the open fields and high-ways, where none but God took notice of them. Yet I did often beg at poor cottages or fo, but to come in to warm me or dry me, or for a draught of fmall beer or fo, which would make fome poor fouls fall a weeping to fee me. But after many dangers and troubles, I footed it as far as Cam-bridge, where I fought from college to college to be but a fizer or poor fcholar, (my little ftock of money being all gone, and the fervitors of King's College, of which I was one before, being difmiffed), but I could have no place, and I had no money, and I wanted bread, and that fo long that all others failed to do anything for me, infomuch I was forced for life to try all things, and eat leather, and drink water, and eat old quills and pens where I could pick them up out of the duft, roafted in a few coals which were left in

Greater
afflictions.

Almoft ftarved
at Cambridge.

---

* His father was "turned out of doors" alfo about this time (1642) by the Puritans.

the chamber where I was, and I aſſayed ſometimes to eat graſs, and did it ; yea, I grew to that height of penury and famine that I ſometimes tried to eat my own fingers, biting them till I could endure it no longer ; then tearing my hair and crying, I had recourſe to prayer, whereby the paſſion, it may be, would away for the preſent ; but this continued ſo long that I met with temptations in the wilderneſs to turn ſtones into bread ; and the Devil did often tempt me to ſtudy Necromancy and Nigromancy, and to make uſe of Magic, and to make a league with him, and that then I ſhould never want, but ſhew me as 'twere upon the pinnacle the glory of the world, ſo repreſented to me in my fancy, bidding me but obey him—that is, fall down and worſhip him, and I ſhould have both my bags of money by me and be honoured of all men and owned by all my friends, and go home with great riches and in great reſpect. But God would not ſuffer me to hearken to him, but to tell him, " Thou art a liar from the beginning ; away, thou malicious accuſer of the brethren, tempt me not." And then I prayed and read the Scriptures, and writ holy meditations and ſoul-ſoliloquies on the 88th Pſalm, all in verſe very pathetical and ſuitable to my condition ; and I began Dives and Lazarus here, and Lazarus and Dives hereafter, two books which I ſoon after concluded, uſing in it Engliſh, Latin, Italian, French—being very tragical, and all in verſe very ſuitable to my condition under ſeveral temptations ; all which I had thoughts, with ſome others which I have by me, to have printed for public profit, but wanted a purſe ; ſo that inſtead of Magical and Aſtrological ſtudies I bent my mind to holy meditations, ſoul comforting, Angelical and Evangelical contemplations. Yet I continued under ſtrong temptations ; but, to the praiſe of God I ſpeak it, I think never was I a more growing Chriſtian than after Satan had theſe repulſes. But yet I muſt not omit to tell you that I had one other temptation firſt, which was almoſt irrecover-

Temptations ſtrong.

The Devil tempts to yield to him.

Is repulſed.

The Devil tempts another way.

Life and Opinions of a

able. For, finding myfelf almoft ftarved and pined to death, my ftrength almoft gone, my eyes funk deep in my head, and wearing death's colours, I was almoft at my wits' ends, for now one temptation got ground and came on audacioufly, and grew ftrongly upon me, fo that I could not efcape it but it followed me. I took up the fkin of my wafted hands and arms with a refolution to tear it off for hunger, but in vain. The Devil had fo befotted me that I could fee no ways to evade death ; for I had been

beholding to all the fcholars I could find any courtefy in, to bring me fcraps, or fkins of falt fifh, or fomething or other, in their handkerchiefs or pockets, which kept me alive awhile, till at laft they were all weary, and I wafted almoft to death and afhamed to beg openly about ; and I was blinded as to any way that I could find to recover out of this condition. Wherefore after violent and never-ceafing temptations, I drew my knife, whetted it fharp, opened my doublet and fhirt, and in the midft of the room where I was alone kneeled down to prayer to furrender my foul up into the

hands of God, my knife lying by me prepared, and I prepared for the act ; when, behold, a door which I thought was bolted all the night before was but fhut to, which

a fcholar opens, and with the fcreeking of it made me ftart up and throw my knife into the chimney in hafte, as afhamed of what I was doing ; and in comes the fcholar to tell me of a place in Huntingdonfhire to teach gentlemen's children, at my Lord Brudenel's houfe, and how one of our college was fent to but refufed it ; by which means I was recovered out of that eminent danger, and after the fcholar was gone did exceedingly reprove and check myfelf for fuffering this temptation to grow fo upon me for want of

faith, and was much afflicted at it ; but, being now night, I went, as I ufe to do, fupperlefs to bed (after duty), but my heart melting into abundance of tears—firft for the fin that I was about, and then for the love of God and his care appearing for me ; until, with an heart full, and head full, and eyes full, and all, I was fallen into a deep ſleep, and viſited with an extraordinary token from on high, both in dream and viſion, which hath been ſince accompliſhed (as I take it), and the laſt in Ireland the laſt year. The dream was this : That I was walking home to my Father's houſe with a ſtaff in my hand ; and fearing left I ſhould be out of the way, I looked for the path, which at firſt I could ſcarce diſcern was a path, and began to look about and to queſtion it, till by and bye I perceived ſome footſteps of ſome that had gone that way ; with that I went forward, and the further I went the plainer I perceived it to be the path, and that I was in the way, and I could ſee no other ; at which I rejoiced, and went on confidently as if I feared no evil nor enemy, till I came to a fine, glorious, beautiful houſe and building on the left hand of me, out of which came forth a beam which reached a little croſs the way I was to go in ; ſo that I being at a little ſtand at firſt, yet would not ſtoop under this beam, but ſtepped aſide and ſo paſſed away, laying my hand on it as I ſtepped by the ſide of it ; but the houſe I thought was all in a flame of a ſudden ; ſo that, being ſomething troubled thereat, I paſſed on in the way, wondering in myſelf what this ſhould be, till I was overtaken by ſome rude, violent, malicious men, that laid to my charge the ſetting this houſe on fire, and would not hear me ſpeak, but were harſhly haling me away to priſon, with which, being ſufficiently frighted and all my fleſh ſet a trembling, I awaked, and was offended with myſelf for being troubled at a dream—a fooliſh fancy ; ſo I laid me (it being yet dark) and fell aſleep again, and was caſt into the ſame dream again word for word ; and at my right hand I thought there was a grave, ancient man, full of white hairs like wool, a long white beard, who ſtood by me and bid me cheer up. " Fear not ; for the Lord hath ſent me to comfort thee,

Comforted and confirmed in dream and viſion extraordinarily.

The dream is reiterated.

The dream interpreted in ſleep.

How firſt
called to the
Miniſtry in his
ſleep.

and to tell thee that He hath choſen thee to preach His
word and Goſpel of Chriſt, which is the ſtaff that thou
haſt in thy hand, and which ſtaff (that is, the word of God)
thou ſhalt walk home with to thy Father's houſe, i. e.
Heaven, where is fulneſs of joy. But after a time thou
wilt be troubled with the different opinions and ways of
men, and ſeem at firſt to be at a loſs, but the Lord will be
thy guide. Go on, and as thou goeſt forward the way of
the Lord will lie clearer and clearer before your eyes ; but
the footſteps are the examples of the ſaints that have gone
before you, which will be a great help unto you, and you
ſhall walk cheerfully on in the way which is clear to you

Prophetical.

(than the which you ſhall ſee no other) ; but yet you muſt
meet the fair houſe on the left hand, i. e. the glory and
great ones of the world, who make a great and fair ſhow
to men, as built high, but they muſt fall, and are but on
the left hand of you, whilſt you will deſpiſe them, preach

Partly
performed of
late in Ireland,
as is well
known ; but I
believe not
wholly.

againſt them, and turn your eye looking forward to go on
in the way of God, and turn not about ; but the beam,
that comes out of this great houſe which makes ſo much
ſhow, is meant the powers and opinions of ſuch, which,
whilſt ſomewhat croſs to the way, you ſtep aſide and will
not ſtoop under, they are ſet on fire and inflamed of a
ſudden ; but be not troubled, go forward ; although they
will ſend after you ſaying you have brought this fire upon
them, and they will falſely accuſe you, and ſeek to hale
you away to priſon for this faêt." At which I awaked
again, this being morning, about daybreak, and being
filled with confidence and comfort, I roſe up and writ it
down preſently. And away I went that day towards Did-
dington in Huntingdonſhire, where the Lord Brudenel
once lived, but was then ſequeſtered ;* and one that the

* An ordinance for ſequeſtering notorious delinquents' eſtates was
paſſed April 1, 1643.

Committee put in had gentlemen's children to board with
him, whom I afterward taught. But after all thefe deliverances I did multiply abundantly in gifts and graces, either
to pray, expound, read, fing hymns and fpiritual fongs.
And finding the Lord fo abundantly to endue me from
above, and to qualify me for the call which I had before in
the night for the miniftry, which then I little meant or
imagined could be (it being often refolved againft before
by my father, and my books ordered to be packed up) ;
but finding things following fo fairly to concur, I was
much confirmed in it that the Lord had defigned me
thereunto.

From that time how he grew fit for the Miniftry.

2. Call to the Miniftry.

At this time I came to be convinced of the Parliament's
proceedings and caufe to be more regular and in order to
the great work that God hath to do in nations than the
Kings, by comparing them together and bringing them
to the Word, and then I faw clearly by the Word that God
would do what he hath to be done by them, and for them,
and for the Commonwealth.

It was not long after this that I was, by a godly people
in Tofeland,* earneftly importuned and at laft prevailed
with to preach the Gofpel, and I was foon known in the
country, and after fent for into Effex, where I fettled,
paffing twice through the Affembly on examination and
approbation.† So, although ever fince I have met with
many forts of afflictions and oppofitions, lies, flanders,
threatenings, libels, vows, and endeavours to take away my
life, yet many have added teftimony to the word I have
delivered in all places, the Lord be praifed, to the great
refrefhing of my foul, and towards the making up of my

3. Call to preach.

4. Call.

Vide Epiftle to Purleigh before the 2 Liber.

---

* A fmall parifh near St, Neots.
† He fpeaks elfewhere of having received Prefbyterian orders in " the
very firft claffis that ever was in England." Claffes were fully organized
nowhere except in Lancafhire in the year 1646, and in London in 1647.

joy when I fhall give an account (to their comfort) at the great day."

Either from choice or from neceffity *Rogers* ufually alighted on difturbed diftricts. In 1642, a few months before he was turned out of his father's houfe at Meffing, the civil war had broken out. In Auguft, *Charles I.* had fet up his ftandard at Nottingham, and in October he had fought the indecifive battle of Edgehill. During the following winter thofe counties in which the parliamentary intereft was fufficiently ftrong were forming themfelves into Affociations for mutual defence. The moft influential of thefe was that of Norfolk, Suffolk, Effex, Hertfordfhire, and Cambridge, to which Huntingdonfhire was afterwards annexed. It is known by the name of the Eaftern Affociation, and was placed under the command of *Lord Grey of Wark* and *Oliver Cromwell*. *Rogers* muft have paffed through the centre of this newly-formed affociation between Meffing and Cambridge in the winter of 1642-3. Poffibly he overrates the dangers and troubles of the road; but in truth thofe Eaftern Counties, and efpecially Cambridgefhire, were at that time in a very difturbed ftate, and travellers were liable to inconveniences and interruptions, if not to pofitive dangers. A few months earlier *Sir John Bramfton*, then a young man, had travelled on horfeback through the fame Affociation, on a miffion from his father in Effex to the King at York, and his travelling experiences exemplify the fort of trouble to which *Rogers* alfo would probably have been expofed. " I went," he fays, " from Skreenes thither (to York) in three days, ftayed there one day, and returned home again to Skreenes in three days more on the fame horfe. . . . As we went about Stanford we were directed by the watchman a way to avoid the town, the plague being there. . . . In our return on Sunday, near Huntingdon, between that and Cambridge, certain mufketeers ftart out of the corn, and command us to ftand, telling us we muft be fearched, and to that end we muft go before *Mr. Cromwell*, and give account from whence we came, and whither we were going. I afked where *Mr. Cromwell* was. A foldier told us he was four miles off. I faid it was unreafonable to carry us out of our way; if *Mr. Cromwell* had been there I fhould have willingly given him all the fatisfaction he could defire, and putting my hand into my pocket gave one of them twelve pence, who faid we might pafs."

Autobiography of Sir John Bramfton, Camden Soc. p. 85, 86.

Nor could he have chofen a more unlucky feafon for refi-
dence at Cambridge. In Auguft of the fame year (1642) the
Colleges had endeavoured to fend their plate to the King, and
"one *Mafter Cromwell*, burgefs for the town of Cambridge, and
then newly turned a man of war," was fent by the Parliament to
ftop them. *Cromwell* furrounded the Colleges " while we were
at our devotion in our feveral chapels," and carried away feveral
heads of houfes and doctors of divinity prifoners to London. Towards the end of the year Cambridge was garrifoned for the Parliament, and from that time forward for nearly two years the
Univerfity was haraffed in every poffible way: gownfmen were
ill-ufed by foldiers, King's College Chapel was turned into a drill-
room, other Colleges into barracks, and finally upwards of two
hundred fellows and tutors were expelled. In 1664, *Rogers* thus
alludes to the interruption of his ftudies :—" Ultra jam duos
vigintique annos elapfos doctrinæ ἰατρικῆς hujus hofpes fueram
. . . . . in Athenis Palæftrifque noftris donec inter arma non
tantum leges, fed etiam literæ omnes filebant, quum Bellona tan-
topere matribus truculenta ac formidolofa, matri almæ Cantab.
noftræ bellicofa fuiffet, Minervamque Pieridefque noftras e col-
legiis et poffeffione deturbaffet."

Again, when he left Cambridge, in 1643, and fettled in
Huntingdonfhire, he found that county alfo in a ftate of diforder.
An ordinance of Parliament, dated 18th July, 1643, declares that
" the weekly affeffments for the County of Huntingdon have not
yet been proceeded with, becaufe of the fears and diftractions of
that county ; that the faid county being now become a frontier to
the Affociated Counties of Cambridge, &c. is enforced through
the emergent dangers to make extraordinary provifion of foot and
horfe for the fafeguard of the faid county and the other Affociated
againft the incurfions of the plundering enemy, and that this has
occafioned extraordinary difburfements of money, of which the
committee of that county is utterly unprovided." And three
weeks afterwards *Oliver Cromwell* wrote as follows :—

" *For my noble Friends the Committee of the Affociation fitting at
Cambridge : Thefe*
" Huntingdon, 6 Aug. 1643."

" GENTLEMEN,
" You fee by this Enclofed how fadly your affairs ftand. It's
no longer difputing, but Out inftantly all you can ! Raife all your

Querela '
Cantab. 4, 5.

A collection of
Orders, &c.
publifhed by
authority of
Parliament in
1646, p. 239.

Bands; fend them to Huntingdon; get up what Volunteers you can; haften your Horfes.

"Send thefe letters to Norfolk, Suffolk and Effex without delay. I befeech you fpare not, but be expeditious and induftrious! Almoft all our foot have quitted Stamford; there is nothing to Interrupt an enemy, but our horfe, that is confiderable. You muft act lively; do it without Diftraction! Neglect no means. I am

Your faithful Servant,

Carlyle's Oliver
Cromwell,
Suppl. to 1ft
Ed. p. 15.
OLIVER CROMWELL."

At this time *Rogers* came to be convinced of the juftice of the Parliament's caufe, and probably at this time alfo, and in Huntingdonfhire, he took up arms as a volunteer, and performed thofe fervices in the field againft the common enemy of which he boafted afterwards.

CHAPTER II.

OGERS left Huntingdonſhire and returned to Eſſex in 1647 or 1648. About the ſame time he received Preſbyterian ordination, married a daughter of *Sir Robert Payne, Kt.*, of Midloe in Hunts, and became "ſettled Miniſter," or, in other words, Rector of Purleigh* near Maldon, a neighbourhood in which he muſt have been well known from his childhood. But he was too reſtleſs to "ſettle" anywhere. He hired a curate and betook himſelf to London. There he renounced his Preſbyterian ordination, joined the Independents, became Lecturer at St. Thomas Apoſtle's in the City, and preached violent political ſermons in ſupport of the Long Parliament, which was ſtill ſitting.

In 1650 the Parliament made an order "to ſend over ſix able miniſters to preach in Dublin, and they to have £200 per annum apiece out of Biſhops' and Deans' and Chapters' lands in Ireland. And in the mean time, the Lord Lieutenant to take care that it be paid out of the public revenue; and if any of thoſe miniſters die in that ſervice in Ireland, that the Parliament will make competent proviſion for their wives and children." And in the courſe of the next year *Rogers* was ſent to Ireland by the Council of State on this Miſſion. The government of the country was adminiſtered at that time by the Commiſſioners of the Engliſh Parliament; of theſe *Ireton* and *Ludlow* conducted the military, and *John Weaver, Miles Corbet*, and *Colonel John Jones* the civil adminiſtration. On

Whitelock,
p. 445.
March 12.

---

* Walker ſpeaks of Purleigh as "one of the beſt livings in thoſe parts."
—*Sufferings of the Clergy*, part 2, p. 395.

his arrival, he found fome of the Commiffioners inftalled at
Dublin. The following order teftifies to their care for his
material comfort :—

"Dublin Caftle,
22 Auguft, 1651.

"Ordered that the Commiffioners of Revenue at Dublin do
forthwith enquire what ftipends and tithes or other maintenance
do belong to the Minifters within the feveral parifhes in the City
of Dublin, and do certify the fame to the Commiffioners of Parliament. And they are likewife to provide two convenient houfes
belonging to the Commiffioners, for the pleafant accommodation
of *Mr. Rogers* and *Mr. Wyke* and their families."

Reid's Hiftory
of the
Prefbyterian
Church in
Ireland, ii.
245.

Shortly afterwards the Commiffioners affigned Chrift Church
Cathedral to him and his congregation as a place of worfhip, and
caufed his name to be added to the lift of Independent Minifters
who were empowered to take order that the Gofpel was preached
in St. Patrick's Cathedral.

Ireland was in a very unfettled ftate at this time. It was
more than twelve months fince *Cromwell* had returned to England
after the fhort and bloody campaign which commenced with the
ftorm of Drogheda and Wexford ; but the war ftill continued :
Ireton was befieging Limerick, where he met his death ; while
the Irifh, if not actually befieging, were at leaft haraffing and
alarming Dublin. *Col. Hewfon,** the governor of that city and
of the adjoining diftrict, gives a deplorable account of the ftate of

---

* Col. Hewfon began life as a fhoemaker. When the civil war broke
out he joined the army as captain, "fought on ftoutly, and in time became
a colonel." In 1645 he commanded a regiment in the campaign of Sir
Thomas Fairfax, and "manfully led the forlorn hope," at the ftorm of
Bridgewater. In 1649 he fat in the High Court of Juftice, and figned the
King's death-warrant. In the fame year he and his regiment accompanied Oliver Cromwell to Ireland, where he did good fervice, and was
appointed Governor of Dublin. He was a member of the Barebones and
other Parliaments, of the Council of State in 1653 and 1659, and was
knighted and raifed to Cromwell's Houfe of Peers in 1657. Shortly
before the Reftoration he made himfelf very notorious and unpopular, by
fuppreffing a riot of apprentices in the city with unneceffary feverity.—
Anthony à Wood, Faft. 2, 78 ; *Sprigge's* Ang. Red., p. 70 ; *Whitelock.*

his command, in a letter dated Oct. 11, 1651, and publifhed in
the London newfpapers. The Irifhry were ravaging the Englifh
territory, intercepting the Englifh convoys, and ftorming the
Englifh garrifons. *Fitzpatrick* had made ufe of the hay that lay
about Caftle Jordan to fire that Caftle, and fo " our men were all
taken prifoners ;" nay, " in my abfence they engaged my own
troop, took 25, and killed 27." The letter, in fhort, contains a
catalogue of difafters, relieved, however, by the intelligence that
Independency was flourifhing. " The Gofpel takes bleffed effect
in this city ; here is one church gathered, and they have chofen
Mr. Winter for their paftor, and another church embodied this
day that have not yet chofen their paftor, but I fuppofe they
will pitch upon *Mr. Rogers*—both godly men."

Mercurius
Politicus, Oct.
16-23, 1651.

Governor *Hewfon* and his wife joined the church of *Mr.
Rogers*, and delivered in an account of their religious experiences,
which may be read ftill in " Bethfhemefh." On the other hand,
Rogers beftowed his affiftance upon *Col. Hewfon* in the field,
boafting afterwards before *Cromwell*, that in Ireland, as well as
in England, he had " engaged in the field and expofed his life to
great dangers freely " for confcience fake. *Hugh Peters* had fet
him a notorious example in this refpect.

But the patronage of thefe great perfonages was of no avail
againft fectarian animofities. The Anabaptifts were now very
powerful in Ireland ; and a *Mr. Thomas Patient*, one of their
preachers, who had been an army chaplain under *Cromwell*, and
had fettled at Waterford, created a fchifm in *Rogers'* congregation
on the queftion of adult baptifm. *Rogers* was willing to concede
a great deal, but he never would allow that it was neceffary to re-
baptize thofe who had been already baptized as infants. *Patient*,
on the other hand, and the Waterford Anabaptifts, fent a letter by
the hands of *Adjutant-General Allen* and *Captain Vernon*, to divers
of the Chrift Church Congregation, urging them to admit none to
communion who allowed infant baptifm. " The Jews," they
faid, " might as well have admitted uncircumcifed perfons to eat
the Paffover." Eventually *Rogers* became fo annoyed by thefe
diffenfions that he threw up his appointment and returned to
England, leaving *Mr. Thomas Patient* to preach at Chrift Church
in his place.

On his departure he received from the Commiffioners for
Ireland the following certificate :—

"Dublin Caſtle, 22 March, 1652.

"Whereas *Mr. John Rogers*, Miniſter of the Goſpel, was ſent over and recommended to us by divers worthy members of the Council of State for preaching the Word of God in Ireland, where he hath continued for the ſpace of — months, and being now deſirous to return for England, we thought fit to certify whom it may concern, that the ſaid *Mr. Rogers*, during his reſidence here, hath been painful and induſtrious in the work of the miniſtry; and we ſhall be glad that ſuch laborious, faithful inſtruments may receive encouragement to repair to this land for the refreſhing of poor ſouls, and for the propagating and carrying on the intereſt of Jeſus Chriſt there."

On his return to England he declared his opinion of thoſe with whom he had been aſſociated in Ireland with his uſual freedom. He had no fault to find with the civil authorities; indeed, their example was one which the Engliſh might follow in ſome refpeéts with very great advantage. "I am bound," he ſays, in an epiſtle to the Commiſſioners for the affairs of Ireland, "I am bound to bear teſtimony to your integrity and fidelity, and wiſh no worſe to England than your orderly and Goſpel-like way of maintaining the miniſtry in Ireland; not only that they have enough and to ſpare, as I know by experience of two hundred pounds* per annum, a very large allowance, and paid them tax free and without fail, quarterly, out of the Treaſury of Revenues, but in that they are not troubled with the thing called Tithes, nor with Pariſh cures,† not being placed as Pariſh Miniſters in pariſhes. So that their conſciences are not tied up to pleaſe men or malignant humours, as Parochial Miniſters and Tithe-mongers here do. The Lord ſend us ſuch an uſeful and orderly proviſion for the Miniſtry in England too, which will be the beſt means to ſet an honeſt, able, ſound, holy, and powerful Miniſtry amongſt us, and to caſt down thoſe wandering meteors, roving runagates, and thoſe unworthy, wicked Preachers in the nation, who are fatted with Tithes and good liquor, but very lean and

---

* Said to be equal to about four or five times that amount of the preſent currency.

† A violent agitation againſt tithes and the parochial ſyſtem was being carried on in England at this time.

Reid, ii. 260.

Bethſhemeſh, p. 28.

Great encouragement for Miniſters in Ireland.

The way to rout the rank, corrupt national Miniſtry.

corrupt in good lives. But fuch as thefe will up as long as Tithes and Parifhes are up, having the old corrupt lives and fottifh fuperftitions and opinions of their parifhioners to be their guard and wall of defence round about them. And by this means will malignant humours be maintained in the nation, and Parifh Churches and orders and ordinances, and Common Prayers and croffings and cringing, and fuch accurfed ftuff, be in moft malignant parifhes provided for; whilft in Ireland thefe trumperies muft tumble for want of maintenance, and the Godly Miniftry hath the more thereby, for no others are allowed falaries or ftipends by the State, but fuch as are fo reputed and approved of for godly and able.''

But the compliments *Rogers* paid to the Commiffioners of Ireland were not extended to the religious world of Dublin. During his fojourn there he wrote a book, and on his return to England juftice to his own reputation conftrained him to publifh it, for his enemies, not content with affailing him in Dublin, were flandering him by their emiffaries in London alfo. A few extracts culled from this vindication will difclofe not only what he thought of his adverfaries, but alfo what they thought and faid of him, exemplifying a ftate of feeling between paftor and flock by no means uncommon then, and one which he in his own perfon very ufually provoked.

"The author writ this" (among other reafons) "for names' fake. It is time to refcue my name and reputation from thofe baylies that have arrefted and roughly handled it at the Devil's fuit out of malice. I have met with men like college butlers, who have fet up apace upon honeft men's names, and charged them to the full (with full-maliced and foul-mouthed afperfions) which they will never wipe off again without I pay them (foundly) for it, which in time I may do more fully, before good witnefs too. So did fome in Dublin, afperfing my perfon and traducing the truth, poffeffing fome people with ftrange opinions of me, as if I held many errors, who therefore looked upon me as an outlandifh man, made up of ftrange fafhions. . . . . And indeed there was fuch a neft of hornets (which I knew not of, till ftirring one I angered all) who came out all at once upon me fo faft that many feared I would lofe my life ere I got away; and indeed it is much mercy that I efcaped them fo well as I did, by the means of the moft honourable Commiffioners

Why the Author writ this? For name's fake.

The Author's fufferings by evil tongues.

Bethſhemeſh,
p. 50.

of Parliament's care of me and countenance to me. But now
theſe perſecuting and unchriſtian ſpirits, not being ſatisfied to
drive the poor, painful bees out of one hive into another, and
from one nation to another, as they have done ſome, but to
have the honey, which they would have, they will burn the
bees ; and therefore it ſeems they have ſent ſome (more
anointed with brimſtone than with the unction of the Spirit)
hither, to purſue here what they have begun ſo ungodlily there.
I will not for a world deny my daily failings, for which my ſoul
is kept continually low ; I muſt have many grains allowed me
to make me weight. ' Quiſnam ſine crimine vivit ?' Gold
hath droſs ; ſome gravel will ſtick on the toes coming out of
the pureſt bath. A good horſe may trip, too ; but is it not
better that the waters run, though they run but muddily, than
not at all ? Sibbs ſays it is, in his ' Smoking Flax,' p. 115.
Why, then, do theſe crows light ſo upon the carrion ? I will
confeſs it to my diſgrace, as much as any man will have me,
that I am ſubject to paſſion, and my heart is very proud and
deceitful, and too ſelf-ſeeking, the Lord knows ; and I hope I am
ſo far from juſtifying my corrupt ſelf in the leaſt, that I am always almoſt charging it upon myſelf, and can as heartily complain
of myſelf as any enemy I have in the world, even for thoſe things
they ſay, as of pride, paſſion, &c.

The Author
charges his
own ſelf as
much as they,
and makes no
account of
himſelf, but as
he is in a new
ſelf.

"But, merciful friends! deal not too rigidly with me ! . . . .
Scotus, that famous ſchoolman, in a fit of apoplexy, was, by the
cruel kindneſs of his over-officious friends, buried before he was
dead. And ſo it ſeems I muſt be (might ſome have their wills)
by the over-officious and cruel unkindneſs of ſome ſudden cen-
ſures. But, pray ſtay ! It is not the interpoſition of ſome clouds
that hinders or fruſtrates the motion of the ſun. And, beſides,
there is ſome light in the very ſpots of the moon ; and ſo
there may be in thoſe things which they account my ſpots, as
paſſion (perhaps), it may be zeal, &c. For when I met with
them, and took them by the hand, and prayed that there might

Great miſtakes
in their reports
of the Author.

be love, they called this hypocriſy. When I preached upon
Job xxiii. 10, in Chriſt's Church (the Cathedral is ſo called),
before the Commiſſioners in Dublin—viz. ' The Lord knoweth
the way that I take, and when he hath tried me I ſhall come
forth as gold,'—why ? becauſe they had abuſed me abroad in
the names of Pope, Hypocrite, Prieſt, Proud, Paſſionate, &c.—

they faid I preached myfelf and fought myfelf, with hundreds
of fuch paffages, as would obviate any unbiaffed underftanding,
and inform them how thefe reproaches are but the abortives of
malice and mifinterpretation. Notwithftanding, I fay, I will not,
nor can I, free myfelf from thefe that they accufe me for, nor
would I recriminate : and yet I muft fay I met with numberlefs
provocations. Now the moft exact archer, in fhooting at the mark,
may fail much when a man jogs him. And would it not vex a
fcrivener, after he had fpent many hours in writing a large leafe
or patent, that one juftling him purpofely makes him blot fo at the
laft word or line, that he muft be forced to write all over again
and to lofe all his labour? Such a plot there was to make me
blot. But, bleffed be God, Satan, I am fure, loft by it. . . . .
And albeit they fay I was not patient, I confefs (when a very little
fpark made them like gunpowder fly in my face) I felt a fore affliction to try my patience, to which ten for one have given a ' pro-
batum eft ' under their hands. But as the hufband that told his
wife he had one ill fault, viz. that he was given to be angry
without a caufe—' O,' fays his wife, ' I will remedy that, I
warrant ye ; fear not that fault, I fhall do well enough with you
for all that, for I fhall give you caufe enough,'—fo I have often
acknowledged it to them that I was given too much to be
impatient ; but they have as often made it appear that they were
as much given to give caufe enough—I fhould not want for that.
And, indeed, for flandering they excel all that I know of.

   Thus, dear friends, in a time of troubles and afflictions, diftractions and difturbances at Dublin, I began this treatife."

   In truth, *Rogers* found himfelf at Dublin in a falfe pofition ;
his old-fafhioned views, as they were confidered, on Infant Baptifm alienated one half of his congregation, and his new-fafhioned
views on other points, e.g. on religious toleration and the rights
of women, alienated the reft. For, "indeed in Dublin they did
no fooner efpy an opinion with a ftrange face, which they were
not ufed to, within their doors, but they afked whence he came
and what he did there, and bid him be thruft out by head and
fhoulders, or elfe carry him to the magiftrates, to be laid by the
heels ; and thus they dealt with thofe truths whofe face they were
not ufed to."

   On his return from Dublin *Rogers* re-eftablifhed himfelf at St.
Thomas Apoftle's ; fhortly afterwards his parifhioners in Effex

Bethfhemefh,
Epiftle to the
Churches, p.
43—54.

Bethfhemefh,
p. 48.

F

cited him for non-refidence. The cafe was argued in Court, was decided againft him, and he was deprived of the living. This kind of ufage very much troubled him; and he petitioned the Lords Commiffioners for his reftoration, but without fuccefs. He bade farewell to his parifhioners in an epiftle, which he publifhed a year afterwards in "Bethfhemefh," and of which the following is the principal part:—

An Epiftle to the Parifh of Purleigh, in Effex, nigh Maldon, wherein the Author was fettled Minifter till of late:—

Bethfhemefh,
p. 229.

DEAR FRIENDS,—

I call you dear, not only that I found you at a dear rate, but I am forced to leave you fo; yet fome of you are very dear to me and in my heart, and whom I can freely bear in my bofom to the Father. But becaufe the death or departure of a Minifter from his people fhould be his laft fermon, I muft therefore fay in general to you this, that my greateft grief for moft of you is, that, like the cyprefs, the more you were watered the more you withered. Would it not grieve you, hufbandmen, to fee your good feed every year to be loft and to lie and rot under huge hard clods, and never to bring forth fruits or to come up? So how can it but be my complaints before my Lord and Mafter when I give up my accounts (Heb. xiii. 17), and fay, Lord, I have preached! prayed! catechized! expounded! conferred for above this five years at Purleigh to fuch a people, and they have not believed nor obeyed thy word, but many of them are as ignorant, arrogant, bitter, profane ftill, ungodly and oppofers of Chrift and his Gofpel ftill as ever. O fad! what comfort can I have of this! Ah, it is too notorioufly known that I have taken much pains to little purpofe amongft you; and yet, O! what plottings and confpiracies there were againft me! what lies and libels were invented! what fcandals raifed! what fcoffs and fcorns I continually met with! what huge taxes and troubles you caſt upon me! what backbitings and railings every day! what variety of defigns were hatched in the midſt of you to afflict me!—yea, with plotted and premeditated malice and menacings to undo me! what work you made to render me contemptible to all the country, before magiſtrates, miniſters, people and all; yea, the children and ſervants ſet upon me to abuſe me! yea, to ſtone me! yea, to ſwear to take away my life from me! All which forced me to be much abſent from you. And O, friends, do ye think God will not viſit you for theſe things? Have ye not ſuffered your ſervants and children to laugh and ſport in the public places openly in the ſight of all the people whilſt the Word hath been preaching, and when I have mildly reproved them, to make mows and mocks at me in the open church—yea, to lay dog-whips and what not on the pulpit cuſhion when I was to preach? What kind of injury and abuſes have you not returned to me for all my love and pains, and care and continual prayers for you! Hath there one poor ſoul of us in Church communion eſcaped your malice and menacing, and your diligence to raiſe ill reports, and to cauſe wrongs to befall them? Have ye not vowed not to leave us till you had rooted all of us from you, and not left a Roundhead or Independent to dwell nigh you? Have ye not confulted with all the Malignants about how to bring to paſs theſe defigns, yet in the midſt of all theſe troubles and every-day new trials and wrongs from ſome or other of you, yet the Lord will one day witneſs what a care I had of you, when I could not be with or durſt not, how I provided for you, and how ye were the travail, as well as the trouble, of my ſoul. Yet when you had not worried me away with all this, how often did many of you defign to ſtarve me from you. And though like a bird kept in a cage without meat, yet I muſt do my duty, and ſing, though the thorn were ever at my breaſt. Still I followed you with love, patience, pity to your poor miferable fouls (O that ye knew it!) and with fweat and fwink, praying, preaching, and expounding, in feafon and out of feafon.

But as I have heard of the Seminary in Lancafhire, riding difguifed, that loft his glove, one that found it rode galloping after him to reftore it; but the Seminary fearing he was a Purfuivant, put fpurs to horfe and flew from him as faft as he could, and for fear he fhould be overtaken, he makes his horfe take a hedge, and fuddenly fkipping over, fell full into a defperate deep pit, wherein he was drowned prefently. O fo, Sirs, the fafter I have followed you to do good, to recover you, to help to fave you, why, alas! the fafter you fled away into fin, after fin rejecting all offers and opportunities almoft, refufing to come to hear the Word on the week-day, and many of you not coming above once on the Lord's day. Oh, alas! for the Lord's fake, hear, make not fuch poft-hafte in fin, to the ruin of your foul, body, and all; but, O, remember, the pit is but on the other fide; ye may foon be in it, but have a care left you perifh. Have I not fpent out my own bowels, and, like a candle, confumed myfelf even out to give you light? Have I thought my life too dear for your fouls? O no, but you would not regard it. Some pretended I was young, to keep them off; but alas! this was but a colour. Did not young *Solomon* give good counfel, young *Daniel* difcern much, young *Jofeph* fill the granary with plenty, and excel all the grandees and gravities in *Pharaoh's* Court for wifdom and judgment? Did not young *Timothy* preach the Gofpel powerfully and profitably? But indeed the main offence you know was my zeal for God, for filence is the bafeft tenure a Minifter can hold his living by. I could not be filent, but tell *Israel* of his fins and *Jacob* of his tranfgreffions.

Thus having ftood fentinel all this while among you, though I muft be juftled afide now from you, I have given you warning, and fo will leave you. And being thus to part, I fhall fay with *Synefius*, I carry nothing from Purleigh (of πῦρ and λαὸς, fire and people) but "bonam confcientiam et malam valetudinem," — a good confcience, an ill conftitution, and an empty purfe (being denied by you the bread I have earned with fweating brows). Yet the Lord fhow you mercy and melt your hearts. And fo farewell, dear hearts, farewell.

The Author's leave of Purleigh, and he may fay of England.

> Your affectionate friend and late your Minifter in the hot bowels of love to you, yet ready to ferve the meaneft and worft of you in the work of my Mafter Jefus Chrift, in and for whom I am
>
> JOHN ROGERS.

From my Study at Thomas Apoftle's,
Lond. March 25, 1653.

Rogers returned from Dublin to London in March or April, 1652 —that is to fay, about feven months after the defeat of *Charles II.* at Worcefter, about twelve months before the diffolution of the Long Parliament, and a few weeks before the beginning of the war between the Englifh and the Dutch.* In England the ftruggle between the Independents and Prefbyterians had ended in the afcendancy of the former; in Parliament a feries of defertions, "feclufions," and profcriptions had left fcarcely any but the Independents fitting; and in the army, both officers and men, from the *Lord General Cromwell* downwards, were of the Independent or of fome kindred fect. But, though the Prefbyterians had been purged out of Parliament and the army, they were ftill ftrong among the lawyers and parochial clergy; and now the Independents and other fectaries began to clamour loudly for law reform and the abolition of tithes. If thefe two meafures could be carried, lawyers and clergy would fall, and the triumph of the Independents would be complete.

---

* The Dutch ambaffadors took their final departure from London on the 30th of June, 1652. But the firft naval engagement between *Blake* and *Van Tromp* had taken place in May.

Befides the conteſt between Preſbyterians and Independents, there was heart-burning alſo between the Parliament and the Army. The Parliament propoſed to reduce the Army; in retaliation the Army preſſed for " a new Repreſentative "—that is to ſay, for the diſſolution of the exiſting Parliament and the election of another.

Rogers threw himſelf into all theſe ſtruggles with his whole force, ſiding, of courſe, with the Independents againſt the Preſbyterians, and with the Army againſt the Parliament. He wrote books againſt the Preſbyterian Clergy, he preached and propheſied againſt the Parliament, and he both wrote and pleaded againſt the Lawyers.

His enemies aſſerted that his animoſity againſt clergy and lawyers originated in perſonal reſentment againſt *Serjeant Maynard*,* the eminent lawyer, and *Zachary Crofton*, a Preſbyterian Miniſter. *Maynard* had been counſel againſt him in the Purleigh caſe, had obſtruƈted his preferment on another occaſion, and, moreover, had inſulted him, as he conceived, in open court. *Rogers* had a keen ſenſe of any injuſtice or indignity offered to himſelf, and the account he gives of this laſt affront ſhows perhaps that the allegations of his enemies againſt his temper were not wholly groundleſs.

Corrupt
lawyers. " Little leſs ſaid one of the corrupt lawyers, viz. *Mr. Maynard*, to me laſt March, before the Lords Commiſſioners of the Seal,† in the Parliament Chambers at the Temple, whilſt he was pleading the law for a Delinquent, Malignant Patron, over and over an open notorious enemy and cavalier againſt God and State, yet, having compounded, he muſt have the power to preſent a man of a wicked, malignant ſpirit—none elſe, and known for ſwearing, company-

---

* *Serjeant Maynard* was born at Taviſtock in 1602, was member for Totnes in the Long Parliament, and one of the managers of the impeachment of the *Earl of Strafford*, " whom," ſays *Anthony Wood*, " he baited to ſome purpoſe in the name of the Commons of England." Afterwards he performed the ſame office by *Archbiſhop Laud*. He, with other Preſbyterians, withdrew from the Long Parliament before the King's death. *Macaulay* deſcribes him as being, in 1689, " by univerſal acknowledgment the moſt ſubtle and the moſt learned of Engliſh juriſts."—*Hiſt. of Engl.* iv. 32.

† The Lords Commiſſioners of the Great Seal at this time were *Whitelock*, *Keeble*, and *John L'Iſle*.

keeping, and other vices; and he muſt force ſuch an one upon the poor people that never heard him ſo much as preach, to the joy of all the malignant, godleſs wretches in the country all about. . . . This *Mr. M.*, (one of the caſt-out members of the Houſe, I hear), pleading for this cauſe of the Devil (for I dare call it no other), much offended me, inſomuch that I was urged in conſcience to ſay before the Lords Commiſſioners, ' Sir, the Acts of the Apoſtles had been your beſt ſtatute book in this buſineſs about ſouls; you uſe not God's word.' But before I could go further, he punched me aſide, with ſome abuſive, foul-mouthed language, (as I hope ere long to declare to the world), ſaying, ' What do ye tell us of the word? we have the law,' &c. So the lawyers puſhed me aſide. But what a ſad thing is this, that ſuch laws and ſuch lawyers ſhould be ſuffered; and how can a good Reformation be laid upon ſo baſe a foundation? They are the lawyers all this while that have hindered the Reformation, and ſo they will as long as they have ſuch influence upon the Parliament.''

    Zachary Crofton's offence was of a deeper dye. On his return from Dublin *Rogers* had eſtabliſhed a Friday evening exerciſe or lecture at St. Thomas Apoſtle's, to which he attracted a large congregation. Shortly afterwards an anonymous pamphlet was publiſhed, entitled, " A Taſte of the Doctrine of Thomas Apoſtle,'' in which he and his exerciſe were ſeverely handled; the author-ſhip was attributed, apparently with truth, to *Crofton*, the Preſby-terian Miniſter of Garlick Hythe. It was imprudent to attack anonymouſly a man who was ſo regardleſs of conventionalities and ſo unſcrupulous about perſonalities as his antagoniſt; and *Zachary Crofton* found himſelf dragged into light as the author of the pam-phlet with the leaſt poſſible delay. " *Memnon*, the General of *Darius* his army, hearing a mercenary ſoldier with vile language revile *Alexander* and exclaim againſt him, he ſtruck him with a lance, ſaying he hired him to fight againſt him, not to rail upon him. Clamours againſt a very enemy require rather reproof than praiſe; and I think there was no man much commended, but much condemned that poor, empty, wide-mouthed libeller of Garlick-hithe for his pamphlet he put out lately, whereby he hath brought himſelf into the report and reproof of all that hear his name, which may be eminently up and famous ere long in London, as it is in Cheſhire and other places. I had, I confeſs, a full character of him indeed by *Maſter Mainwaring*, one that

They mock at the Word.

Lawyers hinder reformation.
Bethſhemeſh, p. 220-3.

As that libeller that put out The Taſte of Doctrine at Tho. Apoſtle's.

Bethſhemeſh,
p. 226-7.

knew him well in Cheſhire, at my *Lord Bradſhaw's* table lately; whilſt *Sir William Brereton*,* with an eminent Miniſter that knows him highly too, was by, and gave ſo good account of him that I cannot but wonder how he could end in one lying, impudent pamphlet, and like a ſquib too dry, it ſeems, flaſh all out at once."

About this time the Fifth-Monarchy-Men were attracting much attention. *Rogers* joined their ranks, and became quickly one of their leading miniſters. They were a ſmall but determined body of men, recruited chiefly from among the more enthuſiaſtic Independents. They believed that the age of the four firſt monarchies—the Aſſyrian, Perſian, Greek, and Roman, had paſſed or was rapidly paſſing away, that *Chriſt* was now coming to reign perſonally and viſibly in the fifth, and that when he came he would utterly deſtroy all thoſe anti-chriſtian Kings, Prieſts and Lawyers who now ſat on his throne and uſurped his powers. Then the ſaints would poſſeſs the earth, ruling it under *Chriſt* as his miniſters, and executing juſtice upon all his enemies. They believed alſo, and declared that, in anticipation of his coming, the preſent work urgently incumbent on the Saints was "to bring things as near as might be before *Chriſt* comes to what they ſhall be when he is come."

Old leaven
purged out,
p. 56.

They were in hot haſte to commence this preparatory work; and paſt ſucceſs had ſo intoxicated them that they ſaw no appalling difficulty in it. The ſword of the Saints had overthrown an anti-chriſtian church, had beheaded a bloody tyrant, and had conquered three kingdoms. That ſword, they thought, was in their hands; and here in England nothing remained to withſtand them but Preſbyterian prieſts, corrupt lawyers, and a ſuperannuated Parliament.

When the ſaints had firmly eſtabliſhed their dominion in England and had pulled down Antichriſt there, then they would wage war againſt the enemies of *Chriſt* and the oppreſſors of his people over the whole earth. Never ſhould the curſe of Meroz be applied to them—" Curſe ye Meroz; curſe ye bitterly the inhabit-

---

* *Bradſhaw* and *Brereton*, as well as *Mainwaring* and *Crofton*, were Cheſhire men. In 1644 *Sir William Brereton* was authorized by Parliament to eject all ſcandalous and ill-affected miniſters in Cheſhire, and to nominate others in their place.—*Scobell's Acts and Ordinances*, pt. 1, p. 67.

ants thereof, becaufe they came not to the help of the Lord, to the help of the Lord againſt the mighty."

Of courfe it was more eafy to juſtify thefe viſions from the Old Teſtament than from the New ; and accordingly it was in the Old Teſtament that they fought for laws, maxims, precedents, and examples. There, too, they found thofe texts which, when neceſſary, they could wreſt into their fervice, either to palliate a piece of folly or to fanĉtify a crime. Such were, for example, "The faints ſhall take the kingdom and poſſefs the kingdom ;"* "The fword of the Lord and of Gideon ;" "Curfed be he that doeth the work of the Lord deceitfully ;"† "Overturn, overturn, overturn ;"‡ and the latter part of the 149th Pfalm—"Let the faints be joyful with glory, let them rejoice in their beds ; let the praifes of God be in their mouth, and a two-edged fword in their hands, to be avenged of the heathen, and to rebuke the people ; to bind their kings in chains, and their nobles with links of iron : that they may be avenged of them, as it is written, Such honour have all his faints."

As the Gofpel of the Fifth-Monarchy-Men was to be propagated with the fword, fo the feĉt itfelf feems to have originated in the army. Many officers of the higheſt reputation belonged to it, or at the leaſt fympathized with it. Such were *Major-General Harriſon, Colonels Alured, Overton, Okey, Rich,* and *Danvers,*

---

* "But the faints of the Moſt High ſhall take the kingdom, and poſ-fefs the kingdom for ever, even for ever and ever. . . . . And the kingdom and dominion, and the greatnefs of the kingdom under the whole heaven, ſhall be given to the people of the faints of the Moſt High, whofe kingdom is an everlaſting kingdom ; and all dominion ſhall ferve and obey him."—*Dan.* vii. 18, 27.

† "Curfed be he that doeth the work of the Lord deceitfully [in margin 'negligently,'] and curfed be he that keepeth back his fword from blood."—*Jer.* xlviii. 10. South fpeaks of Harrifon as being "notable for having killed feveral after quarter given them by others, and uſing thefe words in the doing it—'Curfed be he,' &c."—*South's Sermons,* ii. 422.

‡ "Thus faith the Lord God, Remove the diadem and take off the crown ; this ſhall not be the fame ; exalt him that is low, and abafe him that is high. I will overturn, overturn, overturn it, and it ſhall be no more, until he come whofe right it is, and I will give it him."—*Ezek.* xxi. 26, 27.

Quartermaſter-General Courtney, Adjutant-General Allen, and others; beſides men of inferior rank, ſuch as *Spittlehouſe, Cornet Day,* and *Buttiphant,* of *Cromwell's* own life-guard—active, intriguing men, of conſiderable influence amongſt their equals. Theſe men generally were notorious as men who would neither ſpare their own blood nor the blood of others in the " Good Cauſe." *Cromwell* grudged no pains to gain them over to himſelf, and the baits he offered were the downfall of clergy and lawyers, and " No king but Jeſus."

This general account of the Fifth-Monarchy-Men would not be complete without more particular reference to *Major-General Harriſon,* their leader ; both becauſe in ability, reſolution, and reputation he far ſurpaſſed all other members of his party, and becauſe he will appear hereafter in perſonal and familiar aſſociation with *Rogers.*

The ſon of a grazier in Staffordſhire, he received a fair education at Nantwich, and was indentured afterwards to an attorney in Clifford's Inn. When the war broke out he joined the army of the Parliament as a cornet of horſe, and ſteadily roſe to diſtinction. In 1645 he ſerved the campaign under *Fairfax* as major, and afterwards colonel of *Fleetwood's* regiment, and is particularly mentioned in connection with the battle of Naſeby and the ſtorm of Baſing Houſe. *Hugh Peters* ſays, in a narrative of what fell under his own eyeſight after the ſtorm of Baſing Houſe :—" In the ſeveral rooms and about the houſe were ſlain ſeventy-four, and only one woman, the daughter of *Dr. Griffith,* who by her railing provoked our ſoldiers, then in heat, into a further paſſion. There lay dead upon the ground *Major Cuffle,* a man of great account amongſt them and a notorious Papiſt, ſlain by the hands of *Major Harriſon,* that godly and gallant gentleman, and *Robiſon* the player, who a little before the ſtorm was known to be mocking and ſcorning the Parliament and our army." Readers of *Sir Walter Scott* will remember *Roger Wildrake's* verſion of the death of " poor *Dick Robiſon* the player " by the hand of the butcher *Harriſon.*

In 1647 he received the thanks of the Houſe of Commons for his ſervices in Ireland. But perhaps his behaviour to *Charles I.* in 1648-9 is that by which he was then beſt known, and may ſtill be beſt appreciated. In 1648 he was charged with the reſponſibility of guarding the King as a priſoner from Hurſt Caſtle to

Sprigge's
Anglia
Rediviva, p.
139.

Windfor. The following account of the journey, condenfed from *Anthony Wood*, will not perhaps be thought wholly inadmiffible, in confideration of the light it throws on the charaƈteriftics of a man who was to his party the hero, faint, and martyr of their caufe. *Major Harrifon* reached Hurft Caftle, where the King was confined, unexpeƈtedly and at midnight. The noife awakened the King, who was in fome marvel to hear the drawbridge let down at that unfeafonable hour. When he heard the caufe, he told *Herbert*, his groom of the chambers, that this was the man who intended to affaffinate him, as he had been informed by letter. The major tarried two nights at Hurft Caftle ; and when it was dark, having given orders for the King's removal, he departed to the place from whence he came. A week afterwards the King was conveyed by a party of horfe from Hurft to Windfor. Near Farnham *Major Harrifon* appeared at the head of another party, to the end that he might bring up the rear. His party was drawn up in good order, by which his Majefty was to pafs ; and the major in the head of them, gallantly mounted, with a velvet montier on his head and a new buff coat on his back, with a crimfon filk fcarf about his waift, richly fringed. As the King paffed by on horfeback with an eafy pace, as delighted to fee men well horfed and armed, the major gave the King a bow with his head, a foldade which his Majefty requited. This was the firft time that the King faw the major ; at which time *Thomas Herbert*, groom of the chambers, "from whom" (fays *Wood*) "I had this ftory," riding a little behind the King, his Majefty called him to come near, and afked him who that captain was ; and being told by him that it was *Major Harrifon*, the King viewed him more narrowly, and fixed his eyes fo fteadily upon him as made the major abafhed, and fall back to his party fooner than probably he intended. The King faid he looked like a foldier, and that his afpeƈt was good, and found him not fuch an one as he was reprefented ; and that, having judgment in faces, if he had obferved him fo well before he fhould not have harboured that ill opinion of him. That night the King got to Farnham, where he was lodged at a private gentleman's houfe ; and a little before fupper, his Majefty, ftanding by the fire in a large wainfcoated parlour, and in difcourfe with the miftrefs of the houfe, the King, notwithftanding the room was pretty full with army officers and country people that crowded in to have a fight of him, did at length fee the major at the farther

Athenæ, ii. 590. Fafti, ii. 76.

end of the parlour, talking with another officer; whereupon,
beckoning to him with his hand to come nearer, he did fo accordingly with due reverence; and his Majefty, taking him by the
arm, drew him afide towards the window, where for half-an-hour
or more they did difcourfe together. Amongft other things, the
King minded him that he had received information concerning the
murder that he had intended on him in the Ifle of Wight, which,
if true, rendered him an enemy in the worft fenfe to his perfon.
The major, in his vindication, affured his Majefty that what was
reported of him was not true, yet he might report that the law was
equally obliging to great and fmall, and that juftice had no refpeét
of perfons; which his Majefty finding affeétedly fpoken and to
no good end, went to his fupper, being all the time very pleafant, which was no fmall rejoicing to them there, to fee him fo
cheerful in that company and in fuch a dolorous condition.

    Harrifon conduéted the King fafely to Windfor, and again
from Windfor to St. James's, in order to his trial, and fat with him
in the coach with his head covered, and talked with little or no reverence to him; and when the King propofed to him, " What do they
intend to do with me, whether to murder me or not ?" the major
made anfwer that there was no intention to kill him : " We have
no fuch thought; yet the Lord hath referved you for a public
example of juftice."

Clarendon, vol.
vi. p. 224-6.
    According to Clarendon, the officers about this time confulted
frequently what to do with the King. Some were for depofing
him, others for taking away his life by poifon; a third party,
headed by *Ireton* and *Harrifon*, would not endure either of the
other ways, and urged his being brought to juftice in the fight of
the fun; and this party carried their point.

    Harrifon fat in the High Court of Juftice, and figned the
King's death-warrant.

    In 1651, when *Oliver Cromwell* was in Scotland, *Harrifon*, as
major-general, was left in charge of Cumberland and the borders.
When the Scotch army marched into England, he attended and
haraffed it. Afterwards he and *Cromwell* united their forces
before Worcefter, where *Charles II.* and the Scotch army were
finally defeated. *Harrifon* with the cavalry had charge of the
purfuit.

    At the time of the diffolution of the Long Parliament, he was
M.P. for Wendover and Aylefbury, and a member of the Council

of State. Clarendon fays, " There were few men with whom *Cromwell* more communicated, or upon whom he more depended for the condu&t of anything committed to him."

Clarendon, vi. 220.

Baxter fays of him, that he was like *Cromwell*, who would not openly profefs what opinion he was of, but was moft inclined to Anabaptifm and Antinomianifm. " He would not difpute with me at all," fays *Baxter*, " but he would in good difcourfe very fluently pour out himfelf in the extolling of free grace, which was favoury to thofe that had right principles, though he had fome mifunderftandings of free grace himfelf. He was a man of excellent natural parts for affe&tion and oratory, but not well feen in the principles of his religion ; of a fanguine complexion, naturally of fuch vivacity, hilarity, and alacrity as another man hath when he hath drunken a cup too much, but naturally alfo fo far from humble thoughts of himfelf that it was his ruin."

Reliquiæ Baxterianæ, pt. i. p. 57.

Harrifon ufed to fcandalize the Puritans by the gaiety of his attire. *Mrs. Hutchinfon*, who was ftrongly prejudiced againft him, tells a ftory of his perfuading *Colonel Hutchinfon* and others to come to the Houfe of Commons on fome great occafion in plain black fuits, after which he appeared himfelf " in a fcarlet coat and cloak, both laden with gold and filver lace, and the coat fo covered with clinquant (foil) that one fcarcely could difcern the ground : and in this glittering habit he fet himfelf juft under the Speaker's chair ; which made the other gentlemen think that his godly fpeeches the day before were but made that he alone might appear in the eyes of ftrangers. But this was part of his weaknefs ; the Lord at laft lifted him up above thefe poor earthly elevations, which then and fome time afterwards prevailed too much with him."

Mem. of Col. Hutchinfon, p. 348.

The hiftory of the diffolution of the Long Parliament (April 20, 1653,) has been told fo often, and is fo well known, that it would be unneceffary to repeat it, except for the fake of fhowing how *Oliver Cromwell* made ufe of the Fifth-Monarchy-Men in preparing the way for his defign, and of *Harrifon* in executing it.

Contemporary writers ftate that *Cromwell* at this time made " higher pretences to honefty than ever he had done before, thereby to engage *Major-General Harrifon, Colonel Rich,* and their party to himfelf. To this end he took all occafions in their prefence to afperfe the Parliament as not defigning to do thofe good things they pretended to, but rather intending to fupport the corrupt interefts of the clergy and lawyers." And he " did induf-

Ludlow, ii.
449.

trioufly publifh that they were fo in love with their feats that they
would ufe all means to perpetuate themfelves." " Every other day
almoft more fafts or fome fuch religious exercife was managed by
Cromwell and *Harrifon,* who mainly promoted the fame propofals for
a new Reprefentative, in order to the perfonal reign of Chrift ; and
that therefore it was high time the Government was placed in the
hands of his faints, for all the prophecies thereof were now ready
to be fulfilled ; and this was cried up as the doctrine of the times.
Cromwell feemed to be of the fame judgment and of that Millenary
principle. . . . . So that he had abfolutely fooled *Harrifon* into
a confidence of his good intentions, and that he aimed not at his
own greatnefs ; and thereupon all the party *Harrifon* could make,
which was *Feak's, Rogers',* and *Simpfon's* congregations, were impatient to have the Parliament outed, and their fine module to
take place, wherein righteoufnefs and holinefs fhould be exalted in

Heath's
Flagellum, p.
124, 125.

the kingdoms of the world." " Divers of the clergy from their pulpits began to prophecy the deftruction of the Parliament, and to
propofe it openly as a thing defirable. Infomuch that the General,
who had all along concurred with this fpirit in them, hypocriti-
cally complained to *Quartermafter-General Vernon,*＊ " that he was
pufhed on by two parties to do that the confideration of the iffue
whereof made his hair to ftand on end. One of thefe," faid he,
" is headed by *Major-General Lambert.* . . . . Of the other
Major-General Harrifon is the chief, who is an honeft man, and
aims at good things, yet, from the impatience of his fpirit, will not
wait the Lord's leifure, but hurries me on to that which he and

Ludlow, ii.
449.

all honeft men will have caufe to repent." *Cromwell* joined " with
Major-General Harrifon, being confident that when he had ufed
him and his party to diffolve the prefent Government, he could
crufh both him and them at his pleafure ; and though it was no
difficult matter to difcover this, yet thofe poor, deluded, however

Do. p. 454.

well-meaning men, would not believe it."
    In the meantime the fitting members of the Long Parliament
had feen that a diffolution was inevitable ; but they hoped to anti-
cipate the defigns of *Cromwell* by a bill which they had prepared
themfelves. This bill, however, contained claufes which were

＊ Quartermafter-General Vernon (fometimes called Captain Vernon)
was a rigid Anabaptift, and a ringleader of the party which drove Rogers out
of Ireland (*vide* p. 29). He preached violently againft the Protectorate.

wholly incompatible with *Cromwell's* plans ; and accordingly, he was refolved that it fhould never pafs. On the morning of April 20th, 1653, Parliament met as ufual at Weftminfter, and *Sir Henry Vane* arofe and preffed for the paffing the bill immediately. At this time *Cromwell,* with fome of his officers, was in council at Whitehall ; while *Harrifon* and others were in their places in Parliament. By thefe laft a meffenger was hurried off to fummon *Cromwell.* *Sir Henry Vane* fat down, and *Major-General Harrifon* rofe, and "moft fweetly and humbly defired" the members to lay the bill afide, fhowing them the danger of it. *Harrifon* fat down, *Vane* rofe to reply, and *Cromwell* arrived. Calling to *Harrifon,* who was on the other fide of the Houfe, to come to him, he told him that he judged the Houfe ripe for a diffolution, and this to be the time of doing it. The major-general anfwered, (as he fince told me, fays Ludlow), "Sir, the work is very great and dangerous ; therefore I defire you ferioufly to confider of it before you engage in it." "You fay well," replied the General, and thereupon fat ftill for about a quarter of an hour ; he faid again to *Major-General Harrifon,* "This is the time—I muft do it ;" and fuddenly ftanding up, made a fpeech wherein he loaded the Parliament with the vileft reproaches, charging them not to have a heart to do anything for the public good, to have efpoufed the corrupt interefts of Prefbytery and the lawyers, who were the fupporters of tyranny and oppreffion, accufing them of an intention to perpetuate themfelves in power, had they not been forced to the paffing of this act, which, he affirmed, they defigned never to obferve ; and thereupon told them that the Lord had done with them, and had chofen other inftruments for the carrying on his work that were more worthy.

Cromwell then called in the foldiers ; "whereupon the fergeant attending the Parliament opened the doors, and *Lieutenant-Colonel Worfley,* with two files of mufketeers, entered the Houfe ; which *Sir Henry Vane,* obferving from his place, faid aloud, 'This is not honeft ; yea, it is againft morality and common honefty!' Then *Cromwell* fell a railing at him, crying out with a loud voice, 'O, *Sir Henry Vane ! Sir Henry Vane !* the Lord deliver me from *Sir Henry Vane !*' Then, pointing to the Speaker in his chair, he faid to *Harrifon,* 'Fetch him down.' *Harrifon* went to the Speaker and fpoke to him to come down ; but the

Marginal notes:

"Several Proceedings in Parliament," April 14-21, No. 186.

Ludlow, ii. 455.

Do. p. 456.

Do. p. 457.

Speaker fat ftill and faid nothing. Then *Harrifon* went and pulled the Speaker by the gown, and he came down. It happened that *Algernon Sidney* fat next to the Speaker, on the right hand. The General faid to *Harrifon*, 'Put him out.' *Harrifon* fpake to *Sidney* to go out; but he faid he would not go out, but fat ftill. The General faid again, 'Put him out.' Then *Harrifon* and *Worfley* (who commanded the General's own regiment of foot) put their hands upon *Sidney's* fhoulders, as if they would force him to go out. Then he rofe and went towards the door. Then the General went to the table where the mace lay, which ufed to be carried before the Speaker, and faid, 'Take away thefe baubles.' So the foldiers took away the mace."

Leicefter's
Journal, p.
141, quoted in
Forfter's Oliver
Cromwell, ii.
63.

In the afternoon of the fame day *Cromwell*, attended by *Lambert* and *Harrifon*, came to the Council of State, where *Bradfhaw* was prefiding, and diffolved that alfo.

Whitelock fays the diffolution of Parliament " occafioned much rejoicing in the King's party, who now daily expected the deftruction of *Cromwell* and his party and army, yet made great applications and congratulations to him. Thofe of the Parliament's party were at a ftand ; divers fierce men, paftors of churches, and their congregations, were pleafed at it, and generally the officers and foldiers of the army."

Whitelock,
April 20,
1653, p. 555.

Cromwell convened a meeting of the chief officers of the army at Whitehall, on the 21ft, the day after the diffolution ; and during the next ten days he and this Council were " bufy in confultation to find out a new Government and Governor for their Commonwealth." The creation of a Council of State was the firft difficulty ; and the propofals made when the fubject was debated were very characteriftic of the times and the men. " *Major-General Lambert* moved that a few perfons, not exceeding the number of ten or twelve, might be entrufted with the fupreme power. *Major-General Harrifon* was for a greater number—inclining moft to that of feventy, being the number of which the Jewifh Sanhedrim confifted ;" and *Okey* and others were for thirteen, in imitation of Chrift and his twelve apoftles.

Do. p. 555.

Ludlow, ii.
462.
Forfter's
Oliver
Cromwell, ii.
129.

While the officers were debating, *Rogers* was writing ; and, five days after the diffolution of Parliament, he publifhed his opinion of the crifis, with a fcheme of his own for a new Government. It muft be obferved that the following, and the four fimilar letters which will appear hereafter, although not encumbered with the ufual figns of omiffions, contain yet little more than fcanty extracts from the letters originally publifhed :—

To his Excellency the Lord General Cromwell : *a few pro-pofals relating to Civil Government, humbly offered by* John Rogers, *an unworthy fervant of Chrift, and preacher of the Gofpel, now at* Tho. *Apoftles, London.*

RIGHT HONOURABLE,—

Whilft my foul is boiling over into earneft prayers to the Great Jehovah for wifdom, counfel, and courage for you in this exigency of importance, as the great deliverer of His people through God's grace out of the land of Egypt, I am vifited with that word in Exodus (xii. 42), "It is a night to be much obferved unto the Lord for bringing them out of Egypt. This is that night of the Lord to be obferved of all the children of Ifrael in their generations." So this is the day (viz. April 20, 1653) to be much obferved, the rather for that in the revolution of times the changes will run their round out, and then the Lord will come to reign.

But, my Lord, my heart is full. I am preffed in fpirit, and fo are many others (after a folemn meeting of prayers with hundreds of this city at Thos. Apoftles, London, about this change, and to feek God for you), to prefent you with thefe following propofals :

I. That your Excellency do choofe the men that muft govern this Commonwealth (being that it is the judgment of many faithful difcerning Minifters that you are called thereunto by God). So *Mofes* did choofe able men to be Rulers in Exodus (xviii. 25, 26). And they judged the people at all feafons, but the hard cafes they brought to *Mofes.* And *Jofhua,* the next General (with 's officers), commanded the people. "The Lord faid to *Jofhua* (though in another cafe), take you twelve men out of the

1ft Propofal.

H

people, one of a tribe," &c. After this *Gideon*, the General of that little army of three bands that deftroyed the huge hofts of the Midianites, was offered by the Ifraelites the government (Judges viii. 22), for he had won it; and *Nehemiah* (chap. vii. 2) gave commiffions out to men fearing God to govern, and fo all the Governours that ever were victorious in the Word were either Rulers themfelves, or elfe chofen to be fuch, or elfe chofe fuch. Wherefore we fay as *Ezra* (vii. 25), "And thou, after the wifdom of thy God that is in thine hand, fet magiftrates and judges, which may judge all the people that are beyond the river, all fuch as know the laws of thy God, and teach ye them that know them not."

2 Propofal.

The fecond propofal, as to the number of perfons that fhall govern, I humbly propofe either a Synhedrin, Parliament, Council of Seventy, or elfe one of a county; for that in the Commonwealth of Ifrael (which is our beft pattern) they had three forts of Courts—the Upper Court, or Synhedrin, which confifted of feventy. The fecond fort of Synhedrin was called the Lower Court, and confifted of twenty-three; and the third Court confifted but of three Judges in fmall cities. But fecondly, or elfe choofe one of a county reprefenting that county, as one of a tribe did reprefent the tribe (Numbers i. 4), "And with you there fhall be a man of a tribe." But if the prefent juncture of affairs requires a quicker defpatch that in the interim twelve worthies may be chofen as prefent Governors (Jofhua iv. 1, 2; Numbers i. 4), like to Ifrael's twelve Judges.

3 Propofal.

The third propofal, as to their qualifications. They muft be men fearing God (Nehem. vii. 2; Exod. xviii. 21); lovers of truth and juftice (Deut. xvi. 18); hating bribes and covetoufnefs (which corrupt juftice), (Deut. xvi. 19; Exod. xviii. 21); not refpecters of perfons (Deut. i. 17, and xvi. 19); wife (though not politic), and underftanding in the times and feafons (Deut. i. 13). They muft govern as the fervants of Jefus Chrift, but not as Lords over Chrift, left the nobles be like Oreb and Zeb, and the princes as Zeba and Salmunna, that take the houfes of God (i. e. Chrift's government and jurifdiction over churches and confciences) into their poffeffion. Such are fet as on a wheel upon the run till they have run themfelves all to pieces; and this was openly declared would be the ruin of this Parliament at Tho. Apoftles, Feb. 18, unlefs God prevented : a day when we and the Navy were engaged all day long.*

The fourth propofal is, that the righteous of the worthies of the late Parliament may be owned with honour.   *4 Propofal.*

The fifth propofal is, that the Rulers be fet folemnly and publicly apart by prayer to God.   *5 Propofal.*

Thefe five propofals (Right Honourable) put in practice, with God's bleffing, fhall ferve as five fingers for the work, and will fhew that the hand of the Lord is with us, wherefore confult with the Saints (Deut. i. 13), and fend to all difcerning fpirited men for their propofals.

And I befeech your Excellency to accept thefe few from a faithful Commonwealth man, and one who defires nothing of your Excellency for himfelf but to be one of the meaneft of your fervants for Chrift and this Commonwealth,

JOHN ROGERS.

From my Study, Tho. Apoftles,
  25th day of fecond month Zin, 1653.

Subfequent events fhowed that thefe " five-fingered propofals," as they were afterwards called, were not put forward without a pretty accurate foreknowledge of the Lord General's intentions. A few days after their publication *Cromwell* and the Council of Officers decided that the Council of State fhould confift of *Oliver Cromwell* himfelf and of eight officers and four civilians, amongft

---

* " 1653, Feb. 18. A terrible fight near the Ifle of Wight and Portland, and the Dutch beaten."—*Hiftorian's Guide*, p. 36.

See Oliver Cromwell's Speech, Carlyle, ii. 217.

whom the worthies of the late Parliament were confpicuoufly owned. *Rogers'* concluding recommendation of confulting the Saints was then fully complied with; minifters in various parts of the country, on whom the Council could rely, were directed to take the fenfe of the Congregational or Independent Churches in their feveral counties, and to fend up to the Lord General and his officers the names of perfons "able, loving truth, fearing God, and hating covetoufnefs," whom they judged "qualified to manage a truft in the enfuing government." This being done, *Cromwell* chofe his own Parliament. He gave it the form of a county reprefentation, excluding all cities and boroughs except London; he impofed no other qualification than that "of fearing God and of approved fidelity;" and within a week of their meeting his no-minees in Parliament had fet apart a day for feeking the direction of God, and had paffed a refolution to ftir up the godly of the nation to the fame effect. The only point, in fact, in which *Rogers'* programme was not accurately followed, was that of numbers. The Council of State confifted of 13 inftead of 12,

Forfter, ii. 139. Thurloe, i. 395. "Exact Relation," in Somers' Tracts, vi. 2;7, 266.

and the Parliament of 140 inftead of 70. The Council met for the firft time April 29, 1653. A prefident was chofen weekly : *Lambert* was the firft, *Pickering* the fecond, and *Harrifon* the third. Five weeks, however, elapfed between the nomination of the Council of State and that of the new Parliament, and in the mean time *Rogers* addreffed to *Oliver Cromwell* a fecond letter. It occurs as a dedicatory epiftle to one of his controverfial works. The following extracts will give fome notion of its ftyle and contents :—

Bethfhemefh, p. 1.

The Epiftle

to the

Right Honourable his Excellency

the

Lord General Cromwel,

With an humble Requeft of John Rogers, *Preacher of the Gofpel.*

MY LORD,—

    I was bold to prefent your Excellency, fome five weeks fince, with a handful of propofals, fetched from the Commonwealth of Ifrael, for which it is well known to God and man what uncharitable cenfures, rigid reprehenfions, fcurrilous, keen-tongued, and cutting calumnies, my way lay in that (and fo doth in this), through both from feeming friends and ferious foes.

Thus far, my Lord, I am entered the lifts, and though in the midft of thefe hot engagements, and without a partner too but Chrift, yet have I and fo do I lift up my voice aloud, which I hope fomewhat moves your Excellency to fay, Be of good cheer, for we will engage with you— i. e. for Chrift in the quarrel againft Antichrift and the bloody Beaft. Wherefore that my words and your works may be fteeped all over in the unction with fpread fails for good fuccefs, prayer comes with them and compofes them thus :—

Firft, that your Excellency's eyes may fee the fall of Antichrift and of mere national interefts, the fame as they rofe up.

Secondly, as to the Commonweale. That your Excellency (with the others of the Lords Worthies) go on in the name of the great Jehovah Elohim, in looking out for and then overlooking of the Governors of this Nation ; and feeing running waters are always fweeteft, that there might be a yearly election (or fo) of officers in greateft truft or power, leaft they fhould in time affume an abfolutenefs to themfelves, and become oppreffors. O deliver the Lord's people from proud, confronting *Pharaohs*, *Tobiahs*, and *Sanballats*, and fuch abominable, malignant Committee-men as are in the countries ; and from the intolerable oppreffions (which fqueeze out the very hearts of thoufands) both of the Norman iron yoke of corrupt lawyers, that live by fin, and from the wills, humours, paffions and lufts of men, efpecially of fuch as grow rich by our ruin, of which many godly men and women of feveral parts of this nation have bitterly complained, and with tears told me how the lawyers had undone them and then laughed at them. And alfo from the oppreſſion of that Babylonian, brazen yoke of tithes ; as alſo of pariſh church conſtitutions, ſoul-tyrannizing advow-ſons and preſentations, which make a mere ſale of ſouls and keep up a national, antichriſtian, corrupt intereſt in miniſters and people, as appears in the following treatiſe. And, in-deed, as to maintenance, I do as heartily ſeek the Lord that miniſters might not have too much, as that they might not have too little. And to ſpeak for one, I do profeſs it from my heart that the greateſt temptations I ſhould fear falling into (if I know my own heart) would be great honour, eſteem, place, preferment, or means too much and unfit for me.

Thirdly and eſpecially. Every tongue is now tipt with talk of a treaty with the Hollanders and other nations. But if you make leagues, O let not Chriſt be forgotten! to covenant for your ſelves or national intereſts and forget his! O ! a peace upon the account of Chriſt, to engage together againſt Antichriſt, Rome, prelates, enemies in all nations—to ſtand and fall, live and die together, in one cauſe, for the bare and very intereſt of Chriſt, would be a bleſſed peace indeed, without a penny from the purſe of them to boot. But without this it is not all their treaſures and eſtates that can make us a comfortable peace or league. For in Judges ii. 2, " Ye ſhall make no league with them, but throw down their altars," &c.

But now, Right Honourable, I muſt beſeech you—

1. To ſhun thoſe ſhelves, ſands, and rocks which your predeceſſors (viz. Kings, Lords, and the late Parliament), ran aground againſt and were broken all to pieces by ; I mean in matters of religion ; for believe it, however ſome ſay, that if men will uſurp Chriſt's power therein, they will find it a ſtone that will grind them to powder (Zach. xii. 3).

2. Countenance all you can (in your orbs, civil and military) the Congregational churches, as the gates and

palaces of Sion. For true zeal and devotion will take no pleafure to dwell flovenly, like *Galba's* wit, under a deformed roof (as in mixed congregations or antichriftian church-ways). But—

3. Left we lofe the fubftance for the fhadow, there be, my Lord, a hidden number of faints (fo called in Ps. lxxxiii. 3), that you muft be a fhield to, too, in your capacity. They are as yet fcarce known in the world, as they will be ere long, when the elements are a little clearer.

For thefe ends and ufes the Lcrd our God, we truft, hath anointed and appointed you; wherefore let thefe lines be accepted by your Excellency, and ferve for refrefhment to you in your fubfecive hours, and when you can, to take a turn or two in this treatife, among fuch trees of righteoufnefs as are of the Lord's own planting (in his gardens), which will lead you with delight (if the Lord give but light) to James's* (the Apoftle), yea, beyond, till you come to make Sion's Houfe for your Excellency's habitation. Some compare *Queen Elizabeth* to a fluttifh houfewife, who fwept the houfe, but left the duft behind the door. But now you, my Lord, have fwept the whole houfe indeed, even whilft they were faying, "We fhall never be moved, but ftand fure as a mountain," Ps. xxx. 6, 7, as fome Parliament men have fince acknowledged it in difcourfe with me. O, then, fet not afide the broom now, (for new brooms fweep clean). Go on untill you caft all the duft and filth that lay behind the door (in the late Parliament) out, as fitteft for the common fewer. As faft as may be to it, my Lord, and the Lord fend you good fpeed!

But the moft wife God guide you! And that he may

---

* In Feb. 1650, the Houfe of Commons had refolved "that the Lord Lieutenant of Ireland (Oliver Cromwell) have the ufe of the lodgings called the Cock-pit, of the Spring Garden and St. James's Houfe, and the command of St. James's Park."—*Carlyle*, i. 507.

double the fpirit of your predeceffors upon you, viz. of *Mofes, Jofhua, Gideon, Nehemiah,* and all others whom he hath anointed for the Government of his people, is and fhall be the prayer of one who is willing to be anything till he be nothing, and would be nothing, though in a dungeon or on a dung-hill, fo that his Lord and Mafter Chrift may be all, who is in him,

Your Excellency's unfeignedly

Humble Servant,

JOHN ROGERS.

Thomas Apoftles, Tamuz, the 4th month, the 3rd day, 1653.

Cromwell's new Parliament, which has been already defcribed, was fummoned on the 8th of June, five days after the date of this dedicatory epiftle, and met at Whitehall on the 4th of July. It conftituted what was called by its friends "the Little Parliament," and by others the " Barebones Parliament," from *Praife-God Barbone,* a leather-feller in the City, one of the feven members for London. One hundred and thirty-eight members attended out of the one hundred and forty who were fummoned; and by the inftrument of Government handed to them by *Cromwell* and his officers, they were empowered to fit until November 3, 1654. Three months before their diffolution they were to make choice of other perfons to fucceed them, who were not to fit longer than a year, and were to provide for a further fucceffion in Government. At one of the earlieft fittings it was voted that the bufinefs of tithes fhould without delay be taken into confideration; and prefently afterwards a fimilar refolution was carried in regard to the law. Committees were appointed, and tithes and law reform became again the prominent queftions of the day.

Whitelock, p 559.

CHAPTER III.

N the courfe of this year *Rogers* publifhed his two chief controverfial works on the great religious and political queftions of the day. One of thefe books, from which I have already quoted largely, was called "Bethfhemefh," and the other "Sagrir." The firft was written againft the Clergy (Prefbyterian), and the fecond againft the Lawyers. "Bethfhemefh" was anfwered, in its own ftyle and fpirit, by *Zachary Crofton*, in "Bethfhemefh Clouded." The following account of thefe books will throw light on the perfonal character and hiftory of the controverfialifts, as well as on their ftyle of controverfy and their peculiar and antagoniftic tenets. But the reader for whom fuch difputes have no attraction may omit the whole of this chapter and pafs on to the next, without any interruption to the thread of the narrative.

"Ohel or Bethfhemefh, a tabernacle for the Sun, or Irenicum Evangelicum, an Idea of Church Difcipline," was written before, and revifed and publifhed immediately after, the diffolution of the Long Parliament. It profeffed to prove that the Congregational form of church government adopted by the Independents was that which was moft in accordance with Scripture, with primitive practice, and with reafon. It contained, amongft other things, moft of the materials for a hiftory of the author's life up to the period of its publication, a confeffion of faith, and a full exhibition of his opinions and feelings on the points of immediate controverfy between his party and the reft of the Chriftian world, or at leaft thofe divifions of it which he enumerates as containing his probable opponents. "Of this number," he fays, "are Epifcopalians, Prefbyterians, Papifts, and Anabaptifts (I mean the

moſt formal and furious of them,) and Ranters, yea, and the very
formal and prelatic proud ſort of Independents too will join iſſue
with the reſt as diſcontented perſons. The Preſbyterians," he adds,
" I encounter moſt with, and the hotteſt conflict comes at laſt, in
chap. 9, lib. 2, though every foot we fall a pickeering before, and

Bethſhemeſh,
Epiſtle to the
Churches,
p 56.
P. 350.

now and then have pretty hot ſkirmiſhes."

The confeſſion of faith it may be worth while to tranſcribe in
extenſo. It is as follows :—

1 Cor. viii. 5,
6 ; John viii.
17, 18, 19 ; 1
John v. 5-9 ;
Matt xxviii.
19, 20.

" I acknowledge and profeſs from my very heart, before
the Lord and you all here preſent, that I do believe there is
but one God, who is omnipotent, omniſcient, omnipreſent,
and an infinite and all-glorious Being, and diſtinguiſhed into
three ſubſiſtences, or (if that word offend) I will ſay into three
perſonal proprieties and relations, according to his ſeveral
operations and adminiſtrations, namely, of the Father, Son,
and Holy Ghoſt. The Father is of himſelf, the Son pro-
ceedeth from the Father, and the Spirit from them both.
And although the ſaints cannot take hold of God as God
incomprehenſible and inapprehenſible, yet they know him

Rom. i. 19,
20.

as a Father, as a Son, as a Spirit dwelling in them, and ſo
far as his ſeveral attributes makes him known to them.

1. The Father.
Iſa. xl. 28 and
xliii. 15 ; 1
Peter iv. 19 ;
Rom. iii. 6 ; 2
Chron. xx. 6 ;
Ps. lxvi. 7.

" Firſt, concerning the Firſt Perſon (ſo called) of the
Trinity, or God the Father ; that He is the Great Creator
and Governour of all things in heaven and earth, eternally
diſtinct (as in Himſelf) from all creatures (as creatures) in
His abſolute Being and abſolute Well-being, and that this
God ſhall judge the world.

2. The Son.
Acts x. 42,
43 ; Iſa. xlv.
21, 22 ; 1
John v. 20 ;
Iſa. ix. 6, 7 ;
1 Tim. ii. 5 ;
1 John iv. 2.
3 ; 2 John 7.

" But, ſecondly, concerning the ſecond in the Trinity,
the Son, *Jeſus Chriſt*, of whom *Moſes*, the Prophets, and
the Apoſtles wrote, and in whom all the Scriptures are and
ſhall be fulfilled, I believe him, as he is both God and
man, making a complete mediator ; and as God, equal to
the Father, as man, of the tribe of *Judah*, the line of *David*,
the ſeed of *Abraham*, and born of *Mary*, &c. and as both
the only mediator between God and man. And he was

from everlafting, (and yet) as man from the womb he was feparated, called, appointed, and anointed moft fully with all gifts and graces neceffary for all mankind.

" Concerning his offices—that he is King, Prieft, and Prophet.

" Firft, as the Prophet, he hath revealed his Father's whole will, fo far as is neceffary for falvation, in his word and ordinances, and fpeaks it to his Church and faints by his word and Spirit.

" Secondly, as Prieft, being confecrated for us he hath appeared to put away fin, and hath offered himfelf the facrifice for the fins of the people, once for all, laying down his life for his fheep; and he hath abfolutely abolifhed all legal and ceremonial rites and fhadows, and is now entered into the Holy of Holies, and fits at the right hand of Glory making interceffion for us.

" Thirdly, as King in general, all power is given him in heaven and earth; and he doth exercife his power over men and angels, good and bad, for the fafety of his faints, and deftruction of his enemies, till he hath made them all his footftool.

" In particular, that Chrift is King over his Church, and fhall reign on earth fpiritually in the hearts of his faints and by his word and Spirit. He gathers all his peoples together from idolatry, fuperftition, darknefs, &c. into his own fpiritual way of worfhip and holinefs, and brings them to the Father; and by his Spirit he makes them a peculiar people, a royal priefthood, a holy generation, and inftructs and governs them by his laws prepared for his Church and people.

" Thirdly, concerning the Spirit (the third of the Trinity), that he is fent by the Father and the Son to make application of the whole work of Redemption to thofe whom the Father hath given to the Son by His decree, and whom the Son hath brought to the Father by his blood, according

His Offices :
(1). Prophet.
Mic. v. 4 ;
Mal. iii. 1 ;
Deut. xviii. 15 ;
Acts iii. 22,
23 ; Ifa. liv.
13.

(2). Prieft.
Heb. ix. 12,
14; x. 3, 10;
Ephes. v. 2 ;
1 Pet. ii. 24 ;
John x. 15;
Colos. ii. 14,
15; Ifa. liii.
12; Heb. xii.
24.

(3). King.
Firft, in general.
Matt. xxviii.
18; Ps. ii. 6;
xlv. 6 ; Heb. i.
8; Ifa. ix. 6,
7 ; Rev. ii. 26,
27.

Secondly, in particular.
Matt. ii. 2 ;
Luke i. 33,
74, 75 ; xix.
27; Phil. ii. 9;
Haggai ii. 7 ;
Heb. xii. 27,
28 ; Ifa. xlv.
22 ; Mic. iv.
2, &c.

3. The Spirit.
John xvi. 13,
14; Eph. i.
13; 14 ; iv.
30; Zach. ix.
11; Mal. iii.
1 ; Heb. x. 29;

to the everlafting covenant made between the Father and the Son, which the Spirit carries on to us as the covenant of free grace for our falvation. By the operation of this Holy Spirit in me this grace was begun firft by and through the Law, which awakened me fo as that I faw I was loft and undone for ever, and then by the Gofpel, whereby Chrift was revealed to me (and in me by his Spirit), and his righteoufnefs cleared up mine. (But of this hereafter).

" This Spirit applied Chrift Jefus (as far as I knew him) manifefted to and in me, by which I was brought at length to clofe with Chrift, and that fo unfeignedly that I refolved
to lofe all before Chrift. So fuch are—firft, by Chrift's righteoufnefs juftified; fecondly, by his Spirit adopted fons; thirdly, by his grace fanctified and really changed to the piety and purity of God's holy image (gradually); and fourthly, glorified and changed from mifery to happinefs, which begins in the inward fenfe of God's foul-melting love to them in Chrift, from whence is the hope of glory
and affurance of falvation, joy, peace, and happinefs within, &c.

" Fifthly, concerning the Scriptures in Old and New Teftament, they are the Word of God, as they were writ and indited by the Holy Spirit, and that they are the ftanding rule left us both for our knowledge and practice, doctrine and difcipline here below.

"Sixthly, I believe that by the firft *Adam's* difobedience we all fell, and that we are all by nature the children of wrath, dead in fins and trefpaffes; and that thofe who live and die in their fins cannot be faved, nor any without regeneration or new birth.

" Seventhly, concerning the Church of Chrift, I know it is but one body Univerfal and Catholic, and that it is of all faints, paft, prefent, and to come, invifible and vifible, yea fpiritual and formal. But this I alfo believe, that God hath left a rule in his Word for Particular Congregational

Churches here upon earth as the vifible, to make up his one entire and univerfal body.

"Eighthly. Now, concerning Chrift's particular Churches I believe, as I have preached and proved, fuch a church to be a fellowfhip called out of the world, and united to Chrift as members to the head, and all one with another according to the word, for the worfhip of God and the edification one of another; and that fuch muft be feparate from falfe ways, worfhips, Antichriftian fuperftitions, obfervances, &c. and willingly join in Chriftian communion and covenant or refolution of cleaving clofe to the Lord in this his way with purpofe of heart and by free confeffion of their faith and fubjection to the Gofpel; and therein I fpecially believe that the ordinances of Chrift are to be freely and frequently difpenfed—as preaching, praying, prophecying one by one, finging of pfalms, hymns, and fpiritual fongs, facraments, cenfures, offices and officers, and often and ordinary exercifing of gifts.

" And that there is a choofing of and fetting apart officers by the whole body, and that none doth orderly do the office of minifter among them but fuch; and befides, to omit many other things and bring all up in this rear, I do really believe that fuch orderly churches have privileges royal, oracles and feals, and precious promifes of God's love, prefence, and protection in a fpecial manner, more than all the world befides. And although particular churches be diftinct and independent bodies, even as cities compact, temples, houfes, &c. yet all churches muft walk by the fame rule, and have counfel and comfort and help from one another when need requires, as being all members of one body, of which Chrift is the head.

" And, to conclude, I am fully perfuaded in my very foul that at the day of judgment, when the dead fhall arife, that I fhall arife alfo, and fhall rejoice in Chrift Jefus my Saviour, and reign with him for ever, and fing Hallelujah

8. Churches vifible and Congregational. 1 Cor. xii. 20; Col. ii. 19; Eph. ii. 21, 22; Matt. xxxiii. 20; Eph. iv. 29; 1 Thes. v. 11; John xv. 19; 2 Cor. vi. 16, 17, 19; Rev. xviii. 4; Ps. cx. 3; Ifa. ii. 2, 4; 2 Cor. viii. 5; Acts xi. 21; Mal. iii. 16; Jude 20; Heb. x. 24, 25; Acts vi. 3; xiv. 23; Exod. xx. 24; 1 Kings ix. 3; Ifa. iv. 5, 6; xxv. 6, 7, 8; Ps. cxxxii. 13, 14, 15; Rev. ii. 1; 2 Cor. vi. 3; Cant. iv. 16; vi. 2, 3; vii. 12; Ifa. xxxiii. 17, 20; Ps. cxxii. 3.

John v. 28; 1 Cor. xv. 19; Acts xvii. 30, 31; 2 Tim. ii. 18; Heb. xii. 23.

for all eternity in the congregation of the firft-born, where
the fpirits of juft men are made perfect.

" And this is my faith, fetched from my very heart, and
prefented in the hearing of a heart-fearching God and all of
you here prefent."

The controverfial part, that is to fay, the bulk of the book,
arofe of courfe out of the circumftances of the period. At this
time the parifhes and parochial churches of the country were,
generally fpeaking, in the hands of the Prefbyterians, whofe fyftem
of church government had been fanctioned and to a certain extent
eftablifhed by Parliament. According to this, England was to be
divided into parifhes and provinces, and church government was
to be carried on by Prefbyteries and Affemblies, which were to
be either parochial, claffical, provincial, or national. Each parifh
was to have its parochial prefbytery for parochial purpofes ; a
certain number of adjoining parifhes were to combine to form a
claffis with a claffical affembly ; thefe claffes were to be united
into provinces with provincial affemblies, and the provincial affemblies to fend reprefentatives to the national affembly.
But, in fpite of the letter of the law, the Prefbyterian fcheme
was nowhere completely carried out except in Lancafhire and
London.

The whole fyftem of Prefbyteries and Affemblies fubordinate
one to another was an abomination to the Independents, whofe
inftinct it was to repudiate authority, whether in Church or State.
With them each feparate congregation was a Church complete,
felf-fufficient, owing no obedience or allegiance to any authority
whatever external to itfelf ; in a word, every congregation was or
ought to be, in fact as well as in name, an " Independent Church."
If the Prefbyterian fcheme of government was an abomination to
them, the Parochial fyftem, on which it was bafed, was fcarcely
lefs fo. The Independents laughed at or utterly ignored the exclufive claims of a parochial clergy ; thefe claims they maintained
were not ·only mifchievous and ridiculous, but effentially Antichriftian, inafmuch as they were founded on the Antichriftian
notion that the Church was a mixed multitude of believers and
unbelievers—finners and faints indifcriminately, whereas in their
opinion the Church was a felect and exclufive fociety of the faints.

" Bethfhemefh " is divided into two books, " Chathan " and

Challah." In "Chathan" the author conſtructs an elaborate definition of the Church, maintaining that " Congregational," i. e. Independent Churches, are alone true Churches, and that " Parochial," i. e. Preſbyterian (or Prelatic) Churches, are falſe and Antichriſtian Churches.

The following is his definition of a true Church :—" The true Church of Chriſt is, 1. A ſociety of believers ſanctified in Chriſt Jeſus ; 2. Separate from the world's falſe ways and worſhips, united together into one body, Independent, or having a plenary power within itſelf, without the leaſt ſubordination to any but Chriſt ; 3. Having the ſpecial preſence of God in the midſt of her ; 4. And being ordered and gathered by Chriſt's rule alone ; 5. All her members freely and voluntarily embodying without the leaſt compulſion, having communion with the Father and the Son ; 6. All ſeeking the ſame end, viz. the honour and glory of God in His worſhip." Such are Independent Churches.

Bethſhemeſh, p. 137.

Each clauſe of his definition ſupplies him with a ſtage from which to aſſail the Preſbyterian churches and the Parochial ſyſtem—1. Parochial Churches are a mixed multitude of the world, including ſaints and ſinners, believers and unbelievers indiſcriminately ; 2. Parochial Churches are neither ſeparate from ſinners without nor united amongſt themſelves within, they are ſubordinate to cathedrals and convocations, ſynods, claſſes, and aſſemblies ; 3. Have not the beautiful and peculiar preſence of God ; 4. Are ruled and ordered by ordinances and directories ; and 5. Are kept alive by ſtocks, priſons, fines, pillories, and puniſhments ; Finally, 6—they are full of profanity, excommunicate, and they rob God of His glory.

Book ii. ch. i.

Having defined the Church in the firſt book, the author proceeds in the ſecond to deſcribe how in any particular locality a church may be gathered, embodied, and perpetuated. In the firſt place, perſons deſiring to enter into church ſociety muſt be quite ſure that they do ſo on good grounds, and that they act on their own free and unconſtrained will, without any compulſion whatever, ſocial, civil, or eccleſiaſtical. Having thus reſolved to unite, they give effect to their reſolution in a ſolemn, orderly manner, ſuitable to the occaſion. Great ſcandals have ariſen from neglecting this. " The godly," he ſays, " muſt needs be much offended at the practice of ſome that run prepoſterouſly into a way of fellowſhip on a ſudden, in an hour's warning or two, and in ſome place

Book ii. ch. iii.

or other, too, that is unknown to any but themfelves. They write down their names together, choofe officers, and all at once or fo, in an hour or two's time, make up a body and call themfelves a church ; and then all that will be joined muft be joined to them that are thus jumbled together in a moft undecent and undue order." As a means of checking fuch diforderly proceedings, the author offers the following order for church embodying which had been tefted by his own experience, leaving others to be guided by it or not, as they pleafed :—

Firft, then, in order to a communion of faints in a Gofpel church-ftate, thofe that are godly muft meet often to fpeak and pray together, and make mention of the Lord with favoury fpeeches tending to edification.

After this, being affe&ionately defirous to walk together in this way, and having agreed to it, they do write and give up their names to one whom they appoint to receive them.

In the mean time they moft unanimoufly appoint a day of humiliation, or more, on which day they do lie low before the Lord and lick the duft. (Neh. i. 11). This they do by themfelves, feparate from others.

On fuch a day they appoint another day when they fhall make a church body and unite, and if any be nigh, they fend and feek for the affiftance of fome other church to bear teftimony with them and give them the hand of fellowfhip and familiarity, not of lordfhip and authority.

On the day appointed, they judge it more to the honour of Jefus Chrift to appear in public (unlefs there be perfecution) in fuch a place, where any that will may come to hear and carry away anything they can.

The day is begun and kept on for fome hours with the prayers of the faithful. They pray not in a flight and formal manner, but with a holy violence, and " bounce hard," " even until the room or houfe is ready to fhake again."

After this, there is fome preparatory fermon or fpeech made by one that is able and appointed thereto, and it is fit that the book of Chrift's Law be at that time read openly, unto which he that preaches and exhorts is principally appointed, in a pulpit of wood (Nehem. viii. 4), in the public place or elfewhere.

Then the rules that the church is gathered by, and the grounds on which it is embodied, are laid open.

Next is the confeffion of faith begun by him who is appointed thereunto as the ableft to lead. This brother befides gives an account of the works of grace upon his heart, holding out at leaft fome of his experiences.

After this brother hath delivered himfelf at large, having the more liberty becaufe he leads as it were the others, then follow fome other of the ableft of the brethren (for herein care muft be had in public left the weaknefs of a brother give advantage to them without) who lay down the grounds of their perfuafion, and render a reafon of the hope that is in them by Confeffion of Faith, Experiences of the work of grace, and the like.

Then as many as are appointed for that day go on, one by one, and poffibly for this day but few as eight or ten, or more or lefs, be appointed, becaufe the work is this day the moft difficult and the moft public.

Some will then have a formal covenant in writing ; but this is not effential. After all this their names againft whom no exception is taken are written down in a regifter, and thefe by prayer together give themfelves up to God and to one another willingly.

To conclude this bufy day, they pour out prayer and praife in fuch a meafure that as it was faid of Ifrael in Ezra—when the foundation of the temple was laid they could not difcern the noife of the fhout of joy from the noife of weeping, both were fo great, fo here it may be faid the faints are fo filled with praifes and prayers that the noife of the one can hardly be difcerned from the noife of the other.

As to other brethren and fifters that are to be admitted, they do make their confeffion and declare the work of God on their hearts in private when they are enchurched among themfelves, feparate from the mixed multitude, fo that the world may not take notice of their weaknefs in utterance or expreffion, and upbraid them and the truth.

After a church has been thus embodied, it admits members from time to time, as need requires. On thefe occafions the following order may be obferved. The candidate muft acquaint the church of his defire, and his name is placed on the firft record, and fome elders or brothers are deputed to inquire concerning him and confer with him. If their report is fatisfactory, a fpecial day is appointed for his admiffion ; then if he be very unable to fpeak in public in the church (as fome maids and others that are

Book ii. ch. iv.

K

bafhful) the church indulgently choofes out fome to receive in private the account of his faith and experiences, which they take in writing and deliver in to the church. But in ordinary cafes the candidate appears in perfon and delivers publicly by word of mouth a confeffion of faith and an account of the work of grace on his heart. Great liberty of opinion is to be allowed in the matter; believers of all judgments are to be received, and none are to be rejected for difference of opinion in matters indifferent. (As an example of a confeffion of faith, the author offers that which was delivered* by himfelf by word of mouth at Dublin in 1651.) But befides this confeffion, every perfon to be admitted muft produce fome experimental evidence of the work of grace upon his foul for the church to judge of whereby he or fhe is convinced he is regenerate and received of God. This may have been given either by extraordinary ways in dreams, vifions, voices, and the like, to a poor foul under extraordinary fad temptations or foul-miferies, or elfe by the ordinary operation of the Spirit in the changing effects of grace upon the judgment, will, and affections. Thefe experiences the Saints ought to declare in open congregation, becaufe by them the Church is able to judge of fuch as are godly, and becaufe they are a warning piece fhot oft in the ears of others, for "God teacheth by them as well as by precepts" (faith *Mr. Rogers* in the " Good Samaritan," p. 222).

As models and examples the author inferts at full length the experiences of forty perfons, moft of whom were members of his congregation at Dublin, and amongft whom are *Col. Hewfon*, the regicide, Governor of Dublin, and his wife, with feveral minifters and officers of the army. He concludes with his own experiences as delivered in at Dublin, and thefe fupply the account of his early life which has been already given.

To return to the candidate for church memberfhip. After he has delivered in his confeffion of faith and account of experiences, he is queftioned by thofe that have any doubts, for none can deny that liberty; but fhould he be weak and imperfect in utterance, the queftions muft be eafy and difcreet, for " we muft take heed of grieving tender hearts in expecting too much from them," or of turning away for a form. Then he withdraws, and the queftion of his admiffion is debated. If approved, he is again called in, and

Book ii. ch. v.

Book ii. ch. vi.

Mr. Nehemiah Rogers, my honoured Father, in his Parables.

Book ii. ch. iv.

* See page 58.

received by the right hand of fellowſhip and a ſhort exhortation by the Paſtor or other perſon in the name of the whole church. The ceremony ends with prayer and praiſe.

In the courſe of enunciating his ſyſtem of church diſcipline, the author takes occaſion to ſtate and maintain his opinion on ſeveral other controverted queſtions, and eſpecially on thoſe three which had led to the diſruption and diſſolution of his Church at Dublin. Theſe were, the proper relation of the civil magiſtrate towards the Church (including the queſtion of liberty of conſcience), the validity of infant baptiſm, and the rights of women in Chriſtian churches. On theſe three points he claimed the glory of having been perſecuted for the truth's ſake.

As to liberty of conſcience, the Preſbyterians had conſiſtently maintained that thoſe who tolerated error were little better than thoſe who held or propagated it, and that both ought to be dealt with by the civil magiſtrate. In "A Teſtimony to the Truth of Jeſus Chriſt, and to our Solemn League and Covenant, as alſo againſt the Errors, Hereſies, and Blaſphemies of theſe times, and the toleration of them," ſubſcribed by the [Preſbyterian] miniſters of Chriſt in London, and publiſhed in 1648, there is claſſed among the errors which they "utterly loathe, execrate, and abhor," "the error of toleration, patronizing, and promoting all other errors and blaſphemies whatſoever under the groſſly abuſed notion of liberty of conſcience," and they mention particularly the error "that little can be done unleſs liberty of conſcience be allowed for every man and ſort of men to worſhip God in that way and perform Chriſt's ordinances in that manner as ſhall appear to them moſt agreeable to God's word, and no man puniſhed or diſcountenanced by authority for the ſame." The Preſbyterian miniſters pray that "ſome effectual means" may be found "by authority of Parliament for the utter abolition and extirpation of" theſe errors "out of the Church." *Rogers* joins iſſue with them, and maintains at ſome length that magiſtrates have nothing whatever to do with ſchiſmatics, heretics, blaſphemers, and the like, as ſuch, unleſs they commit ſome action worthy of puniſhment; that God alone is the Lord and Judge of conſciences, and that until magiſtrates keep their own proper ſphere, and meddle only with civil matters, miniſters meddling only with ſpiritual, "we ſhall be far from a good reformation, and muſt look only for a lamentable check."

As he had been perſecuted by the Preſbyterians on one ſide

Book i. ch. xiii.

Book ii. ch. iv.

Book ii. ch. viii.

for his advocacy of religious liberty, fo he was perfecuted by the Anabaptifts on the other for his advocacy of infant baptifm. In fupport of his own practice of not requiring thofe who had been baptized as infants to be re-baptized as adults, he proves in " Bethfhemefh,"—1. That the Apoftles only baptized thofe who had never been baptized before ; 2. That the baptifm of infants, as generally adminiftered, even if we admit it to have been corruptly adminiftered, is notwithftanding true Baptifm in the effential points of matter and form, and therefore is not to be repeated ; 3. That although immerfion may perhaps be preferable, inafmuch as it is more fignificant, yet afperfion is fufficient; 4. That even if we have been baptized by a corrupt adminiftrator, ftill " his corrupt hand doth not invalidate the ordinance." And finally, he declares, 5. That when we find the fruit and effect of baptifm to follow the ordinance on thofe who have been baptized as infants, we are fatisfied "this covers all failings, and the outward is fwallowed up in the inward."

The third queftion, to which he devotes a whole chapter in " Bethfhemefh," is the queftion of the rights of women in a Chriftian Church, and " this was one thing which helped to fet at a diftance the two focieties at Dublin." " The furies and harpies are flown up very high upon this point, and moft men do arrogate a fovereignty to themfelves which I fee no warrant for." He, on the other hand, alleges prophecy, precept, and reafon to fhow that fifters ought to have equal liberty with the brethren in fpeaking and voting, afking and anfwering, confenting and objecting, in the congregation of the Church. For prophecy he appeals to *Joel*, *Ifaiah*, and *Jeremiah*. For precept he quotes " Go, tell it to the Church." Papifts fay this means, tell it to the Pope and his Cardinals ; others fay, tell it to the Prelates ; Calvinifts fay, tell it to the Synod ; fome Independents fay, tell it to the brethren. We fay, tell it to the whole body, which confifts of women as well as men. Women, he fays, bare office in the Primitive Church ; women were chofen to look after the poor ; women laboured with *St. Paul* in the Gofpel ; *Phœbe* was a deaconefs, and *Philip's* four daughters were prophetefies.

Again, women have frequently furpaffed men for piety and judgment. Prudent *Abigail* excelled her hufband ; for knowledge *Prifcilla* excelled *Apollos*, though a preacher ; for faith, the Canaanite, of whom Chrift faid, " I have not feen fo great faith, no,

not in Ifrael." For affection and zeal, " the Queen of the South
fhall rife up againft the men of this generation." *Mary Magdalen*
for piety and fpirit outran and outreached the twelve difciples.
So we read how *Jael* excelled in courage, *Deborah* in thankful-
nefs, *Lois* and *Eunice* in faith and obedience, *Lydia* in entertain-
ing the word. The Shunamite in faith, and zeal, and underftanding excelled her hufband. So the Samaritanefs the reft of
the citizens. We read of women exhorted to win their hufbands
to the truth. Yea, and in *Manoah's* wife you fhall find a founder
faith and judgment than in her hufband. " I remember I have
read in *Jerome's* days of many holy women that exceeded others
in learning and abilities, and in the ftudying of the Scriptures, and they had their commentaries upon them of their own
making."

A further reafon is taken from their ftrong affection to the
truth, when once they be in the way of Chrift. Hence it is that
Satan fo often makes the firft trial of women for his turn and
fervice, feeing where they take their affections are ftrongeft ; and
he fped fo well at firft that he can't forget it. So he found out a
Dalilah for *Sampfon*, a *Jezebel* for *Ahab*, *Pharaoh's* daughter for
Solomon, &c. For where they are bad they are exceeding bad,
but where they are good they are exceeding good ; for, as the gold
fooner receives the form than iron or fteel, fo are women more
readily wrought upon and perfuaded into the truth than men;
and as gold, fo women many times take the faireft ftamp and
fulleft impreffion.

" Yet before I conclude I muft fpeak a word or two both to
men and women. Let not men defpife them, or wrong them
of their liberty of voting and fpeaking in common affairs. To
women I fay, I wifh ye be not too forward, and yet not too backward, but hold faft your liberty ; keep your ground which Chrift
hath got and won for you, maintain your rights, defend your
liberties even to the life ; lofe it not, but be courageous and keep
it. And yet be cautious too, *feftina lentè*—not too faft ; but firft
be fwift to hear, flow to fpeak : your filence may fometimes be
the beft advocate of your orderly liberty, and the fweeteft evidence of your prudence and modefty. And yet ye ought not by
your filence to betray your liberty, trouble your confciences,
lofe your privileges and rights, or fee the truth taken away
or fuffer before your eyes. But, I fay, be not too hafty nor

too high; for as the note that comes too nigh the margin is in
danger to run into the text the next impreſſion, ſo ſpirits that run
too high at firſt may ſoon fall into diſorder and irregularity.
    In a word, I ſay to all, ' Thoſe whom God hath joined to-
gether let no man put aſunder.' "

    Rogers, as he ſays, had " ſome pretty hot ſkirmiſhes " with the
Preſbyterians incidentally in the earlier part of his book ; but he
reſerves his direct and ſyſtematic aſſault upon them for the laſt
and longeſt chapter, in which, hardly acknowledging their right
to be ranked among Chriſtian churches, " properly ſo called," he
exhibits, by way of reductio ad abſurdum, a long catalogue of the
points in which they agree with the Papiſts.   The compariſon is
intereſting, as ſhowing in ſome detail how far the Preſbyterians
of the day had diverged from the Epiſcopalians, and had been
themſelves left behind by the Independents.
    Papiſts and Preſbyterians agree with each other, and of
courſe differ from the Independents, in diſcipline, doctrine, and
practice.
    They agree in diſcipline.   1. In dividing the Church into prin-
cipal and leſs principal—firſt the Pope and his Cardinals, or the
Aſſembly and claſſes, and ſecondly the people ; 2. In ſaying that
the Catholic Church always has been viſible ; 3. In aſſerting a
twofold headſhip to the Church—firſt Chriſt, and then the Pope or
the Aſſembly ; 4. In ſaying all belong to the Church who make
profeſſion of Chriſt, whether Saints or not; 5. In calling all who
ſeparate from them ſchiſmatics, heretics, or ſeparatiſts, they themſelves being neither ſeparate out of Babylon or gathered and at
unity in Sion ; 6. In laying the foundations of their Church not on
Chriſt but on *St. Peter*, or on confeſſions of faith ; 7. In perſecuting all who differ from them ; 8. In giving the power of the
keys not to the congregation, but either to their prelates or
to their claſſes ; 9. In various points connected with ſynods and
aſſemblies, as to their neceſſity, power, or the like.
    They agree in doctrine.
    1. The Papiſts keep off the people from reading the Scriptures,
find fault continually with the vulgar tranſlation, affirm Scripture
to be moſt hard, difficult, and obſcure, and that it requires to be
expounded by Fathers, Councils, &c. and make tradition neceſſary
over and above.   And ſo not only Prelates, of late, but the Preſbyterians are too rigid to keep off the poor people from the Scrip-

tures, fearing .they would excel their teachers, and take their pulpits from them. To fee fuch in their pulpits as have not had hands upon them, O, how they fcreech for fear! (See this in that frothy, namclefs pamphlet of a lying libeller and fcandalous Philocompos, that is· much cried up by that party for his volublc tongue. It is entitled, "A Tafte of the Doctrine of the newly-erected Exercife at Thomas Apoftle's.") Like the Papifts, they fright the people from the Scriptures by telling them they want the original ; others declare their Claffes, Synods, &c. muft determine the fenfe of the Scriptures, and add their authority thereto, or Fathers, Commentators, and fuch as are accounted orthodox : about which I have been in the lifts with many. We diffent from both, and affert that the vulgar tranflation of the Scripture is fufficient in matters of faith for knowledge ; that the Scriptures are to be believed, not becaufe Synods or Councils tell us they are true, but becaufe the Spirit tells us fo ; that we fhould fin againft our confciences if we fat down content with the expo-fition of others, inftead of feeking further and fuller ; that the Scriptures are neceffary to be known, and that it is not enough to hear the minifter preach ; that all things neceffary to falvation to be found in Scriptures ; and laftly, that the Scriptures are not fo dark and undifcoverable as they would urge upon the people. 2. They agree about Baptifm, impofing it as neceffary to fal-vation, maintaining that infants ought to be brought to Baptifm becaufe they have the habit if not the act of faith, and becaufe of the faith of their parents, and adopting the Jefuitical doctrine that Baptifm wipes away fins going before. All this the Independents deny, affirming that the children of the faithful that are holy are holy before Baptifm. 3. They agree as to the ordinance of the Lord's Supper, in bidding men prepare themfelves for it, and faft the day before they receive it (while we Independents fay the pre-parations of the heart are of the Lord, and account fafting before the Lord's Supper to be mere foppery), in difpenfing indifcrimi-nately to all, in bidding the people fall down before it, or keep devoutly on their knees, or fit or kneel or ftand at a diftance from it. Some of them, too, affirm that all have had Chrift who have had the facrament ; and fome of them cut the bread inftead of breaking it, which deftroys the nature of the ordinance. 4. They agree, too, about the doctrine of works, affirming the neceffity of works to falvation, crying up an inherent righteoufnefs in man ;

and they agree in preffing works and duties for fear of hell and for hope of heaven, roaring out with fire and lightning about the ears of the people to fright and fcare them, and there to leave them. "They can fay little elfe but hell and damnation to fuch as are afflicted, inftead of ufing every means to bind up the broken, and pour in wine and oil into their wounds." 5. They agree too much about the merit of works. 6. Laftly, they agree in giving the civil magiftrates too much power over the Church.

They agree in practice.

Firft, as to Ordination. (1). Papifts make impofition of hands effential; fo do Prefbyterians. We affirm it to be a mere ceremony. (2). Papifts fay ordination is to be difpenfed by the Bifhops; the Prefbyterians fay by the Prefbytery or claffes; we fay by the congregation. (3). Papifts and Prefbyterians fay firft ordain a man, and then let him be called and chofen; we fay they put the cart before the horfe. The Church muft firft choofe him, after trial and examination, and then ordain him. "And I affirm that, as ordination Popifhly difpenfed does not give the effentials to the outward call of a minifter, fo the Prefbyterian ordination, which I now difown before God and men, as being in the fteps of Popery and fucceffively from it, (though I was once, through dimfightednefs, under it, in the very firft claffis that e'er was in England, if I miftake not), yet I fay it is antichriftian and diforderly, as preceding the election of the people of God, and not giving the effentials to the call of a true minifter of Chrift."

Next, as to diftinctions and differences.

1. The Prefbyterians, like the Papifts, keep up a diftinction between themfelves as minifters and other people, and they would have no other dare to touch their facred function or to enter their pulpits on pain of anathema. We deny the diftinction between clergy and laity as Popifh; there is no difference between minifters and the people, except it be to exceed them in knowledge and holy life. 2. Papifts make a diftinction of their Priefts by garbs, gowns, caps, garments; fo did the Prelates, and fo do the Prefbyterians, which we think a fuperftitious foppery. 3. Papifts give fome of their clergy principality or power over others of them; fo do the Prefbyterians in their claffes, but we affirm no fuperiority among paftors any more than among churches. 4. Papifts

and Prefbyterians are too alike about tithes; they both fay the payment of tithes is of abfolute duty. We affirm three things—(1). That the Parliament, or any other fupreme power, may throw down tithes; (2). That a competent maintenance and comfortable allowance to all able Gofpel minifters who live foberly is of divine inftitution; but, (3). That this ought to be in as voluntary a way as may be, fo that the people ought to be free in the manner of payment. 5. Papifts and Prefbyterians are too much alike in their names of days, months, and feafons. Such names as "Sunday" and "Monday," "January" and "February," "Chriftmas Michaelmas, Candlemas," &c. muft be reformed, as fprung from Popery or Paganifm. 6. Their practice is too like the Papifts about their public meeting-places, which they call "churches." (1). The Prefbyterians at this day hold what they can neither prove nor dare openly own—that there is a fpeciality in their churches, as if they were holier than other places; from whom we diffent, and affirm their churches to be no better than ftreets or barns in themfelves, and fo fay all Proteftants againft Papifts. (2). The Papifts dedicated their churches to faints, and though the Prefbyterians cannot for fhame own thefe Popifh decrees, yet what do they lefs than approve of their churches being fo dedicated when they call them by their names as fainted—*St. Mary, St. John, St. James, St. Thomas Apoftle.* "Therefore it would do well that our State would declare againft thofe churches as no churches, that they might never be eyed or owned more than any other places, further than for conveniency's fake, fo that as hot, violent minifters might not approve, fo not appropriate them as they do. For, indeed, fome proud, felf-conceited, hot-fpirited Prefbyterians I know (that account thefe churches their own inheritance) will keep or folely command the keys, and fuffer none to preach but themfelves, or of their own feather, gang, and fancy with them, and on the week days keep the door fo clofe that a moufe may hardly get in, for fear of too much preaching, which they account dangerous, unlefs on their rounds on Sunday. So that they threaten to arreft fuch as dare preach in their pulpits or churches (as they fay) without their confent. O fad! fuch doings we have in the countries yet; and are forced to preach under hedges or on mountains (which I have done myfelf, when we have not had a twig to fhelter us from the rain). But woe be to them, for they have taken away the key of knowledge, and have not entered in themfelves, and them that were entering in they have hindered. But if thefe places muft be dedicated to Saints, let them be dedicated to the ufe of faints living, and for the churches that are fo indeed to meet in."

"Laftly, Papifts and Prefbyterians are too alike in their accurate fcrutiny which they have of us, to obferve what differences they can find among us, to make their advantage and outcry againft us. This is an old Popifh trick. We muft acknowledge too many differences amongft us, and that about forms too. But there may be unity where there is not uniformity. And though we have too, too many divifions and differences amongft us, God knows, which is our daily grief, yet they are not fo many or fo dangerous as the bitter brethren would have all believe by looking into their magnifying-glaffes. But thofe few that are, are not about points of faith, but for the moft part forms, which are by fome too hotly and haftily preffed and purfued."

The author concludes with an earneft exhortation to unity, which will be the refult, he thinks, of three things now coming on the churches,—a fhort but fharp time of trial, a large pouring out of the fpirit, and the near approach of the great and notable day of the Lord. Finally, he afferts and endeavours to prove that the Gofpel order of the Congregational Church way, or, in other words, the Independent form of church government, is one of the great promifes of thefe latter days, in which Chrift alone fhall reign and an earthly paradife be reftored.

" τὸ θέλειν, τὸ τέλειν."

In "Bethfhemefh," the greater part of which may be affigned to the laft days of the Long Parliament,* the author exhibits himfelf as an advanced Independent; allufions to the Chara&teriftic Fifth-Monarchy do&trines are comparatively few and faint. But in his next book, "Sagrir," which was publifhed while the Barebones Parliament was in full vigour, he not only makes his ufual onflaught on clergy, tithes, and lawyers, but he declares alfo, or developes, thofe views on foreign policy and a military millennium which were the chara&teriftics of the Fifth-Monarchy-Man. The

Oct. 20, 1653.

* Moft of the dedicatory Epiftles are dated March and April, 1653. The book itfelf had been written in Dublin in 1651-2.

foreign policy advocated by the Fifth-Monarchy-Men, and enun-
ciated in "Sagrir," was eminently warlike and aggreffive, and at
the fame time eminently calculated to advance the interefts of
Cromwell. *Macaulay* fays truly, "There was nothing which
Cromwell had for his own fake and that of his family fo much
reafon to defire as a general religious war in Europe. In fuch a
war he muft have been the Captain of the Proteftant armies.
The heart of England would have been with him. His victories
would have been hailed with an unanimous enthufiafm unknown
in the country fince the rout of the Armada, and would have
effaced the ftain which one act condemned by the general voice of
the nation has left on his fplendid fame."

It was for fome fuch war as this that the Fifth-Monarchy-Men
thirfted ; a war for the defence and extenfion of the Proteftant
faith over the whole world. To what extent *Cromwell* prompted
them it is impoffible to fay, but it is worth remarking that he
actually made England " the moft formidable power in the world "
by afferting within rational limits thofe very principles which they
were then proclaiming with fuch exaggeration and extravagance,
and that he infifted on almoft incredible demands from other
nations on the plea that " his people would not be otherwife fatif-
fied." In fact, *Cromwell* availed himfelf of the clamours of the
fanatics againft foreign nations juft as he had availed himfelf of
their clamours againft the Long Parliament, the clergy, and the
lawyers, to ftimulate his friends, to intimidate his enemies, and
to prepare the way for a policy which was, after all, entirely
his own.

"Sagrir," which appears to have been written in the autumn
of 1653, is a volume of nearly 200 pages, and contains an Epiftle
to *Cromwell,* an Epiftle to the Reader, a violent denunciation of
exifting laws and lawyers, and lengthy digreffions on tithes, foreign
policy, and the Fifth Monarchy. Its tone and temper are very
fairly reprefented in its title-page, in which, however, the date
feems to be wrongly printed : it was certainly publifhed in 1653.

Macaulay,
Hift. of Engl.
i. 144 (Ed.
1858).

Macaulay, i.
143.

Clarendon, vii.
300.

סַגְרִיר *Sagrir,*

OR

Doomes-day drawing *nigh,*

With Thunder and Lightening to LAWYERS,

In an *Alarum*

For *New Laws,* and the *Peoples Liberties* from the
Norman and *Babylonian Yokes.*

Making Difcoverie

Of the *prefent* ungodly *Laws* and *Lawyers* of the *Fourth Monarchy,*
and of the approach of the *FIFTH ;* with thofe godly *Laws,*
Officers and *Ordinances* that belong to the *Legiflative Power* of the Lord *Jefus.*

SHEWING

The *Glorious Work* Incumbent to *Civil Difcipline* (once more) fet
before the *Parliament,* Lord *Generall, Army* and *People* of *England,* in
their diftinct *capacities* upon the *Account* of *Chrift* and his Monarchy.

Humbly prefented *to them by* JOHN ROGERS, *an unfained* Servant
of Chrift, *and this* Common-wealth *in their beft* Rights, Laws
and Liberties, *loft many years.*

Bread of Deceit is fweet to a man, but afterwards his mouth fhall be filled with Gravell.
Prov. 20, 17.
Whofo ftoppeth his ears at the cry of the poor, he fhall cry himfelf, but fhal not be heard.
Prov. 21, 13.
They are Braffe and Iron, they are all Corrupters, the Bellows are burnt the Lead is con-
fumed of the fire, the Founder melteth in vain, for the Wicked are not plucked a-
way. *Ier.* 6. 28, 29.

נִשְׁמְטוּ בִידֵי־סֶלַע שֹׁפְטֵיהֶם וְשָׁמְעוּ אֲמָרַי כִּי נָעֵמוּ׃ when

their Judges (or the greateft Lawyers) are thrown down into ftony places, they fhall
hear my Words, becaufe then they are fweet. *Pfal.* 141, 6.
Caufidicis, *Erebo,* Fifco, *fas vivere rapto ;*
Militibus, Medico, *Tortori, occidere ludo ;*
Mentiri Aftrologis, *Pictoribus, atque Poetis.*

LONDON,

Printed by *R. I.* to be fold by *Giles Calvert* at the *Black Spread Eagle,* at
the *Weft end of Pauls* 1654.

" *To the Right Honourable the* Lord General Cromwell, *the people's Victorious Champion in England, Ireland, and Scotland.*

MY LORD,

His Excellency the Lord Jefus hath fent out his fummons to other nations alfo; and the blade of that fword whofe handle is held in England will reach to the very gates of Rome ere long, but by what inftruments we know not; yet for what end we know, (Ps. lxxii. 2, 4, 13) viz. to break in pieces the oppreffor and to deliver the poor and needy. Now, my Lord, hitherto he hath honoured you in his war. Let him alfo do fo in his work, which the war hath made way for, viz. in throwing down of tyranny and oppreffion, which as you have begun to do, fo this treatife hath unavoidable reference to yourfelf to carry on, as our conqueror upon Chrift's and the Commonwealth's account, and not upon your own. Therefore are the eyes of thoufands upon you, to fee what you will do for their fafety and freedom, according to the juft rights and liberties of the people of this nation, which they had before the Norman tyranny and conqueft; for it is far better for us, my Lord, now to hang us than not to help us againft thefe unfufferable laws and lawyers, which rob us of juftice and righteoufnefs, as it is obvious in this treatife. It is without malice to a man of them, and merely out of confcience to engage againft fin and enemies to Chrift and this Commonwealth that I muft make fuch a character of them as I do. It may be I fpeak fpiritfully yet not fpitefully; though oppreffion makes a wife man mad, fays *Solomon* (Eccl. vii. 7). And indeed, if it be madnefs to engage againft fin, I will be fo: for—

' Si natura negat facit indignatio verfum.'

Wherefore, my Lord, I befeech you contemn not the

(margin note:) There is a prediction, which fays C. fhall found within the walls of Rome.

clock that tells you how the time paſſes. A mean herald may go on great errands ; and on this errand he is contented to be mean and contemptible who is ſent to you, and prays unfeignedly for you that you may never be ſet aſide, but be of ſingular uſe yet in this generation ; and then, and not till then, reſt from your labours as *David* did (Acts xiii. 36).

The ſword of the Lord and of *Gideon** together gets the loud ſuffrage of your ſuffering yet

> your heartily humble
> ſervant in the ſervice
> of our Lord Jeſus,
> JOHN ROGERS.

From my Study, the 8th month, 20th day.
Thomas Apoſtle's."

Some of theſe ſufferings are connected with his unceaſing proteſts againſt the iniquity of tithes. He gives the following account of them in his Epiſtle to the Reader :—

"I confeſs I was occaſionally the fourteenth day of the ſeventh month at the Committee of Tithes,† in the Chequer

---

* *Gideon* was a favourite example, and "the ſword of the Lord and of *Gideon*" a favourite watchword with ſuch men as *Rogers ;* for *Gideon* with his handful of men firſt routed whole hoſts of his enemies, and then cut off the heads of their kings ("Bethſhemeſh," p. 171). On the other hand, to ſuch men as his father, *Nehemiah,* "the ſword of the Lord and of *Gideon*" was ſignificant only of religious intolerance, cruelty, and rebellion. "Theological hatreds as one termeth them are moſt bitter hatreds. He that ſtrikes for religion ſtrikes with a razor ; the other thruſts with a foil. When a battle is fought ' by the ſword of the Lord and of *Gideon*,' then it ever proceeds with the greateſt cruelty ; and rebellion never proves ſo loud and dangerous as when religion is pretended."—*The Figleſs Fig-tree*, p. 280.

† The Committee of Tithes appointed by the Barebones Parliament conſiſted of thirty-two members. The firſt, third, and fifth names on the liſt were thoſe of *Major-General Harriſon, Sir Anthony Aſhley Cooper,* and

Chamber, where was a rude rabble, and amongſt them many lawyers and miniſters of the city and country too, to tug for tithes; and finding liberty given to any to ſpeak, I being deſired ſo to do by ſome Parliament men, I accepted of the call, for that I could not in conſcience be ſilent, ſeeing I had ſuch a ſeaſon to make my blow at Antichriſt and to ſpeak for Chriſt; but finding that the liberty was limited to what could be ſaid as to or againſt their propriety by the law, I only laid a foundation for a future diſcourſe, which I took up on the 16th day. And becauſe *Maſter Jacob*, being of a like conſtitution and complexion in principles with the prieſts, with the aſſiſtance of one of his brethren, that foul-mouthed ſcandalous fellow of Garlick-hithe, cenſoriouſly and raſhly condemned me as full of impertinences therein, although they were well rebuked for their rough, proud ſpirits, and the Committee took *Mr. Jacob* up ſharply for his folly, impertinency, and impatience (for he wanted his note-book); yet, to ſatisfy ſome of the precious ſervants of God, I ſhall here inſert what I ſaid.

Quef. Whether the preſent clergy have right by the laws of this land to tithes? Before my anſwer I premiſed that, without fee, preferment, or bye-end, I ſhould offer my judgment, being brought hereto by a good conſcience, as perſuaded that I appeared for Chriſt againſt Antichriſt, ſo that I would not be daunted by the threats of any given out againſt me. Then I digeſted my diſcourſe into four heads:—

Anſ. Neg. 1 (*ab origine*).— From the riſe of thoſe common laws that they plead to give them this right, i. e.

The Author's ſpeech at the Committee, Sept. 16.
The preſent Miniſters no right to Tithes by the law proved.

Anſ. 1. Becauſe common laws which give the right are down.

Praiſe-God Barbone. The Committee was ordered to ſit in the Chequer Chamber. "This Committee hath power to puniſh ſcandalous miniſters, and to prefer godly miniſters in their place."—*From " A New Liſt of all the Members of this preſent Parliament.* 1655."

canon, or Chriftian law fo called. If the canon or ecclefiaftical law is down, and gives them no right, then the
common laws, which arofe therefrom, are down and fallen
with them. But the canon law is down, &c : ergo, the
confequence is clear. . . . .

Anf. 2. Becaufe there the laws look on men ordained in another way.

Anf. 2 (*ex objecto*). The laws which they plead and
pretend for propriety look on fuch only as were ordained
according to the Popifh canons then in force when thofe
laws were made ; but the prefent clergy difown thofe canons
and ordination—ergo, the laws that refer thereto. . . .

Anf. 3. The end of the law is loft by thofe laws which grant tithes.

Anf. 3 (*a fine*). From the end of all honeft laws, which
muft be preferred before the letter of the laws, viz. the
public good and freedom of the people. . . . .

Anf. 4. The foundation of fuch is fand, and unfound.

Anf. 4. From the foundation of the laws, which ought
to be the eternal law of God. . . . .

Thus their propriety to tithes is proved rotten and in-
valid by their own laws, as to the principle, object, end,
and foundation of them ; and if God do not honour our

To the Parliament.

prefent governours with fuch a ftripping of the ornaments
and pulling away the black patches of the impudent harlot as
this does, I fear they will hardly be the men then that muft
tear her flefh from her bones and burn it with fire. . . .

This is the fubftance of what I delivered by word of
mouth, (which I had a copy of in writing, whence I have
taken this), and afterward in writing by an honourable
member of Parliament. But that the fpirit of Antichrift
might appear for itfelf, there was fuch uncivil talking,
hiffing, mocking, threatenings, railings, and crowding me,
whiles I was fpeaking to the Committee, to interrupt me,
that the Chairman, with many members, were forced to
check them, and to rife up to chide feveral times. After
we were withdrawing by order from the Committee, *Mr.
Jacob* exclaims againft me. With that I turned back, and
heard him fay I offered many impertinencies, and he was
glad the truth had fo many weak enemies as I was. Let

him and all my enemies know that I truſt I ſhall be a very
weak enemy to truth as long as I live ; I deſire to be ſo,
and rather to die than be any enemy at all to truth.   But
yet tell him that Antichriſt, againſt whom I engaged in this
buſineſs of tithes, which the blood of the martyrs will
witneſs with me (Fox, p. 494, ii., 80, and 537, &c.) I
ſay, tell him that Antichriſt ſhall find ſtronger, and abler,
and faithfuller, and more undaunted, reſolute enemies than
I am to this traſh, and trumpery, and relic of Antichriſt ;
and it is my joy to be one, though a weak one, that engages
for Chriſt herein, though I was grieved to be alone among
ſo many adverſaries of the clergy, lawyers, and rude rabble
at that time.   But my anſwer to *Mr. Jacob's* affront was
this—that he ſpoke like himſelf (meaning a Preſbyterian,
and one that would have been *Mr. Love's* ſucceſſor) ; and
that as Auguſtine once ſaid he was content to ſpeak falſe
Latin, ſo he might but win their ſouls to Chriſt, ſo I ſaid I
was welcome to ſpeak fooliſhly and impertinently, ſo I
might but ſerve my maſter Chriſt therein, as I truſt I had ;
which ſince, among many others, ſome Parliament men and
honeſt miniſters, too, and members of the army, have with
thanks told me was well.   But after he was reproved by
the Committee, we withdrew, where a huge conflux of rigid
clergy, ſolicitors, and rabble fell a railing and aſſaulting me
(among whom was *Crofton,* the preacher of Garlick-hithe,
threatening and abuſing me) ; but I was through mercy
reſcued by ſome friends and members of the army, and
carried away to a friend's houſe to refreſh my ſpirits, which
were much ſpent with their violencies.   But I did not feel
the hurt which I had by their crowdings, punches, and
pulling about, and getting me (as they had once that day)
under their feet till I cried for help ; I felt it not till the
next day ; and then, what with inward bruiſes and outward
ſoreneſs and ſickneſs, I fell into a fierce fever, when, amongſt
others, *Colonel Rathbone* came to viſit me, and told me how

M

the rabble the day before fell upon him alſo, upon the ſame account of engaging againſt that garbage of Antichriſt; and for applauding what I had offered to the Committee they fell upon him, and he was ſtabbed twice, once in the forehead and the other was in his ſide, ſo that he hardly eſcaped with his life; and as ſoon as he was dreſſed by the chirurgions, he ſaid, he came to give me warning of them, they were ſo incenſed againſt me it would be dangerous to ſtir abroad for ſome time, ſeeing my life was threatened.

By this it appears what a ſpirit it is that pleads for tithes; infomuch as I wonder nothing at their lying, railing, and abuſing me about this city, and in Martin-in-the-Fields, where the Preſbyterian profeſſors follow their old trade of venting and inventing to the amazement of honeſt men. . . . . But for all this ſtorm their tithe muſt tumble, and the ſtanding, too, of thoſe nationaliſts ere long.

Clergy and Lawyers. There be two ſorts of men that muſt and will be my profeſſed adverſaries, viz. the national clergy and the Norman lawyers. Whiles I am engaged againſt the Babylonian and Norman yokes, and ſtrike at the block or body of them (as I have done at the firſt in a treatiſe of Church Diſcipline, and do at the laſt in theſe lines of Civil Diſcipline), the fierce chips fly about mine ears; but they muſt into the fire ere long, with the beaſt and falſe prophets (Rev. xix. 20). Some brats of this brood are very bitter Backbiters and Preſbyters. B * * * biters as well as P * * * biters; but I am poſitive, with *Jo. Huſs*, that all the (National Corrupt) Clergy muſt be quite taken away ere the Church of Chriſt be truly reformed, or Antichriſt fall. I hear ſome are purſuing me with the rage of the Red Dragon (Rev. xii.), and in chief the forenamed ſcandalous libeller *Crofton*, of Garlick-hithe, the fitteſt man for ſuch a buſineſs I know of. He is, it ſeems, full of arts, and ſciences, and tongues too, for wronging and ſlandering; and whiles he dialogues with his noſe, his communication is mere ſmoke. This is he that calls all Independents Devils, and fays they are damned that are fo. This is he that preacheth they were damned that took the Engagement (as I have it to fhow under an honeft minifter's hand). This is he that, on pain of damnation, and as they will anfwer it before him at the day of Judgment, requires the people to hear him only, and not ftir from him to any other man. This is he that is fo notorioufly known for a fcurrilous and fcandalous Prieft in many counties, and is moft groffly Popifh, both in doctrine and practice, as doth appear to many, and may ere long to more. This is he that is always flandering and perfecuting the people of God, calling them naufeous names and making lies of them in the pulpit; yea, of fuch as are afleep in the grave, whom he inhumanly flanders, and what not that is ignoble and unworthy. Far, much worfe I might fpeak, but I fhall fpare him and the reader."

Rogers concludes this part of his book with a few words on the approach of the Fifth Monarchy, of which he fpeaks more fully afterwards.

. . . . " Schoolboys look after holydays, worldly men after rent days, chapmen after market days, travellers after fair days, profeffors after Lord's days, and the people of God long for thefe days of Chrift, viz. the end of the four monarchies (Dan. vii.), that the Fifth may come, wherein Chrift and his faints fhall rule the world. Mark it, by Anno 1656 the flood begins; and, as in *Noah's* flood, after the doors were fhut up there was no mercy, though they came wading middle deep, fo let this be an alarum to all men to make hafte while the door of the ark is open. In few years they will find it fhut; and then, though they wade through and through much danger, whether Parliament men, Army men, Merchant men, Clergy men, Lawyers, or others, they may find it too late, and that their delays have bred dangers; for the door will be fhut

What days we look for.

1656. By that year Hafte—Hafte—Hafte.

shortly.   My aim herein is to awaken them all up to their
work, in the restoration of God's laws and government, the
people's liberties and privileges, the Commonwealth's
comfort and advantages, in Christ's kingdom and appear-
ances, which is and shall be the mark of my arrow, yea the
rainbow of my cloud that looks on the sun, and that which
my soul shall pump out apace in all my prayers to God in
Christ for this Commonwealth, whose honest, faithful
servant I am in my heart, without the cunning politick or
artificial composition of compliments, though I must and
do suffer for my sincerity and simplicity."

The character of the foreign policy which *Rogers* and his
party advocated is exhibited in the following digression, which is
introduced into the first part of his book, and opens the way for
the main attack upon Lawyers.

A digression.   " Let me digress a little now, for the public's sake, in
this my discourse, to acquaint the Governours of our
Nation how much the message from Bourdeaux in France,
or any other nation concerns us ; for we are bound by the
To assist our   law of God to help our neighbour as well as ourselves, and
neighbours.   so to aid the subjects of other princes that are either persecuted for true religion or oppressed under tyranny.   What
mean our Governours to take no more notice of this?
How durst our army to be still, now the work is to do
abroad?   Are there no Protestants in France and Germany
even under persecution?   And do not the subjects of
France.   France that lie under the iron yoke of tyranny send and
seek and sue to us for assistance?   Well, woe be to us ' if
we help not the Lord (Judg. v. 23) against the mighty ;'
for it is the Lord hath sent for us thither, and calls for a
Holland.   part of our army at least into France or Holland.   Therefore, ' Cursed be they that do the work of the Lord
negligently,' or but by halves (Jer. xlviii. 10).

Wherefore, let me tell our army and ſtateſmen that if they belong to the Lord yet, and if God hath good to do by them yet, that then they ſhall not be able to ſit ſtill long ; for if they will not take their work abroad they ſhall have it home, as ſure as God lives and is righteous. For where the kingdom of Chriſt comes, there is no ſuch thing as bounds, or limits, or rivers, or ſeas, that ſhall cage up or confine the fervent zeal and flaming affeĉtions of an Army, Repreſentative, or People ſpirited for the work of Chriſt, which is more and more public, and looks beyond ſeas now. O no ! no more than the bounds or limits of a pariſh ſhall confine a miniſter of the Goſpel to the ſpiritual work of Chriſt.

A word to the Army.

The work will go beyond ſeas.

So, as it is againſt the law of nature for the King of France to be worſe than an enemy to his own citizens and ſubjeĉts, ſo it is as much againſt the law of God, ſhould they ſupplicate to us for aſſiſtance, to be worſe than neighbours ; and then ſuch profeſſors and pretenders for the kingdom of Chriſt as we make a noiſe of in the world to be, if we ſtrike not now in for the intereſt of Chriſt, and take not the opportunity to viſit thoſe coaſts, and to view the condition of the Proteſtants and oppreſſed ones in that kingdom.

The Gadites deſired to be at reſt and to go no further, but to ſtay on the other ſide Jordan and to live there ; which though *Moſes* aſſented to, yet it was with this proviſo, that they ſhould go on and aſſiſt their other brethren with their whole work, and go thorough-ſtick with it, now they had begun it, until the Iſraelites had conquered the land of Canaan—yea, and to go firſt out, as in the van, becauſe they would firſt ſit down ; and if they refuſed to do this, then they were anathematized and deſtined to deſtruĉtion, like them that were adjudged rebels at Cadeſh Barnea, and none of them by the decree of God were ever to enter into the land of Canaan. So ſuch of the Army, Repreſentative,

Gadites—who, now.

and Commonwealth that have no heart to go further beyond
the feas (Jordan), but would be at reft on this fide, fhould
hear a *Mofes* fay, What! What! your brethren go on and
fight further for Canaan, and you fit ftill and live lazing and
idling at home! No, no! away, you that would firft fit down
and lay down your arms and live in peace, get you firft out
beyond Jordan ; for you fhall not return to your cattle and
corn, and fine, finical fig-leaves, to be coached and compli-
mented into effeminacy and fooleries ; no, nor yet to dwell

When 'tis time
for the Army
to reft.

at home in England with your wives, until the Lord hath
driven his enemies before you, and granted a place to your
brethren beyond Jordan, as well as to you on this fide
it ; and then you fhall return in peace and with welcome,
and be innocent before the Lord and his people Ifrael, and
abide in quietnefs, and not till then.

    And let not men difpute fo much whether it be lawful
to defend or ftrike in for another's liberty and deliverance,

Our warrant
for this.

if it were lawful to do fo for our own, feeing we muft love
our neighbour as ourfelves. If we love Chrift in our own
nation, why not in another ? and if juftice, and peace, and
piety, and righteoufnefs among ourfelves, why not among
others ? O! for fhame, firs! let's rub our eyes and look
about us. And after the wicked lawyers have had a bang,

An alarm.

let us beat a march and alarm the whole world (Jer. l. 2).
' Declare ye among the nations and publifh, and fet up a
ftandard ; publifh and conceal not, (till ye) fay Babylon is
taken.' ' Who is on my fide, faith the Lord — who ?'
' Come againft her from the utmoft border (even Ireland
and Scotland), open her ftorehoufes, caft her up as heaps ;
deftroy her utterly—let nothing of her be left. Woe unto
them, for their day is come, the time of their vifitation.
The vengeance of the Lord our God, yea the vengeance of
his Temple (or Churches).' Jer. l. 26—29.

    I intended not this length, but the Lord would have it
fo ; and fo I come in again to the Lawyers.

The two plagues of this nation rose up both from the bottomlefs fmoke, and are the Priefts and the Lawyers. Both alike they keep up a corrupt, carnal, antichriftian intereft. The Priefts would fill the cup of the harlot for the nation to drink of, and the Lawyers would clothe her with fcarlet. But woe be to us if either be fuffered to trade; 'for becaufe thou haft let go them that I have appointed to utter deftruction, therefore thy life fhall go for theirs, and thy people for theirs' (1 Kings xx. 42). They muft fall together, feeing ever fince Edward III. his time in England they were advanced together, as to their height and intereft. The Lawyers, who are tyrants and oppreffors of the civil ftate, may as well be compared to the locufts, mentioned Rev. ix. 3,* &c. as the Priefts the tyrants and oppreffors of the Ecclefiaftical ftate. For—

1. Out of the fmoke which darkened the air as well as the fun, earth as well as heaven, and fo out of that Antichriftian darknefs which arofe upon the ftate, civil as well

Priefts and Lawyers the two plagues that rofe together.

Lawyers locufts.

1. Arifing out of the bottomlefs pit fmoke.

---

* "And he opened the bottomlefs pit, and there arofe a fmoke out of the pit as the fmoke of a great furnace; and the fun and the air were darkened by reafon of the fmoke of the pit. And there came out of the fmoke locufts upon the earth, and unto them was given power as the fcorpions of the earth had power; and it was commanded them that they fhould not hurt the grafs of the field, neither any green thing, neither any tree, but only thofe men which have not the feal of God in their foreheads. And to them it was given that they fhould not kill them, but that they fhould be tormented five months; and their torment was as the torment of a fcorpion when he ftriketh a man. And in thofe days fhall men feek death and fhall not find it, and fhall defire to die and death fhall flee from them. And the fhapes of the locufts were like unto horfes prepared unto battle; and on their heads were as it were crowns like gold, and their faces were as the faces of men. And they had hair as the hair of women, and their teeth were as the teeth of lions. And they had breaftplates as it were breaftplates of iron; and the found of their wings was as the found of chariots of many horfes running to battle. And they had tails like unto fcorpions, and there were ftings in their tails; and their power was to hurt men five months."—Rev. ix. 2-10.

as ecclefiaftical, came thefe locufts (ver. 2, 3,) upon the earth, and Lawyers into this kingdom (vide *Malmſbury*). In William II. his time they proceeded from the Roman Clergy.

2. Unclean creatures.

2. Locufts are unclean creatures, many times tranflated grafshoppers; and the Midianites and Amalekites which came againft Ifrael in *Gideon's* days (Judg. vii. 12) were faid to be like grafshoppers, which, fays *Cooper*, fignifies bodily oppreffors, Egyptian plagues (as Exodus x. 13, 14.) Grievous! Such are the Lawyers all over the nation.

3. For multitude.

3. Locufts have their ftrength in their multitude. O, what heaps of this noifome vermin may you fee at a time in the Temple or Weftminfter Hall. Thefe do make up the numerous army of Antichrift in this ftate againft Chrift, and are to torment men (Rev. ix. 3, 5, 7); and fo, Exodus x. 14, they cover the earth.

4. For their variety of orders.

4. Locufts have their variety of orders, and ye may fee them noted in their feveral colours and marks. Thus have Antichrift's laity—I mean Lawyers, as well as Antichrift's Clergy—I mean Priefts. It were but loft labour to enter into this number of his name, or to reckon up the variety of orders and degrees of this brood of the beaft, diftinguifhed by feveral forms, fects, and habits of divers fafhions.

5. For their earthly difpofition.

5. Locufts are of earthly difpofitions, greedy devourers, infatiable for covetoufnefs, always defiring, but never delighting to work, fow, labour, nor plough, but to eat up the fruits of other men's labours, and to fall or feize upon and take poffeffion of the beft meadows, vallies, and pleafant places of the land. Now the Lawyers, as well as Priefts, are fuch a plague of locufts.

6. For their leaping.

6. Locufts have a leap like grafshoppers, and fo have the Lawyers; for like the leopards they get their prey faliendo, by leaps, which are fometimes very large; and as to the things of God, or religious exercifes, we fhall find few of them frequent them unlefs by leaps now and then.

I always except fuch as were Lawyers and are con-verted. But fuch are not many. . . . . As to the feƈt of them in general, (excepting fome particular rare ones — fuch *Zenaſes* as are honeſt and godly amongſt them), theſe locuſts may leap to a little honeſty it may be on Sundays, but all the days after they follow their old trade of lying and oppreſſing, and eating up the greens of the land. ' Subitos dant faltus fed protinus in terram cadunt.' Their ordinary going is but higgle-haggle, here and there, this way and that, on this fide and on that too, for any cauſe or client, fo they meet but with an angel* in the way.

7. Theſe locuſts that help to make up the army of Antichriſt had a power like to fcorpions given to them (Rev. ix. 3); and fo have the Lawyers. (1). ' Scorpio eſt blanda facie fed cauda pungit occulte.' The fcorpion hath a flattering face, and fo theſe locuſts (Rev. ix. 7, 8); ' their faces were as the faces of men, and they had hair as the hair of women.' But (ver. 10) their tails were like to fcorpions, that had ſtings to torment men. All this ſigni-fies their hypocriſy and craft, as well as cruelty to hurt us. (2). As fcorpions, ever fince they were curſed, in Gen. iii. 14—' Thou art curſed above every beaſt of the field, upon thy belly ſhalt thou go and duſt thou ſhalt eat all thy days,'—I fay ever fince, with their tails (which torment us) they gather up the duſt of the earth, and feed altogether upon earthly things as their meat. So they, like the unclean beaſts under the law, creep on all four upon the earth, and all this upon their belly too. O bitter curſe! they cannot abide the things above. And this makes them ready to receive petitions, opinions, cauſes, complaints, many hours together, about bodies and eſtates, but cannot abide a peti-tion that concerns fouls; which lately I tried their patience with before the Lords Commiſſioners, but upon the naming

Margin notes:

Titus iii. 13.

7. Like fcorpions.

(1). Flattering faces full of craft and cruelty.

(2). They eat the duſt.

They cannot abide a plea out of Scripture.

---

* The " angel " was worth originally 6*s.* 8*d.*

of a Scripture or two they would not hear it; at which, drawing my Bible out of my pocket, and telling them that that was the ſtatute book to be uſed in ſuch caſes, and be-ginning to open ſome Scriptures I came to that in Ezek. xxii. 27—' Her princes are ravening wolves, they ſeek to deſtroy ſouls, to get diſhoneſt gain,' &c; but they fell a chafing and fuming, and would not hear it. But (3).

(3). They ſting deadly, and by degrees.

Scorpions ſting, but not dead at firſt, but the wound works by degrees. The Lawyers, like them, ſting deadly; and it were better they killed us right out (Rev. ix. 6) than to conſume, perplex, pain, grieve, afflict us to death by degrees; the plague of them is the worſe. Thus theſe locuſts are like ſcorpions.

8. Monſters.

8. Theſe locuſts were monſter-form, and that multi-form, being made up of many ſorts of creatures. So theſe Lawyers are foxes for ſubtlety, vipers for venom, dogs for

(1). In their bodies.

mouthing it, but tigers for tearing it and cruelty. But (1) in their body, ' Horſes prepared for battle,'—horſes not common, but kept up, and fed, pampered — jades that work not but feed hard, and eat and drink of the beſt. (2)

(2). Their heads.

' On their heads as it were crowns;' ſo are theſe locuſts or Lawyers Antichriſt's army of crowned men in ſtate matters, as well as the Prieſts and Clergy his army in eccleſiaſtical matters, not only in their wear of caps like crowns, but in that they get the legiſlative power, and have (more regum), in the manner of kings, lords, and ſuch like perſons, impoſed laws and ties to conſciences, tyrannizing and oppreſſing all the people of God as their vaſſals and

(3). Their faces.

ſubjects. (3). They had ' faces like the faces of men '— that is, (leſt men ſhould loathe and abhor them for their cruelty and curſed diſpoſition), they inſinuate into great places, Kings' courts and palaces, &c. by ſimulation and fine glozing, flattering ſhows of humanity and great humi-lity—having learned the art of diſſembling in their Inns of Court, having it infuſed as a principle, which Kings and

rulers held by their authority, that none was fit to rule
unlefs he can diffemble. Thefe Lawyers never more diffemble than when they refemble the faces of men; for they
put the faireft faces on the fouleft actions. There be
no greater flatterers in the world. But foft, firs. (4).
'Hair as the hair of women' (Rev. ix. 8); that is, as
Cotterius notes: 1. 'Varias fraudes,' their variety of art to
deceive and infinuate; 2. 'Ornatum illicitum,' their unlawful attire, to make a great fhow with fine, foft, and delicate ornaments; and 3. 'Effeminatos mores,' their effeminacy and womanifh fancies and fafhions. And, like women,
O how they love their long hair and 'delicate comam alunt,
pingunt, mulcent,' powdering and painting it. (5.) 'Their
teeth as the teeth of lions' (Rev. ix. 8). Such an expreffion is in Joel i. 6. 'Voraces et truculenti funt,' that is,
they are ravenous and cruel; fo that in the defcription of
them there is 'falfi boni fimulatio et veri mali diffimulatio
et aperta fævitia,' a femblance of good in their faces, a
diffemblance of evil in their hair; but 'dentibus crudelitas
fignificatur,' by their teeth is figured out open cruelty and
tyranny; and be fure thefe ftate locufts or Lawyers, where
they cannot get what they would with the firft or fecond,
they bring in the third, and fhew their teeth to the purpofe
in tearing away men's eftates, liberties, and lives too, if they
can. 'Omnia rapiunt, æraria exhauriunt, domos devorant,
agros vaftant, crudeles et fævi funt in pios qui in manus
eorum incidunt,' making themfelves rich by others' ruin.
(6). 'They had habergeons of iron,' Rev. ix. 9. That is,
their outward defences, whilft corrupt laws and Lawyers
have been a long time, efpecially in thefe five months that
they have fo fearfully tormented us (I mean for the 150
years laft paft), kept up by fecular powers, fo that there was
no oppofing them. (7). 'And the found of their wings
like the found of chariots.' This ftate army of Antichrift
being, as we heard before, fo crafty, cruel, fierce, ftrong,

With their art
of diffembling.

(4). Their
hair.

(5). Their
teeth terrible.

(6). Haber-
geons of iron.

(7). Their
wings and
privileges.

forcible, and armed with fecular powers, they have wings, that
is, fuch things, advantages, and privileges, with which they
fly high in boldnefs and ambition and are elevated exceedingly and lifted up, and efpecially to the terror of honeft
people. *Beda,* writing on this place, fays, ' Expavefcendum
magis quam exponendum.' It is rather trembled at than
interpreted, how the army of thefe locufts increafe; for with
their wings they make fuch a huge noife as amazes and
amufes men and makes them afraid of them.

The army of locufts.

For the noife is firft confufed, like the found of many
chariots, uttering no diftinct noife, terrifying the people
with horror at their loud, clamorous voices, lamentable
lying, pleadings and difputes, and violent janglings and
indiftinct voices which others muft not rightly underftand.

Noife of their wings—what.

Secondly, it is comfortlefs, for they neither found glory to
God nor peace to men, but all vexation, fuits, troubles,
mifchiefs that may be. As King Jabin (Judges, iv. 2, 3)
had nine hundred chariots of iron, and for twenty years
vexed Ifrael fore; but thefe have a hundred and twenty
years vexed England fore, fo that nothing but ruin and
undoing is looked for from them, and a man needs no more
trouble than to be within the found of their chariots and
laws, I'll warrant him his heart will ache and quake too. For
as ' diverfi currus diverfis viis cum impetu currunt,' &c.
Divers chariots run divers ways, and all furioufly to battle,
fo do thefe Antichrift's ftate locufts, in divers ways perplex

Lawyers perplex us—how.

us and fling us out of one court into another, with unreafonable reftleffnefs, till they have run over us or ruined us
with violent contentions or torments, and that which is
worft is, that they are fo numerous and run fo many ways
that we can by no means efcape them. 8. Thefe mon-

(8). Stings in their tails.

ftrous locufts ' have ftings in their tails,' (Rev. ix. 10),
not only the priefts and prelates, and fo Antichrift's ecclefiaftical army, have their tails as officials, commiffaries,
proctors, regiftrars, and fuch like, that did grievoufly afflict

and torment men, but alfo the lawyers, Antichrift's ftate army, have their long tails too, with terrible ftings, and fuch are folicitors, clerks, bailiffs, ferjeants, gaolers, and fuch like, and it is fo much to their advantage in tormenting men to have terrible tails that they will have none to execute their warrants, writs, orders, or the like (as near as they can), but the moft curfed, gracelefs villains they can get, and by this means are men (in the country, above all places) abufed by bloody villains, drunken fots, who fit night and day drinking and fwilling upon an honeft man's fcore whom they have ferved with a warrant or fo, and yet ufe him (it may be), if he be a man fearing God, worfe than a dog, in beating, bruifing, pulling, threatening, and abufing him all manner of ways, if he do not fill their pouch with money and their paunch with liquor up to the throat. Thefe torment fo with their tails that fome men had better be hanged right out than fo ufed, and (v. 6) 'feek death but cannot find it,' 'Mors optanda magis,' whiles clubs and canes lie thumping upon the backs of poor people that once come under the bailiffs, being fo cruelly plagued, pulled away from their wives, hailed up and down by head and ears, bereaved of their relations, and robbed and fpoiled of their eftates and comfortable fubfift-ence. Oh! how fad is the torment of their tails, as thou-fands can teftify to this hour. So that all the lawyers' eftates cannot make amends for the world of mifchief they have done and yet do daily with their tails, which are moft violent, virulent, and venomous.

Thus are they defcribed in their monfter-formity, or monftrous deformity :—

9. Thefe locufts have a limited power; As, 1, to per-fons (Rev. ix. 4), 'that they fhould not hurt the grafs, nor the green things, nor the trees ; 2, to time (v. 5), 'they had power to hurt but five months.' 1. To perfons. The Saints, who are of three forts, refembled (1) by grafs,

Side notes:

Such multitude of clerks, &c. are againft juftice and true law.—Mir. of Juft. fol. 246.

Judge Arnold was hanged for faving a bailiff from death who had robbed the people with diftreffes and extorted money from them. See Mir. of Juft. 241. And now the bailiffs do it daily, and no juftice.
9. Their limited power.

To perfons.

χόρτος, weak, yet fappy, and (2) by green, χλωρός, flourifhing things, and (3) by trees of the higheft and talleft ftature in Chrift, viz.—Fathers, young men, and children (1 John ii). Yet all are to abftain from lawyers, and the lawyers are to have nothing to do with them, for, as the Apoftle fays, 'Dare any of you go to law before the unjuft,' but as it is in 1 Tim. i. 9, the law is not made for the righteous man, but for the lawlefs and difobedient, for ungodly and for finners, for unholy and profane, fo it is Rev. ix. 4, for them that have not the feal on their foreheads. 2. To time. But five months. . . . taking in Scripture fenfe a day for a year (Num. xiv. 34) at thirty days for a month, yet five months is but 150 years, which is a fhort time. But to this I think Bullinger fays well that the allufion is made to the time of the locufts or graffhoppers coming forth, which is about April, as we fay, and continues to September, i. e. the five hot months. So thefe locufts have a fummer time of doing mifchief for about the fpace of 150 or 155 years, which will be a hot time for them. They fing, and leap, and devour.

> Don Pluto dares not to affay, though he be Prince of Hell,
> So much as lawyers dare, though they their fouls to angels fell."

He proceeds to argue that we muft not reckon from the firft time of power, for that is of long ftanding, i. e. from Edward the Confeffor and William the Conqueror, but from the time when the weather began to grow warm upon them, i. e. from 1369 until H. 7, 1504.

" Then their fummer months to do mifchief and to torment the people came on apace, and continued hot to them, that they had and did almoft what they lifted ; but now their five months, i. e. 150 years, are upon expiring, and their power to torment will be no more by a year or two, their September is hard by, and a weft wind will remove them out of thofe places wherein they have fat, and fung, and plagued us for five months.

But to conclude this chapter, we might well wonder how the lawyers yet ftood, feeing the priefts, and prelates, and fuch like locufts were fwept away, but that their five months we find began here in England after the priefts and prelates, yet now the day of their deftiny draws nigh. 'Wherefore, gird up thy loins,' faith the Lord, 'and fpeak unto them all that I command thee. Be not difmayed at their faces, left I confound thee before them.'"

This invective is given at much length, though alfo with much condenfation, both as a fpecimen of *Rogers'* detailed application of prophecy, and becaufe Law and Lawyers, fupplying as they did one of the two great political queftions of the day, were the fubject of his book. From it he proceeds to declare the advent of the Fifth Monarchy.

The Fifth Monarchy now hard by.

Daniel tells us of four Beafts. The laft of thefe beafts had ten horns, amongft which rofe another little horn, and this little horn perfecuted the faints till the judgment fat, when they took away his dominion and deftroyed it for ever.

Now the four Beafts are the four great Monarchies; the ten horns are the ten European kingdoms which arofe out of the laft of thofe Monarchies. As concerning the little horn, "with much affurance and clear fight," he afferts it to be *William the Conqueror* and his Norman fucceffors, all fierce perfecutors of the faints, but cut off at laft and for ever by "the Judgment, which was anno 1648 in that High Court of Judicature erected for the King's trial." \ After this comes the Fifth Monarchy. By 1660 the work of this monarchy is to get as far as Rome, and by 1666, is to be vifible in all the earth. It will come myfterioufly, fuddenly, and terribly, and will redeem the people—1ft, from ecclefiaftical bondage, decrees, councils, orders, and ordinances of the Pope, prieft, prelate, or the like; 2, from civil bondage and flavery, thofe bloody, bafe, unjuft, accurfed, tyrannical laws and fin-monopolizing lawyers as now opprefs and afflict the people. And fo he calls on the Parliament—the Barebones Parliament, then fitting — to prepare everything for the entry of the Fifth

The little horn —i. e. William the Conqueror.

The manner how. For the Redemption of the people— from ecclefiaftical flavery of fouls— from civil flavery of bodies.

1. To model all for the Fifth Monarchy.

2. That the laws agree with God's laws.

3. To do all for Chrift and his monarchy.

In the Fifth Monarchy.

To avoid faction and parties.

The pretty defign of the former Parliament.

Monarchy; and, in order to this—1. To appoint none except the faints to place or office. 2. To abolifh all thofe unjuft and cruel laws, and to pull down thofe courts, terms, and lawyers, yea, and tithes, too, which have occafioned fuch actions, continued complaints, and vexations to the people, and wrongs to God and men, good and bad. 3. To fet up God's law alone, being that in Deut. vi. 1.

" Thefe are the Commandments" (i. e. the ten in two tables given to *Mofes* on Mount Sinai, Exod. xx.) " the Statutes," (i. e. the feveral cafes arifing out of each Commandment tending to eftablifh and confirm each command) " and the judgments," (i. e. the fentence upon the breach of every law, how, and what, the punifhment muft be). Now this law, ftatute-book, and judgment-feat of God muft be fet up in the Fifth Monarchy, and then fhall we be reftored to (1) God's laws ; (2) in our own language, (3) read, and expounded, and made known to the people, (4) at free coft, without charge, (5) juftice will be had at home then, and judges fit in all the gates of the cities, (6) and every man plead his own caufe, (then no need of lawyers), (7) juftice will not be delayed, but fpeedy, (8) and executed without gainfaying, according to the law (fet) of God, and without refpect of perfons, (9) then judges fhall be as at firft, and juftice alfo in every city, and (10) then the Lord will be our only lawgiver, and the law abide for ever, without alteration, as there is now, and ought to be, in the forms of men. " Wherefore, if you be men whom the Lord will own and honour in the work, up then and about it. . . The Lord Jefus awaken you with the noife of the Monarchy which is fwift in motion and now nigh us, left you be furprifed."

Laftly, he urges them to avoid making of parties and running into contentions, as the former Parliaments had done.

" O what hot contefts were between the two parties in general of Prefbyterians and Independents (befides particular parties) in the Parliament before. What ways they had thereby to advance and advantage themfelves and friends was obvious to every eye, and by this pretty artifice they fhared the Commonwealth almoft between them. Befides private cheats, what abundance of open ones, by gifts, rich offices, and employments in committees and treaſures they obtained ! And in pretence of ſerving the public, too, they ſhuffled the trumps into their own hands, and how artificially have they confounded the accounts by laying on numberleſs taxes and aſſeſſments, whilſt the multitude of money ran through ſo many muddy channels, committees, officers, and collecting lickfingers, as it is impoſſible to make any public account thereof. So that, notwithſtanding all fair promiſes to the people, no accounts are or ever will be given of thoſe many millions of money which were made by King's lands, biſhops' and deans' and delinquents' eſtates, arrears, excise, aſſeſſment, and the like, which ſome have licked up ſo handſomely into inſatiable tubs, εἰς πίθον τετριμμένον, &c. that they bought great manors and lordſhips of many hundreds a year, whilſt poor *publica fides* is but *Punica fides*.

Thus by their factions they had their ſeveral deſigns for themſelves and intereſts of their own, and with their Hocus Pocus could conjure up and carry their own for the public, and in pretence of the public, with honour and wealth enough, they did gladly ſacrifice the public peace to their own private intereſts, and when they had ſet all on fire, as ſeveral times they did in the nation by troubles and wars, they would with joy warm their own hands at thoſe unhappy and unhallowed flames which themſelves kindled. Witneſs *Hollis, Stapleton, Maſſey, Sir John Clotworthy*, and many others more lately whom I forbear. But ſee thus the iſſue of parties and factions in the Parliament, to the hindrance and hurt of the public ; and O how do honeſt men's hearts ache already to hear what factions, ſchiſms, and parties are in this Parliament. Yea, about the poor, petty, Popiſh traſh and trumpery of tithes, which ſhall tumble in due time, when ſelf-intereſt is more laid aſide, and Chriſt is with more unanimous concurrence accepted of ; for the harlot ſhall be ſtripped, though Babylon's birds lament it ſo. But in the interim, we truſt our good God will give theſe

So now parties about tithes.

governours a new clue to lead them out of this labyrinth.   .   .   .

But to conclude, the day of our deliverance is dawned.
Let the priefts and lawyers, Antichrift's Church and State
fervants and folicitors, fit and howl, and as many as trade with
Babylon and gain thereby.   Let them look and lament by
fifty-five next, and caft duft on their heads (Rev. xviii. 19),
for the hour of their torment makes hafte.   Wherefore,
woe! woe! woe! to them that hear the voice which now
warns them, and yet will not beware and come out."

1655.

"Bethfhemefh" and "Sagrir" attracted a hoft of critics, of
whom *Zachary Crofton* was the moft eminent, and his book alone
has defcended to pofterity.

Crofton's criticifms on "Bethfhemefh" are minute, perfonal,
and pedantic. Commencing with reflections on the fize, the price,
the frontifpiece, and the title-page of the book, he arrives by
degrees at the dedicatory epiftles, and with the materials they
fupply he attacks not only the political and religious opinions, but
the perfonal and bodily infirmities of the author; not only his
"pride, paffion, and infolency," but the weaklinefs of his conftitution and the colour of his face. A very few extracts will fhow
that in his attacks on the Prefbyterians *Rogers* did not attack men
who were unwilling or unable to retaliate in kind, and will fhow
alfo the eftimation in which he, his books and his "Exercifes,"
were held by contemporary and unfriendly critics. The following
is *Crofton's* account, not perhaps a very unfair one, of *Rogers'*
ftyle of controverfy :—

"Let any ingenuous man read his reafoning, and they
fhall find him railing beyond the bounds of modefty, as the
denominating parochial conftitution an antichriftian, corrupt,
Chrift-crucifying, Chrift-flighting, and Chrift-deftroying
Church ftate, and all parifhes fynagogues of Satan ; without
any demonftration that they are fuch, more than that they
differ from his fancy. So alfo, the reviling the late Affembly
as lordly ufurpers of Chrift's power, bold brazen-faced myf-

tery of iniquity, compofers of a doctrine for affes, and fuch-like epithets doth he ufe for all Prefbyterian Affemblies and Minifters, which modefty doth blufh to mention. Amongft others, he fingles out by name but one antagonift, and takes notice of one only piece oppofing his doctrine. Yet the weapons with which you fhall find him fighting are no other than the flanderous traducing of the fuppofed author, calumniating him with the titles of lying, poor, empty, wide-mouthed libeller, fcandalous philo-compos, violent comet, Jefuitical Prefbyter, furious-pated, and one outed of his place for fcandal and malignancy ; and the work itfelf, though no other than a modeft propofal of juft exceptions, by denominating it a frothy pamphlet, malicious, fpurious, and frog-like froth, not rendering the leaft anfwer to any one objection in it, nor reafon for fuch reviling terms, other than mere falfities and pofitive untruths."

The Author of the Tafte of the Doctrine of the Exercife at Thomas Apoftle's.

And this is *Crofton's* own ftyle of rejoinder :—

" His Firft Epiftle is to the *General Cromwell*, in which we may obferve thefe few confiderations. . . . He faith, ' I do profefs it from my heart, that the greateft temptation I fhould fear falling into would be great honour, efteem, place, preferment, or means too much or unfit for me.' A fair profeffion. But a little to expoftulate with the Rabbi. Do any that know your proud and ambitious genius, even your intimate friends that ob-ferve the very frame of your heart, give credit to the fame ? Will the Commiffioners of Ireland, from your infulting carriage and infolent conteft, nay, almoft any that knew you in Dublin, conclude this to be true, who generally reprefent you to be of a contrary difpofition ? Doth your holding Purleigh, in Effex, when you embraced another place not far thence, or of inferior means, when you offered you know who thirty or forty pounds per annum to be

" Bethfhemefh Clouded."

your curate in the one, or of your holding Purleigh and
receiving the State's falary of £200 per annum, tax free, (as
himfelf confeffeth in page 28) in Ireland, nay Purleigh and
Thomas Apoftles, London, fince at the fame time, fupplying
the one by *Mr. Needham;* nay, will your folicitous feeking
after great benefices, your rage againft *Mr. Maynard* (a
known faithful man), but for being a juft inftrument to
ftop your purfuit, or yet your fubtle obtaining of the Great
Seal for Martin's-in-the-Fields, to the fupplanting of *Mr.
Sangor,* poffeffed of it, and unjuft impofing of yourfelf
and miniftry on the people, not only undefired and un-
called for, but expresfly refufed and denied, conclude or
proclaim to the world that the falling into great places and
means is the great temptation you fear? For fhame, man!
—recall your profeffion or publifh better demonftration,
left you be not believed. . . . .

I fhall pafs from this briefly to his next epiftles, which
are all of them fo full of levity, falfity, vanity, and loqua-
city, for method indigefted, for matter various and varioufly
repeated, for manner—fometimes complaining of his own
mifhaps, and I doubt juftly incurred troubles and felf-
created oppofition, proclaiming his own pride, paffion,
infolency, as made obvious in every place whither he
came—fometimes, Momus-like, carping at and condemning others, with unjuft criminations, railing and reviling,
more than rationally convincing; and herein fometimes he
reflects on the Prefbyterians in general, then on the late
Affembly of Divines, fometimes on fome in Ireland, then
on the men that carry on Blackfriars Exercife, fometimes
on particular perfons, as *Mr. Maynard* and myfelf;
fo that, in a great, high-flown, furious fancy, he falls
on all to clear himfelf; whilft he doth but more fully
manifeft his ignorance, impudence, imbecility, impertinencies and what not, that may proclaim a man fwelling
with pride to boil over in paffion; and fo indeed prefents

himfelf much more *Zoilus* than *Zealous* (though he abundantly affeƈt the latter); fo that the very foam and froth
that he difgorgeth in his Epiftle is fufficient to render his
tabernacle diftafteful to any civil, modeft, ingenuous,
rational man, though of his own judgment."

 Crofton proceeds to accufe his adverfary of being aƈtuated by a
fpirit of obfcurity and darknefs, a fpirit of error, a fpirit of felf-
contradiƈtion, a fpirit of felf-condemnation, a fpirit moft grofsly
abufing authors whom he pretendeth to produce, and moft pal-
pably abufing the Scriptures, with which he jingles and makes a
ftir as if every text were the very principles he fancies, when
many of them, to a due obferver, will be found altogether imper-
tinent to the thing to which they are annexed as proof. All this
it is unnecefsary to exhibit. But in the Appendix to "Bethfhemefh Clouded" *Crofton* gives an account of the original difpute
between himfelf and *Rogers*, which affords us, at no unreafonable
length, a life-like piƈture of a denominational fquabble of the
time.

"A Vindica-
tion of 'A
Tafte of the
Doƈtrine of
Thomas
Apoftle's' and
of its Author."

 " In the foregoing treatife," fays *Crofton*, " I have endeavoured to refcue the truths and churches of God from *Mr.*
Rogers' fancies and falfe cenfures: give me leave a little to
refcue my own name from his flanders, and reprefent to you
his dealings with me in particular ; wherein I may fay of
him, as *Dr. Rivet* of *Bifhop Montague*, 'This man cannot
fo much as motion any man from whom he differs in
opinion, though it be but in the flighteft matters, without
reproach.' That I may be brief, I fhall, in order to my
own vindication, lay before you the caufe and calumny or
matter he urgeth againft me.

 1. In reference to the caufe, you muft underftand that
about December laft there was ereƈted, then a new, already
become a late exercife, at Thomas Apoftle's, London, on
Friday evenings, at the firft of which *Mr. Rogers* preached,
and with a loud cry called into his tabernacle or church
way. Againft which exercife, and in fpecial *Mr. Rogers'*

fermon, there was fome juft exception taken; and in a little book entitled ' A Tafte of the newly erected Exercife at Thomas Apoftle's, London,' firft fignified to the Rabbi, and fo indeed to the world; and this was that which provoked *Mr. Rogers* againft me, for till this he heard me and embraced me.

Well, many men wonder why the coming abroad of this pamphlet fhould fo much provoke, for the modefty of its ftyle may be fubmitted to the judgment and cenfure of the meekeft Independent; nay, and withal it bears not my name upon it. Aye! but upon a convention of faints at his houfe, it muft be judged my work, for two reafons, which muft be fent for to hear. (1). The words ' faith of affurance' and ' faith of adherence' had been in my mouth on the Lord's day, and in this on Friday following; ergo, it was a judicious reafon. (2). I faid to *Mr. Corken*, ' I would break this exercife;' and this was the way to it, to publifh this paper. That the exercife was broken up I was and am glad, but that I fo fpake I denied. Yet, indeed, when I faw the countenance of the fatherlefs child, I offered to be its nurfe, though I called not myfelf its father. I did and do aver the exceptions therein to be juftly laid and modeftly propounded, and fuch as fhould be maintained againft their fury; and this was the caufe of laying this book at my door and fathering it on me as its author, and flying in my face for its exceptions— from which confider thefe. (1). That difference of opinion is the caufe of his rage. This is very fuitable to his liberty of confcience for all opinions, and unity among faints of all judgments. (Lib. 2).

(2). That modeft exceptions are anfwered with violent calumniations of the author, not one reafonable anfwer being given to any one exception, but railing on the poor paper—branding it as a frothy and namelefs pamphlet, malicious, fpurious, frog-like froth.

(3). For this he muft fly in my face, on mere conjecture that I was the author. Suppofe I had been, was there
caufe thus to whip home the poor babe, and with Billingfgate weapons to fly in the face of the father? Was this
author the only exceptor againft his doctrine? Witnefs the
voice from the gallery the firft night, and in the chancel
the fecond night, excepting againft his doctrine. Oh, but
thefe were Anabaptiftical brethren, and therefore to be
indulged. Nay, again, had I not caufe to have publifhed
it, to the refcue of my name from the repute of falling in
with fuch a fanatic fociety which began to arife?—for that,
on a paper fubtlely conveyed to me when in the pulpit,
amongft the bills exprefing the wants to be prayed for, I
had (being, indeed, fuddenly furprifed), given notice to my
hearers of a lecture to be held at that place by minifters of
Weftminfter and London, though not one that I know of
appeared; and for that alfo, expecting the lecture to be
accordingly performed, I was amongft them as a hearer,
unto the offence of fome which fpake to me of it; fo that
I fay, had I as the author figned it with my name, what
caufe had there been of fuch retort?—but much lefs can
fuch dealing with a man on mere conjecture be commended.
But to pafs from the caufe of the Rabbi's rage to the matter
which he chargeth on me. The matter charged is twofold; firft, that which concerns the book and its author—
fecondly, that which concerns my perfon."

After defending his book, *Crofton* charges *Rogers* with fetting
about to deftroy his character.

" In order to which, he lays about and enquires all
Chefhire men out that he can hear of that there have
known me, and he ftrictly enquires of them concerning my
carriage in that country—whether I were not a malignant
or fcandalous man, and endeavours to get depofitions before
the Committee for plundered minifters. The truth of this

you may conjecture from his dealing with *Mr. Sam. Baxter*, Minister of St. Olave's, Silver Street, London, whom he sent for three several times to his house ; and when he came to the same, he assisted with his learned colleague *Rabbi Walker*,* he requires his answers to certain interrogatories, composed for the purpose, concerning me and my carriage in Cheshire and those parts. Nay, and to deter him into accusations of me, he threatens the calling him before the Army—terrible judges, to give in evidence against me. And yet, *Mr. Baxter* not regarding his threats, and so not (as indeed he could not) answering his expectations, he goes to Westminster, and from thence sends a deterring summons to *Mr. Baxter*, signed by *Mr. Shepherd*, deputy of the ward of Martin's Vintry, wherein he was required forthwith to appear before him, to give in evidence against *Zachary Crofton*.

Is not this meekness—with a Mahometan spirit, to advance his principles ' vi et armis,' by force and fury ?"

So much for a theological quarrel, which probably received considerable attention in the year 1653.

Somers' Tracts,
iv. 439, note.

* Henry Walker was originally an ironmonger, and afterwards a student at Queen's College, Cambridge. He was ordained deacon by the Archbishop of Canterbury. When Charles I. went to the city to demand the five members of the House of Commons who had taken refuge there, Walker, from the crowd, shouted " To your tents, O Israel !" and threw a pamphlet with that title into the King's coach. He took a very active part against Laud in his adversity, publishing " Canterbury's Pilgrimage," " Canterbury's Dream," &c. During the Protectorate he incurred the bitter hatred of the Fifth-Monarchy-Men as the editor of the Government newspaper.

CHAPTER IV.

HILE *Rogers* was vituperating lawyers, and *Crofton* vituperating *Rogers*, the Barebones Parliament came to an end. Viewed as a Revolutionary Convention, which it was, and not as a Parliament, which it was not, it hardly deferved the amount of ridicule it has received. *Carlyle* thus fums up the hiftory of its doings and the caufe of its fall :—" In their five months time they paffed various good Acts ; chofe, with good infight, a new Council of State ; took wife charge of the needful fupplies ; did all the routine bufinefs of a Parliament in a quite unexceptionable, or even in a fuperior manner. . . . But, alas, they had decided on abolifhing Tithes, on fupporting a Chriftian Miniftry by fome other method than Tithes ;—nay, far worfe, they had decided on abolifhing the Court of Chancery ! Finding grievances greater than could be borne ; finding, for one thing, Twenty-three thoufand Caufes of from five to thirty years continuance lying undetermined in Chancery, it feemed to the Little Parliament that fome Court ought to be contrived which would actually determine thefe and the like Caufes ;—and that, on the whole, Chancery would be better for abolition. Vote to that effect ftands regiftered in the Commons Journals ; but ftill, for near two hundred years now, only expects fulfilment.—So far as one can difcover in the huge twilight of Dryafduft, it was mainly by this attack on the Lawyers, and attempt to abolifh Chancery, that the Little Parliament perifhed. Tithes helped, no doubt ; and the clamours of a fafely fettled Miniftry, Prefbyterian-Royalift many of them. But the Lawyers exclaimed : ' Chancery ? Law of the Bible? Do you mean to bring-in the *Mofaic difpenfation*, then; and deprive men of their properties? Deprive men of their properties; and us of our learned wigs and lucrative long-windednefs,—with your fearch for 'Simple Juftice' and 'God's Law' inftead of Learned-Serjeant's Law?' There was immenfe 'caroufing in the Temple' when this Parliament ended; as great tremors had been in the like quarters while it continued."

The attack on the lawyers was doubtlefs the main caufe of the fall of the Barebones Parliament, but the immediately preceding caufe was the Tithe queftion. On Saturday, the 10th of December, Parliament paffed a refolution by a majority of fifty-fix to fifty-four, which was confidered equivalent to a vote for the abolition of tithes. This was the time for *Cromwell* to interfere. The Parliament had previoufly alienated the army by backward-nefs in voting its pay; it had now made deadly enemies of the lawyers, the clergy, and the lay impropriators of tithes. *Cromwell* and his party fpent Sunday in confultation. On Monday, December 12, they packed the Houfe, and before the oppofite party had fully affembled it was moved and carried, " That the fitting of this Parliament any longer, as now conftituted, will not be for the good of the Commonwealth, and that therefore it is requifite to deliver up unto the *Lord General Cromwell* the powers which they received from him." Whereupon the Speaker rofe " in an irruptious way," and with many members of the Houfe departed to Whitehall, where they refigned their powers into the hands of *Cromwell. Major-General Harrifon*, who with fome twenty-feven others remained fitting, was expelled from the Houfe—very much as he had expelled others—by a file of mufketeers.

Thus perifhed the " Barebones " or " Little " Parliament, after fitting from July 4 to December 12, 1653. *Cromwell*, according to his cuftom in fuch cafes, convened a council of his officers, who, after feveral days feeking of God and advifing therein, refolved that a Council of twenty-one godly, able, and difcreet perfons fhould be named, and that his Excellency fhould be chofen Lord Protector of the three nations. " In purfuance hereof," continued the Government newfpaper, " feveral perfons of eminency and worth are already made choice of to be of the faid council, and on Friday laft [the 16th] His Excellency came down to Weftminfter and was inftalled Lord Protector of the three nations."

The Fifth-Monarchy-Men were furious. They execrated the government of any and every "fingle perfon," whether pope, prince, or protector. England's work and their own was not to raife up but to throw down principalities and powers; they had fought and bled, they had preached and prayed, they had caft out and brought in, that they might have "no king but Jefus," and now they were outwitted, betrayed, and were likely to be oppreffed by the very man whom they had moft trufted.

Cromwell was fully aware of the fury of the Fifth-Monarchy-Men, which, indeed, they did not attempt to conceal. It is faid by *Oldmixon*, in his Hiftory of the Stuarts, that the chiefs of their party were at this time *Major-General Harrifon, Colonel Rich*, and *Mr. Carew* among the laity, and *Rogers, Feake,* and *Simpfon* among the clergy. The three firft were fummoned at once before *Cromwell*, and when they refufed to engage not to act againft him, *Harrifon* was ordered to his houfe in Staffordfhire, *Carew* was imprifoned in Pendennis Caftle, and *Rich* committed to the cuftody of the Serjeant-at-Arms. The minifters would have been unmolefted if they could have remained filent, but filence in that day of rebuke and blafphemy was to them not only a fin but an impoffibility. The Barebones Parliament refigned on the 12th of December, the Protectorate was announced on the 16th, and two days afterwards, that is to fay, on Sunday, the 18th, *Feake* and a certain *Vavafor Powell* declared open war, and told their hearers in Chrift Church, Newgate, that *Oliver Cromwell* was "the diffemblingeft perjured villain in the world, and defired that, if there were any of his friends there, they would go and tell him what they faid, and withal, that his reign was but fhort, and that he fhould be ferved worfe than that great tyrant the laft Lord Protector was, he being altogether as bad, if not worfe than he." The next day, Monday, the 19th, the Lord Protector was proclaimed by the heralds in Weftminfter and the City, and *Vavafor Powell* preached againft him again in the fame ftrain. Two days afterwards, on the 21ft, *Feake* and *Powel* were fummoned before the Council, and committed to the cuftody of the Serjeant-at-Arms, but they were releafed on the 24th, in time for *Powell* to preach againft *Cromwell* for the third time on Sunday the 25th.

Nor was *Rogers* idle. On the very day (Dec. 21) on which his brethren were fummoned before the Council, he publifhed the following epiftle to *Oliver Cromwell*:—

P. 423.

Thurloe, i.
641.

"To his Highness Lord General Cromwell,
Lord Protector, &c.

*The humble Cautionary Propofals of John Rogers, Minifter
of the Gofpel according to the Difpenfation of the Spirit
(now) at Thomas Apoftles, London.*

My Lord,

It is the great Jehovah Niffi, or Lord Protector of his
people, who hath awakened me morning by morning, who
would not let me reft day nor night fince you were proclaimed Lord Protector, until his Spirit had fet me upon
my feet in thefe following propofals with cautions.   Now
becaufe none elfe is upon this errand, which is fo eminently
for Chrift and his intereft, and fo many are up and jocund
already for the intereft of Antichrift, therefore I can find no
truce nor peace within me till I become obedient to the
Lord God which hath opened mine ear, and I will not
rebel.   Therefore have I fet my face like a flint, for I know
that I fhall not be afhamed.

1ft Propofal.   Take heed of Protecting the plantations
of Antichrift or the Towers of Babylon, which muft fall,
and with fury too, upon the heads of their Protectors, as
Ifaiah xxxi. 3, ' When the Lord fhall ftretch out his hand,
both he that helpeth (or is their Protector) and he that is
holpen fhall fall with him.'

2nd Propofal.   Take heed of being guided or governed
with the old State principles of carnal policy, for Antichrift
works now more in a myftery of iniquity than ever.   And
what the Beaft could not do with his horns here in England (by cruel pufhing) which we hope are off, yet he
hopes to do it with his heads (by cunning plotting) which
we fear are on.   This principle of policy was fatal to *Jehu,*
Ahithophel's counfel came to nothing, and *Antiochus* could
not Protect himfelf.

Fifth-Monarchy-Man.

3rd Propofal. Take heed of carnal counfellors, I mean fuch men as feek themfelves more than Chrift. *Darius* had fuch counfellors, who flattered him to his face (Dan. vi. 6, 7); but they were enemies to *Daniel*, the true prophet (who had an excellent fpirit). Therefore, my lord, let them give you counfel that are converfant with the fecrets of God and the vifions of thefe days. *Belfhazzar* did fend for *Daniel* to open the vifion to him that concerned him, fo when you find, my Lord, all the wife men of the world to fail you in the vifions of thefe times and feafons by their liberal arts and fciences, philofophical notions or rules, then fend for the *Daniels* (of an excellent fpirit) to confer with upon the prophecies. Befides, my Lord, it concerns you, you will find fome day, to have a high efteem of thofe moft honourable members of the laft Parliament that proved faithful to Chrift againft Antichrift and his caufe.

4th Propofal. Take heed of meddling with the Protection of men's carnal, cruel, heathenifh laws, guilty of tyranny, oppreffions, perjury, cheating, injuftice, perfecution, and much innocent blood, and moft of them contrary to the laws of God, whofe laws are to be reftored and made republic law in thefe latter days, as Ifaiah xlii. 21, 22, ' for his righteoufnefs' fake he will magnify the law, and make it honourable.' His are the beft in all cafes that ever were made, which muft be known to all, (Deut. xxx. 10, 16).

5th Propofal. Take heed of Protecting the carnal,*

---

* " There was a paper delivered to his highnefs from one *Mr. Rogers.* The perfons and titles of orthodox divines do feem to be much difpleafing to him. I fhall here give it to the difcreet reader for novelty's fake :— ' Take heed of protecting the carnal, national, antichriftian clergy,' " &c.— From the *Weekly Intelligencer*, Dec. 27 to Jan. 3, 1653—4.

This paragraph feems to have been inferted in the newfpapers for the fake of fecuring the fympathies of the orthodox, i. e. the Prefbyterian Divines againft *Rogers* and his party. The firft four " propofals " are fuppreffed, while the fifth is copied at full length.

national, Antichriftian Clergy, though they come in the
name of orthodox or learned. . . . . So *Ahab* (a
notable politician) did Protect his national Clergy, or Prophets (who were his not the Lord's), and by their fuggeftion
hated and perfecuted the true Prophet *Micaiah*, which
proved his ruin.

Make hafte, my Lord, for Chrift's Protection againft
the plagues that are (as fure as God is righteous) coming
upon Babylon, and all that will cleave to her in intereft.
Luther was not too bold, in the name of the Lord, to tell
his Lord Protector, the *Elector of Saxony*, 'Judico Celfi-
tud. Veftr. plus a me præfidii et tutelæ habituram effe quam
mihi præftare. Huic caufæ nullus gladius confulere aut
opem ferre poffe'—that by his prayers he had gained him
more fafety and Protection than he had received from him;
and that the caufe of Chrift needed not his Protection, but
he needed that's Protection. And 'Sive id credat C. V.
five non credat,' (fays he), whether you believe it or no,
yet this way I will undertake to fecure and Protect your
Highneffes foul, body, eftate, and all, (viz. by faith and
prayer), if you engage freely in the caufe of Chrift againft
Antichrift. So fay I, my Lord, in that name which fent
me, which fills me with courage and confidence, that if you
will freely oblige for Chrift and his intereft, the faith and
prayers of the faints, which were never higher than now,
fhall Protect you fufficiently in all emergencies; but if you
will engage for Antichrift and his interefts, the loud-crying
faith and inceffant high-fpirited prayers of the faints will
all engage againft you, and never give Jehovah-Niffi, the
Lord our Protector reft, till the excellency of *Jacob* have
prevailed. (2 Chron. xix. 6). 'Take heed what you do.'

Thus the Lord hath ftirred me up by an irrefiftible and
reftlefs power (once more) to lay his work before you,
for that he hath ufed you as a moft glorious inftrument in
the three nations (by the faith and prayers of this people),

to make way for this work, which if you reject will
reject you, and be the infallible forerunner of your fall;
which that God may prevent is the fervent prayers of
the faithful people night and day, whose fouls mourn in
fecret for you, whofe hearts ache and bleed abundantly
on your behalf, as for a man moft dear in their fouls, but
under moft defperate temptations and dangers. I have
freely expofed myfelf, in this my Mafter's fervice, by whofe
Spirit I am, I hope, full of power, to all the fharp cenfures,
reproaches, revilings, and hard meafures that I can meet
with from men or devils, choofing rather to have my peace
within me than without me. ' Ruere cum Chrifto quam
regnare cum Cæfare.' It may be men will judge me
proud or felf-feeking, as they thought of *Luther*. . .
But in thefe propofals, I am fure I have kept my fphere,
and followed the ftrong impulfe of God's own Spirit in me
and many others, however it be taken. Wherefore, the
great God awaken you to his work; elfe the time will
come when God will fay, ' Let him alone, he is joined to
idols.' (Hos. iv. 17).
    Now, that the hand of the Lord may be with you, fee
what thefe five fingers point at to you, which, if you practife, will be able to Protect you as well as direct you in this
dreadful day of the Lord's Controverfy for Sion. They
concern you, my Lord, more than *Cæfar's* paper did him.
Now, that they may not prove a handwriting againft you
and a cup of trembling put into your hands, they are
ftrengthened with a divine generofity, and fhall ftruggle
with you in the faith, tears, and prayers of many who pray
and mourn for you, and amongft others
                   Your afflicted, faithful fervant,
                For the intereft of my Lord Jefus,
                               JOHN ROGERS.
From my Study, the 21ft day of Tebeth,
    or the 10th month.''

Rogers was probably as active in preaching as in writing ; for it appears that on Monday, the 9th of January, 1654, about three weeks after the date of his Cautionary letter, he and *Vavafor Powell* preached fo violently againſt the Government in their church in Newgate market, that *William Erberry*, another Independent Miniſter, was conſtrained in confcience to remonſtrate.* It appears, from the letter *Erberry* publiſhed, that *Rogers* chofe for his text Jerem. xlii. 20—" For ye diſſembled in your hearts when ye fent me unto the Lord your God, faying, Pray for us,'' &c. " This he [*Rogers*] interpreted as the diſſembling of fome in power to aſk the prayers of the Prophets and people of God in their troubles, who now act contrary to their own profeſſed purpofes of no perfonal rule." It is difficult to fuppofe that he would have allowed his congregation to overlook the two verfes which immediately follow that from which he took his text—" And now I have this day declared it to you ; but ye have not obeyed the voice of the Lord your God, nor anything for the which he hath fent me unto you. Now therefore know certainly that ye ſhall die by the fword, by the famine, and by the peſtilence, in the place whither ye defire to go and to fojourn."

On the 23rd of January, 1654, a fortnight after the date of this fermon, *Cromwell* and his Council publiſhed an ordinance declaring what offences ſhould be accounted treafon. Thefe were—" to compafs or imagine the death of the Lord Protector ; to raife forces againſt the prefent Government ; to deny that the Protector and the people aſſembled in Parliament are the fupreme authority of the nation, or that the exercife of the chief magiſtracy is centred in him ; or to affirm that the Government is tyrannical, ufurped, or illegal, or that there is any Parliament now in being ; alfo the proclaiming or in anywife promoting any of the poſterity of the late King to be King or Chief Magiſtrate." All fuch ordinances iſſued by the Protector and Council had the force of law.

Notwithſtanding its laſt claufe, this ordinance was confidered by the Fifth-Monarchy-Men to be levelled directly at them ; and their anger was further inflamed when *Feake* and *Simpfon* were

Godwin's Hiſtory of the Commonwealth, iv. 34.

---

* " An Olive Leaf ; or, fome Peaceable Confiderations to the Chriſtian Meeting at Chriſt Church in London, Monday, Jan. 9, 1654. By *William Erberry*."

arrefted under its authority, on Jan. 26, and fent to Windfor Caftle a few days later.

But in truth it was high time for the Protector to take precautions for the fecurity of his perfon and government. At that moment plots were being hatched by the Royalifts and Fifth-Monarchy-Men againft both ; and fuch plots were a fource of continual uneafinefs to *Cromwell* and his family for the reft of his life.

The following is one of the many informations received by *Thurloe*, who had the management of this department :—

Whitelock, p. 580.

"A LETTER OF ELLEN ASKE.

MR. R. NELSON,—

May it pleafe your worfhipe to acquaint his highnes . . . . that I am able to difcover many of my lords deedly and deftructive enemyes, and thofe that latly upon a faft day in London did gather together in a place that I can difcover, becaufe then there prefent, and did there moft ftrangly rayle againft his highnes and faid the plage of God confound him, calling him 'round-heded doge, I would I had his flefh between my teeth,' and much more as bade ; . . . . and one of them faid ' now he is gone to pray let us go charge and bind him.'

Furder I have harde of a fecrett plot of many who refolve to have a runing army againft my lord his highnes for blood, and have as I underftand horfes bought redy for that purpofe, and my frinde . . . *Ifaac Wellis* doath know the man which I confave can defcover very much of this great plott which doath, I feare, drawe nere to be executed by a people called a 5th monirchy peopll ; and that there is a gentillwoman who did tell me that that work would not be accomplifhed until fhe went, for fhe fhould be one of them that fhould pull him down or help down with him, was the word faid. Whereas I am afraid to fpeak with any but my Lord or your worfhipp; the refon of it is, becaufe there are in my Lords houſe or thereunto belonging them that doe declare to *Mr. Rodgeres,* and ſo to *Mr. P heake* and oatheres, what allmoſt ſoever is ſpoken in my Lord's one houſe. I being not long ſince a herer of *John Rodgeres,* did underſtand much, and had almoſt been deſtroyed or ſwalowed up with deluſions that my Lord was not a man that ſtood for truth and peace. So with my humble ſarvice preſente to you, ... I reſt your Sarvant,

ELLEN ASKE."

"THE EXAMINATION OF ELLEN ASKE.

That *Mr. Rogers* told her that one *Rachel* or *Abigal* —— that lives about the Tower is very intimate with a gentleman that waits conſtantly on his Highneſs, and uſually at his elbow when he is in his chair at dinner, that publiſhes all he hears or knows to be done in his Highneſs's family to the ſaid *Rachel* or *Abigal.*

That *Mr. Aſke,* now in the 'Elizabeth' of London, at Graveſend, ... hath a liſt of the names of all thoſe that ſubſcribed for the raiſing of horſe againſt his Highneſs and this preſent Government.

The ſaid *Mr. Aſke* only named *Major-General Harriſon, Rogers, Feake,* and one that was a commander in ſome great place, that ſhould have been the Commander-in-Chief; but he could not remember his name. . . . . Many other particulars ſhe told me, of horſes that were bought for that purpoſe, and to be lodged in the town, to be put in execution by way of ſurpriſe. . . . .

This examination was taken Feb. 17, 1654, by me,

RO. NELSON."

In conſequence, probably, of this information, the "powers" cauſed *Rogers'* houſe to be ſearched, and his papers ſeized, which elicited his fifth and laſt letter to *Cromwell.*

Mene, *Tekel,* *Perez,*

OR,

A little Appearance of the

HAND-WRITING

(In a Glance of Light)

Againſt the Powers and Apoſtates of the

T I M E S.

By a Letter written to, and lamenting over

Oliver Lord *Cromwel.*

BY JOHN ROGERS.

In this woful Howre of his Temptation, and of
Sion's ſore pangs, and *Solemne* Appeals; and of the precious *Saints* im-
priſonments and perſecution for *this* moſt *Glorious,* betrayed,
denyed, and crucified *Cauſe* of *Chriſt Jeſus*

KING OF SAINTS AND NATIONS.

There ſin is written with a Pen of Iron, and the point of a Diamond (ungue
adamantino עצמן) *whiles there Children remember their Altars and
Groves again.* Jer. **17. 15.**
*Why do ye perſecute me, as God? and are not ſatisfied with my fleſh? oh that my
words were now written! oh that they were printed in a Book! that they were
graven with an iron pen in the Rock for ever! For I know that my Redeemer
liveth, and that he ſhall ſtand in the Latter end upon the EARTH, &c.* Job
19. 22, 23, 24, 25, *&c.*

Heu pietas! ubi priſca? profana o tempora! Mundi!
Fax! Veſper! prope Nox! O Mora! Chriſte Veni!
Sinite Virgam Corripientem ne ſentiatis Malleum Conterentem. Bern.

"A WORD BY THE WAY TO THE READER.

Since the time that I was lately fo illegally and arbitrarily plundered without any caufe fhown or known by this unrighteous felf-created powers that is got uppermoft, I have with the words of Jeremy (ch. xx. 8, 9) 'cried out violence and fpoil ! becaufe the word of the Lord is made a reproach and derifion daily. Then I faid, I will not make mention nor fpeak any more in His name. But His word was in my heart as a burning fire fhut up in my bones, and I was weary with forbearing, and I could not ftay,' but conftrained in fpirit wrote this letter. Yet feeing by feveral meffengers I have affayed, and that feveral days together to get it delivered, and finding it fo difficult that it is doubtful whether it be fafely conveyed to him or no, you find it printed as the moft probable means of having it prefented to his eye, for that many flatterers are ready to run with the news to their mafter (as v. 10). 'Report, fay they, and we will report it. All my familiars watched for my halting, faying peradventure he will be enticed, and we fhall prevail againft him, and take our revenge on him.' Well, if they do fo, we come, Crofs of Chrift, for my next petition to ' Thy Kingdom come' is ' Thy will be done in earth as it is in heaven.' Yet who knows but this weak word may awaken him a little. . . . . But whether this do or not, my confcience is now fo well fatisfied, my heart refrefhed, and my fpirit fo warmed in the ftrength of our dear (defpifed) Chrift, that I hope to go on with Jer. xx. 11 : 'For the Lord is with me who is the terrible one, therefore my perfecutors fhall ftumble, they fhall not prevail, but they fhall be greatly afhamed, for they fhall not profper (long), and their everlafting confufion

fhall never be forgotten.' This is the victorious, over-
turning,* already triumphing faith of hundreds (bleffed be
Jehovah) befides

JOHN ROGERS."

"My Lord,—

While the fouls of many of the Lord's dear fervants
(who fit weeping over you) are in travail and ftruggle for
you in the hour of temptation, I moft humbly beg, as
upon my knees, for your own foul and family, and for the
poor afflicted faints' fake, that you will but weigh thefe few
lines of our prefent lamentation in the balance of your
heart and confcience, one part of an hour which you may
beft fpare and be moft ferious in, which, if the Lord whom
I ferve require it, I think I could as freely write with my
own blood as with ink, in tears and gall of grief. O, our
bowels! our bowels! Our hearts ache and are pained
within us to hear the doleful groans, and crys, tears,
prayers, and folemn appeals of godly people in the nation
round about to the Righteous Judge of the whole earth,
which doubtlefs will be anfwered with a dreadful difpenfation and fevere decree upon thofe that be found the enemies
to the Lord Jefus and his exaltation. The apprehenfion
whereof hath fo feized upon my fpirit that I fhould fin if
fome way or other I gave you no notice thereof, for that
your own perfon is (yet) fo dear in our very fouls that
bowels of affection are frequently feen to you in mourning,

---

* See Oliver Cromwell's Speech to Parliament, Sept. 4, 1654. He
fays, in allufion to the Fifth-Monarchy-Men, "Whilft thefe things were
in the midft of us, and the nation rent and torn from one end to the other,
family againft family, parent againft child, and nothing in the hearts and
minds of men but 'Overturn, Overturn, Overturn,' a Scripture very much
abufed and challenged by all men of difcontented fpirits."—*Whitelock's
Memorials,* p. 599.

praying, and wreftling for you (if poffible) to recover you
out of thofe bottomlefs fnares wherein you are fo deeply
enfnared by the evil counfel of parafites, fubtle and felf-
feeking flatterers, Dawbers and Deceivers, who have not that
lively fenfe to the Lord Jefus, His poor faints, and intereft,
nor yet to your foul (fo defperately engaged, we humbly
conceive) as we who are counted enemies for the truth's
fake, as the Lord will witnefs, have, of whom, as Philip. iii.
18, 19 : 'I have told you often, and now tell you again,
even weeping, that they are the enemies to the Crofs of
Chrift, whofe end is deftruction, whofe god is their belly,
and whofe glory is in their fhame, who mind earthly things.'
Jer. ix. 1, 2 : ' Oh, that my head were waters, and mine
eyes a fountain of tears, that I might weep day and night
for the flain of the daughter of my people, and go from
them, for they be all adulterers, an affembly of treacherous
men.' I cannot fpeak with you in perfon, therefore I befeech you, read thefe words, which our tears and prayers
are the ambaffadors and forerunners of, ' mittamus preces
et lacrymas cordis legatos' (Cyprian), for that we have
not the leaft grain of ill-will, hatred, or malice (as fome
fuggeft and fay) againft any perfon, but only againft the
fin and evil of this change of government, which God
will (and if righteous, we are fure muft) judge, and then,
as once you faid in your letter to the Kirk of Scotland,
' God, who knoweth us, will in His due time manifeft
whether we do multiply thefe things as men, or do we them
for the Lord Chrift, and his poor people's fake.' Wherefore,

Your own declarations.   Firft, be pleafed, we befeech you with weeping tears, to
compare a little prefent tranfactions with former engage-
ments, and with the Army's declarations, &c. as that of
June 14, 1647, page 6, declaring that you took up arms in
judgment and confcience for the people's juft rights and
liberties, and refolved to affert and vindicate them againft
all arbitrary power, violence, and oppofition, and againft

all particular parties and interefts whatfoever, fo page 7, that it is no refifting of magiftracy to fide with juft principles. . . . So page 9—that ' we are fo far from defigning and complying to have an abfolute arbitrary power figned or fettled for continuance in any *PERSONS WHAT-SOEVER*, as that if we might be fure to obtain it, we cannot wifh to have it fo in the perfons of any whom we ourfelves could moft confide in, or who fhould appear moft of our principles and opinions.' . . . .

Secondly. Be pleafed, my Lord, a little to revife or reafon with the rife of this change upon the breaking up of the late Parliament, taking its being but for this end, to keep up the carnal interefts the Parliament had voted down, viz. of clergy, carnal church-ftate, tithes, prefentations, &c. . . Now, for the Parliament to do that which the army and good people round the nation have declared to be their duty, viz. to take off the civil dependence of the national clergy with their national Church-State, and to vote a new model of the law, viz. lefs intricate, uncertain, tyrannical, and unjuft, and more confonant with God's word and ftatutes, and judgments, and right reafon, and more plain, eafy, and clear ; and to take away corrupt and fimonious prefentations, whereby fouls and people are bought and fold to great men's lufts ; for this, formerly judged to be their duty, to be diffolved and broken, yea, at that time, too, when this longed-for mercy after many years was brought to the birth . . yea, and after the long-fitting Parliament was broken, too, for their neglect of thefe very things (with others), feems ftrange to us, and the more diffatisfies us for that we fee this power fucceed for the fupport and upholding of thofe things which that Parliament had voted down, and what the army and good people had fo often declared props of Antichrift. . . . .

O, my Lord, that the opening and bleeding of our

Againft abfolute government in one perfon.

The rife of this G. upon the ruin of the laft Parliament.

Rev. xviii. 13, being merchandize of Babylon.

bowels for thefe things might be a little regarded and pitied.

Thirdly. May you be (moft humbly, and as upon our bended knees) entreated to take a little account of the already fruits and effects of this alteration, (which the Lord knows we bitterly bewail before the great God as more heavy to us than the precedent changes) in fhutting up the doors of our public meeting-places, hindering us in God's worfhip, imprifoning our dear brothers and friends, plundering, reproaching, and grieving them, (and them only) that have been all thefe wars, and yet are (and we hope ever will be) faithful to the Caufe and Kingdom of Chrift, threatening to take away their lives, and endeavouring to ftone and ftab them, afperfing them with moft palpable, loathfome, and notorious falfities, to poffefs good people in the counties with prejudice againft them, as if they were againft all Magiftracy, Minif-try, and Property, which with a wonderful and wicked confi-dence fome write and fpread about (the Lord lay it ferioufly to their hearts and humble them for it) but we cannot be fuffered to print the truth or to anfwer their cruel calum-nies or accufations, whilft we defire no other weapons (the Lord knoweth) for our warfare but the word of truth, which fhall be our defence ; yet we are not fuffered to print, but are plundered of our notes and writings, while all manner of lies, flanders, and malicious reports are printed and divulged of us. . . . .

Laftly, my Lord, may you be pleafed but to fee a little in the midft of our trouble and agony how like this prefent government looks to that which the Lord (by the faith and prayers of his defpifed people) hath fo eminently engaged againft, laid in duft, and ftamped upon with difdain. . . . And muft we not pray that you may be freed from fuch as have fubtlely enfnared you, and do, prelate-like, poffefs you and others againft us that we are fanatic mad-men, fools, and heady enemies to Magiftracy, Minif-

The already effects and fruits of this change moft grievous to the faithful and godly.

How alike this G. is to it which God hath thrown down before our eyes.

Our weapons of warfare and our adverfaries —what they are.

try, and all, &c. for which our hearts are pained within us, whiles we ponder thefe things and our fpirits grieved that men of fo much former merit and eminency fhould fo finfully and unchriftianlike condemn and accufe us of things our hearts abhor and loathe within us, and call for feverity under the name of juftice, and dealeth perfecution againft us in the matters of our faith and confcience, merely and alone for the exalting Jefus Chrift. . . . . .

But, my Lord, may the prefented truth (or poor crucified Jefus) beg this favour, to give it as much favour as His adverfaries have for their grofs lies or falfities in printing or otherwife, therefore will you be pleafed (though but for a little time, a month or two) to releafe thofe laws which hinder the publifhing of the truth. Let our brethren or any that will oppofe us, convince or conquer all they can with the good word of God, and we fhall be fatisfied to try it out with them fo, but not with the weapons of the world, as they have them (now) all on their fide, to imprifon, perfecute, or put to death, for that is Antichrift's not Chrift's way of warfare. . . Therefore, as *Luther* wrote to the *Dukes of Saxony*, fo do we humbly to you, my Lord. 'I would not,' faith he, 'but all have free liberty, yet if any tranfgrefs Gofpel bounds, and would raife up feditions or wars againft you, then you may reprefs them.' . . So, my Lord, if we ftir up people to rifings, tumults, or carnal warfare, as men falfely charge us, then punifh us as you pleafe, for it is contrary to our principles fo to do.

Furthermore, O that you would not believe every report of the Boutefeus or Fireblowers of thefe our new troubles againft us. . . . Will you be pleafed to perufe a little thofe writings taken out of my ftudy, and fatisfy yourfelf concerning the truth of them, and not believe thofe bits and parts which fome fycophants probably will acquaint you with. . . . .

But if we have no hopes left to prevail with you, yet

our hearts are filled with hope, and sure we are to prevail with God. Our appeal is in heaven, and the faith and prayer which are up (as high as ever since the world stood) either will bring forth your conversion (for *Luther* saith the Church converts ' totum mundum sanguine et oratione ') or your confusion. For the death and destruction of the persecutors was, as it was said of the death of *Arius*, ' precationis opus non morbi.'

But if it be asked what we would have you to do, our present answer is—

What to be done in order to return.

First, advise with the Lord about your former declarations. . . . .

2. And then proclaim a fast, a solemn day of humiliation for the errors and sins past, as 1 Kings xxi. 27-29— ' It came to pass when *Ahab* heard those words he rent his clothes and fasted, and lay in sackcloth, &c. And the Lord said, Seest thou how *Ahab* humbleth himself before me. Because he humbleth himself before me I will not bring the evil in his days.' . . . . Let out the Lord's prisoners whom the Churches are robbed of, viz. *Mr. Feak* and *Mr. Simpson*.

Let out the Lord's prisoners, Mr. Feak, Mr. Simpson, Han. Taprel in Bridewell.

And that they may open to you the present vision of God given them in these things according to the dispensation of the Spirit, O, hear them once at least preach to you the power of Jesus . . . . let them have, though but for a month or two, and though but half so much liberty to open the word of the Lord to you as your chaplains have. . . . . But if you will yet go on, ' ad exitium potius quam ad exercitium,' after all our bleeding entreaties, and be hardened up by the dangerous counsel of your own reason or them about you, then, my Lord, our souls shall mourn in secret for you as for one desperately

Our resolution.

lost indeed, and we shall proceed to bear our testimony against the sin of the times, for our appeal hangs in Heaven and we cannot recall it. Yea, as *Luther* once said, ' Quo magis illi furunt eo amplius procedo,' the more men rage the more refolute we hope to be in our appeals, faith, and prayer. . . . .

So far as I may,
Your true fincere Servant,
JOHN ROGERS."

On the 20th of March, 1654, two months after the Ordinance of Treafon, another ordinance was publifhed, which was fcarcely lefs offenfive to the Fifth-Monarchy-Men. It was called an ordinance for the " Approbation of Public Preachers," and provided that every perfon who had been admitted to a benefice within the laft twelve months, or who might thereafter be admitted, fhould be "judged and approved by the perfons hereafter named to be a perfon for the Grace of God in him, his holy and unblameable converfation, as alfo for his knowledge and utterance, able and fit to preach the Gofpel." Such as were approved received from the " Triers," as they were called, an inftrument in writing, without which no one was to be deemed lawfully poffeffed of any living or benefice, and by virtue of which, when obtained, the holder was put in as full poffeffion as if he had been admitted by inftitution and induction. Thirty-feven Commiffioners (or Triers) were named, and the partial and oppreffive way in which they ufed their power was bitterly complained of both by Royalift clergy on the one fide, and by fuch men as *Rogers* on the other.

Scobell's Acts and Ordinances, part ii, p. 279.

The authorities do not feem to have noticed Mene, Tekel, Perez, or the fermons which preceded it. To requite their forbearance, *Rogers* held a folemn fervice of humiliation over their fins, and as a preliminary he publifhed the grounds on which he acted.

" *The Grounds of Meeting at Tho. Apoftle's, the 28th day of the firft Month* [*March*], 1654, *in folemn humiliation before the Lord, beginning at 7 o'clock in the morning.*

1. The manner of the coming in of the prefent G—— with the fudden breaking up of the laft Parliament, for that they would have changed the prefent National Miniftry, lawyers, prefentations, taxes and oppreffions, and

for that they would have ruled as Saints—therefore driven out of the houfe.

2. The prefent grand apoftacy of profeffors, churches, preachers, and eminent perfons of the nobles of Judah in the Army, city and country, from their former engagements, declarations, profeffions and promifes for Chrift and his kingdom, caufe and intereft.

3. The profecution of the faithful remnant that threatens them, wherein we may fpread before the Lord thofe new-made laws of treafon, &c. which look too much like tyranny, according to which the fervants of the Lord are imprifoned at Windfor, and others threatened.

4. The manifold tentations abroad, both here and in the country, which are of divers forts, as adverfity, imprifonment, lofs of friends, liberties, &c ; on the other fide, offers of places, preferments, honours, &c ; and on all fides the fpirit of delufion by falfe deluding pamphlets, arguments, fallacies, and lies, whereby many good people are blinded in city and country.

5. The prefent deadnefs and flatnefs of fpirit that is upon the little remnant of Saints that are not yet backfliden, as at All-hallows meeting and elfewhere ; that thofe that remain may have a full, free, fit and quickened fpirit, beyond whatever they yet had, to engage with one heart and mind, by conftant faith and prayer, in the prefent teftimony.

6. As to deplore the prefent magiftracy and miniftry, and fuch wicked ones which are heightened in their expeĉtations and exalted into places ; fo alfo to be earneft for the magiftracy and miniftry of the unĉtion according to the promife in the latter days, that Chrift alone may be exalted.

7. To fpread before the Lord the animofities, jealoufies, heartburnings and divifions, that are amongft the Saints and Churches, about forms, opinions, or points of judg-

ment, and that the Lord would make an union in the
Spirit.

8. On thefe and divers other grounds which we might
mention, as hypocrify, pride, and oppreffion; to mourn
alfo for the prefent unfeafonable weather and drought,
which threatens famine and mortality, that the Lord would
remove caufes that the effects might ceafe."

Thurloe, ii. 196.

It was very ufual in thofe days for the more zealous members
of the congregation to take fhort-hand notes of their minifter's
fermons. This cuftom enabled *Thurloe's* fpies to provide themfelves, in the fame way, with the following abftraft of the fermon
which *Rogers* delivered on this occafion.

"INFORMATION AGAINST MR. ROGERS.

*May** 28, *at Thomas Apoftles;* in his prayer thefe and
fuch like paffages. Haften the time when all abfolute
power fhall be devolved into the hand of Chrift, when
we fhall have no Lord Protector but our Lord Jefus,
the only true Protector and Defender of the Faith. Let
our faith have fo much of the grain of muftard feed as to
fay to that great mountain, ' Be removed,' and it fhall be
removed.

Look 'n mercy upon thy faints at Windfor, that are
imprifoned for the truth and teftimony of Jefus ; be thou
their freedom and enlargement, &c. Remember thy
handmaid,† who is brought to town, and threatened by
the worldly powers, who crucify Chrift Jefus in the fpirit
every day. Hear the blafphemies of the Court, and regard
their ridiculous pomp and vanity. And now Chrift Jefus
is proclaimed King, pour forth thy vials on the worldly
powers, the powers of Antichrift.

---

* The date "May 28" in Thurloe is probably a mifprint for
"March 28." † Probably Hannah Taprell.

Then he bleſſed God, that had yet reſerved himſelf a remnant, who had not bowed their knees to *Baal*.

He named his text out of the 5th chapter of the letter of Matthew, 25th verſe—'Agree with thine adverſary quickly.' By the adverſary, he ſaid, was meant Chriſt, whom the apoſtate profeſſors and wicked ones of this world had made their adverſary; and ſo made this his doctrine. 'Tis the concernment of all adulterous, apoſtate profeſſors to make a ſpeedy agreement with their adverſary. And becauſe the kingly office of Chriſt was at this preſent time moſt eminently oppoſed, he would ſpeak to the preſent powers, who are the oppoſers of it in their Government, in their prieſthood, in their armies.

The apoſtate profeſſors of this age have openly broken all God's commandments, as I ſhall ſhow in their order.

1. To the firſt. 'I am the Lord thy God, that brought thee out of Egypt; thou ſhalt have no other God but me.' But, as Iſrael of old made themſelves calves, and ſaid, 'Lo theſe are our Gods, which brought us out of Egypt,' ſo the men of this generation ſay, Lo this, and lo that; lo our ſtrength and lo our armies have brought us out of bondage from under monarchical government, &c.

2. 'Thou ſhalt not make to thyſelf any graven image.' But the preſent powers have ſet up graven images, that is to ſay, the works of men's imaginations. They have lately ſet up Triers at Whitehall—a new ſet of doctors, worſhippers of the inventions of man; a new com-miſſion-court to give out tickets and ſeals, and inſtruments and picklocks to open houſes and pulpits, and pig-ſties and hen-roofts, to fetch thence eggs and geeſe, and pigs and tithes—a moſt ſottiſh and ridiculous foppery, nay, mere idolatry. 'Tis an horrible ſin in any to own them or receive commiſſion from them. The laſt Parliament would have proved a reformer and have pulled down this image, but that the powers of this world interpoſed. And I believe

one day they muft give a fad account for it. If any have
received fuch commiffion from them, let them return it,
and quickly agree with the adverfary.

3. 'Thou fhalt not take the name of the Lord thy
God in vain.' But the men in prefent power have eminently taken God's name in vain, by applying his attributes
to finifter ends. Their pretenfions were for the honour of
God, for the intereft of Chrift—what more frequent in
their mouths ? Well! God took them at their words,
gave them many a victory in truft, to fee what they would
do with it after fo many promifes and pretences. But at
laft, what God gave them only in truft, for the advancement of his glory, they have purloined and abufed to the
advancement of themfelves, breaking all oaths, promifes,
covenants, engagements, declarations. When they go to
fight another battle, they cannot give that for a word any
more, 'No King but Jefus'—a word which won them
more than their fwords. No, they have fet up now a
King of their own.

4. 'Remember thou keep holy the Sabbath.' They
are guilty of the breach of this commandment who do their
own works. Thofe who have no foul-reft cannot keep a
Sabbath. Such are they that gape after court honour,
privileges, preferments, advantages.

5. 'Honour thy father and mother.' To obey the
world before God makes us guilty of this commandment.
God will fay to the men of this generation, 'Go to your
Governour, go to your Protector.' 'If I be a father, where
is my honour?'

6. 'Thou fhalt do no murder.' There is a heart
murder ; thofe that hate the fpirit in the faints are murderers. Thofe who have it in their intent and defire to
murder the faints, though for fome refpects of their own
they refrain from the outward act, they are murderers
before God. Some in the prefent power are guilty of this

murderous intent. Before, nothing but the laws of Chriſt
and the intereſt of Chriſt ; but now 'tis a particular and perſonal intereſt, the intereſt of a man, the cauſe of a man.
Thoſe who were ſlain for the cauſe of Chriſt their blood
cries aloud ' let Chriſt reign ;' but thoſe who ſay, ' let us
reign,' make themſelves guilty of that blood, and ſo are
murderers.

Then he converted his diſcourſe againſt ſpies and tale-
bearers, recounting out of the Book of Martyrs and other
ſtories God's remarkable judgments againſt them.

7. ' Thou ſhalt not commit adultery.' There is a
heart adultery, as Chriſt alſo expounds it. He that looks
upon pleaſures and honours and profits, and luſts after
them, this luſt of the heart is adultery. The preſent
powers have committed adultery with all intereſts, with the
cavalier party, with the army, with the clergy.

8. ' Thou ſhalt not ſteal.' They are thieves and
robbers which take away violently that which is not their
right, that which does not belong to them. We have
great thieves and rich thieves, army thieves and clergy
thieves. A poor pirate was brought before *Alexander the
Great* for robbing ; and being demanded the reaſon, the
pirate anſwered him, ' This is the ſole difference 'twixt you
and me ; you are the great thief, and I am but the little one.'
' Do violence to no man,' ſaid *John the Baptiſt* to the
ſoldiers ; but our ſoldiers do violence to all men. What
right have thoſe men in the throne to it ? The Cavalier
party will ſay *Charles Stewart* has a right ; but I ſay there's
no man breathing has more right to it than the meaneſt
child that walks the ſtreets. The kingdom is the Lord's
and his Chriſt's. They which detain what they have
unjuſtly taken are thieves. Why do they not make reſti-
tution of their ſtolen powers, their ſtolen thrones and
dignities, reſtore them to the ſaints whom they deſpiſed
and caſt out, under the name of Fifth-Monarchy-Men.

They that make unlawful hafte to be rich are thieves and robbers. (Then he directed his fpeech to my Lord Protector.) Certainly he is in a defperate condition. No wonder we hear fo much of plots—two or three already; though, for my part, 'tis the defire of my foul that he may not be taken off by any of them, but rather that he may repent, and God recover him again to himfelf. Becaufe he hath oppreffed and forfaken the poor, becaufe he hath violently taken away a houfe which he builded not, furely he fhall not feel quietnefs in his belly, he fhall not fave of that which he defired (Job xx. 19). Oh, thou black Whitehall! thou black Whitehall!—fah! fah! it ftinks of the brimftone of Sodom and the fmoke of the bottomlefs pit! The flying roll of God's curfes fhall overtake the family of that great thief there—he that robbed us of the benefit of our prayers, of our tears, of our blood; the blood of my poor hufband will the widow fay, the blood of my poor father will the orphan fay, the blood of my dear friend will many fay. Thefe fhed their blood for the caufe of Jefus Chrift and for the intereft of his kingdom; but that which they purchafed at fo dear a rate is taken from us by violence; we are robbed of it, and the caufe of Chrift is made the caufe of a man.

He would have proceeded to the two other commandments, but that time prevented him.

At the conclufion of his difcourfe he produced a letter from *Mr. Feake* at Windfor, giving a large account of what betided him there; how he had preached to fome foldiers of the guard, and that they were much affected with what he fpake; how he was remanded to his chamber by the governor, and a long dialogue betwixt them on that occafion. All which he diftinctly read to the people, being a very numerous affembly. And thus clofed all,—In fum, my dear friends, you may fhortly expect a new book of Martyrs. The faints are worfe dealt with by the powers of this age than they were by the heathens of old. *Paul* was fuffered to preach at Rome, but they now are forbid to preach the Gofpel.

Afterwards a hymn was fet, compofed for the occafion, which the people fung very affectionately. It began thus— ' Come, glorious King of Sion, come to defend thy caufe againft all earthly powers, and to work deliverance for thy captives,' and much to that purpofe."

Thurloe, iii. 483.

This information was preferved and was afterwards produced, but it was not inftantly acted upon. *Rogers* remained at large until July. The following extracts from the Order Book of the Council of State, and from the London newfpapers, will explain what happened next.

" Council of State, *July* 25, 1654.

His Highnefs prefent.

Mr. Laurence, L.ᵈ Prefident. Maj. Gen. Lambert, L.ᵈ Vifc. Lifle, Col. Fiennes, Mr. Rous, Gen. Difbrowe, Col. Mackworth, Col. Montague, Sir Gilbert Pickering, Col. Sydenham, Col. Jones, Major-Gen. Shippon, Mr. Major, Mr. Strickland, Sir Charles Wolfeley.

Appr. in pfon.

Ordered—That *Hannah Taprell*, formerly committed to Bridewell, be fet at liberty, and that a warrant to the Mafter of Bridewell be in that behalf iffued.

Appr. in pfon.

That *Mr. John Rogers* be fent for in fafe cuftody, to anfwer fuch matters as fhall be objected againft him, and that a warrant to the Serjeant-at-Arms be in that behalf iffued.

Entry or Fair Order Book of the Council of State, No. 103, in the Public Record Office.

That *Col. Jones, Col. Sydenham, Col. Mackworth, Mr. Rous, Sir Charles Wolfeley*, or any two of them, be a committee to examine *Mr. Rogers* and the matters charged on him, he being ordered this day to be fent for in cuftody."

" *July* 27, 1654.

Mr. John Rogers, of Thomas Apoftle's, London, was this day apprehended by a meffenger, touching fome things by him preached and written againft the prefent power. He was before a committee of the Council, and remains in the cuftody of a meffenger, but did much defire to have been in prifon."

Several Proceedings in State Affairs, No. 253.

" *Auguft* 10, 1654.

Mr. John Rogers, prifoner at Lambeth, preacheth daily to people that come to vifit him, whither many do refort. But *Mr. John Simfon,* who now owns and prays for the prefent powers, hath been there with him."

Several Proceedings in State Affairs, No. 255.

The following letter (from *Thurloe,* iii. 485), has neither date nor fignature. It was probably written at this time by *Serjeant Dendy,* * who was Serjeant-at-Arms to the Council of State, and was refponfible for the cuftody of his kinfman *Rogers* in Lambeth Palace.†

---

* Serjeant Dendy, earlier in life, executed warrants for the Star Chamber. In 1637, with a warrant from Archbifhop Laud, he broke open Mr. Burton's houfe at midnight and arrefted him, for which he was cenfured by Parliament in 1640. In January, 1649, he was appointed Serjeant-at-Arms to the High Court of Juftice, which condemned Charles I. In this capacity he proclaimed the Court in Weftminfter Hall, and took charge of the King as a prifoner at the bar. On January 29, after fentence had been paffed, it was ordered " that the officer of the Ordnance at the Tower of London, in whofe hands the bright execution axe for the executing malefactors is, do forthwith deliver the fame unto Edward Dendy, Efq., Serjeant-at-Arms attending the Court, or his deputies."

† Moft of the Bifhops' palaces and houfes in and near London were converted into prifons in 1642-3.—*Walker's Sufferings of the Clergy,* part i. 57.

"A LETTER TO THE PROTECTOR CONCERNING
MR. ROGERS.

MAY IT PLEASE YOUR HIGHNESS,—

Having for thefe five or fix years had more opportunities
to read *Mr. Rogers* than many others, I humbly conceive
it not altogether improper (efpecially at this time) to give
your Highnefs as true a character of him as his actings and
my flender obfervations thereupon hath led me to.   .   .
Now, that your Highnefs may know *Mr. Rogers* of Thomas
Apoftle's from that man which he defcribes and would have
others to think him to be, by his book called a ' Tabernacle,' I fhall, in as few words as I can, difcover more of
the man than the Chriftian in him ; that fo your Highnefs
may in fome meafure difcern him from fome others, and
that before the change of Government, againft which *Mr.
Rogers*, with a pretended zeal of God, hath fo furioufly
appeared.

About fix years fince *Mr. Rogers* married *Sir Robert
Paine's* daughter, late of Huntingdonfhire, who was the
relict of *Mr. Smyth*, of St. Neot's, where for fome time he
taught fchool, and from whence by Providence he was
called to a living at Purleigh in Effex, worth, as I have
been informed, above £200 per annum, where the people,
as in many other places, being but children in underftanding, and fuch as, I have heard him fay, did not know
how to value men for their abilities, the faid *Mr. Rogers*—
I fear overprizing his gifts, did thereupon turn non-
refident ; and, hiring another to fupply his place at
Purleigh, he came to London ; and endeavouring to get a
lecture, which in fhort time he obtained at Thos. Apoftle's.
Thus neglecting his charge at Purleigh, about 33 miles off
London, it pleafed God to ftir up the patron and parifh
againft him, fo that he was ejected thence.

Mr. Rogers, hereat being exceedingly troubled, petitioned the Lords Commiffioners for a reftoration, from whom not obtaining his defires, and meeting therein with oppofition from *Serjeant Maynard*, he thereupon, as incenfed againft lawyers, writ a pamphlet; and how he vented his fpirit in that quarrel I prefume your Highnefs is not only a ftranger to.

After the lofs of Purleigh, *Mr. Rogers* folicits hard for the rectory of Martin's, and to that end endeavours the removing of one *Mr. Sangor*, a godly man; and being afked why he would do fo, he replied that *Mr. Sangor* had a living of £100 a year in the country—forgetting that it was lately his own cafe in Purleigh, when yet he had a lecture in London and lived there. But, not feeking a way of God, his endeavours here alfo proved abortive.

Whereupon *Mr. Rogers* puts forth a book called ' A Tabernacle for the Sun,' and according to the dedication of it prefents one to your Highnefs, not doubting but that this book would have attracted your Highnefs' efpecial favour to him; but the Lord, who weighs the fpirits and ponders all men's goings, did, for ought I know, caufe your Highnefs to fee more of *Mr. Rogers* than he could of himfelf. Whether a difappointment herein hath not been a ground of *Mr. Rogers* his difcontent (that I fay not malice) I will not pofitively affirm, yet fear (as the Apoftle fpeaks of a young novice) that he hath been lifted up of pride and fallen into the condemnation of the devil. For, faith the fame Apoftle, ' The fervant of the Lord muft not ftrive, but be gentle unto all men, apt to teach, patient, in meeknefs inftructing thofe that oppofe themfelves,' &c. My Lord, I could fay much more, but am unwilling to trouble your Highnefs; only I befeech your Highnefs to permit me to fpeak my heart in one thing, which is this—viz. that if your Highnefs fhould ftudy to pleafe *Mr. Rogers*, you cannot do it in a more direct line than by imprifoning of him. Not that I believe he hath any principle wherewithal truly to glory before God, nor doth he fimply delight in being reftrained; but, my Lord, by this means he gets great ftore of money, having many vifitants, and fome of quality. Wherefore, my Lord, I humbly fubmit it to your Highnefs' confideration, whether, after a fober and fharp reproof, it would not be well to give him his liberty ; for, my Lord, in reality and truth his defign is not for the Fifth Monarchy, but how to get money. And to that end he hath for above thefe two years given it out, that it hath been ftrong upon his heart that he fhall die a martyr, though, I fear, none of thofe whom Chrift hath as yet owned. And therefore, what other comfort he hath by imprifonment than getting money, I underftand not : for certain it is he acts not in the fpirit of Jefus ; and being not conformable to Chrift in his death and fufferings, furely the Spirit of Glory, nor of God, doth not reft upon him. Wherefore, my Lord, I befeech you confider whether it would not be beft yet a little longer, by gentlenefs and meeknefs, to heap up coals of fire upon his head ; and if he turn not at fuch a reproof, which God ufually takes up to reduce finners, then certainly the Lord hath not called your Highnefs to bear the fword in vain : and yet, if he perfift in the forwardnefs of his heart, I hope when the Parliament fits they will call him to an account; which I confefs I would rather they fhould do than your Highnefs, of whofe uprightnefs I hope the Lord will bear further witnefs to, notwithftanding all gainfayers.

I defired to know of *Mr. Secretary* whether all comers might be admitted to *Mr. Rogers*, who told me that he had no directions at all therein. The laft Lord's Day I am informed that there was at the leaft a hundred perfons that went to fee him ; neither can I reftrain them until your Highnefs' pleafure be known herein."

Thurloe, iii. 485.

While he was in prifon *Rogers* wrote two books,—

1. " Prifon-born Morning Beams ;" or, a Hiftory of his Sufferings at Lambeth. The Introduction only was faved, and this
was printed as part of his fecond book,—
2. " Jegar Sahadutha ; or, a Heart Appeal:" a Hiftory of his
fufferings at Windfor and elfewhere.

He was very much annoyed at the difficulty he found in
fecuring a printer in the face of the Ordinance of Treafon, and at
the cowardly mutilations to which his books were fubjected. Of
courfe they were printed fecretly, and, fo far as the printer was
concerned, anonymoufly. It muft be remembered always that
when thefe books were circulated he was ftill in prifon, wholly
and entirely at the mercy of the authorities, the gaolers, and the
foldiers whom he fo fiercely reviles.

Accompanying the book is a fhort Preface, of which the following is a part :—

" FROM A FRIEND TO A FRIEND.

The books mentioned by the author are very ftrangely
mifcarried ; only the Introductory part to the firft treatife,
or ' Prifon-born Morning Beams,' are preferved and gotten
together, as the occafion of his falling upon fo large a
fyftem, fo fome part of his fufferings at Lambeth until
Windfor, which therefore we have added unto his ' Heart
Appeal,' (having been hardly kept and collected) that
the view of prefent perfecution may be the more clear,
and his Hiftory the more complete, though to my knowledge many things are omitted, paffages left out, fleeced,
and fheered round, befides much more which in time may
be added, if need be, as fome of us hear, of feveral reafon-
ings between him and O. P., him and foldiers, him and
minifters, him and many adverfaries, befides what fufferings
have been added fince thefe papers came from him to this
chain.

It may be thefe fufferings may work upon fome that
hear them ; they have on fome that faw them, yea, even
amongft the foldiers, for we hear that one of them formerly

bufy is now wounded and touched in confcience for it, and others have left them for their cruelty to thefe, whiles the Cavaliers can have liberty to drink, fwear, or anything, it feems, and live as they lift. And thus, fay the foldiers, may our friends too, fo they be for their Lord Protector and his G——, whom the Lord protect us from, and from their wickednefs in high places."

    The next chapter, compiled from various parts of the Introduction to " Prifon-born Morning Beams," will give an account of his arreft and his imprifonment at Lambeth.

CHAPTER V.

MORNING BEAMS; OR, THE VISION OF THE PRISON PATHMOS.

LIB. I.

CHAPTER I.—HAGAH.

The Introduction, with the cauſe accidental of the following Diſcourſe upon the preſent truth and teſtimony.

IT is none of the leaſt part of our priſon Threnodies in the preſent tragedy, which the bloody Beaſt by a new guiſe hath acted again upon the ſtage of Great Brittanny, the trampling under foot the preſent truth and teſtimony of Jeſus, ſo as that ſcarce one interpreter of a thouſand durſt entertain or own it ſimply, which at beſt hath but a paſſport from many, and ſo is whipped away from one to another, from poſt to pillar, according to the Court law for a vagrant, with warrants like to Pope Euge-nius, 'hoc eſſe verum, ſi ipſe velit, ſed non aliter.' This or that is true if he, His Holineſs (or His Highneſs) will have it ſo, but not otherwiſe. Who then can find the faith or courage to expoſe his life, or at leaſt his liberty and eſtate to ſo prodigal a hazard, as he muſt do who will fetch it from under the Beaſt's foot, and feel the acrimony or cruelty of his ſharp clunch, claw, or horn piercing him to the very heart.

The General Introduction by way of Lamentation.

T

Well may our prifons found and refound with exaggerated night groans, for the Court and country increafe in lying and tranfgreffing, and falling backwards, perpetrating iniquity at fo high a rate as will fuddenly fill up their meafure. This I fee evidently from my iron bars. And yet none intercede for the truth ; not one will run after it, follow it, meet it, or to the face of all own it. O what a lamentation is this! if one doth like Wifdom's child but a little juftify it . . . he that doth fo expofes himfelf to be fpoiled, plundered, imprifoned, and made a prey of to the ravenous beaft that eats bones and all. (Zeph. iii. 3).

Alfo when I advert the height of the controverfy already between the Lamb and the Beaft (precious blood of faints having fealed thereto) and the vials fo lately poured out upon the King, lords, prelates, and corrupt powers of this State ; alfo our late zeal againft Common Prayer, Croffes, Painted Windows, Rails, Surplices, Corrupt Minifters, Magiftrates, and the like; O! my foul even bleeds within me to behold the prefent apoftacy of fpirit, principles, and perfons, not only among mercenary profeffors, but the little remnant whofe coldnefs, cowardlinefs, and careleffnefs is almoft incredible, at this time of day too. And were it not to fulfil the word of God (Rev. xi.) that this prefent death is upon us for thefe three years and an half, I fhould be fo aftonifhed at it as not to know what to make of it.

But when I am venting my burthen with thefe like words or paffions, ' Lord, where is the fpirit of old, yea, the fpirit, and faith, and courage that we ourfelves had fome ten, twelve, or fourteen years ago, among the good old Puritans? Yea, the fpirit of Englifhmen and rational men among us. O! what a change it is ! What fheepifhnefs, what fleepinefs, what deadnefs, what darknefs, what timoroufnefs, and what tamenefs is now feized upon us!' The light ariſing in darkneſs doth put an end to ſuch reaſonings and ſyllogiſms, giving reſt to my ſpirit till the time of the end, which is at hand.

Now, if ever there were a time to hear the grave-groans of the living and the dead, of thoſe who are in priſon-graves, and of thoſe whoſe ſkulls and bones we left behind us in the field, and of thoſe under the altar, who cry, 'How long, O Lord, holy and true?' (Rev. vi. 10). Yea, the ſhrill heaven, heart, and earth tearing call of ſaints, paſt, preſent, and to come, from the days of Abel to this day, to maintain their cauſe, to revenge their blood and the Lamb's, and to be UP AND DOING for the Lord Jeſus, the King of Saints, it is NOW within a year or two, as we ſhall ſhow you.

Woe to them that are at eaſe (Amos vi. 1), yea, to the very women that are careleſs (Iſaiah xxxii. 9, 10, 11, 12), for they ſhall lament; and if ye will be all ſilent, the very graves ſhall open, the dead ſhall live, the dry bones ſhall live, the ſtones of the ſtreet ſhall ſpeak, and the beam of the timber utter it, the witneſſes will ariſe, and the earthquake come to take vengeance againſt this apoſtate generation of four profeſſors.

But, ſay ſome, ſeeing the priſons are ſo deeply ſenſible, and bear ſo heavy a burden for us, how falls it that before now your exonerating groans and ſighs got not a free paſſage abroad in the nation?

1. To which I muſt anſwer, that for above a year's impriſonment now, partly more at large and partly cloſe, I have been under the preſſure of the ſpirit, as if my heart would break within me at times, to ſee ſo ſervile and degenerate a ſpirit, as yet, among the ſaints. Yet, with patience, purpoſing to wait and poſſeſs my ſoul, as unwilling to write what few if any were able to bear, though moſt honourable truth, I kept in as long as I could, not knowing but there might have been before this a kindly recurrence among

1ſt reaſon why the priſons are ſo ſilent.

some of those retrograde motions which so tremendous and fearful a wrath as I easily foresee follows the heels of. Besides, so great is the servile spirit and fear which possesses the hearts of men against the glorious cause and controversy of Christ, for which we are imprisoned, plundered, exiled, or persecuted, that what we write to ease our hearts and consciences, with the greatest sobriety and simplicity, we cannot carry through the press or get printed upon any terms almost in the language, life, and favour of the present anointing from the Holy One which is upon us and teaches us all things. That new-found engine of the Beast (the Ordinance of Treason for words and imaginations) hath put them into so panic and foolish a fear that above an hundred sheets preparing for the press, to enlighten the deluded, abused people of this nation as to us and our cause, or rather Christ's (while they give out we suffer not for conscience) have been either betrayed by Iscariot kisses, plundered from me, or stifled before they were born, and all this left the people should have light into the sufferings of our consciences, or conscience of our sufferings, viz. the truth of the Fifth Kingdom, or to receive a right information of the apostacies, hypocrisies, perjury, cheating, persecution, and unheard-of baseness of such as are gotten into power.

2nd Reason.
The prison opprobries, abuses, and injuries, especially at Lambeth.

2. The marvellous trials which I have encountered with in the flesh since imprisonment have much impeded my appearing in public until now. But the truth, cause, and persecuted saints do expect some account at my hands, it seems, of the particular harsh usage I and my family met with under this power in Lambeth House (and since), where I was for above five and thirty weeks, and then sent to Windsor Castle the 31st day of first month, 1655, with two messengers, who delivered me up prisoner here a little before noon.

I was fetched out of my bed the 27th day of fourth

month in 1654, early in the morning; and at night, after
all day waiting, I was fent to Lambeth Prifon, being very
ill and diftempered with a fever; yet for all that, at eleven
in the night, did a meffenger rap at the gates, called another
of the meffengers, who was going into his bed, made him
put on his clothes again to affift him, and fo they came
both, with *Harding* the under-gaoler, to carry me at that
time of night I knew not whither (nor would they tell me).
But being very ill on the bed, and my wife alfo unready, I
told them I was not able, prayed them to let me alone for
that one night—told them the righteous man was merciful
to a beaft, and were a beaft of theirs, horfe or cow, fo ill
or little able to ftir, they would be more merciful—with
many more arguments I and my wife alfo defired them to
forbear that night; but they faid they had orders from
Serjeant Dendy to remove me prefently, and I muft not
ftay, one of them fpeaking very high and threatening. The
iffue was, they made me rife, and my wife to make herfelf
ready; and I, fcarce able to go, my head being light with
the fiercenefs of the fever, was forced that time of night to
one *Leadbeater's** houfe, a meffenger, into a little low dark
room, where was very little air, which I much needed, and
for which I rather wifhed to be in the other prifon. The
next day at night new orders came to carry me to Lambeth
again, where I continued, till *Serjeant Dendy* procured my
removal. Of which place I fhall choofe principally for the
prefent to give a fhort hint or abftract account, leaving the
whole hiftory for a fitter feafon, that the obftreperous falfe
reports may be obviated, our fufferings (a little) known and
fympathized with, His poor fervants prayed for, their faith
and patience owned, their God be glorified, and his enemies

---

* Jofhua Leadbeater was appointed one of fourteen men to attend the
Council as Deputies to the Serjeant-at-Arms, 26th Dec. 1651.—*Order
in Council of that date.*

Worfe than heathen tyranny to us.

1. Uncon-demned and without law.

This is contrary to all or moft of their declarations, where they call this tyranny in the King and Bifhops, and incongruous with the laws of God, of nature, and of nations.

found liars and afhamed of their worfe than heathen tyranny to us. Which appears in thefe particulars,

1. By the law of the heathens (the Romans) none were to fuffer before the law had judged and condemned them. This is the rule of reafon, contrary whereunto our perfe-cutors now practife, having put us into prifon thus year after year, with worfe ufage and more clofe than the worft Malefactors, Cavaliers, Plotters, Ranters, Blafphemers, or offenders they put amongft us. For all the while I was, by order from *Serjeant Dendy*, kept out from the air of the common hall, the wicked crew of Cavaliers, Plotters, Ran-ters, Roarers, drinking, curfing, fwearing, finging, fiddling, gaming, and blafpheming day and night, had the benefit of it. Yea, for above thirty weeks they would not fuffer me to ftir out of the gate for air; but the worft of all other prifoners had their liberty with their keepers every day. And when order was to let but three at a time to come to fee me—yea, not to fuffer man, woman, or child to come at me, nor one of my family to ftir out for neceffaries for me, the worft of men befides had all that would come to fee them, yea the moft loofe fort of people that could be, to fit up healthing, hooping, ranting, and revelling with them at the higheft rate in the moft hideous manner about mine ears. Thefe had abundance of liberty to fin, when we could not have liberty to pray together, or to have any holy affembly but at the prifon grates, when I put my head out at the iron bars to my dear brethren and fifters in Chrift who ftood in the ftreet. And all this without any law condemning, any crime charged formally upon us, any witnefs againft us, any trial of us, or licence given us to anfwer in any open Court. Only the fixth of the laft month the laft year I was carried to Whitehall into a chamber, (where what was objected was denied to be any charge againft us), and fo remanded to prifon again; but by no other law than luft and will—the beafts' law, ' fic

volo, fic jubeo, fit pro ratione voluntas.' ' Take him, gaoler,' being all the trial, law, and fentence.

2. Under the dragon power of Rome, the very gaolers, who are ufually the worft of men, were more civil, courteous, and urbane than ours are to us; for *Paul's* gaoler let who would come to vifit him (Acts xxiv. 23). Yea, their gaoler pitied them, and wafhed their wounds and ftripes, and made much of them (Acts xvi. 33); but our gaolers do add ftripes, aggravate our crimes (pretended), augment our afflictions, accumulate into mountains lies, flanders, vilifying fpeeches and reproaches upon us, invent and inform what they can, with any colour, againft us, daily going to Whitehall for that purpofe, and every way more to us than to the worft malefactor they had. At Lambeth we found it fo, from the upper to the under, from the mafter to the man gaoler; whiles others found very fair quarters and civil courtfhip who fed them with round fums, which we could not buy at fo dear a rate, and therefore, befides other reafons, were forced to coarfer fare. For after a few weeks, word was brought to my wife that I muft pay in fees fomewhat more than fix pounds a week (which I was not able to do, having no eftate in the world, and what I had being all taken away from me), and this for the rooms to *Serjeant Dendy*. About a week's fpace after this one of *Serjeant Dendy's* men, old *Meazy*, came up at candle-light into my prifon chamber in the name of *Serjeant Dendy*, faying he came from him to demand the money which was due to him, for his fees and the chambers for fo many weeks; faying I was to pay but ten fhillings a day fees for myfelf, for although it was twenty fhillings a day, yet the Parliament put down ten fhillings a day of it; and for that *Serjeant Dendy* would ufe me courteoufly, he would have but fourteen fhillings a week rent for the room where we kept a fire for my family while they were with me, and for the little inward lodging room, where was no chimney,

2. Our gaolers worfe to us than the heathens. A hiftory of fome few paffages for an inftance.

where I lay, I fhould know that when I came out. I
told him I was not able to pay fo much, nor did I judge it
reafonable, being in prifon upon will, and nothing brought
to my charge ; and therefore thofe that imprifoned me muft
pay him. Yet this I would do willingly : if *Serjeant Dendy*
will choofe one honeft man I will choofe another, and what
they think meet for me to pay, as God fhall enable me, I
will, faying withal I would know the *loweft* which I muft
pay. He faid £4 4*s.* a week was the loweft, at which I
told him I was not able to do it, nor did my brother *Feake*
at Windfor pay fo much, but as I heard, but fo much in a
quarter as is demanded of me in a week ; and that it was
worfe than tyranny to take away all I had to live on, turn
my wife and children, poor fucking babes, out of doors,
when the Lord allows a fnail a fhell, yet my poor wife and
babes had not a fhell to live in but my prifon ; yea, and to
hinder thofe that would to minifter to our wants, and to
demand £4 4*s.* a week too, was wonderful unjuft. But
the old man, being techy hereat, flew from me with thefe
menaces, ' You muft and fhall pay it, before you go out
from hence.'

But becaufe the carriage of this bufinefs was fo cruel,
mercilefs, and unchriftian, *Serjeant Dendy* was afhamed to
own it to good men, ftoutly and often affirming that neither
he nor any for him did ever demand it of me or threaten
me about it. But with how little modefty and grace, and
that ye may fee what wide mouths ravenous fifhes have, it
follows under the hands of fome prefent in the prifon
chamber when the old man came for the money, two of
them being church-members :—

' We whofe names are hereunder written do certify to
whomfoever it may concern, that old *Michael Meazy* came
as he faid from *Serjeant Dendy* (whofe fervant he is) into
the chamber where *Mr. Rogers* is prifoner now at Lam-

beth, and in our hearing demanded of *Mr. Rogers* the fum of ten fhillings a day for fees for himfelf a prifoner to *Serjeant Dendy*, and of fourteen fhillings a week for his chambers (in all £4 4*s.* a week) : and for that *Mr. Rogers* made fcruple to pay fo much at prefent, the faid *Meazy* told him he muft and fhould pay it before he went out from thence. This we witnefs by our hands, who heard him demand that fum of him, and can depofe it.

DOROTHY HILL,
ALICE LEWIS,
ANN EVINGTON.'

Notwithftanding, with fo ftrange a face they denied this, and faid I was no minifter of Jefus Chrift if I affirmed it, and they would publifh in newfbooks againft me, and the like, I can fhew it under *Serjeant Dendy's* own hand, by feveral orders and letters, that the not paying thofe fees and fums of money was one thing that made him fo harfh to me above others. For, foon after, the old man went to Whitehall and told his tale againft me in his own mood and figure, and then followed the enfuing letter from *Serjeant Dendy* to me :—

' SIR,

I took not my houfe at Lambeth to accommodate families, but only fuch prifoners as by order of the Council ftand committed to me ; and therefore, whereas I hear you fay *Mr. Feake* at Windfor hath his wife and children with him, and yet pays nothing, which is not altogether impro- bable, becaufe Windfor Caftle is the State's proper houfe, but fo is not mine nor the goods. Wherefore, inafmuch as I am informed that it is commonly reported that you are at £6 a week charge (though I know not of a penny that hath as yet been received from you) ; and this declared on purpofe to abufe the well-minded, by provoking their charity toward you, of which I wifh you were as capable as fome other. Further, your wife at your firft coming to my houfe, vapouring that fhe would give £5 aforehand, fo you might be accommodated at my houfe (which was more public than others of my deputies, and fo to ferve your defign was rather made choice of), upon thefe confidera-tions, having no allowance at all from the State to defray fo great a charge as my houfe at Lambeth amounts to, I defire you will remove your children and fervants to fome other place more proper for them, to which end I have ordered that you have a week's time from this day to difpofe of them, and for your own particular, and your wife, if fhe be with you, to be treated with all civility, and have as good accommodation as my houfe can afford. So, wifhing that you may be partaker of Chrift's fufferings rather than thofe of evildoers, I reft,

Your loving friend,

E. DENDY.

Sept. 14, 1654.'

I confefs I was much grieved at this letter, for that I knew not whither to fend my poor children from me, two of them being about a year old and very weak, and my poor family being thruft out of all. Befides, the lines were fraught with falfe reports, I perceived, of my wife and me, and pitiful, uncharitable cenfures and fuppofitions, as that I fought to come thither to abufe the well-minded, whereas I knew not of my returning to Lambeth till *Harding* came with a new order ; nor did I otherwife defire it but for air, in the time of my burning fever. I confefs I did defire more air ; and fo my wife faid fhe had better give five pounds than be fo choked up in a little hole for want of air (as *Lead-beater's* houfe was). But then came in confolation from Matt. v.—' Bleffed are ye when they fhall fpeak all manner of evil of you.' So that I thought it beſt to ſpread it before the Lord, and wait with patience ; and ſo I did, without any noiſe, as the ſheep that is bit by the fierce teeth of a dog weeps inwardly moſt, and whines not like a hog. But ere long he ſends a moſt ſevere order to the under-gaoler to take away the beds from under us, yea, to execute his order that night that one of my children lay giving up the ghoſt ; but becauſe the child was gaſping he could not find the heart to execute it ; and the child dying that night, he then ſaid he would not have done it for a hundred pounds, though his maſter commanded him ſo ſtrictly to obſerve his orders. But for all this, and the death of one child and the weak-neſs or drawing on of another,* their immanity without pity was proſecuted upon me ; and to ſhow it ſufficiently the under-gaoler brings me theſe two enſuing warrants :—

' WILLIAM HARDING : †

I am informed one of *Mr. Rogers* his children was carried away laſt night very ſick, and which, for ought I

---

* " 1653. Peter⎫ Sons of John and Elizabeth Rogers, borne and baptized
          Paul ⎭ 28 September.
   1654. Paul yᵉ ſon of John and Elizabeth Rogers, decᵈ yᵉ 12ᵗʰ, burᵈ.
        yᵉ 13ᵗʰ October.
   1654. Peter yᵉ ſon of John and Elizabeth Rogers, decᵈ yᵉ 1ˢᵗ, burᵈ.
        yᵉ 2 of November."
    From the Pariſh Regiſter of St. Thomas Apoſtle's, London.

† Anthony Wood gives the following account of this Harding :—" In the times of Uſurpation, when the Biſhops were put down and their lands ſold, the ſaid palace [Lambeth] was inhabited by ſeveral lay perſons, of whom Tho. Scot, one of the Regicides, and one Harding, were two. Which laſt having the chapel allotted to him as part of his ſhare, he divided it into two rooms. . . . At length, hearing that the corpſe of Archbiſhop Parker had been there interred, he took up the floor and pavement under it, and having ſo done dug up the corpſe, which was put into cere cloth of many doubles in a coffin of lead. The coffin he ſold to a plumber ; and after he had cauſed the cere cloth to be cut open to the

know, may be the fmall-pox, which you cannot but hear the city and fuburbs are much infefted with, and none more liable to take the difeafe than children. Wherefore, in regard of the danger through multitudes of perfons coming to *Mr. Rogers*, I would have you once more let him know that I expect that he remove his children and fervants to fome other place. For I am refolved not to endanger the health of my prifoners any longer. Therefore, if *Mr. Rogers* will not remove his children after fo fair and civil a warning, let the bedding be carried into another room. Herein fail not.

Yours,

E. DENDY.'

But the truth is, the gaoler's children were ill of the fwine-pox, whereby we and other prifoners were in danger, but, bleffed be the Lord, not one of ours; and the child we fent away one night, for fear he fhould catch it in the houfe, the next day we had him home again to the prifon; for we had not, nor have we any other earthly home but a prifon now. So that my family was forced to be with me, which was according to the law of God and nature (the child being in good health); nor was there the leaft ground to fufpect fuch a difeafe in my family.

And indeed, the warning, which he calls civil, to fend my children from me (and the Lord knows I knew not whither) I could not fee civil or Chriftian, and therefore refted rather contented to have the bedding pulled from

---

flefh (which he found frefh as if newly dead), he conveyed the corpfe into an outhoufe where he kept poultry, and there privately tumbled it into an hole. About the time of the Reftoration of Charles II. that bafe fellow, the brute that removed it, was forced to difcover where he had laid it; whereupon it was brought into the chapel, and buried juft above the Litany defk, near the fteps afcending to the altar."—*A. Wood*, Athen. Oxon. i. 689.

under me, and to lie in pads of ſtraw with my poor children, than to be ſo mercileſs and unfatherly to them as he
commanded. Beſides, there were very few priſoners then
in the houſe, and abundance of rooms ſtood empty for
want of gueſts, they not having a third part of the priſoners
(I hear) are there now. Nor had we any more chamber
room than one priſoner who was in before us, a plotter.

With this he delivered me another at the ſame time,
which follows :—

‘ WILLIAM HARDING,

It’s not unknown to you the great charge I am at for
my houſe, &c. and particularly for my goods, for which I
pay ſeven pounds a month, which by the year is £91. All
which I perceive *Mr. Rogers* and his wife are not ſenſible
of, otherwiſe they would not take upon them to appoint
what lodgings my priſoners ſhould have, as that they ſhould
not lie two in a bed but ſingle, ſo as the priſoners’ wives
might come and live with them ; which freedom I ſhall not
deny to any priſoner, although I might do it. So I hereby
again order you to remove *Mr. Rogers* his children and
ſervants forthwith. And if the printer’s wife do come, let
them lie in the chamber within *Mr. Rogers*, or in the
outward room, which he will. For I ſee no reaſon that I
ſhould find bedding for *Mr. Rogers* his children and ſervants, when he refuſeth to pay me for it. I do expect that
my orders ſhould be better obſerved by you than hitherto
they have been, otherwiſe I ſhall ſee that directions be
followed more to my quiet. If you find that *Mr. Rogers*
or his wife will not remove their children and ſervants, let

Mr. Brown.*

Mr. Chap-
man’s.
The lodging
room where I
lodged.

---

* Two perſons of this name, “ papiſts,” were amongſt the Royaliſt
“ plotters ” impriſoned in June, 1654, for Gerard and Vowel’s plot.

me know it, and I ſhall diſpoſe of *Mr. Rogers* to ſome
other place ; being reſolved to free my houſe of ſuch domi-
neering ſpirits.

Yours,

E. DENDY.

Oct. 20, 1654.'

Theſe two together founded very harſh to my very
heart, at that ſeaſon too, whiles another ſweet child was ſo
near the grave too, very weak, and died within three or
four days after. I confeſs the trials were very great ; but,
for that I perceived this was a matter of money, and nothing elſe would ſtay the ſurges and ſources of this raging
ſea, I ſent my wife after candlelight to Whitehall, with five
pounds, which I was glad I could get together for him (not
being able to ſend him more then), who carried it ; but at
that time they thought it not fit to receive it, but to accoſt
her with coarſe courtſhip and dialect, and ſo to ſend her
home to priſon again, telling her that we domineered in his
houſe, and took upon us to appoint lodgings for his priſoners, &c. How ſuch ſtories could be coined or invented
I wondered, when for three, four, or ſix weeks together I
ſtirred not out of my room or ſpake with one priſoner or
gaoler, perceiving how they were ſet together againſt me—
the priſoners for reproving their ſins at ſo high a rate day
and night when I had liberty to preach and pray. Seeing
I was in priſon with ſo wicked a blaſpheming, curſing,
ranting crew—' hominibus perfrictæ frontis '—with men of
ſo much impudence and immodeſty, with raving beaſts, with
very brutes, I judged it beſt not only to keep out of their
company, but out of their ſight, as much as might be ;
inſomuch that they could not tell, I am perſuaded, but on
the Lord's day, or when I preached or prayed in family, or
the like, whether I was in the priſon or no, but by hearſay.
Yet it ſeems, the night before this laſt warrant he ſent me,

Mr. Chapman and *Mr. Spittlehoufe** were brought in prifoners, who fupped with me in my prifon-chambers. That night at table, in difcourfe they faid they lay both in one bed. I faid I thought, if they would, they might have each of them a chamber, one within the other ; for that all the other prifoners had fo that I faw. But the gaoler's boy liftening, as fome one or other frequently did for ftories at my chamber door, carried down, as unhappy boys ufe to do, what he could make of it to his father, who carried it or fent it next morning betimes to Whitehall, which occafioned the aforefaid's words, as I conceive.

After, I put pen to paper and wrote thefe enfuing lines :—

' COUSIN DENDY,

I have received feveral meffages from you which have been very harfh and unexpected, and indeed, I think, un-deferved. I had wrote unto you long before, had not my wife defired to come to you, as fhe did late laft night, and had done it long before had not my children been fo ill. One of them is dead, and another very weak ; and having but two left alive, I did hope for more mercy. I befeech

---

* Live-well Chapman was the printer of moft of the books publifhed by the Fifth-Monarchy-Men. Col. Barkftead, Lieutenant of the Tower, fpeaks of him as " the owner or at leaft a fharer in the private prefs, which hath and doth fo much mifchief."—*Thurloe,* iv. 379.

Spittlehoufe publifhed, about this time, "Certain Queries propounded to the moft ferious confideration of thofe perfons now in power, or any others whom they may or do concern. By John Spittlehoufe (late of the Army), whom the Lord hath ftirred up (in the abfence of Mr. Feake and Mr. Rogers, now prifoners of the Lord Jefus), to mind our prefent Rulers and Army of their Perfecutions and Apoftacies, and what is likely to follow them for fo doing if they repent not. London : printed for Live-well Chapman, in Pope's-head Alley. 1654."

you, coufin, be not too ready to receive falfe and unworthy reports, &c. &c.   .   .   .   .

With our real and true refpeéts to my coufin, your wife, and all our friends with you, I am

Your unfeignedly loving, though

Afflicted and oppreffed kinfman,

JOHN ROGERS.

Lamb (i' th') Prifon,
Viz. Chrift in this Mount with me.   Oct. 21.

Poftfcript.—Here *Harding* denies that ever I or any of us domineered or faid anything of the prifoners about other rooms or lodgings. *Mr. Meazy* alfo denies that ever he told you I faid *Mr. Feake* pays nothing.'

I confefs I wrote brokenly, my mind being fo diftracted, but not fo as might minifter any juft occafion to ufe me and my poor family as they did afterwards, infulting over us, and adding affliction to our bonds daily.   A while after this old *Meazy* came again for money, who had £5 of us, being all that we could then get him, which bought us quiet for a few days ; but then finding us unable to lay down the full price for it, we loft the manfion.   And be-fides we bought our provifions, and had our drink at the beft hand from abroad, which made our gaolers, upper and under, more enemies to us than before ; for the gain which *Harding* had, and which it is faid he pays out of every barrel of beer to his mafter, is great from prifoners.   So that now nothing but evaporating wrath, curfing and fwearing to be revenged, fetting all the wicked prifoners upon us, who put their wits upon the tent-hooks, to that purpofe inventing and coining new ways and words, faying they hoped to fee me dance in a rope and fwing in a halter, calling us Hypocrites, Liers, Deceivers, yea, Rogues and

Queans and Devils, and what not, affronting me to my face if I went but down ftairs, which made me feldom ftir down for air, not above once or twice in a quarter of a year. When *Paul* was in danger of his life, his Gaoler, the Captain, came and refcued him from the Jews, and after loofed his bonds; but thefe are fo far from pity, ingenuity, or Chriftianity, that their frequent dialect is bitter, bloody, malicious, and menacing, as if they longed to have our blood, fwearing to run me through if I offered to ftir, putting Cavaliers, Ranters, Blafphemers upon it to plot againft me for my life, to gather up articles againft me from what they overheard or invented, from my praying or preaching, or finging of hymns, writing down all they could make for their purpofe, and then fending them to *Serjeant Dendy*, or to Whitehall to *Mr. Thurloe*, againft me. The firft informer they got up againft me was one *Abdy*, a high Ranter and Blafphemer and Atheift, who was ftabbed to death that day that he was promifed and expected his reward at Whitehall for his good fervice againft me, and his were fome of the articles they read againft me at Whitehall. This man did frequently confult with the Devil, calling him his God, and, as I heard, in the chamber below me conjured him up in a perfonal fhape. When he heard me at prayer in my family he would come to the door, fhrieking, yelling, and fcreaming with a moft hideous noife, thump at the door, open it, and come in among us, finging, roaring, fmoking tobacco, curfing, fwearing, blafpheming, blowing horns, and the like, on purpofe to difturb us. Three days before he was ftabbed, and after he had fent in his forged articles, which he gathered againft me to take away my life, he made a moft blafphemous fong. This fong he and fome more of the fame fort came to my door with finging it together in the tune of a pfalm or hymn, fcoffing, laughing, fwearing, and blafpheming moft hideoufly between whiles. Befides him fome other of the prifoners were put on this practice, and a little before I was called to Whitehall laft, old *Meazy* came, he faid, from *Serjeant Dendy* to bid them get all their papers they had ready, who faid they would, and immediately went together one day after another until they had gathered up articles into two or three fheets, as I hear, againft me, bragging what they would do, and fo fent them to *Serjeant Dendy*, and he appointed his man to carry them to *Mr. Thurloe*. They were grown fo high then as to come into my chamber upon me and invade me, my wife and family there, with violent and moft virulent invectives, ftabbing words and threats, οἱ ὀδόντες αὐτῶν ὅπλα καὶ ἡ γλῶσσα αὐτῶν μάκαιρα ὀξεῖα, infomuch as they being defperate, our lives we thought were in danger by them. So that I fay we received not Roman civility, or fo much as fober Heathen ufage from them, and were by many degrees more brutifhly and barbaroufly treated than the verieft mifcreant Cavaliers, Ranters, or Blafphemers they had. For they had the liberty of any room in the houfe ; of any of their friends, though ever fo rude, to fee them ; yea, the Cavaliers at this day, courted by *Serjeant Dendy* and his wife, offering to fend down-bedding if they lay too hard, giving them liberty to go abroad when they will, by day or by night, yea to go to Taverns when they lift, yea to take the key and let who they will in and who they will out, and to keep my friends out, as if they were the gaolers, fcoffing and mocking them by the name of holy fifters and holy brethren, and what not.

3. The prifon company with us worfe than in the Heathens' days.

3. They furpafs the Roman tyranny, yea, of Nero too, in this, that *Paul* was prifoner in his own hired houfe two whole years, and he was fuffered to dwell by himfelf; but we are torn out of our houfes like beafts out of holes, and brought as I was into fuch a company and crew at Lambeth, with them that were brought in there, that for drinking, fwearing, revelling, fiddling, finging, roaring, and

blafpheming, day and night, I never heard the like among
the worft Cavaliers or wickedeft of men, making the Prifon
to me a very Portraiture of Hell and Horror and hideous
Blafphemy among the damned ones, as I may have a feafon
to acquaint the world with ere long, for now I do but hint
and inftance in things for proof. They were fo wicked
that befides all their moft hideous mockery and contemning
the ordinances of Chrift, and forefaid living in fin day and
night, they would affault my family, get the key, and
folicit them to Taverns if they could, take the children,
threaten them, and force them to fwear, curfe, and call vile
names. Yet thefe were the informers againft and accufers
of me. Though I expect to fuffer the fharper for telling
this little of the truth, yet Jehovah is on my fide, of
whom fhall I be afraid ?

4. The Roman power under Dragon government did
give liberty to all *Paul's* friends to vifit him and minifter
to him ; but our friends and acquaintance are forbid as to
their coming. The 18th of the laft twelfth month they
let in a godly maid, after long waiting to fee me, who went
into the kitchen, the way up to my chamber; but there
they fell upon her, and beat her about the head and body
moft fadly, whiles others looked on, laughed at it, and
made them fport with it, and then turned her fo abufed
out of doors again without feeing me. Another they refolved to let in on purpofe to pump him, feveral of the
Cavaliers with the Gaoler having agreed it, as we hear ;
but the man hearing of it, prevented them, and never durft
come to fee me there after that. As to their miniftering
to us, they do ufe very ftrange and incredible lies, reports
and means, for all that I can fee, to ftarve us and keep
others from miniftering to us, for they have taken away
all, and yet exact heavy fees, and fay they afk none, and
report high mountains of lies, either to make us odious
that none might regard us, or elfe if a friend but come and

4. To hinder
friends vifiting
and miniftering
to us worfe
than the
Heathens.

dine with us, reporting we fare fo bravely and better than their *Lord Protector*, and that all the churches in England had gathered for us, and that the church of Hull* had fent me thirty pounds at Lambeth, with abundance more of fuch abominable untruths, on purpofe to poffefs our friends with thefe reports, and to bind up their hands from miniftering to us, who have, may they be believed, fo little need, and had they been believed, the Lord knows we might have ftarved. *Serjeant Dendy* was very diligent to vent fuch reports to fuch friends as have told me of it again with grief when they faw them fo untrue. Sometimes too they fay we are kept high in prifon, and it makes us proud, and that for this reafon we will keep in ; and at other times that their *Lord Protector* gives us a large table and liberal allowance. The truth, or rather the untruth, is foon known : neither doth their *Lord Protector's* charity reach to us, fo far as to allow us bread and water, for all that he hath taken away our livelihood from us and our little ones, which is far more cruelty than King, Prelates, Papifts or Heathen did fhow, for they gave an allowance to every traitor, befides what friends miniftered to them. Yea, *Bonner*, as bloody a beaft as he was, fent provifion to *Mr. Philpot* and others into his Coal-houfe. But we know whom we ferve ; yea, when bread fails, faith feeds hard, (Ps. xxxvii. 3,) ' pafcere fide,' as Junius reads it ; for faith fetched *Daniel* his dinner into the den, out of *Habbacuc's* belly too, if the ftory be true, whiles the Lions lacked, and fo faith fetches in food and raiment and outward things for us, fore againft our enemies' and perfecutors' minds, it feems (Ps. xxiii. 5 ; xxxiv. 10), by opening the hearts and minds of fome poor Saints to fave it out of their own bowels for us, though there be but few, and

---

* His friend Colonel Overton had been the Governor at Hull, and Cann, the Fifth-Monarchy-Man, the Minifter of a church there.

thofe all poor, that dare or do own us at fuch a diftance.
' Dat bene, dat multum qui dat cum munere vultum.' But
I fpeak for the difcovery of that unreafonable fpirit which
is in our perfecutors, who report every mite or morfel of
bread a mountain, upon a defign to ftay the hands of the
Saints from miniftering unto us, and fo to tire and ftarve
us into an Apoftacy and yielding from our principles with
them. But ' fides famem non formidat,' for as one fays ' if
thefe perfecutors and purfuivants, tyrants and gaolers, will
take away my meat, I truft my God will take away my
ftomach, and fo 'tis all one ftill,' for this I am fure of, that
we fhall be fatisfied when our enemies fhall want and be
afhamed (Prov. xiii. 25 ; Ifa. lxv. 13). Amen, fays faith,
who fetches this in alfo.

But thus far for the fourth particular, which proves
their inveterate malice and hatred to the caufe and me.

5. They fall fhort of heathen civility, in the allowance
the Romans gave; yea, *Nero,* as notorious a tyrant as he
was, to *Paul* (Acts xxviii. 31), 'preaching the kingdom of
God and teaching the things which concern the Lord Jefus
Chrift, no man forbidding him;' yea, and this at Rome,
too, under *Nero's* nofe. But we are forbidden to preach in
prifon, and our friends forbidden to come to us to hear us.
Yea, *Serjeant Dendy* fent a letter at large, which I have by
me, to forbid it. Yea, the church fociety I walk with are
not fuffered to come at me to pray or exercife with me ;
and after, they had an exprefs order to turn me out from
the air and ufe of the common hall in Lambeth, becaufe I
preached and prayed there. They faid alfo, they had order
to keep prifoner any man that fhould dare to pray with me
in my chamber. The fame day, when *Jonathan Taylor,* of
Warwick Church, was with me and prayed, they gave
warning thereof; and after that they took ftrict notice of
any that looked like a gifted brother. Here alfo at
Windfor we have like experience, having been beaten,

5. To hinder praying and preaching to poor fouls is beyond the Tyranny of Heathens.

abufed, and clapped up clofe for it, as we fhall fhow ere long. This is doubtlefs fo high a crime, among Chriftians too, that *Nero* fhall find more mercy at the Day of Judgment, and it fhall be eafier for him than for thefe men, in this matter. But, 'fignum eft mihi majoris gloriæ ut omnes impii (fere) me deteftantur.'

I might mention other particulars, too, wherein our perfecutors and gaolers are worfe to us than heathens or Romans under the Dragon Government, or Papifts and Prelates under the Beaft's Government; and to us too, who have all along fought in the field, raifed men, fpent our eftates and ventured our lives, and for the very truths and upon the fame principles we now fuffer in. All this is the aggravation of the threnody.

Much might we fay of *Paul's* plea of freeborn (Acts xxii. 28), and as we are the conquerors and never yet the conquered, though cheated and deceived fide; and much more I might fay, but that the fword as it is hath neither eyes nor ears, and therefore can neither pity us as Englifhmen nor as Chriftians. 'The foldiers' counfel was,' Acts xxvii. 42, (and is it not?) 'to kill the prifoners.' But ftay, Brother Redcoat! we except againft thee; for we will have no butcher for a juryman.

The main caufes which moved *Serjeant Dendy* to be fo long a fuitor, as I hear, to the Council for my removal to Windfor—according to his feveral threatenings by letters, meffages, word of mouth at Whitehall that day I was before them—was the complaint the prifoners made, being afraid to take that freedom and excefs in fin day and night as they would do, whiles I was there; and then the gains which he loft by my being there, both in fees and otherwife. As Acts xvi. 19, 'When they faw that the hope of their gains was gone, they caught *Paul* and *Silas* and drew them to the market place to the rulers, and the rulers caft them into prifon' (ver. 23, 24); yea they were 'thruft into

the inner prifon.' But there they fang praifes; and fo do
we our 'antelucanos hymnos,' and fo we will, till the
foundations of this earthly government rend. Amen,
Hallelujah! Yet I can tell them, that with a better confcience, which is my continual feaft, I can look out at thefe
iron bars and fing, whiles the thorn is at my breaft to keep
me watchful, than they can at their belconas or rattling
coaches, or ruffling in their gold and gaudinefs, died in the
blood of faints, and gotten by hypocrify and cozening.
No wonder they are alarmed with continual fears, whiles
we poor worms in prifon need none of their courts of
guard, but can fleep fweetly and fecurely, though madmen,
drunkards, and devils are about us day and night. Thou
proudeft tyrant, thou canft but batter the veffel, thou
canft but hurt the bark; but my life is hid with Chrift in
God. Amen! and Lord keep it there, that I faint not.

   3. Another reafon why I appeared not publicly from 3rd Reafon.
prifon before was impreparation, having been in the valley
for the vifion many days and months before I could come
to this; and I muft confefs I did deliberate with too much
flefh and blood, at firft contenting myfelf more with the
heavenly prifon and prefence of waiting than of writing, of
praying than of publifhing anything to the world, fo that I
might run the lefs hazard to life, liberty, fame, or eftate,
&c. But I was foon roufed up out of this contentation and
kind of contemplation whether I will or no, by a loud call
to me for what is already born of God in me about the
work of this age, yea, of the forty-five enfuing years after
this, wherein the Lamb's followers and fufferers under the
banner of Chrift are to know their places, maintain their
watches, keep their motions, continue their marches, renew
their charges, till they rout Babylon, and deftroy the
Beaft's dominion root and branch, yea, until they do
wonders in this old world. For the years of wonders
(Dan. xii. 6) are now entering, upon the defcenfion of the

Spirit of Life from God. And in order, I am to found the
enſuing trumpet to the two witneſſes and remnant of the
woman's feed, for it is no time to dally; the danger is
great, the day is come, and we are engaged (there is no
going off); live or die, ſtand or fall, fight or flight, is at
hand. So that, after a long and humble attendance at the
Throne for my preſent work, I am put upon this; whatever I muſt do or endure for it, ſo Jeſus be but magnified,
my ſpirit is pitched, having ſo manifeſt and manifold a call
for it thus.

The order of
the Author's
call to this
treatiſe.

1. A meſſage brought to me the 10th of this month
by our S. *H. T.*,* who had a week's cloſe communion and
conference with the Lord, in heavenly viſits and viſions—
ſinging, praying, contemplating, communicating, and receiving amongſt other things a meſſage to deliver me in the
priſon, which I had to this effe-ct:—That the Lamb's Book
ſhould be unſealed and the viſion opened to me, bidding
me be of good cheer, for I ſhould ſhortly know my own
work and what Iſrael ought to do.

1. A ſpecial
meſſage from
the Lord
brought by a
choice ſervant
of Chriſt and
his Church.

Beſides, upon the firſt day of the third month laſt, after
a very ſolemn faſt all day with my concaptive, to know our
work and what we ſhould do, the ſucceeding night in my
ſleep, I thought I lay under the ſhadow of a great mulberry
tree, which hung full of great ripe mulberries." . . .

[He dreams that the mulberries fall into his mouth, whereby
he is abundantly refreſhed.]

* Probably "our Siſter Hannah Taprell." (See p. 123, margin.) The
newſpapers of the day report of her that ſhe was "a maid that lived at Hack-
ney, and a member of Mr. John Simpſon's church. She appeared to be in
a trance for a fortnight at a time; and ſome ſay that what ſhe does is by a
mighty inſpiration. Her cuſtom is to pray ſometimes an hour and ſometimes
two hours, and then ſings two hymns in two ſeveral tunes, and then prays
again, and ſometimes ſings again. Her prayers are in exceeding good
method and order, and her matter is various."—From *Several Proceedings*,
Jan. 16, 1654.

. . . . "And when I awaked I was fo indeed, full
of joy, and could not hold, but told my wife of it prefently, and afterwards my friends. But before noon the
fame day I received a letter from the aforefaid perfon with
thefe lines :—' Truly, brother, I have feen you frequently
in the Divine bofom, and have fung abundantly Hallelujah
for the cordials which I faw poured down your throat,
which made you, I apprehended, like a champion, and
like a triumphing conqueror. Go on, thou champion;
for He hath faid He will ftand by thee who ftood by *Paul*
at his firft anfwer, when none ftood by him,' &c. Some
may mufe at my admitting of thefe things, but I do affure
them it is neither to boaft of them nor to build upon
them, which is very dangerous; but it is to obferve the
concurrence and good effects of fuch paffages. For though
I am as far from taking notice of, or having dependence
upon dreams or vifions as any man alive, yet I muft not
omit the night teaching of the Spirit, nor fuch dreams or
vifions which bring forth bleffed effects upon the fpirits of
men, or are ratifications of the truth and mind of God.

2. To fecond that fervant of God, the very next day,
and fince, many days in a week, have men of much wifdom,
grace, holinefs and integrity come unto me, to tell me that
it is the expectation of the choiceft faints in London, and
fome in the country alfo, the Remnant of the woman, to
hear fome news of the prifon vifion ; yea, that they have
kept praying by whole days and whole nights for that
purpofe, being very high to hear from us, that they, who
are ready to give proof of their faith for the Lamb with us,
in the very fame battalia and teftimony againft the Beaft,
might be provoked by us in the prefent work, watch, and
warfare.

3. The variety of reports, and of unfatiable reporters,
which have run about city and country ; yea, their very
preachers, to make us monfters in the eyes of the poor

2. The incef-
fant expectation
of the people
of God.

3. The flying
reports which
pafs and repafs
upon our

deluded people, report ſtrange things of us as they uſe to do
of dogs—firſt ſpread abroad they are mad, and then hang
them. Thus are we reported, and their inhuman tyranny
upon us is in the pulpits reported to be no perſecution, but
an act of juſtice. But how any of the preſent friars, chaplains or parſons can prove our ſufferings ſo, or dare utter it
with ſuch boldneſs for orthodox doctrine to their poor
deluded people, had not they the ſpirit of the Beaſt, and
forehead of the Whore newly painted, I profeſs I ſhould
have wondered ; or how the people can be willing to hear

ſo high pulpit lies at their prieſt's mouth is as much to be
admired, were they not ſuch pitiful ſlaves in ſoul and body.
For can there be an act of juſtice without a trial, or trial
without crime, or crime without a law, or the like? Yet
without all or any of theſe we lie in priſons year after year,
only for preaching the truth, as their own conſciences can
and do tell them, and all the world knows, and no formal
charge againſt us to this day. So that the Prelates and
Papiſts, who had a law of the land, &c. had more colour of
juſtice than theſe men. Beſides them, and the fore-men-
tioned at Court, there be others, too, ſet a-work by Satan,

viz. falſe brethren of the Churches we walk with—eſpecially
two withdrawn from for ſcandal and ſin (whoſe names I am
loath to make too public, for who knows but thcy may repent
and be other men, which would be a great rejoicing to me),
have moſt unchriſtianly reported, if not invented, ſuch
things as my very ſoul abhors, which is publicly ſpread as
far as Lewes in Suſſex—yea, the paſtor of the church told
me, for all he knew, as far as Edinburgh in Scotland. And
this makcs me mention it the more particularly, becauſe no
author can be found for it, and the Cauſe of Chriſt is ſo
much concerned in it : which makes the Devil ſo buſy at
this day, by divers inſtruments, after the aforeſaid two, to
report me to have played at cards in Lambeth Priſon (a
very vile ſlander) thc laſt Chriſtmas, as they call it. The

Cavalier prifoners, and the reft of the ranting crew in that prifon, did play, drink, and game day and night all the time ; but for my part, I neither faw nor touched a pair of cards all the time, nor to my knowledge any one of my family ; and to take off all fcruple, I have had a kind of antipathy to cards ever fince my fufferings with the Puritans (fo called by the Prelates) when I was yet but a child, being then led to it by their example when I knew no other reafon, and cannot endure to fee a pair of cards ; and if I fee but any anywhere that I can lay hands of, I burn them.

4. Another degree of the call is the proud, flaunting, and Goliath-like challenge made us by fome of the Court-catchers and boafters. One of the late Clerical Commiffioners hath twice preffed it upon me in the prifon to print fome-what ; faying he would warrant I fhould have liberty to do it without offence and without danger, print what I would, withal that I fhould have an anfwer ; which, with a kind of boafting and infulting, being urged fo hard upon me, for the truth's fake was a notable inducement to point my pen, for I hope to find a little ftone fit for the purpofe.

4. The Challenge of fome of the Court Champions.

5. I find, befides all faid before, cafes of confcience come thick upon me, and fent apace unto me, for refolves in the work of the day about the witneffes, the time, the ftreet, the rife, the order and effects of their rifing ; alfo about the vials and about the Beaft's dominion, the firft and fecond Beafts, with their characters, and about the number of the Beaft's name, and who is the man that makes up the laft character of the Beaft, viz. 666 ; and feveral queries, which I may fay fome fcores of faints fent or brought to me—to whom I fhall minifter my light in the enfuing treatife, having a fufficient call (whatever it fhould coft me) in my place as a minifter of the Gofpel to anfwer all cafes of confcience.

5. The many cafes of confcience fent me alluding to this fubject.

6. The frequent news brought us of that unsteadiness, darknefs, and indeed malignity and contradiction of doctrine which is delivered at London, whereby abundance of precious hearts have told me they are fo confounded that they know not what to fay, and can fee no light in their doctrine, which makes them take fo long journeys to the prifon for information; for that fome of our brethren, inftead of fnuffing the candle, put it quite out, and fo leave our wonted hearers in the dark.

7. . . . .

8. To name no more, I was fomewhat dejected, yet not fo as to defpond or doubt of affiftance, to fee the moft tremendous and dreadful wrath of God, which is to begin within two or three years upon this apoftate generation, to pafs before me. Some temptations feized upon me, (through felf-diffidence and bodily diftemper), *as* at the apprehenfion of the inextricafy, depth, and incomprehenfivenefs of thofe deep prophecies which I have to ferry over or pafs through, wherein fo many more able have funk and fallen before me, *fo* at the fierce looks, bellowing threats, and atrocity of the Beaft now up in England, who will not be able to bear the tidings of his deftruction. But as the firft part of the temptation was obviated and deforced by the former promifes, fo the other by what follows. For this morning, being the 18th of the 10th month, to make all the way clear, a full commiffion was given me, and ' quietus eft,' figned and fent to me thus. Firft, I faw in my fleep a great Dragon of large fize." . . . .

[He dreams that the Dragon perifhes without power of hurting, &c.]

" Yet I objected. But, Lord, though I have a call from circumftances and faints, &c. yet what have I from the Scriptures?

Then came into my mind tumbling abundance of Scriptures and promifes one upon another, as Ifaiah xxxv.

3, 4; xl. 1, 2; yea, that of Luke xxii. 32 was flung in forcibly upon my fpirit, with abundance more.

But I objected further, What particular call have I, who am in prifon, to publifh to the world anything that reflects fo fharply upon the prefent powers, perfons, armies, or the like? *Objection.*

But that of James v. 10 perched upon me in that point immediately—' Take the prophets who have fpoken in the name of the Lord for an example;' for they feared not, in or out of prifon, the powers or perfons of Kings or the like. *Anfwered.*

Then I fell upon my unfitnefs, fewnefs of years, fmall-nefs of light, fhallownefs of judgment, weaknefs of faith, and the like. *Objection.*

But was prefently filenced by God's words to *Mofes* and *Jeremiah* fuggefted unto me (Exod. iv. 11, fo Jer. i. 6, 7)—' Say not I am a child; for what I command thee thou fhalt fpeak (and write abroad, and) be not afraid of their faces; for I am with thee to deliver thee, faith the Lord.' Do not I, the Lord, take when, where, and whom I will, and give of my Spirit, power, and ability to whom I will? Now therefore arife, and my Spirit fhall be with thee, the pen of a ready writer. With which word my heart did exult and leap within me, being as full as I could hold. *Anfwered.*

But, Lord, faid I, what is it that I muft write? What meffage fhall thy poor worm have for the world? When prefently, before I afked almoft, much fell upon me at once. ' The day of the Lord is at hand! It is his day! the day of his wrath! of his vengeance! and of great deftruction upon the inhabitants of the world! upon this land! upon thefe apoftates and adulterous generation of evil-doers! for they are all turned afide! Blood cryeth unto blood, and the earth fhall cover her flain no more! The Witneffes fhall up upon their feet, and the remnant *The meffage in bulk.*

of the woman's feed do wondrous things; for by the fpirit of *Elijah* they fhall reftore all again—Magiftracy and Miniftry as at the firft, and recover the Holy City from the Gentiles that have trod it under thefe 42 months. They fhall affault the great city, and climb up the wall like men of war; they fhall pour out the vials upon the powers, priefts, and armies of the Beaft, and on all his dominion, and execute the vengeance on all his worfhippers and irrefragable fupporters, fubjects and followers that have his name or mark on their foreheads. Yea, the earthquake fhall rend them up by the very roots, and the little ftone ftrike them up by the very toes; and none fhall fave them from the wrath of the Lamb that is to come.'

Objection.

But ah! Lord, faid I, thefe men in power, haft thou not owned them in the field at Nazeby, Dunbar, Worcefter? and wilt thou now reject them?

Anfwered.

Upon which fell thefe Scriptures upon me: Ifaiah x.— 'Shall the axe boaft itfelf againft him that heweth therewith, or the faw magnify itfelf againft him that fhaketh it? as if the rod fhould fhake itfelf againft them that lift it up, or as if the ftaff fhould lift up itfelf as if it were not wood. Therefore fhall the Lord Jehovah of Armies fend among his fat ones leannefs, and under his glory he fhall kindle a burning like the burning of a fire; and the light of Ifrael fhall be for a fire, and his Holy One for a flame; and it fhall burn and devour his thorns and his briers in one day.' Befides this, that of Jer. xviii.—'At the inftant that I fhall fpeak concerning a nation and a kingdom to build and to plant it, if it do evil in my fight and obey not my voice, then will I repent of the good wherewith I faid I would benefit them.' But efpecially that of Jeremiah— 'Tell *Coniah*, were he as a fignet upon my right hand, yet would I pluck him thence and give him into the hand of them that feek him.'

With thefe things I was fatisfied and flefh was filenced,

and faith fo fupplied and well raifed that I fell forthwith upon this work. Wherein, according to my illumination, I muft defire leave to differ from many of our dear brethren whom I highly honour, that have put us and the prefent work at too great diftance, having fent it to Germany or to other places, from whence it being fent back again to us in Great Brittanny, as I can fhow by letter from foreign parts, where I hold correfpondence with the choiceft lights, who fee the rifing of the Witneffes and ruin of the Beaft's dominion in this our ftreet firft. Thus far for the call to it.

It may be I may be judged none of the wifeft to make fo much ado in the entry of the difcourfe, and to tell fuch a ftory of my Call to this treatife, which few men will heed or hear. Notwithftanding, it is not labour loft; for one may learn wifdom by looking upon a fool; and indeed, I do grant that I am inftructed, and ftudy it every day more and more, to be and to fpeak like them whom the wife men of the times repute fools, i. e. in all plainnefs, fimplicity, and experimental language, and not in the wifdom of words or acts, as the world would have us (1 Cor. ii. 4). I have ftudied to be wife, as well as others; but now I am learning to be a fool, which none will look after, becaufe fuch are the Lord's inftruments, and by fuch he will confound the wifdom of the wife. Yea, fuch affes and idiots as we are (by grace) the King of Saints fhall ride upon into his throne; for, as one faid, ' Afinos et idiotas Chriftus elegit.' And, indeed, I write to and for fuch fools, and not to the wife. But to fuch fools as Jehovah hath made promife to (Ifaiah xxxv. 8) that they fhould not err in the way, I write. And who but fuch madmen and fools, in the world's opinion, would oppofe Powers, Armies, Kings, Councils, Priefts, Lawyers, or the reigning corruptions of the reigning Beaft, as they do? who but they will run their lives, liberties, eftates, &c. into fuch apparent hazard?

We accounted fools and madmen, and how we are fo.

or who but fools would defpife preferments and places—
£200, £300, or £1000 a year—and tread gold and filver
under their feet at this day.? Who be they but fools or
madmen, that dare be fo bold againft great perfons, &c. as
to utter all their minds at once, though they die for it? or
who but fuch will be meddling fo? Who but fools and
madmen, that will be venturing with a *Gideon* army of 300
againft an army of 30, 40, or 100,000 men? And who
but fools that build upon things not feen (Heb. xi. 1) nor
likely in reafon to come to pafs, as if they were already
prefent? and who but they that look on the ends of the
earth? Yet amongft thefe fools for Chrift's fake I am content to be numbered, and for fuch fools and madmen I
calculate and inculcate the enfuing difcourfe; fo that, as the
Apoftle fays, ‘ Wherein any is bold (I fpeak foolifhly) I
am bold alfo.’

Some of the complaints poured forth at Lambeth were tranf-
mitted to Whitehall; the following reply is anonymous, but the
fuperfcription, date, and contents feem to indicate that it was
either one of the papers collefted by the Gaolers from *Abdy* and
other prifoners, or the Gaolers' own vindication of themfelves:—

“ A Vindication againft the Complaints of Mr. Rogers,
addreffed to Edward Dendy, Efq.

Lambeth, Feb. 3, 1655.

Sir,

    In anfwer to yours about the unjuft complaint of *Mr.
Rogers,* we return thefe lines, being part of our juft vindication in brief, and remain ready to enlarge verbally.

    Firft, to his charge that drunkards and fwearers in-
trude into his chamber and fit by his fire, we know of none
but *Mr. Spittlehoufe* (of late a champion creature of *Mr.
Rogers,* though now at defiance), fat in his chamber, as
being ufe to it; but for fwearing and drunkennefs, let

Spittlehouſe clear himſelf. The whole houſe can witneſs us clear from thoſe extravagancies.

We were never in his chamber but at his public ſpeaking, except once, when—ſome three weeks agone—he challenged and ſent for us five or ſix times, as being galled by a relation ſent him from us, occaſioned by his abuſes offered, wherein we diſcovered that we would not have him think us ſo ignorant, but that we diſcerned out of what box he juggled, by his and his ſociety's proceedings, in puhliſhing ſedition, treaſon, rebellion, and therein included hereſy.

For though we hated informing, yet not being ſatisfied if to conceal treaſon were not treaſon, we ſhowed our diſlike thereof to your officers; adding, moreover, that his Highneſs had but bad ſervants if he were not acquainted with theſe odious proceedings, which to us are very ſtrange that a handful of Scum, the very Raff of Billingſgate, Redriffe, Ratcliff, Wappen, &c. ſhall aim at the deſtruction of this Government, as being by *Mr. Rogers* encouraged, animated, inſtigated, and ſeduced, not in any myſtical expreſſions, but in plain words, viz :—

That 'twill be all their own very ſhortly, and the great man at Whitehall muſt ſuddenly be confounded and deſtroyed, averring, with the moſt of ugly expreſſions and confidence, that they are the ſaints that muſt ſhortly enjoy and poſſeſs the glory of the earth, and all men being either ſaints or devils, whoſoever is not of their mind are devils, they being the ſaints.

That the Antichriſt, the Babylon, the great Dragon, or the Man of Sin, *Oliver Cromwell*, at Whitehall, muſt be pulled down, with much ſuch-like fantaſtic ſtuff.

One of them, ſpeaking or preaching in *Mr. Rogers'* chamber, had theſe words : that we did not live in an age to expect miracles, that Babylon cannot be deſtroyed, nor the ſaint at Windſor be releaſed, by only faith and prayer, but you muft be of courage, and make ufe of material inftruments, and proceed by force ; per example, faid he, if this houfe at Lambeth were to be pulled down, you muft make ufe of materials, and not expect 'twill ever fall by faith and prayer.

Another time praying thus—' Lord, when wilt thou trample under feet him that hath ftolen the government into his hands ?'

Another time praying—' Lord, when wilt thou free thy faints from the fear of men ? when fhall they by force redeem the captives of the Lord in Windfor, this place, &c ?' and as I apprehended, one faint at Maidftone by name was expreffed.

We add to this his intentions to raife feditions, treafon, rebellion, and herefy, as by witneffes here can atteft, that *Mr. Rogers* did read a letter openly to his auditors, which he faid came from *Mr. Powel* from Wales, who did affure him of twenty thoufand faints there ready to hazard their blood in defence of their caufe.

Thus much for prefent vindication, forced from us by *Mr. Rogers* his afperfions, occafioned by the aforefaid relation fent him, the heads or chief contents thereof, which fo much difturbed him, and which we, from the premifes and other evidences concluded, which were—

That he had undeceived us from fuppofing his way a blind zeal, by his frequent bloodthirfty expreffions.

That his chief aim was carnal in ftriking at the head of the Government, that he, as counting himfelf the chief of faints, might attain to the height of temporal preferments.

That he was uncharitable, damning and curfing all others not of his opinion.

That his hocus was to feduce the filly multitude, and juggle their means into his pocket, appeared by the continual gatherings at home and abroad, which we think is one chief reafon why thofe journeymen that factioufly join with him do follow his fteps in exclaiming againft the Government, that they might procure to themfelves fuch like profits, and why we judged him a perfect hypocrite, was then related.

We fhall conclude (being all paffages would take up many fheets) with *Mr. Rogers'* relation to his auditors the occafion why *Col. Overton* was fecured, whereby you may judge what edification he hath for his fociety, the whole defign being to turn and wind ftate proceedings by his commenting to their fond fenfe, faying 'twas not only for a private meeting with fome of the faints in the country, and proceeding, charged the *Lord Protector* for injuftice in that.

And, finally, take notice of his felf-made hymns, read by him, and publicly fung by him and his fociety for divine fervice. This one verfe for pattern :——

> For God begins to honour us,
> The faints are marching on ;
> The fword is fharp, the arrows fwift,
> To deftroy Babylon :
> Againft the kingdom of the Beaft
> We witneffes do rife, &c.

This and much more you fhall not only, if needful, have hands for, but from us and others. Aio."

CHAPTER VI.

HE Gaolers' Vindication feems to have been prepared and forwarded to *Secretary Thurloe* on the 3rd of February, 1655, in anticipation of what was to happen on the 6th. On that day *Rogers* was taken by his keeper to White-hall, in order that he and *Oliver Cromwell* might debate face to face, and in the prefence of their refpective adherents, whether *Rogers* was a prifoner for the caufe of Chrift, or whether he fuffered as a bufy-body and evil-doer. In the debate *Kiffin*, the Anabaptift, and others of the Court party, interpofed on one fide, and fundry obfcure Fifth-Monarchy-Men on the other.

The following account of *Cromwell's* policy towards the chief religious parties of the day—extracted from *Heath's* "Flagellum"—will perhaps help the reader to underftand his tone in the debate with *Rogers*. But if he entertained towards the Fifth-Monarchy-Men the feelings here attributed to him, it was not until after his repeated and evidently fincere efforts to conciliate them had proved abortive :—

"We will difcourfe a little," fays *Heath*, "of the prefent ftate of religion, and what opinion *Cromwell* beft afpected. The ortho-dox Proteftants were wholly fuppreffed; and yet fome reverend perfons, as *Dr. Ufher*, the Bifhop of Armagh, and *Dr. Browning*, the Bifhop of Exeter, received fome fhows of refpect and rever-ence from him—which he more manifeftly boafted in the funeral expenfes of the learned *Ufher*, and this to captate a reputation of his love to fcholars and the meek, modeft, and virtuous clergy. The Prefbyterian was rather tolerated than countenanced. . . . The Independents and Anabaptifts he loved and preferred by turns, and was moft conftant to them, as the men that would and did fupport his ufurpation. Only he could by no means endure the Fifth-Monarchy-Men, though by their dotages he had raifed himfelf to this height; and therefore *Feake* and *Rogers* were by him committed to prifon in the Caftle of Windfor, where they continued a long while. And not only fo, but he fet *Kiffin* the Anabaptift (whom he had taken out of defign into his favour) with his party together by the ears with *Feake's*, to the raifing of a feud between them — the balance of his fecurity in the Government. The like he did between the Prefbyterian and Independent, a fubdivided fchifm from the Church of England, as *Feake's* and *Kiffin's* were from Independency."

The following account of what paffed on the 6th of February is taken from the Government newfpaper of the day, and was afterwards incorporated by *Anthony Wood* into his account of *John Rogers*:—

Heath's Flagel-
lum, p. 143.
Athenæ Oxon.
ii. 594, ed. 1721.

" *Feb.* 6, 1655.

Mr. *John Rogers*, prifoner at Lambeth, was this day brought before his Highnefs the *Lord Protector* at White-hall, occafioned by an addrefs laft week made by fome of his friends that had been with his Highnefs to defire his enlargement, who being told how high a charge was againft him, and that he was not a prifoner for the caufe of Chrift, but fuffered as a bufy-body and an evil-doer, did then defire that they might hear it debated by his Highnefs and Mr. *Rogers*, they being by, which his Highnefs confented to, and this night he was admitted to his Highnefs with many of his friends, and being told of an high charge exhibited againft him, Mr. *Rogers* charged them that brought it in to be drunkards and fwearers. His Highnefs afked him which of them? and he could not name one of them that he knew. His Highnefs preffed him for Scrip-ture for his actings. He faid the Scripture is pofitive and privative. His Highnefs afked him which of thofe evil Kings that he mentioned that God deftroyed he would parallel to this prefent ftate? to which his Highnefs having no pofitive but a privative anfwer, fhowed what a difpro-portion there is, thofe being fuch as laboured to deftroy the people of God, but his work was to preferve them from deftroying one another. As, if the whole power was in the Prefbyterians they would force all to their way, and they, the Fifth-Monarchy-Men, would do the like, and fo the re-baptized perfons alfo, and his work was to keep all the godly of feveral judgments in peace, becaufe like men falling out in the ftreet would run their heads one againft another, he was as a conftable to part them and keep them in peace. And when he cried down the National Miniftry and National Church mentioned to be Antichriftian, his Highnefs told him that it was not fo,·for that is to force all to one form that is National, which is not done in this Commonwealth.

Thefe are but a tafte of much more as it was reprefented to me by fome prefent. Afterwards *Major-General Harrifon, Colonel Rich,* and fome others, made addrefs to his Highnefs to defire the releafe of him, *Mr. Feake,* and fome others, or to try them. His Highnefs fhowed how he kept them from trial out of mercy, becaufe if they were tried the law would take away their lives."

" Several Proceedings in State Affairs," No. 280.

The Fifth-Monarchy-Men were very much diffatisfied with this account of the interview between *Oliver Cromwell* and their champion, and publifhed their verfion of the ftory in a " Narrative " of their own. It appears on the title-page of this tract that it was "printed in the year 1654 ;" it muft have been printed, therefore, within fix or feven weeks at the lateft from the day on which the interview took place. The year at that time began, not on the 1ft of January, but on the 25th of March ; according to this computation, the interview took place, not on the 6th of February, 1655, as we fhould reckon it, but on the 6th of February, 1654, and the " Narrative " muft have been printed in the interval between that day and the 25th of March following, when the year 1654 expired.

The following is a reprint of the original tract, except that the fpelling has been modernifed, and fome parts of the introductory matter and a few words of the actual narrative have been omitted, but every fuch cafe of omiffion is indicated to the reader by the cuftomary figns.

The Faithfull

NARRATIVE

OF

The late *Teſtimony* and *Demand*

made to *Oliver Cromwel*, and his *Powers*, on
the Behalf of the

LORDS PRISONERS,

In the Name of the *Lord Jehovah* (Jeſus Chriſt,)
King of *Saints and Nations*.

Publiſhed by Faithful hands, Members of Churches (out of the
original Copies), to prevent miſtakes, and miſreports thereupon.

To the *Faithful Remnant* of the

Lamb, who are in this Day of *great Rebuke* and *Blaſphemy*, ingaged *againſt the BEAST and his GOVERNMENT*, eſpecially, to the *New Non-Conforming Churches*, and
Saints in *City* and *Country*, commonly called by the
Name of Fifth Monarchy-men.

Numb. 16. 5. *Even to morrow the Lord will ſhew who are his, and
who is holy, and will cauſe him to come near to him, even him whom he
hath choſen will he cauſe to come near to him: therefore take you Cen-
ſers*, &c. Gen. 42. 16. *And ye ſhall be kept in Priſon, that your words
may be proved.*

Printed in the year. 1654.

" *To the little Remnant of the Lamb againſt the Beaſt and his Government.*

An Apolo-
getical Epiſtle
to the little
Remnant of
the Lamb. SOME may wonder what we mean, the meaneſt of all the flock, to be ſo public, and it may be our deareſt brethren, the Lord's Priſoners at Lambeth, Windſor, and elſewhere. . . . . But, beſides other reaſons, ſhould we be longer ſilent, the three following would fall foully upon us :— 1. For that ſome of Satan's ſurrogates, the Court pen-ſioners and pamphleteers, have let fly many filthy lies and falſe reports about city and country, to poſſeſs them with prejudicate apprehenſions and miſinformations againſt us. . . . . This we find State policy in all hiſtories and ages, and the practice of proud tyrants, pedagogues, and perſecutors, firſt creating lies againſt the ſaints, and then bringing them into ſufferings, when once they had made them ſufficiently odious, ſo that no eye might pity them. Thus *Iſaiah* was reported for a liar, *Jeremiah* a traitor, *Daniel* a rebel, *Chriſt* a blaſphemer, *Paul* a peſtilent fellow, the Apoſtles ſtirrers up of ſedition and preachers of new laws and doctrine, and ſuch as would ſubvert all magiſ-tracy and miniſtry, laws and cuſtoms, and all then preſent. This principle and practice is revived again under this Government, Nero-like to enrobe the faithfulleſt of the aſſerters of the truth and teſtimony of Jeſus with bear-ſkins, then to bait them with their maſtiffs or bloodhounds, like men that will report their dogs mad when they have a mind to hang them. So, doubtleſs, the lies raiſed againſt the poor ſaints, trampled upon and traduced (now) every-where, eſpecially the Lord's priſoners, *Mr. Feake, Mr. Rogers*, and others, are precurſory to ſome baſe if not bloody deſign againſt them. Therefore it is they give out that they are railers, liars, ſtirrers up of ſedition and

tumults, enemies to Government, magiſtracy, miniſtry, laws, and evil-doers and what not, as perſecutors uſe to do of old. What is pretended againſt *Mr. Rogers* may appear in what follows, who refuſed to make a full or formal reply without it were in an open court, by a juſt and legal trial, according to honeſt and known laws. Therefore, and for no other reaſon, as he declared to them in our hearing, was it that he declined to anſwer, and not becauſe he was non-pluſt, not able or afraid to anſwer, or the like, as the Court creatures, who have made it their employment for ſome days to blaze lies about, have moſt wickedly and untruly reported ; but the truth is, they all ſeem to be given up over head and ears into ſtrong lies and deluſions. . . . .

2. It is and hath been, but now more than ever, ſince the Court-gloſſes have been printed and publiſhed upon it, the earneſt deſire, expectation, and indeed call of many of the ſaints to have as true a narrative of the late teſtimonies as we could publiſh . . . and knowing no other are ſo well accommodated to undertake it as ſome of us who were either ear-witneſſes or writers hereof, we reſolve to publiſh it, and therefore have compared the papers together that were taken in characters, and have given this account, which we believe is as well taken as could be in ſuch a crowd, and among ſuch interruptions, confuſions, and diſturbances, we do not ſay to every individual word, point, or circumſtance, but in all the material paſſages to the beſt of our knowledge, obſervation, or remembrance.

3. It is of ſome concernment to all the Remnant of the Woman's ſeed in city and country to know how far the Remnant in London with this teſtimony of Jeſus and Cauſe have gone and are engaged . . . . left they alſo by their ſleepineſs and ſilence incur the curſe (Judges v. 23), which God forbid ! For theſe and many other reaſons are we ſtirred up to this narrative, ſeeing as *Ahab* did ſend for

Micaiah (2 Chron. xviii.) to fee if he would fay 'Go up
and profper,' as his own prophets did fay to him, and as
Ahab faid (v. 15), 'I adjure thee fay nothing but the truth,'
which when he faid he would not fuffer, but faid (as v. 25),
'Carry him back, put this fellow in prifon, and feed him
with the bread of affliction,' fo alfo was *Mr. Rogers* remanded to his bonds in Lambeth with more feverity than
before, too.

Neither are we without our temptations in this little
bufinefs for the Lamb. . . . We confider how eagerly
our enemies would gape for advantage againft us,fhould they
find the leaft miftake, and poffibly they will find many, for
as there is no pen, fo there is no man without erratas, yet
for the truth's fake (fo far as the copies taken in fhorthand
and our friends have agreed in one, though we confefs it
cannot be publifhed fo exactly as we could wifh, feeing we
met with fo much interruption, as we faid before) the Lord
knows we have been as faithful and impartial as we could
be for our lives, and we blefs our gracious Father, we fear
not what flefh can do unto us as long as the Lord is with
us, and on our fide, and as long as we can claim protection
from Jehovah our King by covenant, intereft, privilege, and
propriety (however fome cenfure that fit at ftern, as if we
were ignorant of the Covenant of Grace; they fhall find
it otherwife, by the grace of our God, ere it be long). . .

This confcience feafts us with very excellent viands
from above, which we believe no caterer in the Court can
provide their Great Mafters withal; but theirs is like to
have but four fauce, though it be but outlandifh, like as
when chirurgions open the dead bodies of epicures, they
find many indigefted crudities, fo will the Ancient of Days
ere long, when He fits to anatomize, diffect, and rip up their
confciences, find many a foul crudity—viz. the fkulls, blood,
and bones of thoufands of the faints to ftick there. But
the Lord have mercy upon them, for the plague is begun,

if they be not paſt recovery or true repentance.   But if
they be, then the righteous and holy juſt God, who is our
God, will appear againſt them and their intereſt ſpeedily,
powerfully, and effectually, according to all the faith, tears,
and appeals of His poor worm *Jacob*, in whoſe hand we believe will be the new threſhing inſtrument viſibly, ere long.
And then this contemptible teſtimony or coarſe barley-cake
of truth will tumble from the *Gideon* camp and ſmite
down all their tents according to the faith and prayer of
Chriſt's and His poor Remnant's deſpiſed ſervants,

> To do or to ſuffer, to live or to die with
> them in this moſt glorious though
> clouded, precious though perſecuted
> Cauſe of Chriſt Jeſus,

Hur Horton.	*Samuel Bradley.*
Chriſtopher Crayle.	*William Bragg.*
Hugh Day.	*William Medley.*
Edward Grove.	*Francis Young.*
John Pugh.	*James Wilſon.*
John Durden.	*Daniel Ingoll.*

' Lift up a banner upon the high mountain, exalt the
voice unto them, ſhake the hand that they may go into the
gates of the nobles.   I have commanded my ſanctified
ones, I have alſo called my mighty ones for mine anger,
even them that rejoice in my Highneſs.' (Iſaiah xiii. 2, 3).

A Faithful Narrative to the Faithful Remnant round the Nation, the New Non-conformiſt Churches and Saints in City and Country that go under the name of Fifth-Monarchy-Men.

THE hope we have of fair weather ariſes from the Rainbow in the Cloud ; though the Cloud be black, the Sun is up and looks full upon it, which hath produced divers colours, and put the poor Saints hard upon faith, groans, and prayers to make up that tremendous Judgment and dreadful Thunderbolt that muſt fall out of this black cloud, and which begins to rattle already over the heads of the preſent perſecutors, as Rev. iv. and the 5. . . . And it is well known the New Non-conformiſts round the nation are at it day and night . . . giving the Lord no reſt, and though many have been as dead as dry bones, yet they begin to gather ſinews apace now, and are like (may we ſpeak it without alaruming the New Court) to be an exceeding great army, for the Witneſſes are warm and begin to ſtir, and benumbed ſenſes by uſe get life apace, ſo that the Remnant of the Woman's ſeed are like to have their hands full, ere long, and long they think it. Among them are thoſe deſpiſed ones of the Lord that walk in fellowſhip with *Mr. Rogers,* now priſoner for the teſtimony of Jeſus at Lambeth, who after ſeveral ſolemn days and whole nights, did find it a preſent duty incumbent upon them (and preparative to future) to go to Whitehall, the revived Court, and demand the Lord's priſoners, and bear their Teſtimony againſt theſe in preſent powers, for their groſs ſins and apoſtacies ; which the whole body agreed to, not one diſſenting, with a loud ſuffrage of joy and alacrity, bleſſing the Lord that they ſhould be honoured by the Lord Jeſus as to be called to this Teſtimony for his ſuffering Truth and Saints at this day.

They fought the Lord earneftly two whole nights
herein, though the firft night they were difturbed by fome
rude abufive ruffians, that feemed zealots for their Protector; they roughly handled, fcurriloufly mifcalled and
abufed fome of the Brethren, that they hurried them away
from prayer to prifon (for night-prayers are reputed dangerous and difturbful to the Court intereft), yet for all that
they kept another night, to have directions from the throne
in the management of fo high and noble a Meffage, and
that they might not in the leaft difhonour the dear name of
the Lord Jehovah, nor the Caufe and Kingdom of Jefus
Chrift that now fuffers. So after they found much of
God's prefence and many fweet promifes to apply, and concluded unanimoufly upon the number of Twelve (which is
the Lamb's number againft the Beaft, and the root and
fquare number of the hundred, forty-four thoufand, in Rev.
xiv.) to deliver the Meffage in truft to *Oliver Cromwell* in
perfon, in the name of the great Jehovah. And now, that
God alone might have the choice of the men, another time
was appointed to feek the Lord, and then they all agreed
to take their call by lot given in the name of the Lord, fo
that after folemn looking up to heaven the lot was given
from the lap (Prov. xvi. 33, and xviii. 18), and fell upon
twelve, but (to obferve the Lord's wifdom) thofe that they
in their wifdom fhould probably and principally have
pitched upon, for parts, utterance, and abilities, were by
the Lord's lot put by; yet this appearing fo undeniably to
be of God, the fame Twelve were fully fatisfied and accepted
their call. Afterward they agreed to go (every one with
his Bible in his hand) upon the Meffage of the Church.
Accordingly, upon the 29th of the eleventh month, a
folemn day of prayer was kept, and they were fent out in
the name of the Lord Jefus. The contents of the Meffage
with which they were entrufted is as followeth :—

THE

MESSAGE

OF THE

CHURCH

To O. C. *by*

the Twelve.*

' WE are ſent unto you, Twelve of us, in the name of our
Lord Jeſus, and of that Church Society whereof *Mr.
Rogers,* now priſoner for the Lord Jeſus at Lambeth, is
overſeer in the Holy Ghoſt, although we be poor
deſpiſed worms, and the weakeſt and unworthieſt of the
Lord's number or of the body to which we are related, and
although we be not ſo able to ſpeak as others of our
Society might have been, yet after much ſeeking the Lord
to be with us, and truſting in the ſtrength and name of our
Lord Chriſt, by which we are come out this day, after the
ſeal of ſome promiſes upon our ſpirits in the ſtrength of
the anointing, we are (as well as the Lord ſhall enable us)
come to deliver our Meſſage to you from the Lord ; and
that—

     Firſt, becauſe the Lot of the Lord is caſt upon us
above others.

     Secondly, becauſe the Lord hath choſen the poor and

---

     * Anthony à Wood ſays that this Meſſage was drawn up by Rogers
himſelf.—*Athen. Oxon.* ii. 594.

moſt deſpiſed things to confound and appear againſt the wiſe and great ones of the world (1 Cor. i. 27).

Thirdly, becauſe we are bound to ſympathiſe with the Saints in bonds (Heb. xiii. 3) in the defence of the Goſpel (Philip. i. 7-14) and the Apoſtle blames them that ſtood not by him in his bonds (2 Tim. iv. 16), but we are reſolved by the grace of our God to own and ſtand by theſe our brethren, the faithful ſervants of the Moſt High, and true and faithful miniſters of Jeſus Chriſt, who are now perſecuted and impriſoned by you and your powers.

Fourthly, becauſe the Primitive Saints, who had a Primitive Spirit (which we pray for and are in daily expecta-tion of) ſpake boldly in the name of the Lord (James v. and the 10), and ſo muſt we to you in the plainneſs, fooliſhneſs, and ſimplicity of the Goſpel, without any politic, ſtudied, or artificial frame of words or expreſſions after the wiſdom of the world or the princes of the world (1 Cor. ii. 6, 8; 2 Cor. ii. 17); therefore it is we dare not give flattering titles to any man whoſe breath is in his noſtrils (Job xxxii. 21, 22), nor come we to make our petition to man, but to God we do, in theſe matters of our Faith and Conſcience, for which we contend this day, and for which our dear Brethren are cruelly impriſoned at Lambeth (meaning our brother *Rogers*) and Windſor (meaning *Mr. Feake*).

1. Wherefore, in the name of our Lord Jeſus, and of that whole ſociety who have entruſted us on this errand, we are to DEMAND the Lord's priſoners—thoſe priſoners of hope at Lambeth and Windſor, as due to Chriſt and His Churches, whom ye have ſo unchriſtianly rent and torn from us (we meaning the churches), and neither we nor they know for what to this day, but we are perſuaded it is for their Faith and Conſcience in the Truth and Teſtimony of Jeſus Chriſt, againſt the foul apoſtacies and ſins of the times in profeſſours, whether in Powers, Prieſts, Armies, or others, that have caſt off the true Cauſe and Intereſt of

Nota.

The teſtimony.

Chrift and have taken up the creature's inftead thereof, which can never ftand. This Demand we make according to Ifaiah xlii. 22 ; 2 Chron. xxviii. 11.

2. And laftly, though we never yet did it in public, yet fo long as you go on thus we dare not but join with our fuffering brethren (viz. in what prifons foever) for their Confciences and this Caufe of Chrift, and declare and teftify againft you and the reft that adhere unto you, whether in power or out, fo long as you are the enemies of Chrift and His Caufe at this day, which we muft do with the words of truth and fobriety, for the Lord will rend you and all up by the roots that are not plants of His own planting, and the great God will appear (ere long) to confound and deftroy this fpirit of perfecution, injuftice, and tyranny, which the poor Non-conforming Saints feel fo forely, and we pray you confider that of *Afa* (2 Chron. xvi.) though a good man and a great general and conquerour, when once he forfook the Lord, relied on an arm of flefh, and began to imprifon the Lord's prophet, the hand of God was againft him (and fo on others), and fo will His wrath be upon you and thofe that belong to you, if you go on thus, and if God give you not a true and timely repentance of thefe great fins, which cry day and night for vengeance againft you and yours, and fo do thoufands of the poor perfecuted faints (however you are made to believe), therefore we pray you fee (if you will yet keep the captives of the Lord) Jer. l. 33, but mark it, *v.* 34; fo Ifai. xxix. 20, 21 ; Ps. cii. 17, 20, 21 ; Ps. xxxvii. 32, 33, 34 ; Ps. lxxix. 11, and faith Chrift, 'What you did unto thefe you did unto me,' and Acts ix. ' Saul, Saul, why perfecuteft thou me ?' fo fee in Matth. xviii. 28, 30, 34; fee *v.* 35 ; Ifa. xlix. 24, 25 ; Mal. ii. 11, 12. Now to conclude. The day of Chrift is at hand which will fet them free, and will, ere long, call you and all about you to judgment for all thefe things that you have done and fuffered

In the prifon Mr. Feake, Mr. Rogers, Mr. Spittlehoufe, Col. Overton, Col. Alured, Adj.-Gen. Allen, with many others. Since that Maj.-Gen. Harrifon, Col. Courtney, Col. Rich, M. Chary, imprifoned the 16th day of this month, befides all in other countries and Scotland thofe there that are like to lofe their lives by bloody trials, all thefe with many others at this day fuffering for and with the Teftimony of a good confcience againft men that have betrayed the caufe of Chrift ; others have been imprifoned, as Mr. Vavafor Powel, Mr. Jo. Simfon, Col. Okey, &c.

to be done againſt the Lord Jeſus and all His Saints, and for all the blood of the Saints that hath been ſhed againſt this intereſt, and theſe evil things which you have ſet up again to the joy of the wicked, the grief of the godly, and reproach of pure religion and undefiled. This is the ſum of our Meſſage which we are ſent to deliver to you in the name of the Lord, and whether you will hear, or whether you will forbear, we leave it with you and to your conſcience, before God, the righteous Judge of heaven and earth.'

After long waiting they obtained acceſs, and all Twelve being preſent together, one, as the mouth of them, delivered the meſſage, but the word DEMAND would not go down well, but the *Lord Cromwell* told them that *Mr. Feake* and *Mr. Rogers* ſuffered not for conſcience, but as evildoers and buſybodies in other men's matters. One of the Twelve then ſaid, ' If ſo, why were they not tried by ſome known and juſt law, and convicted for evildoers ? but to keep them there in ſo long and cruel impriſonment, without ſhowing cauſe, was contrary to God's law and the juſt laws of men ; beſides, they were ſick and weakly men.' But he ſaid he would put it to an iſſue, upon Friday or Tueſday (as he ſaid) *Mr. Rogers* ſhould be brought before him. On the ſixth day of this twelfth month, being the third day of the week, the brethren and ſiſters (many of them) of the Society met together, and with much difficulty got into the priſon to pray with *Mr. Rogers*, which they continued till between three and four of the clock, and then they were called away by the gaoler to go to Whitehall, according to his *Lord Protector's* order, ſo that in the name of (another) the Lord Protector of heaven and earth, the great Jehovah (whoſe face they had ſo ſolemnly and ſo often ſought for His preſence with them) *Mr. Rogers* ſet out of Lambeth along with *Harding*, his keeper, and the reſt from the Church Society (twenty brethren being the

Feb. 6 laſt, 1654 [5].

B B

moft) going along with him, much rejoicing as they went
(according to Acts v. 41) that they were fo honoured to be
called before men for the Name, Faith, and Caufe of Jefus;
and when they came to Whitehall Bridge others of the
dear Saints of feveral Churches, waiting with tears, and
prayers, and acclamations, partly of joy and partly of grief,
to receive him, and with an unanimous fuffrage, and fignal
tokens of love to him and to this bleffed Caufe he fuffers in,
they prayed the Lord's prefence to accompany him.   So
we paffed by, and *Mr. Rogers* was by his Keeper carried
into the chamber hard by the Council Chamber; but the
keeper only had admittance into the long Gallery to give
notice that the prifoner was there; but by and by he came
out again and told *Mr. Rogers* and his friends that they
muft all go down again, and go through the Guard Chamber, but *Mr. Rogers* anfwered that was ftrange, being come
fo near where the Great Man was they muft now go down
to go through the Guard Chamber and about again; but
the Keeper anfwered they muft do it, he had order for it,
which he did, not in the leaft refifting, but the main end
was, as they found afterwards, to try whether they were
fword-proof or no. So by force *Mr. Rogers* and his friends
were carried the other way back again through the Guard
Chamber.   Many other people flocked about them, the
Keeper going foremoft, *Mr. Rogers* and his wife next to
him, and his friends following clofe after him, until they
came up to the Guard Chamber door.   Immediately was
the word of command given to the Guard, who, as foon as
they faw them and us coming in, fell foully upon us with
their fwords and their halberds, faying, 'Keep back, keep
back!' to which *Mr. Rogers* anfwered with all his heart he
would go back, but his Keeper would not let him.   We
alfo faid if they would give us liberty we would go back as
faft as we could, but they would not hear us, but fell upon
us with a word and a blow, flafhing and ftriking in a moft

The harfh
ufage of the
poor perfecuted
Fifth-
Monarchy-
Men.

violent manner, calling us rogues, damned rogues, and
evacuating the moſt venomous words in their bellies, &c.
but we told them not one of us had a weapon, but the
Bible in their hands ſome had, and ſo we told them ; but
ſome ſaid the ſword of the Spirit would be too hard for
them one day, which occaſioned them to be the more violent, who ſtruck (to chooſe) at their Bibles, hands, and
heads, and ſo followed them, fighting, flaſhing, and beating the poor naked Chriſtians all the way into the court
again, and there laying about them too, and ſaying they
cared not for their Bibles, ſtill inculcating, inſulting, and
calling us damned rogues and curſed dogs, and the like;
but *Mr. Rogers* and two or three more were ſhut in among
their ſwords, whiles the reſt of the brethren were kept
without in the court, and did with very much patience bear
all their railings, reproachings, ſcoffs, ſcorns, flouts, jeers,
and injuries offered them all the while by the ſoldiers and
others of the Court Creatures.   In the mean time *Mr.*
Rogers with two or three more were brought into the Chamber of Henry the Eighth, where were many gentlemen of
the Court complexion, ſome excuſing the aforeſaid violence
and aſſault, ſaying it was by accident, to which he anſwered
he conceived it not, but that it was rather a plot, and for
aught he knew there might be a deſign to murder ſome or
other, for the word was given to fall on, and it is conceived
by moſt that they did it on purpoſe to raiſe us to a mutiny,
that ſo they might have had, at leaſt in appearance or pretence, ſome (or a more juſt) cauſe againſt *Mr. Rogers* and
his friends in Church fellowſhip with him, for the Guardians
confeſs they did but as they were commanded.   Whilſt
ſome were excuſing this affront put upon Chriſt and His
perſecuted Churches, others ſaid it was good enough for us,
and it was pity we were not worſe uſed than we were.
Mr. Rogers in the interim was talking with others, and
two of the Guard told him how ſorry they were their fellows

were fo rough, and drew their fwords, flafhing fo fiercely, and what a mercy it was no more mifchief was done, feeing they had the command given them to do what they did, and that it was the readinefs of fome amongſt them againſt us, efpecially the outlandifh. There was a fhort difcourfe between Mr. *Rogers* and fome others.

A. S. 'Why did you come up there?'

Nota.

Mr. R. 'We were fent for and commanded to come, yea, brought by force upon you, and by your Mafter's command, who fell a flafhing us with your fwords, fo that it is probable it was a defign againſt us on purpofe, elfe why fhould peaceable men that had no kind of weapons in their hands or about them, without fword or ſtaff, but only the Bibles with us—poor naked men and women—be forced by order and command to come before your Mafter, and be thus abufed, affronted, flafhed, and driven into dangers? But the Lord is righteous, who will judge.'

W. F. 'But why came you with fo many?'

Ro. 'We were fent for and commanded, and thofe that came are Chriſtians and Church members, no ways uncivil or diforderly.'

A. S. 'Well, it's well it was no worfe.'

Ro. 'It was the Lord that made it fo, in whofe name we came; and He hath delivered us from your fury and the rage of the fword, for they ſtruck with rage, fury, and high purpofe to do more mifchief than they did, but it is Heb. xi. "By faith they obtained promifes, efcaped the edge of the fword, &c." and fo have we efcaped yours, though fome do bear the mark; but the Lord Jefus will reward them when He comes.

For fo it was to the late King and his Court, where his Meſſengers and Guardmen

And you fee, gentlemen, your fword cuts bluntly, and doth little execution upon the poor Fifth-Monarchy-Men, though they be but naked and unarmed; but it may be this bufinefs will be ominous to you in this place.'

A. S. 'We wonder to fee fo many women, and what they meant.'

Ro. 'And are ye fo fearful? It may be it is true, then, what we hear, that the barking of a dog lately running about the yard gave you a very great alarm, feeing the fight of a few women hath frighted you fo pitifully as to draw your fwords upon them and hurt them. Alas! poor hearts! you are pitifully affrighted, it feems. What would you have done, then, at the fight of weapons, if a few white aprons makes you fly to your fwords and halberds?'

But by and by came a Gentleman Meffenger to *Mr. Rogers,* faying that his Lord was at leifure to fpeak with him, but the keeper at the door fuffered none to go in with him fave whom they lifted. One of the Twelve that was fent for, going in with *Mr. Rogers,* a Guardman ftanding by took him by the fhoulders in a very hoftile manner and tore his cloak off his back and abufed him. But *Mr. Rogers* and three or four more went into the chamber where their Great Mafter was, to whom fome of his Court fyco-phants had told fuch tales as they ufed to do to juftify themfelves, and complained firft, which is the Machia-vellian policy and principle, as if we had intended a tumult, which was a thing our fouls abhorred, and a moft impudent untruth, for there was not one had a weapon or ftaff with them, or fpake one uncivil word ; but after *Mr. Rogers* with three or four more were brought into the room by *Serjeant Dendy,* the Great Man had with him two gentlemen more, who ftood by the fire-fide, and a piftol lay prepared at the window where he himfelf at firft was. Then he came to the firefide in great majefty, without moving or fhowing the leaft civility of a man, though all ftood bare to him and gave refpeft. By and by he fpake, and bid one call in two or three more of the Church Society, or of the Twelve that had been with him before, when the DEMAND was made. Whiles they were gone for them faith he,—

fell upon the Citizens with their fwords at the Gate, there was his blood fhed.

O. C. 'I fent for fome of you, *Mr. Rogers* and fome more of the Church ; but you bring with you about two hundred and fifty men to make tumults and rifings, therefore fend them away, or I will not fpeak one word.' To which *Mr. Rogers* anfwered, and to give him a civil refpeᏨ, faid, 'My Lord'—

Ro. 'You are ruled much by informations which you take upon the reports of them about you, whether true or falfe, which brings the Lord's people into fo much trouble by you, but there is no fuch matter.'

O. P. 'Ha! You will talk, I fee, although it be nothing to purpofe. Who fpeaks to you?' With that he turns to one of his Creatures, faying, 'What fay you—is there not fo many ?'

Servant. His fervant anfwered, 'Yes, and it pleafe your Highnefs, there's above an hundred below, and it is to be feared they might have made a tumult.'

Ro. 'If they muſt be believed, they muſt. Yet this I may fay, I think there are not thirty men that belong to us ; and befides, they are all peaceable Chriftians, related to us in the faith of the Gofpel, all unarmed, apprehending your order and command to reach them, and they are only thofe with us as have been this day together feeking the face of the Lord, and now, according to your order, at four o'clock attending here.'

The Room fil's with the Courtiers. But by this time company was coming in apace into the room at both doors, but all were Court Creatures, to the number of fourfcore or more, as we conceive, either of the Council, army men, lawyers, and councillors, or of his creatures that were his minifters, or new made gentlemen, or the like ; but not one of them related to *Mr. Rogers* or that Church Society, till at laſt, with much ado, two or three more were crowded in of them ; but all the reſt were left waiting below in the yard, abufed, fcoffed, hiffed and hooted at by fome of the foldiers, as will appear by and by.

O. P. 'I promifed to fend for you, for fome of your

friends came and fpake fharply to me, as if I had apoftated from the Caufe of Chrift, and perfecuting godly Minifters, naming *Mr. Rogers* and *Mr. Feake*, and fpake other things that were fharp enough. You might have had patience in your words. Now you have liberty to fpeak to thofe things, but do not abufe your liberty. You told me *Mr. R.* fuffered for the Gofpel. I told you he fuffered as a Railer, as a Seducer, and a Bufybody in other men's matters, and a Stirrer up of Sedition, which rulers, led by juft principles, might fupprefs. I told you *Mr. Rogers* fuffered juftly, and not for the Teftimony of Jefus Chrift ; and, indeed, in fome degree it is blafphemy to call fuffering for evil-doing fuffering for the Gofpel ; and if he fuffers for railing, and defpifing thofe that God hath fet over us, to fay this his fuffering is for the Gofpel, is making Chrift the patron of fuch things ; but if it were fuffering for the Gofpel fomething might have been faid, yet not fo much as faying uncharitably he fuffered for evil-doing; fo that I fay this is the thing in Scripture, and if we fhow you that you fuffer for tranfgreffion, then you abufe that Scripture, which I have often thought on, that it is " to make a man an offender for a word." I wifh it were better underftood in the plainnefs of the fpirit, for (to interpret that Scripture) it was the evil of thofe times, which was to lie in wait for words on purpofe to catch at words without actions, and that is a fin ; but fome words are actions, and words are conjugal with actions, for actions and words are as fharp as fwords, and fuch things I charge you with, and you fuffer not for the Teftimony of Jefus Chrift. I fpeak—God is my witnefs—I know it, that no man in England does fuffer for the Teftimony of Jefus. Nay, do not lift up your hands and your eyes, for there is no man in England which fuffers fo. There are thofe that are far better than *Mr. Rogers*, though comparifons are not good, and not near his principles, yet if they fhould fuffer

He begins his long fpeech with manifeft reproaching and manifold untruths.

And is it not the evil of thefe times ? fo that he is condemned out of his own mouth, as in Luke xix. 22.

It feems when he faid fo, " he called G d to witnefs," Mr. Rogers lifted up his hand, and his eyes appealing to witnefs alfo, at which pofture he was offended.

for the Teftimony of Jefus: But there is fuch liberty, I wifh it be not abufed, that no man in England fuffereth for Chrift, and it is not your fancy, you muft bring ftrong words to acquaint me of your fharp expreffions.'

After he had fpake, and all were filent, *Mr. Rogers* defired to know of him whom he expected to reply, whether himfelf or fome other—the anfwer to, ' Who would.'

Rogers. ' Do you expect me to anfwer? I will premife this, before I fpeak further. I have been twenty-feven weeks a prifoner (my brother *Feake* above a year), and there hath been no charge againft me; but now I am brought before you, I defire to know in what capacity I ftand before you—as a Prifoner, or as a Freeman; as a Chriftian to a Chriftian, with equal freedom that others have, or as a flave?'

O. P. ' A Prifoner is a Freeman, as Chrift hath made you free, and fo you are a Freeman.'

Ro. ' It's true, indeed, my Lord; and yet I muft fay, as fome gentlemen here prefent know I did before I was imprifoned, and when they would have had me meet in Coleman Street to difcourfe our principles upon which we fuffer, that it is unreafonable to defire it at the difadvantages we meet with, feeing they who are our antagonifts have the advantage of a law new made, which they call

Mr. Rogers told him that Ordinance making Treafon for words was fuch as Queen Mary herfelf, as bloody as fhe was, would abhor, as appears in Hollinfhed in the firft year of her reign, which made

an " Ordinance of Treafon," to lafh us with, as a mafter hath a rod in his hand overawing his fchoolboys; fo that it is a very unjuft and unequal thing that they fhould fpeak as freemen and we as flaves under an overawing; but if that law be repealed, though but pro tempore, during fuch debates, and we be reftored to our juft and equal liberty with the adverfaries, fo as to engage on even ground, we are ready to argue it with them when and where they will; but till then it is unreafonable, for every word we fpeak may be a fnare to us.'

O. P. ' I know not what fnare may be in this. Are you

ſo afraid of ſnares? What need you fear, that will ſpeak ſo boldly?'

Ro. 'I bleſs the Lord I fear them not, nor the force of any men or devils, in theſe matters of my Faith and Conſcience, for which I ſuffer; yet I ſhould be loath to run into ſnares, which diſputes have been to the people of God; for *Stephen*, (Acts vi.) before he was tried for his life, he was firſt enſnared by diſputes and then brought to the Council, tried and arraigned for his life, and they murdered and deſtroyed him. And in *Queen Mary's* days, before they put any to death, they began it cunningly with enſnaring diſcourſes in the Convocation houſe, and ſo gathered matter to take their lives away and murder them.'

O. P. 'You are afraid of ſnares and advantages taken for your life, when there is no ſuch a thing; but I tell you, upon your friends' Petition I ſent for you, to ſatisfy them you ſuffer as an evil-doer.'

Ro. 'Say you ſo, my Lord? that is more than ever I heard before. Nor dare I take this liberty upon that account of Petitioning for it; but that I believe the Lord will help me by his own Spirit to anſwer, as indeed I have not ſtudied a form of words for you, though you have prepared matter againſt me, I hear; but I am, in the ſtrength of the Anointing, ready to anſwer.'

O. P. 'Ah, we know you are ready enough.'

Ro. 'Yea, although I have made no other preparation than faith in the promiſes, however ſome may ſcoff at them, yet I have, I bleſs the Lord, the comfort of them, and hope

---

their tyranny worſe than the Roman tyranny.

That they ſeemed to do all this in juſtice and by appeal and free courts. At this they were vexed, and look on one another.

O. was troubled at that word, and ſaid, Preparation! ha! what! but it is well known what for ſeveral days were the informations (ſome lay on

---

the table) a gathering againſt him; and the priſoners put in for plotting had by one Meazy a charge to get all their papers ready upon the 30th day of the 11th month laſt, who were very buſy to get them, and are we hear a gathering more; for when Mr. Rogers is forced to preach out at the window to the members of the church and thoſe that come to hear him, theſe wicked and bloody beaſt-like men have liberty to come into a room under him to write what they can catch or forge or patch together, though all the week long they are in another room at the further end of the houſe day and night, ſinging, ſwearing, ranting, fiddling, blaſpheming, d?y and night, to go out in the night, yea without a Keeper, to carry on the deſign.

I fhall have the benefit of that promife which I have the feal of in my heart, in Matt. x.—" Take no care what to fay, for in that hour fhall it be given unto you ;" therefore I doubt not but to fpeak to you and them about you in the name of the Lord Jefus, and in the demonftration of his Holy Spirit.' (He was interrupted).

O. P. ' Take heed you do not abufe the Scripture. If you be fuch a difciple, then that promife fhall be made good unto you, and then you may fay you fuffer for Chrift.'

Ro. ' I doubt not but that will appear that I am His difciple who made me that promife ; and if we be not able to make it out to unbiaffed men that we fuffer for Chrift and a good confcience, by God's holy word, then chop off my head. But indeed, my Lord, we can clear it to all the world, would they hear us, and not handle us fo roughly as you do ; for we have had a very dangerous paffage to you this day, an " ardua via " through fwords and halberds.'

O. P. ' Indeed ?' (fays he in a fcoff) ; ' and I pray who was wounded ?'

Ro. ' It was a mercy there were no more hurt, though many were bruifed, beaten, and hurt, and among others my wife ; but who the reft be, as yet I know not.'

O. P. ' No, fo I think ! But I have no time to difpute thofe things.'

Ro. ' Why, then I fay, as I faid before, my way muft be clear before I can proceed further ; for if they *Petitioned* I have done, and dare not anfwer a word on that ground, becaufe I reprefent thoufands of the poor Saints, who are one with me in this Caufe, whofe truft I cannot, I dare not betray.'

O. P. ' Then we have done : for I tell you you came here by a defire. I told them I would put it to the iffue this meeting, and that I would prove it you fuffered for evil-doing.'

Ro. ' That will not be fo eafily done. But, my Lord, I

ſpeak as, I hope, I am a civil man, and in ſome meaſure a
rational man, and I truſt through grace I am a Chriſtian,
nor doth Chriſtianity deſtroy civility ; and yet I muſt ſay
again, that [if] I came hither by the deſire or requeſt of
my friends, I ſhall not, I will not ſpeak a word any farther
than to tell you my reaſons. For I would not have any
friend *Petition* for me, wherein and to whom I cannot with
a good conſcience Petition for myſelf. Now, in the
matters of faith and truth, for which we ſuffer, we cannot
Petition to you, for we are not debtors to man but to
God, who is the lawgiver and only proper judge therein,
and therefore we Petition to the Lord Jehovah our Judge.
Then, 2. If they did ſo, they did not anſwer the truſt the
Church whereto they are related repoſed in them ; for it
was ſet upon their hearts as an incumbent point of duty
to Chriſt and his Churches to make *Demand* of the Lord's
priſoners in the name of the Lord Jeſus, whom you and
your powers have ſo unchriſtianly, and indeed with worſe
than Roman tyranny, rent and torn from the Churches ; ſo
that if they made a *Petition* to you I am ſilent, and ſhall
ſay no more, as I ſaid before.'

    Brother C. (one of the Twelve). 'I ſhall lay open the
whole ſtate of the buſineſs, for we are entruſted with a
Meſſage from our Society, and did but according to our
truſt make the Demand and bear our Teſtimony, and made
no requeſt at all to you ; but when you ſaid our brother
Rogers ſuffered as an evil-doer, we ſaid then, Why do you
not make it appear ? and you ſaid you would on Friday or
Tueſday, and this was all.'

    O. C. 'Well ! who ſays it is more ? Who ſays you
Petitioned ? I told you he ſuffered as an Evil-doer, as a
Railer, as a Seducer.'

    Ro. 'But your words are not proofs, my Lord. But
yet, ſeeing my way is more clear now, I ſhall ſay ſomewhat
more ; there is no law of God nor yet of man that makes

Life and Opinions of a

me fuch an offender but yours, which is worfe than the
See their
Ordinance for
Treafon.
Roman law and tyranny, that makes a man a Traitor for
words.'

O. P. 'Who calls you a Traitor? I call you not. See,
I believe you fpeak many things according to the Gofpel,
but you fuffer for evil doing.'

Ro. 'The Gofpel of the Kingdom may occafionally be
fo accounted and judged ; for, as Chrift our Saviour faith
"I came not to fend peace but the fword," the doctrine of
Chrift by the powers of the world hath ever been reputed
fedition, railing, lying, and fpeaking evil of dignities.'

O. P. 'I grieve that you call this the Gofpel ; for every
one is ready to come and fay, This is the Gofpel, with words
in their mouths, and fay this is the meaning of the Scripture ; but there wants the power of godlinefs, for Chrift
and his difciples will not fpeak evil of no man.'

Ro. 'Yea, they did fpeak againft finners as finners, which
is no evil-fpeaking. But who made you the judge of the
Scriptures, my Lord ? Whatever you fay, it fhall never
appear, I truft, to the Saints or unbiaffed difcerning men
that I fuffer as an evil-doer. Whatever you fay or fuppofe, I can make it appear it is an effential fundamental
What the
teftimony is
they fuffer in.
principle of faith, which is now under perfecution, and for
which we fuffer, viz. the Kingly Office of Chrift ; and
thofe that deny that truth, for and in which we fuffer, are
indeed heretics, and not we. It is true this prefent Teftimony for Chrift's Kingly Intereft hath two parts, viz. the
pofitive and the privative ; now, for the laft it is we fuffer,
and not for evil-doing.'

O. P. 'Why, who will hinder your preaching the
How knows he
that? for he
hears him not
preach.
Gofpel of Chrift—yea, His Perfonal Reign ? who will
hinder? You fpeak of high notions, but you do not
preach the Gofpel to build up fouls in Chrift.'

Ro. 'I know, my Lord, that you are a Sophifter. And
With that the
officers and
them prefent
fo it feems, for a part of the truth we may preach, but not

the whole, not the Gofpel of the Kingdom preached for a witnefs, as Matt. xxiv. 14, to witnefs againft the crying fins of men in power or out of power; for that feems to ftrike at your intereft too much.'

fcoffed, and fome gnafhed with their teeth at the prifoner.

O. P. 'Why, what intereft is mine?'

Ro. 'A worldly intereft, which God will deftroy.'

O. P. 'Ha!——And do you judge me?'

Ro. 'Yea, by the word of the Lord, in the majefty, might, ftrength, power, vigour, life, and authority of the Holy Ghoft I can, do, and dare judge you and your actions (1 Cor. ii.) : "The fpiritual man judgeth all things, whilft he himfelf is judged of no man." Befides, I am called by the Holy Ghoft, which hath appointed me to preach the Gofpel, to judge fins.'

O. P. 'And who will hinder you to preach the Gofpel or to do fo—fpeak againft fin as much as you will.'

Ro. You do from preaching that part of the Gofpel which decries the public fins of the times, or of men in powers, armies, &c. Neither is it, as you fay, a railing, lying, or fpeaking evil of dignities ; for the word railing, in Jude 9, is βλασφημία. Now this is no blafphemy, to fpeak the truth, or againft evils ; nor is it railing to call a man as he is. To call a drunkard a drunkard is no railing . . . . to call a thief a thief, to call an apoftate an apoftate, is no railing ; but to call one fo that is not fo is railing.'

O. P. 'To call an honeft man a thief is railing. . . Though I do know you have truths of Chrift in you, yet I will prove you fuffer for railing, lying, and as a raifer of fedition ; and I told them that I would have you fent for to fatisfy them.'

Ro. 'If that you fay can be made to appear, it is fit I fhould fuffer ; but, as *Reygnold* faid, "Nihil eft quin male interpretando poffit depravari.'"

O. P. 'This will appear in the informations that are upon the table there, what a railer you are ; and therefore let them be read,' (fays he to fome by him) 'for there be many of them : the witneffes and the evidences all are ready, it will appear eafily, and out of the prifon fuch informations, evidences there are brought in, let them be read.'

Ro. 'Your informations will not make it appear ere the more to juft men. I looked to have had a fair trial, or a Chriftian debate. But this is otherwife, feeing men that are hired or any other ways bafely fuborned do inform againft me. As for them out of prifon, it is a fign that your caufe is not very good, that needs fuch informers as the prifoners at Lambeth. They are fuch as you yourfelf have put in for plotting againft you, left they fhould cut your throat, and of whom you yourfelf have faid, in your laft fpeech, that they differed little from Beafts ; and yet you can take their informations againft me,—yea, drunkards, fwearers . . . Cavaliers, ranters, any men that make nothing to lye, fwear, drink, curfe, ban . . . and blafpheme day and night, and what not? And yet thefe muft inform againft me, to take away my life. Thefe are but bad evidences, my Lord ; and befides, were they honeft men, it were illegal.'

O. P. 'Nay, they are honeft, godly men, that mourn over you, and that are troubled for you, that will witnefs thefe things againft you.'

Ro. 'I hardly believe honeft men will accept of fuch an office, to inform againft the poor people of God, and to feek the blood of any one of Chrift's little ones; but I rather believe they are fome of your hired men, who feek for any ftuff to gratify your ears. But might I but ftand on even ground, with equal freedom, I would undertake to any unbiaffed Chriftian to make it appear that the fubject matter of our fuffering [is] for the Truth and Teftimony of Jefus, our infirmities excepted, which the Lord knows are many, and therefore we muft overcome by the blood of the Lamb and the word of the Teftimony (Rev. xii.)'

What fort of informers will ferve againft Fifth-Monarchy-Men.

He faid there was no fuch word in his fpeech, but fee it, p. 13 : "It is fome fatisfaction, if a Common-wealth muft perifh, that it perifh by men and not by the hands of perfons" (fpeaking of the plotters) "differing little from beafts."

Meaning now another paper of informations of what was preached at Thomas Apoftle's, that alfo lay upon the table with the other out of Lambeth Prifon.

O. P. 'Nay, but I know you well enough, I know you, and what your principle is too, I know that you never preached the Covenant of Grace, yea, I know it, I have had fome difcourfe with you formerly, I know you are ignorant of the Covenant, nay, for all your lifting up your eyes, it is fo.'

Ro. 'That is ftrange you fhould judge fo. My condition were uncomfortable then, indeed, if I did not know the Covenant of Grace, yea, fruition, whiles it may be fome have a national, difciplinary, or barely intuitive knowledge, there be many can teftify whether I am fo ignorant or no of the Covenant of Chrift, who have been my hearers long ago. It is for a branch, yea a principal branch of the New Teftament Covenant that we are perfecuted (as Acts ii. 30), viz. that part that God hath fworn unto, to exalt Chrift over all His enemies, and to make Him King over all Nations. This Covenant of the Father to the Son makes us grapple with the Beaft, and conteft fo as we do with the powers of the world, though others are ignorant of the Covenant.'

O. P. 'Nay, I tell you, I know you well enough, and I know your principles; though you are but a young man, yet you have been in many places, and are known well enough.'

Ro. 'Yea, I am, fo I hope, known of Chrift too; and amongft other places, I have been in the Field too againft the common enemies, that are now gotten fo high again, where I think I have done more for nothing, in mere confcience for the Lord Chrift's fake (never feeking wages as your mercenary men), than any of your colonels can fay.'

O. P. 'You talk of that is nothing to the purpofe.'

Kiffin. 'I cannot fee, my Lord, there will be any danger to have thofe papers read. We defired to hear how it appears that *Mr. Ro.* fuffers as an evil-doer; and if it pleafe your Highnefs, let thofe informations be read that are

[marginal notes:]

At whofe confidence Mr. Rogers with admiration lifted up his eyes and hands. This being fpoken in fuch confufion of others and the Great Man's heat together, he was hardly heard, but only of them who ftood nigh and wrote. One of his courtiers made anfwer, but he went on in his heat.

Raifing men, arming himfelf and others, engaging in the field in England and Ireland, fpending his eftate, killing his cattle for the army freely, expofing his perfon to great dangers freely.

brought in there, that we may hear how it appears as your Highnefs fays.'

O. P. 'Ah! fo I fay. Let them be read.'

Which gentle-
man was Mr.
Kiffin, who
fince with
fome of his
members hath
flandered him
behind his
back.

Ro. 'My Lord, that gentleman fpake very fmoothly, but we know now by experience the greateft fnares are couched under the fmootheft words; fo there is a great fnare in his, for he defires them to be read, that they may judge thereby whether I be an evil-doer or not, fo that I thank the gentleman for his charity. He feems before-hand refolved to judge me according to them, whether right or wrong, true or falfe, or whatever they be, and whoever informs, and whether they can be proved or no againft me. But I perceive by him he is fome mercenary man, that hath fome dependence upon you, and from fuch I look for no other. But the moft, my Lord, that can be faid againft me is but an evil fpeaker (which, by God's affift-ance, I truft in this matter fhall never be proved againft me neither) and not an evil-doer, for notwithftanding your former words, I can prove that the very heathens them-felves abhorred to make words matter of fact as you do.'

O. P. 'It is matter of fact you are queftioned for, for fpeaking evil of authority, raifing falfe accufations; for

Mark it out of
his own mouth.

if they were as *Nero* you are not to fpeak evil of them, for what hath the Devil his name for, but becaufe he is an accufer of the brethren; and it is not for your good deeds you are punifhed, for what faith Chrift, " for which of my good deeds do you punifh me?" and fo you fay, but you fhall hear if thefe be read, whether it be for your good deeds or for evil doing.'

Ro. 'And as they anfwered Chrift then, fo do you us: it was not for his good deeds they would ftone him, but for his blafphemy, and fo pretended to do it legally, for the law would have a blafphemer ftoned; but that which they called blafphemy was indeed the truth and good, and fo it is now; what you call evil is good, and the Devil, my Lord, hath his name from calumniating, flandering, and lying, and accufing the good, or grace of God, but not for accufing evil or declaring againft fin, the evils of Apoftacy, perfecution, or the like. But if you will read the articles you may, yet expect not a word of anfwer from me, unlefs it be in an open and legal court, before a competent and fit judge, which you are not, my Lord, nor thofe about you ; but thofe things which are my due right granted, I am ready to anfwer them in Weftminfter Hall, where I believe the Lord's Remnant, who are one with me in this Caufe, will ftand by me ; and at laft you can have but a poor carcafe, that is every day dying ; yet I am refolved with the help of God not to throw away my life, nor to betray this bleffed Caufe fo as to anfwer to I know not what fpurious and forged informations or charge in a chamber, grounded on malice or that which is worfe ; nor will I be tried in huggermugger, but if I have offended, it is fit I have open juftice.'

So that the accufer of the good and grace of God is on that fide by the informers and perfecutors.

O. P. ' Who tries you ? and who fays it is a charge ? Who calls it a charge ? I fay not fo ; and fee ! before you hear them you call them fpurious.' (With that he takes up one that was titled from Lambeth, and was going to read fomewhat).

R. ' Yea, and I have good grounds fo to do, feeing they come from fuch kind of informers as they are.'

(Then *O. P.* read one article from Lambeth, as that he fhould call him, *Oliver Cromwell*, that great dragon that fits at Whitehall, pull him out, &c.)

Ro. ' There is fuch ftuff as I abhor to have in my mouth, but I fhall forbear to anfwer, for that it is not worth the anfwering to.'

One Abdy, the chief informer, that very day he came with his Keeper to look for his reward, he was ftabbed in Fleet Street, being imprifoned for Blafphemy, Adultery, Ranting, Atheifm, and the moft horrid fins that ever were heard of.

O. P. ' Thefe things will be proved.'

Brother H. (one of the Twelve) ' We defire the things our brother *Rogers* fuffers for may be publicly known to all, for we apprehend he fuffers for the truth, and the things which you hear you may be mifinformed in.'

Life and Opinions of a

Ro. 'Therefore let me have a fair hearing in a legal court; and I hope the Lord will make me ready for whatever I muſt ſuffer, right or wrong, if it muſt be ſo. But yet, I tell you, my Lord, I fear not anything that you can lay againſt me juſtly and honeſtly, but the truth is you take up anything that your informers can handſomely patch together, who, like the Devil, take a bit here and a bit there, that makes for their turn, and you take it as it lies, for granted preſently. O, my Lord, I cannot but mourn for you and your condition, which is ſad and to be bewailed, and the rather for that you have ſo many about you who for their own ends to get the world into their hands do deceive you; but the Lord will judge righteouſly, ere long, I am ſure, and let appear whether you or we have the beſt bottom to bear us up, for I bleſs the Lord the comforter is with me. I think my condition, through Grace, though a poor priſoner, a great deal better than yours; I would not change with you.'

O. P. 'Well, well, you are known well enough, and what ſpirit you are of. We know you, and to call your ſufferings for Chriſt when they are for evil-doing is not well; yea, it is Blaſphemy; yea, I ſay Blaſphemy again, for all your lifting up of your eyes, and I tell you, yea, you, that in a good box of ointment a little thing—a dead fly— may ſpoil all, yea, a little fly.'

Mr. Rogers, amazed at ſuch language, again lifted up his hand and eyes towards heaven, appealing to God to judge righteouſly.

Ro. 'I dare not, my Lord, juſtify myſelf in my infirmities, but I bleſs the Lord I can apply Chriſt's merits. I beſeech you, ſpeak not ſo reproachfully of the Spirit of God to call it fanatic, or an evil ſpirit, for that is Blaſphemy ſo to do (and ſee Iſai. lxiii. 10), neither call evil good or good evil, for that is prevarication (Iſai. v. 20), that which you judge evil-doing the Lord judgeth well-doing and my duty. Yet I muſt tell you, the Lord never made you a judge over our faith, nor of His Scripture, whereof you take upon you.'

O. P. 'Well, you know that the time was there was no great difference betwixt you and me. I had you in my eye, and did think of you for employment (and preferment) ; you know it well enough.'

Ro. 'True, my Lord; and then you could fay to me you thought no man in England fo fit, but fince the cafe is altered indeed ; but I pray confider who it is is changed. Surely, it muft be Confcience that makes me fuffer, then, through fo many temptations as I have met with. And I have often faid, let me be convinced by good words that I am an evil-doer, as you faid, and I would lay my neck under your feet for mercy ; but till then I muft keep my Confcience.'

One of the Grandees (as we take it it was *G. Defborough*) fays, ' Let the informations be read, let them be heard ;' and then *Scobell* was called to read them, not thofe from Lambeth, but thofe that were brought in from Thomas Apoftle's, from what *Mr. Rogers* prayed, what he preached, and what they fang in hymns. What he prayed was for the prifoners of the Lord at Windfor, and againft the tyranny of all Antichriftian powers, and to that purpofe, and that God would haften his Vials out upon them. What he preached was out of Matth. v.—' Agree with thine adverfary (Chrift) quickly,' and he obferved, ' Apoftate-adulterate profeffors muft agree quickly with Chrift, their adverfary,' applying it to the prefent Powers as fuch, proving they break the Ten Commandments. As the 1ft. In fetting up idols again, a golden calf ; fo the army and flefhly ftrength, and the like are idolized, whilft men fay, thefe are the gods that brought us up out of Egypt.

2nd Command is,—Graven images, and fo are the Tryers, and High Court Commiffioners—fuch the inventions and graven images of men's making with their feals, parchments, black boxes, and picklocks, padlocks and keys for your hog-fties, pig-fties, and goofe-ftalls.

The informations from Thomas Apoftle's read.

The Articles againft Mr. Rogers as well as they could be taken.

Thefe Articles are many of them falfe for matter and form, as can be made appear by hundreds.

3rd Command. Take not My name in vain, &c. Such as have broke all their Declarations, Engagements, and abufed His Attributes, ufing that name of God for the'.r own ends, are guilty of this.

4th Command. Remember that thou keep holy the, &c. fpeaking of foul-reft, and faying that the prefent Powers kept not the Sabbath that refted in their pleafures, flefh, &c. and not in Chrift, but did their own work.

5th Command. Honour thy father and mother, &c. They break this Commandment in their difobedience to God, the heavenly Father.

6th. Thou fhalt not murder, &c. Murderers are of many forts—fuch as have betrayed the blood that hath been fhed againft this kind of Government, &c. And then he converted his difcourfe againft informers that come for blood, and faid, to hate a brother without a caufe is murder.

7th. Thou fhalt not commit adultery, &c. This they did with others, as Army, Lawyer's, Prieft's intereft, and that which they before deftroyed.

8th. Steal not. Now there are great thieves and little thieves (great ones are now in prefent Powers) and army thieves, clergy thieves, lawyer thieves, and the Great Thief now in Whitehall. But the other two he left to another time. When he had done he read a letter from *Mr. Feake*, where was a dialogue between him and the Governor, and then he commented upon it, and faid it is worfe now than it was with the Romans, for then Paul might preach, though a prifoner, but now we are denied it. After that he fung an hymn, and the people joined with great alacrity, againft oppreffion and perfecution, &c.

After this information was read, *Mr. Rogers* faid, ' My Lord, I had a purpofe not to anfwer one word hereto, this being no fuitable place or time to anfwer a charge, and no witneffes appearing againft me to make it good; but yet I fhall tell you this, for I will not, with the Lord's help, fpeak

Now is Mr. Rogers forced to preach out at the iron bars of the prifon on Lord's days.

a word but what I will own to your face, for I love to appear in the fincerity of my foul and confcience for my Lord and Mafter (Jefus Chrift) plain to all men, and to lay open my principles, which I have no caufe (through grace) to be afhamed of. The matter of this is much of it true, but as to the form, there is a great deal of patching and botching put in by your mercenary hirelings which I will not own ; but as to much of the matter of it, I muft dare, and with the Lord's grace I will, though I die for it, and without you fhould cut my tongue out of my head, I fhall continue the Teftimony, up and tell you, moreover, with the reft about you here, that I regard your laws in the matters of my God no more than ftraws, for "Imperia Divina non funt fubjecta magiftratui," faith one of the Martyrs ; and tell you that I will not be accountable to the magiftrate nor fubmit to his judgment in the matters of my Faith, which the civil law can take no due cognizance of.'

One of his Council faid : ' Ha! Imperia Divina !'

Ro. ' So I fay, Imperia Divina.'

O. P. Saith he, ' Are thefe fpurious articles now ? put in by drunkards and fwearers too ? . . . Are they not ? Ha !—ha !—'

Ro. ' My Lord, I know what I fay. Thofe which were fent from Lambeth put in by the prifoners there ; thofe, I fay, are fuch. I did not fay all, but thofe that I fee there, which lie upon the table, titled from Lambeth ; and befides, there is *Serjeant Dendy* knows this that I fay, for he himfelf (I thank him) fent in their informations againft me to *Mr. Thurloe,* which he cannot deny.'

S. Dendy. ' My Lord, I delivered him none.'

Ro. ' I fay not you delivered them, but you fent them by your man, who delivered them according to your directions.'

S. Dendy. ' But my Mother, my Lord, this was my Mother, for fhe catechized me, my Lord, and I told her.'

They would fain have fhifted off them from Lambeth as it feems, as if they were afhamed of them.

Ro. 'So that is true, as I faid before, that thofe from Lambeth prifon are fpurious, wicked, and illegal.'

Mr. Cre. 'Pray, my Lord, let *Mr. Rogers* have a copy of his charge, for the law allows it him.'

O. P. 'No, this is not his trial.'

Ro. 'Why, then let me have it, as you are a Chriftian; for is it fit I be denied a fight of my accufation againft me?' (But he turned away and would not hear).

Mr. Cre. 'Then, my Lord, let us have Liberty of Confcience. Will you not give us fo much liberty as the Parliament gave?' (With that he turned about in anger).

O. P. 'I tell you there was never fuch Liberty of Confcience, no, never fuch liberty fince the days of Antichrift as is now—for may not men preach and pray what they will? and have not men their liberty of all opinions?'

Ro. 'It is true there is liberty enough, and too much too, for drunkards, fwearers, and men of vile debauched principles and evil lives, Common-prayer men, and fuch like, we know, round the nation.' (Then his creatures about him fcoffed).

O. P. 'Ha!—are drunkennefs, fwearing, opinions then?'

Ro. 'I fay not fo, but I fay fuch men may have their opinions, whilft we are perfecuted for the truth. But why do you not, my Lord, let out my brother *Feake* at Windfor with myfelf? Seeing we fuffer in one Caufe, for one Teftimony, and I truft by one Spirit of Jefus Chrift, let us both out to anfwer for ourfelves jointly together, and to make it appear to all uninterefted Chriftians that we are no evil-doers in the matter we fuffer for; which if we do not, then let us fuffer.'

O.P. '*Mr. Feake!* truly, *Mr. Feake!* I think lefs evil may be faid of him than of you; but there are many of different opinions that come to me, and they know they have all their liberty of their opinions.'

Ro. 'Yea, every man almoft that talks with you is apt

He confeffed that Antichrift's Government is now up in England yet, fo that no wonder the Prifons are fo full of precious faints.

to think you of his opinion, my Lord, whatever he be.' (His creatures fcoffed again).

O. P. 'Nay, you do not,' (faith he in anger. His creatures fcoffed and laughed again).

But fome of that opinion do as Mr. T. G. and others.

Ro. 'Some of this judgment do think you fo, although, as I faid before, the privative or negative part of the Teftimony you cannot bear.'

O. P. ' Pifh ! here is a great deal of pofitive and privative to fhow you are a Scholar, and 'tis well known what you are. And where do you find that diftinction ? '

Ro. ' In logic.'

O. P. ' Ha !'

Ro. ' I muft tell you in the name of the Lord Jehovah that your condition is very defperate, and if you confult the holy oracles you will find it ; for the next Vial which is to be poured out is the fcorching hot one, and muft fall upon the Apoftate profeffors, that have forfaken and betrayed the Caufe of Chrift. And look to it, it is like to fall heavy upon your heads and thofe that are about you ; I pray think of that in Hofea i. 4—the blood of *Jezreel* fhall be upon the houfe of *Jehu*—though *Jehu* did obey the Lord in doing juftice on *Ahab* and *Jezebel ;* yet becaufe he fell into the fame predicament of fin, walking in the fame fteps of evil which *Ahab* walked in, the very blood of them fell upon his head.'

They thought Mr. Rogers to be an antic, becaufe he fpake in power and great zeal.

O. P. ' Your fpirit is to judge, but I regard not your words ; look you to your confcience, and I will look to mine. Yet for that of *Jehu*, why, what was that for ? It was for fear left the people fhould go back again to the houfe of *David* and to Jerufalem.' (And fo he was running into the ftory of *Jeroboam*, but he was corrected. Then *Kiffin* faid ' It is fo ;' then faid *Mr. Rogers*, ' It is not fo of *Jehu*, but of *Jeroboam*, which he fpeaks of.' Then he corrected himfelf, and faid), ' Well, but *Jehu*—can you parallel it now ? Why, his heart was hypocritical, and by

policy clave to the fame fin of his predeceffors, and *Baal*
again, to pleafe the people.'

Ro. ' True, my Lord ; and is it not fo now ?'

O. P. ' Hah !'—(faith he, and turned about to his army
men)—' and fo he fpake of the army too.   What can you
fay of them ?'

Ro. ' I fay they are an Apoftate army, that have moft
perfidioufly betrayed the Caufe of Chrift, broken their faith
in fo many Declarations and Engagements, and are odious to
the Saints ; yea, the very name of them will be odious to
the children that are yet unborn.'   (With that the army men
—for many officers were by—were forely vexed, fome grating
their teeth and laying heads together).

O. P. ' I tell you,' (faith he in a chafe) ' I tell you, and
you ! that they have kept them all to a tittle.   Not one of
you can make it appear that they have broke one declaration or engagement, or a tittle of one ; prove it if you can,
any of you.'

Ro. Mr. *Rogers* did earneftly prefs for liberty to inftance in fome, and with much ado faid—' My Lord, if you
would have patience, I would inftance in many.'   (They
fcoff again).

O. P. ' Am I impatient, then ? let them that ftand by
fee !   Nay, it is you are fo full, like the Pamphleteers.'

Ro. ' They that write Pamphlets now never printed
more lies and blafphemies fince the world ftood.'

O. P. ' I think fo too.'

Ro. ' But, my Lord, if you pleafe to let me fpeak, for if
I be extreme, [it] is not " paffio concupifcibilis," as we fee in
fome men who fpeak all for themfelves, whilft we feek only
for Chrift and his kingdom, but rather a " paffio irafcibilis,"
(which it may be is my weaknefs, but fure it is my indig-
nation to fin and felf, and that which I fee fet up inftead of
Chrift) ; but if you will give me leave I will inftance in
declarations, as that in '47, for one, page 9, where they

For there were
many poftures
and actions
tending to
difturb and
interrupt him.

declare againſt any authority or abſolute power in any perſon or perſons whatſoever during life, ſaying the people ſo ſubjected were mere ſlaves, and that you would not have it ſo in any, no, not in any of your own army, or of your own Principles, nor yet of whom you might have moſt perſonal aſſurance, and that it was no reſiſting of magiſtracy to ſide with juſt principles, and much more to that purpoſe. Beſides, in ſeveral others, as in Alban's, and that when the army went to Scotland againſt the Clergy and Tithes.' (But *Maſter Rogers* was interrupted, and not ſuffered to inſiſt on any others).

O. P. ' And who? Hear me: who? — who, I ſay, hath broken that? Where is an arbitrary or abſolute power? (nay, hear me): where is ſuch a power?'

Ro. ' Is not the Long-ſword ſuch? By what law or power are we put into priſon, my brother *Feake* above theſe twelve months, I above twenty-eight weeks, and ſeveral others of our brethren, and we know not for what to this day? which I ſay again is worſe, yea worſe than the Roman law. And is not this Arbitrary? And is not your power with the armies Abſolute, to break up Parliaments and do what you will? But, if you pleaſe, let me inſtance in others.' (But they would not ſuffer him).

One of the army—ſome ſay L. C. *W.** ' Sir,' (ſaith he to *Mr. Rogers*), ' you ſay the army have broken all their Engagements.'

Ro. ' Yea, every one of them ; and if they make another Declaration, they will hardly be believed again by good people.'

L. C. W. ' But I pray by what rule do you reſiſt Powers ſet up of God ?'

Ro. ' Sir, you are miſtaken ; we do not reſiſt ſuch as are

---

* Probably Lieut.-Col. Worſley, of Cromwell's own regiment.

fet up of God, but we refift fin in all men. And as *Luther* faid, " Inveniar fane fuperbus, &c." I may be accounted proud, mad, or anything, but be it fo, " ne modo impii filentii arguar, dum Chriftus patitur," rather than I be guilty of the fin of filence.'

O. P. ' Now, for the Army, they are refolved not to reft till they have performed all they engaged; and they are about it as faft as they can do it in order.' (And much to that purpofe he fpake. But then *Mr. Her.* defired to fpeak).

Mr. Her. ' I defire to fpeak a word.'

O. P. ' Well, do.'

Mr. Her. ' That gentleman' (meaning L. C. *W.*) ' afked by what rule we refift Powers. We defire, then, to be fatisfied by what rule you refifted the King, and warred againft him and his adherents, and deftroyed the Government before, feeing they were accounted too a lawful authority. And confider how much blood cries under the altar, "How long, O Lord, holy and true?" '

O. P. Would undertake to anfwer by a long narrative of the people's grievances, the King's abfolute power, and his feeking to deftroy his fubjects till they were forced to take up arms for their own defence, fo that it was a defenfive War; and the former Powers had broken their Engagements and forfeited their truft. Much more was fpoken by one or other thereto. But faith he, looking upon *Mr. Ro.* ' Ha!'

O. P. ' I fee he is full to fpeak.'

Ro. ' Yea, my Lord, I am, for (ex conceffis) our controverfy is decided, and the cafe is plain on our fide, and feems fo now more than ever; for do not the poor people of God feel a Prerogative Intereft now up? As the old Nonconformifts, or the good old Puritans were perfecuted, imprifoned, reproached, and denied protection from men, and therefore were forced to fly to God by faith and prayer and tears day and night, not ceafing till the Vial of

But Mr. Ro. was interrupted and forced to break off, whiles O. P. procceded.

The Controverfy cleared out of their own mouths, &.

Wrath was poured out upon the heads of the King and his Prelates; fo I fay the new Nonconformifts are abufed, difowned, and denied protection, perfecuted, imprifoned, banifhed, and forced day and night (yea thoufands of them in city and country) to their faith, tears, prayers, and appeals, which are the " Bombarda Chriftianorum," and will prevail, as fure as God is in Heaven, to bring down the next hot, fcorching Vial of His Wrath upon thefe new enemies and Perfecutors.

Befides, 2, in your own declaration, p. 7 of that 1643, you fay it is no refifting of magiftracy to fide with juft principles. And is it not juft to fide with that Intereft which the blood of fo many thoufands of the Saints hath fealed to in the three nations, and fo many Declarations, Vows, and Engagements have been made for, viz. for the Lamb's, and againft this your Intereft, which we have all engaged, prayed, bled, and fought againft? Now, my Lord, let the loud cries of the blood, fhed againft thefe things you have fet up, be heard, and make reftitution of that blood, thofe lives, tears, bowels, faith, prayer, limbs, and fkulls of us and our relations left in the fields and laid out againft this kind of Government, whether in Civil or Ecclefiaftical; or elfe let us have what they were laid out for; otherwife we muft and will, with the Lord's help, fide with thofe juft principles that have been fo fealed to and owned by the Lord. And this will be a moft apparent defenfive war as ever was in the world, to defend what the blood, and bones, and eftates of fo many thoufands of the Saints of God have bought at fo high a rate, which they are wronged [of], for they never thought of fetting up this. And therefore I fay, my Lord, if our God, the Lord Jehovah, do give his call, I am ready, for one amongft the Lord's Remnant, " to fide with juft principles " in the ftrength of the Anointing, whether it be "prædicando, precando, or præliando," by preaching, praying, or fighting.'

Sir Gilb. P[ickering.] 'Said you not "præliando?"'
'Yes,' (fays *Mr. R.*), ' in the Spirit of the Lord, for the
cafe was never fo clear as now it is, in the ftate of the con-

The ftate of
the controverfy
is between
Chrift and O.
P.—Chrift's
Government
and Man's.

troverfy. For the controverfy is not now between man
and man, one Government of the world and another
Government of the world, or King and People, but it is
now between Chrift and you, my Lord, Chrift's Government and yours; and which of thefe two are the higher
Powers for us to fide with and be obedient unto, judge ye.'

This fpeech
feemed to
trouble them
all.

O. P. 'Ha! who denies the cafe to be clearer now?
But I heard indeed it is fome of your principles to be at
it; Why, you long to be at it—you want but an opportunity.'

Ro. 'The Remnant of the Woman's feed muft be at it
when they have the Call. For I befeech you, my Lord, to
confider how near it is to the end of the Beaft's dominion,
the 42 months, and what time of day it is with us now.'
(But *Mr. Ro.* was interrupted).

An Ignoramus
brought in
very honeftly.

O. P. 'Talk not of that, for I muft tell you plainly they
are things I underftand not.'

Ro. ' It feems, my Lord, fo, elfe furely you durft not
lay violent hands upon us for the Teftimony and Truth of
the day as you do.'

B. D. (one of the Twelve). 'Why, then, do you imprifon others for the light, if you yourfelf be fo ignorant?'
But then fome of the Court creatures pulled him by the
cloak, and laid violent hands on him, and called him
ftinking, bafe fellow, faying he knew not whom he fpake
to, nor where he was, giving him many uncivil words.
But afterward one of them faid to him, ' Afk for *Mr. Rogers*
out of prifon; afk for him, and my Lord will let him out.'
But *B. D.* anfwered, ' No, Sir, we came not for that.'

B. P. 'Great men are not always wife.'

O. P. 'See!' fays he, looking upon his army men.

Ro. ' They are not always wife with the wifdom of God,
though they may have much carnal policy, fubtilty, and

reafon of ftate. But the feed of the woman fhall break the ferpent's head.' (Which *Mr. Ro.* fpeaking with a high voice and great alacrity, it made the Courtiers fcoff at him as if he were a madman).

O. P. 'Ha! And thus they talk of the Miniftery and Commiffioners for Approbation, and fay they are Antichriftian.'

Ro. 'Yea, my Lord, we do fay fo, and they are fo, as to their ftanding upon a wrong, un-Gofpel foot of account; and I will prove them, and your Triers (I fpeak not as to their perfons, but as to their ftanding) Antichriftian for matter, and form, and rule, by which they fit, and end for which they fit.'

O. P. 'You fix the name of Antichriftian upon anything.'

Ro. 'Pray, my Lord, make no law againft that name; let it not be Treafon to ufe the name of Antichriftian, for that name will up yet higher and higher, and many things that you think good and Chriftian will be found Antichriftian ere long.'

O. P. (Being angry, looked on his army men). 'See,' (faid he), 'and fo all is Antichriftian, and Tithes are fo too, with you; but I will prove they are not.'

Ro. 'My Lord, you were once of another mind, and told me you'd have them pulled down, and put into a treafury.'

O. P. 'Did I ever fay fo?'

Ro. 'Yea, that you did, in the Cock-pit—the round place there; and faid, moreover, that the poor fhould be maintained, and put to work with what remained of them, that we might have no beggar in England.'

O. P. 'Ha! there be many gentlemen know that I have been for them, and will maintain the juftnefs of them.'

Ro. 'But, my Lord, how can that be that the National Miniftery is not Antichriftian?'

See your Ordinance, March 20, 1653. The ground is upon Patrons' right to prefent to cure of fouls, the Creator is your L. P. Cromwell, the matter men of corrupt principles and practices, and moft of them of the National Church; the end is to fill Parifh-cures and get Tithes —all Antichriftian.

O. P. 'See, now, how you run! It is not a National Miniftery that is now eftablifhed, nor can you make it appear they are Antichriftian.'

Ro. 'Yea, my Lord, without any difficulty: out of your own law, which hath conftituted thefe Triers and High-Court-Commiffioners to eftablifh a worldly clergy.'

O. P. 'I tell you, you and you, that you cannot, for they ordain none.'

Ro. 'No; but if the Pope, Prelate, or Devil fhould ordain them, they muft approve of them, fettle them in their parifhes, and what not, if they be but conformable to——' (He is interrupted).

O. P. 'I tell you—I tell you, it is their Grace they judge of, and not for parts or learning Latin, Greek, or Hebrew.'

Ro. 'And who made them judges of Grace, my Lord? At moft they can but judge of the fruits of Grace, and how dare they take upon them to be judges over Grace? It is not you, but the Lord Jefus, that can make them fuch judges.' (With that he turned away, as very angry).

B. H. 'My Lord, we are very much diflatisfied with what you have done againft thefe prifoners of the Lord Jefus, for fo they are, and we muft count them fo, for you have given us no fatisfaction at all in what you pretend them to be as evil-doers.'

O. P. 'I cannot tell you, then, how to help it.'

B. H. 'For my part, I muft declare againft you, and will venture my life, if I be called to it, with thefe our brethren that fuffer.'

B. Cr. 'As for thofe Articles, we have heard them read againft our brother *Rogers* out of his fermons preached at Thomas Apoftle's, and from what he prayed at Thomas Apoftle's. Set afide but what is put in by your Informers, which we will take our oaths that heard them all preached, were never fpoken by him; only I fay that excepted, we will live and die with him upon thofe Articles, and will own him with our lives.'

' Yea,' faid *Mr. Ro.* ' and I believe an hundred will that heard and writ them.'

O. P. ' Well,' faith he, ' I'll fend for fome of you ere long, but I have loft this time, and have public bufinefs upon me at this time : I had rather have given £500 !—I tell you there wants brotherly love, and the feveral forts of forms would cut the throats one of another, fhould not I keep the peace.'

Ro. ' Thofe you call Fifth-Monarchy-Men are driven by your fword to love one another.'

O. P. ' Why, I tell you there be Anabaptifts' (pointing at *Mr. Kiffin*), ' and they would cut the throats of them that are not under their forms ; fo would the Prefbyterians cut the throats of them that are not of their forms, and fo would you Fifth-Monarchy-Men. It is fit to keep all thefe forms out of the Power.'

Ro. ' Who made you, my Lord, a judge of our principles ? You fpeak evil of you know not what. For that Fifth-Monarchy principle, as you call it, is of fuch a latitude as takes in all Saints, all fuch as are fanctified in Chrift Jefus, without refpect of what form or judgment he is. But " Judicium fit fecundum vim intellectualis luminis "'— (He was interrupted).

O. P. ' What do you tell us of your Latin ?'

Ro. ' Why, my Lord, you are Chancellor of Oxford, and can you not bear that language ?'

B. C. 'My Lord, we have great comfort by the Miniftery of our brother *Rogers*, and great mifs of him, and therefore we have demanded his liberty, and defire to know whether he fhall be at liberty or no.'

O. P. ' I will take my own time ; you fhall not know what I will do.'

B. H. ' Then let us have liberty to hear him preach.'

Life and Opinions of a

And yet for all
S. Dendy's
bafenefs to the
poor perfecuted
people of God,
and his
readinefs to
prevent the
Great Man's
anfwer, he can
let in as many
as will come to
the drunken
profane
prifoners and
plotters, fo that
friends are glad
to ufe their
names (if they
know any of
them) that
come to fee
Mr. Rogers.

S. Dendy. 'It cannot be, my Lord, for I have many prifoners, and 'tis dangerous.'

Ro. 'Pray, my Lord, confider that place in Ifaiah xlix. 24, 25, 26, for the Lord will deliver the lawful captive in that day which is coming. You can but have my blood at laft, and you had like to have had it already in the Prifon ere this. Two of my children have died there fince my imprifonment, and I have been at Death's door.'

B. H. 'It is unreafonable our brother *Ro.* fhould be kept prifoner fo in fuch a place and at fuch a charge, as is for him above £200 per annum, and we know no caufe for it, but his confcience.'

Then *S. Dendy* was fpoken to, to anfwer for himfelf.

S. D. 'Now, my Lord, I fee one of my accufers. I never demanded a penny of *Mr. Ro.* nor of my Aunt, his wife, who is one of *Sir Robert Payne's* daughters.'

O. P. 'I knew her father very well.'

S. D. 'But they have, my Lord, three rooms, and it cannot be allowed.'

Ro. 'No more room than one prifoner had before, being divided into three little rooms, and but one chimney in them all. The Plotter that went out before I came into them had them all. And for the fees, though you in perfon demanded them not, yet your man, old *Meazy,* did for you feveral times, viz. £4 4*s.* per week, which he did before witnefs, as I can prove under their hands, and he faid I fhould not go out till the Serjeant had it. And what befides I was to pay you I was not to know till I went out.'

Mrs. Ro. faid to *Serjeant Dendy*—'It's true, you have had but five pounds yet of it.'

O. P. 'Why, he is your nephew, who was accounted one that loved the people of God.'

Ro. 'So were others as well as he till this trial.'

Mr. Cre. 'My Lord, will you not give us the liberty to

hear him in the prifon then, feeing you will not let us hear him abroad ?'

O. P. 'Is that the liberty you fought for ?' fays he in a fcoff.

Mr. Cre. ' Yes, Sir, and that which we demand.' But then the Great Man would be gone, and as he was going out *Mr. Ro.* defired him to remember he muft be judged, and the day of the Lord was near, and that he would ere long, and thofe about him, find them that now he and they counted falfe Prophets in Windfor and Lambeth true Prophets, and what they have faid they fhould find come to pafs ere many years yet, for that the righteous Jehovah who fitteth on high heareth all our prayers, fighs, groans, and tears. But away he went, and would not hear.

As foon as we came out of the room *Serjeant Dendy* in the gallery threatened what he would do, and how he would fend them further off, and order them ere long, *Mr. Rogers* receiving the threatening without impatience or one word of reply unto him.

That very night a ftrict order was fent after him to Lambeth Prifon that no more than fix may come to fee *Mr. R.* at a time, no fuch order being made for any of the other prifoners, who have of lewd company as many as they will at a time. And fince that the gaoler hath been fo ftrict, efpecially upon the Lord's days, according to his orders from Whitehall, that he will not fuffer one Brother to come in to fee him or to pray with him, that is fent from the Churches of Chrift upon thofe days, if he knows him, to keep a holy reft with *Mr. R.* But to pafs over that, and leave it to the Judge of heaven and earth, who we are fure will not overpafs it.

During this difcourfe between *Mr. R.* and the Great Man above, the brethren that were below in the yard had their fhare of reproaches and abufes. For the members of the Churches of Chrift who could not have accefs with

In the mean time the contumelies, contempt, and opprobrious

abuſes the members of Mr. Feake's, Mr. Rogers', Mr. Raworth's, and of ſome other Churches, met with below in the yard, during the foreſaid diſcourſe with O. Cromwel.

Mr. Ro. were kept below, and encompaſſed about with divers of the deboiſt ſoldiers, who when they heard us declare againſt thoſe barbarous actions which the Guard ſo cruelly acted with their ſwords againſt our naked brethren and friends, thoſe aforeſaid ſoldiers began to queſtion the occaſion of our being there, which when we had told them they began to ſet up their voices, many of them hooting and hiſſing at us, as if we had not been Chriſtians or creatures of the like make with themſelves, telling us we had often riſen, and they had allayed us, and they made no queſtion but they ſhould alſo allay us at this time, if we intended to riſe. To whom we anſwered that there was no ſuch thing in our eye now as to avenge ourſelves by or with external weapons, but ſaid, we have here Swords (ſhowing our Bibles) which we believe will in God's appointed time, being guided and accompanied by his Spirit, deſtroy and cut in pieces your Swords, which now you draw againſt us and it.

Afterwards we further obſerved that whilſt we were waiting below in the open yard for the return of our friend and friends, there being of us, as near as we can remember, betwixt forty and fifty perſons, men and women, that we could find no place in the aforeſaid yard where we might have any quiet, or be free from the uncivil reproaches, ſcoffing, jeers, blaſphemous nicknames, and what not, which ſome of the aforeſaid Foot-guard threw upon us with great contempt and ſcorn, telling us Bridewell and ſuch like places were fitter for us than to be there.

So that we believe the Lord hath a little remnant in the Army alſo, whoſe ſouls do ſecretly mourn for theſe abominations, and it is obſervable that

But in the midſt of their uncivil, unchriſtianlike, and very lewd language to us, we cannot but remember that ſpirit of remorſe and pity which ſeemed to be in ſome of their Officers, to ſee us ſo abuſed, infomuch as ſome of the Officers told us they were ſorry to ſee ſuch things, namely, the uncivil carriage of ſome of their ſoldiers; yet, ſaid they, we cannot expect better where it is not.

Thus for the ſpace of divers hours we were hurried up

and down, not being fuffered to be in quiet in any one place without the company of divers of thofe unruly fellows, whom we fhould have been content to let hear our difcourfe would they have fuffered us to ftand ftill or in quiet. But they fo uncivilly and moft ungodlily fhew their obfcene and filthy fpeeches and actions . . . . ufing fuch words as we are afhamed to utter or exprefs, befides manifold more provocations, revilings, and threatenings, and finful actions, wherein they feemed to take great delight.

But after *Mr. Rogers* and the Brethren that were with him came down into the yard many friends gathered about him. Whiles *Mr. R.* being remanded again to prifon, was going to take water with his keeper, he heard *Major-General Harrifon, Colonel Rich, Mr. Carew, Quartermafter-General Courtney, Mr. Ireton, Mr. Squib,* with many others, were there in the yard, fo that *Mr. Ro.* went to them, and after joyful falutations, he told them he was going to prifon again, and that there were articles put in by wicked men out of the prifon againft him, which he excepted againft as illegal, and as given in by plotters, and men given to drinking, fwearing, and fuch like fins, and fome others which were read againft him from Thomas Apoftle's. But as he was telling this he was interrupted by one that cried out, ' That is falfe! it is falfe!' Upon which he was filent to look upon the man that fo faid, and it was *Mr. Kiffin*, who had crowded among us to liften for tales to carry to his Mafter, who then faid, ' They were not articles put in by drunkards ; that is untrue, &c. but by honeft, godly men, that heard you at Thomas Apoftle's.' To which *Mr. Rogers* replied that the articles were of two forts—thofe read were from Thomas Apoftle's, but thofe unread (which he excepted againft) were from Lambeth, given in by fuch lewd men, and he faw them upon the table, and that his *Lord Protector* befides faid they had informations from the prifon, and moreover read one of them, viz. that of the

the Lord hath by degrees pulled the choiceft of them out of this Apoftate Army, that they might not partake of their plagues, as M. G. Harrifon, Col. Rich, Col. Okey, Col. Alured, Adj.-Gen. Allen, M. G. Overton, Maj. Wiggens, Dr. Day, and many others.

Great Dragon, and *Serjeant Dendy* fent them to *Mr. Thurloe*, as was proved ; fo that it was not falfe, but very true. At which *Mr. Kiffin* was fo filenced that he could not fay a word for himfelf, which fome of the gentlemen by feeing, reproved him for his rafhnefs, and fo *Mr. Ro.* and they parted, perceiving people to flock about them, and without doubt to have fomewhat to inform their Great Mafter againft *Mr. Ro.* or fome of the poor Saints, but that is the principle or practice of felf-feeking fycophants and Court parafites, to make themfelves, and not care how they murder others or what they inform againft them.

Whiles *Mr. R.* was carried away to prifon again, the

M.G.Harrifon,
Col. Rich,
Mr. Carew, *
Mr. Squib,
Mr. Courtney,
Mr. Ireton,
and many
others, con-
tinued up the
Teftimony and
the Demand to
O. P. the very
fame night.

forefaid Gentlemen, of much merit and fingular honour amongft the choiceft Saints, for their unfpotted fanctity and integrity to the betrayed Truth and Caufe of Chrift, went up to the Great Man, although before they could have any accefs the fword was drawn at them alfo, and fet at *Mr. Carey's* breaft, but after eight or ten of them had liberty to *O. P.* they brought him the fame kind of meffage from Jehovah that was before delivered him by the Twelve, making a

---

* Mr. John Carew was the fecond fon of Sir Richard Carew of Antony. His elder brother, Sir Alexander Carew, was beheaded in 1644, by fentence of a Parliamentary Court-Martial, for attempting to furrender Drake's Ifland, in Plymouth Sound, to the King. John Carew figned the death-warrant of King Charles I, for which he was executed in 1660. Mr. Squib was one of the members for Middlefex in the Barebones Parliament.

When Fairfax and Oliver Cromwell vifited Oxford, in 1649, an honorary degree of M.A. was conferred upon the chief officers of their ftaff, and amongft others upon Hugh Courtney. He is defcribed by Anthony Wood as "an officer of note," and ferved afterwards as Quartermafter-General in Ireland. He fat for North Wales in the Barebones Parliament, while a member alfo of the Council of State.

Mr. Ireton was brother to Henry Ireton, the Lord Deputy of Ireland, was member for London in the Barebones Parliament, a member of the Council of State, and Lord Mayor of London in 1659.

Demand of the Lord's prifoners, and bearing their Teftimony to his face againft him and his Government.

In the mean time *Mr. Kiffin* below had got a company
together in *Mr. Rogers'* abfence, railing upon him, and
faying he was a wicked man, and had told what was
not true of the articles, and fpake againft his Lord. But
Mr. G. a precious, godly Chriftian, and a member of
the church at D. then fpake aloud to *Mr. Kiffin,* as *Mr.
Kiffin* did before to *Mr. Rogers,* faying, ' That's falfe, for
I can,' fays he, ' no more be filent for *Mr. Rogers* than you
can be for your *Lord Protector.* What *Mr. Rogers* fpake
was truth, as he made it appear to your face,' and then he
told him how. So that poor *Mr. K.* was filenced again
the fecond time, and could not go on till a more private
and clandeftine meeting among his own kind of timefervers and felf-feekers, where he might tell his untruths
againft *Mr. R., Major-General Harrifon,* and others without
control (as we hear he, with fome that belong unto
him, have done at large), and have them taken upon
the truft and credit of his word at a venture. It is but
reafon and gratitude to his Great Mafter to poffefs all he
can againft the poor perfecuted Saints in the behalf of him
to whom he is fo highly obliged, above any one man almoft
in England, for his large favours and beneficial patentees.
But ere long the Merchants who were made rich (by compliance with Babylon) fhall weep and wail, and fay ' Alas!
alas!' (Rev. xviii. 15, 16).*

It is to be obferved, that very day the fword was drawn Somewhat
obfervable.
twice at the Witneffes and Woman's feed. The Providence
is alfo admirable; at that very juncture, when *Mr. R.*
and the Brethren were before him to maintain the Tefti-

---

* For an account of Kiffin's fubfequent profperity and misfortunes, fee
" Macaulay's Hiftory of England," ii. 488 (Ed. 1858).

mony and Demand made by the Twelve, that on that very day (many affemblies of the Saints in feveral places being hard at the Throne) the Lord fhould call out one (unknown to any of us) whole meeting of the praying number, being about thirty-four men, to go to Whitehall and bear their Witnefs alfo.

The concurrence of the Teftimony and the Demand is no lefs confiderable (feeing one had not the knowledge of the other's Meffage) that *Major-General Harrifon, Mr. Carew*, and the reft fhould fecond the aforefaid Twelve by a mere hand and call of God, which they were obedient unto, which is very exemplary and encouraging to all the Saints and Churches in England, who are faithful to the caufe of Chrift, feeing fo leading and calling a Providence.

The Teftimony up at a high pitch.

The Demand and the Teftimony is of a fudden gotten to a high pitch, which doth mightily raife up the expectations of the believing Remnant.

It is not meet for us to publifh the matter of their Teftimony, being of the fame nature with this Narrative; neither can we do it fo accurately and faithfully as we hope fome others will. The prefent work of the day—to gag the mifreports thereupon, for the quickening and ftrengthening them that are to follow us, calling for the publication thereof without delay, wherever it lies, and the rather for that thofe choice fervants of the Lord Jefus, *Major-General*

M.G.Harrifon, Mr. Carew, and Mr. Courtney fent away, with a troop of horfe, to prifon, we know not whither, the 22nd day of the 12th month [February].

Harrifon, Colonel Rich, Mr. Carew, and *Colonel Courtney*, are fo cruelly ufed for their Teftimony and the Truth's fake, having no fact but their faith to charge them with, and hurried away to prifon with a troop of horfe, we know not whither. So that the man muft needs be wilfully blind indeed now, that will not fee and fay, The Saints are under perfecution.

A word of caution.

Therefore let not the good people of the nation be fo fhamefully abufed and deceived as they have been with lying pamphlets and informers, whiles the Truth cannot, muſt not, dare not be printed, for fear of offending the men in Power and ſuffering a priſon or worſe. Of all, beware of that Abominable Oracle the late Ironmonger, but now Pariſh Preacher, *Walker* (his Weekly Proceedings), whoſe forehead hath for many years been plated and brazened in the trade and art of lying, making it his calling and his living (except the Triers help him more eaſily to the pariſh tithes). This drives the poor man to ſo much pitiful ſcraping among the Court clerks for a few lies to ſell every week at an eaſy rate, that he and his family may live comfortably upon the lying, ſlandering, and traducing the Lord's peculiar ones, who are as the apple of his eyes. How lamentably he hath abuſed *Mr. Feake, Mr. Rogers, Major-General Overton,* and many others, is well known, and one day he muſt anſwer before the juſt Judge of all hearts with a wan countenance and woful conſcience, however he thinks to palliate it at preſent with a ' So 'twas told me.' But, as *Solomon* ſays (Prov. xvii. 4), ' A liar giveth ear to a naughty tongue,' and the curſe is threatened not only to them that make but them that receive and report lies (Rev. xxi). Therefore (Exod. xxiii. 1), ' Put not thy hand to an unrighteous witneſs.'

A man ſo baſe and ſcandalous as makes him horrible, and his name to ſtink among the Churches as very unfit matter to be a member of a Church, but rather fit to be excommunicated and exploded the Society of all the Saints for bringing ſo foul a reproach upon Religion, which he hath formerly pretended to, till he followed this Trade of Merchant for lies.

Theſe things are publiſhed in mere love to the Truth and deſpiſed Saints of God, for whoſe ſake we are contented to become a reproach in the world, and to ſuffer anything, by his grace, that man can inflict upon us, ſo our dear Lord Jeſus may but reign, his Truth triumph, and his Kingdom be exalted. Amen, Amen."

As will preſently appear, neither the " Meſſage to O. C. by the Twelve," nor the reaſonings of *Rogers,* nor the advocacy of *Harriſon, Carew,* and *Courtney* could induce *Cromwell* to releaſe his priſoner. In the mean time *Henry Walker* revenged himſelf on the Twelve for the abuſe laviſhed upon him in the " Narrative," by publiſhing the following account of them in his " Perfect Proceedings :"—

" There are twelve men about London, ſaid to be notorious

impoſtors, who pretend to be of a Society whereof *Mr. Rogers*, priſoner in Lambeth Houſe, is overſeer, but never a one of them are of the church at Weſtminſter, of which *Mr. Rogers* is a member, but no overſeer neither, but another miniſter of great worth and piety. Their names are *Hur Horton*, *Chriſtopher Crayle*," &c. " notable firebrands, concerning whom divers honeſt, godly men are ready to make it appear that abundance of filthy, baſe lies have been raiſed and ſpread about the city by them, ſuch as all good Chriſtians had need to take heed they be not poiſoned with, for it is thought they have ſome Jeſuit or Popiſh prieſt at the helm with them, and they are much of the ſame ſpirit that *John Spittlehouſe*, priſoner at Lambeth, is of, who was once an under-marſhall in the army, and then bloody enough, but ſince he was ſtripped of that, as cunning an impoſtor as the twelve. This is but a touch of them. I have many of their pranks ready by me to make known if need be, but I had rather ſee them turn honeſt men."

See page 179.

Perfeɛt Proceedings, March 27, 1655.

CHAPTER VII.

FTER his interview with *Cromwell*, *Rogers* was remanded to Lambeth Prifon, where he remained until *Serjeant Dendy* procured from the Council of State the following order for his removal to Windfor :—

"COUNCIL OF STATE.

Friday, 30 March, 1655.

His Highnefs prefent.

Lo. Prefi. Laurence, Lo. Lambert, Col. Montagu, Mr. Rous, E. of Mulgrave, Col. Fiennes, Col. Sydenham, Col. Jones, Lord Lifle, Sir Gilb. Pickering, Sir Chas. Wolfley, Mr. Strickland.

A letter from *Serjeant Dendy* to the *Lord Prefident* was this day read. Ordered by His Highnefs the *Lord Pro-tector* and the Council that *Mr. Rogers* be removed from Lambeth Houfe to Windfor Caftle, and that warrants be iffued to the *Serjeant at Arms* to convey him to Windfor Caftle, and to the *Governor* of Windfor Caftle to receive him in Cuftody."

"On the 30th of March, 1655," fays Wood, " *Oliver* and his Council ordered that the faid *Rogers* fhould be removed to Windfor Caftle. Whereupon the next day he was carried there, and his wife rode after him."

Rogers records the hiftory of what he fuffered as a prifoner at Windfor and elfewhere, in the book entitled " Jegar Sahadvtha," from which all the remaining part of this chapter is extracted. As ufual, the title-page of the book is characteriftic of the author; it is therefore reproduced here.

Fair Entry Book of the Council of State, in the Public Record Office.

Athenæ Oxon. ii. 595.

JEGAR SAHADVTHA:

AN OYLED PILLAR.

Set up for Posterity.

Againſt the preſent *Wickedneſſes*, Hypocriſies, Blaſphemies, Perſecutions, and Cruelties of this *Serpent power* (now up) in *England* (the Out-Street of the Beaſt.) Or, a *HEART APPEALE* to HEAVEN and EARTH, broken out of *Bonds* and *Baniſhment* at laſt, in a Relation of ſome part of the paſt and preſent Sufferings of *JOHN RO-GERS* in cloſe Priſon and continued Baniſhment, for the moſt bleſſed Cauſe and Teſtimony of *JESUS;* the ſound of the Seventh Trumpet and the Goſpel of the ſeven Thunders, or holy Oracles (called *rayling* by them in Power) ſealed up to the time of the End.

From Carisbrook Caſtle in the third Year of my Captivity, the Fifth-Priſon, and the third in Exile, having been hurried about from poſt to pillar,
Quia perdere nolo ſubſtantiam propter Accidentia.

Gen. 31. 36, 37. *What is my treſpaſſe? What is my ſin, that thou haſt ſo hotly perſued after me?——Set it here before my Bretheren and thy Bretheren, that they may judge betwixt us both!*

Lam. 4. 3. *The very Sea-monſter (or* תַנִּין *Tannin the old Serpent) drawn out the Breaſt, they ſuckle their young ones (or Protected ones from the root* גוּר *gur, he ſojourned with or dwelt under), the daughter of my people is a cruel one, as the Oſtritch in the Wilderneſſe.*

Lam. 3. 52, 53. 55. *Mine enemies have hunted, hunting me like a Sparrow without Cauſe (or grace of* חֵן *chen), they have cut off my dayes in the dungeon, and caſt a ſtone upon me: I called upon thy name (O Jehovah) out of the under dungeon.*

Non Vindictâ ſed Victoriâ.

" *The poor Prifoner, Pilgrim and Exile in Caines-br-Caftle from the top of Amana, the top of Shenir and Hermon, from the Lion's den, from the Mountains of the Leopards, to all his fellow-citizens in Sion and fellow-feparates out of Babylon, and to fuch as are not afhamed of our chain, efpecially in that Church Society whereof the Holy Ghoft hath made him an Overfeer.*

BECAUSE the cruelty of this Serpent in England (whom effeminate lufting Eve-like profeffors have fallen in and fallen off and fallen down with) from whofe face we fly till the time, times and a dividend (Rev. xii. 14), is hardly heard of, known, or believed abroad, his horns looking fo like a Lamb, but that ye may hear a little how he fpeaks and perfecutes like a Dragon, I have held it a duty for further difcovery of him and his fpirit, to publifh thus much further of his Nimrodian Tyranny and Trading in this kingdom fince the late Apoftafy. That which I have feen and felt of his fury at Lambeth, for fo many months, among monfters rather than men, fo greedy of my blood, I omit here, as being mentioned in my preface to ' Prifonborn,' but that men, if they will, may fee, what an unreafonable, beaft-like Monfter this is that rends, tears, and devours fo, I have added this hiftory of fome paffages fince Lambeth, which I have fuffered for the fake of my dear Mafter Jefus Chrift in this his Caufe.

Now I do declare it, as before the moft Righteous and Holy Judge of Heaven and Earth, fhould any one afk me why I have been, that is as fome fay, upon the civil account, fo long in prifon, hard bonds and banifhment, year after year (which long imprifonment the Martyrs accounted worfe than death) I muft acknowledge an abfolute ignorance in my own confcience before God, angels, and men, let fome Timefervers fay what they pleafe for themfelves, without this be it that I cannot in my confcience turn with the dog to the vomit, and in plain Englifh, lie, diffemble, forfwear, and play the traitor to Chrift, the hypocrite to God, and the knave with men as others have done. I will not deny but my infirmities have been very many, which I think I could weep over the feet of any that fhall reprove me for them, but what I have done worthy of imprifonment and banifhment, (them excepted) I know not, this I can fay from my foul, that I think as I preached, fo I fought nothing but Chrift and his Kingdom. Canutus, King of England, in thofe thick times of popery, did confefs to all his lords about him no mortal worthy of the name of king, fave He to whofe beck, heaven, earth, and fea are obedient (Hen. of Hunt.), and fhall we in thefe days after fuch folemn engagements for a Theocracy, as I have proved, admit of any other King, Lord Protector, or Lawgiver, to ravifh us with their lufts? God forbid!

Wherefore, for Chrift's fake, ftand faft, unmoveable, and abounding in the work of the Lord, and I do profefs, for my part, I will abide by it, for as one of the Martyrs often ufed Vefpafian's faying, 'Imperatorem decet ftantem mori,' it becomes us, that are Kings and Priefts to God, (Rev. v. 10), to die ftanding, not ftooping to the luft of any man, efpecially now the day of Chrift is come. Therefore let us all fall in, and on, and ftand to it, with the Lamb and the twenty-four elders, or the twenty-four orders of the Levites about the throne in this Caufe, by which tribe of Levi are indeed to be underftood the Generation Saints, the firft-born, who like the Levites (before under a curfe, Gen. xlix. 7) obtained the bleffing for executing judgment (Exod. xxxii. 27, 28, 29) with the fword on their brethren and fpared not. So that fuch Generation Saints (the twenty-four) fhall join in one work and fong with the Lamb, and with all the living creatures about the throne, and with the Holy Angels, (Rev. iv. 9-11, v. 11) and altogether in one Hallelujah, Amen. As, Ifaiah lii. 7, 8, which he waits for, who is buried with the body of Jefus in this new Sepulchre, where the foldiers feek to keep down his refurrection, and the hope of your brother,

JOHN ROGERS."

" *A High Witnefs, or Heart Appeal, &c.*

I SHALL take up a few of my fubfecive hours, for the public good, in giving a fhort and fuccinct account of fome few more of thofe barbarous, brutifh acts of this Beaft now up in Great Britanny upon my body, fince my removal from Lambeth prifon to Windfor, and into this Ifle of Wight, where I am now, a poor pilgrim, prifoner and forfaken, banifhed man. As a preface to ' Prifonborn,' or my former treatife out of prifon, I gave a narrative of fome part of my Lambeth fufferings, and as an introduction to this ' Banifhborn' (I intended it) I fhall proceed fo far as I think it my duty.

They brought me into the wide jaw of Windfor Caftle the 31ft day of the firft month, 1655, delivering my body up to that den of Leopards, according to this order from their angry mafters, procured by *Serjeant Dendy*, whom the Dragon hath given a power unto for a time, and times, and a dividend, but he acts as a ferpent full fubtilely :—

' Thefe are to will and require you, to receive into your Cuftody from the hands of *Edward Dendy, Efquire*, Serjeant at Arms attending the Council, or his Deputy, the body of *Mr. John Rogers*, and him fafely to keep a prifoner in Windfor Caftle, until you fhall receive further order from the Council. Hereof you are not to fail, and for fo doing this fhall be your fufficient warrant. Given at Whitehall this 30th day of March, 1655. Signed in the name and by the order of the Council.

HENRY LAWRENCE, *Prefident.*

To the Governor of Windfor Caftle or his Deputy.'

Thus *Serjeant Dendy*, upon monftrous reports of my preaching out of the prifon grates, got this order by folicitation, and to fcrew up his power to the higheft peg of feverity, he fent ftrict orders to his under gaolers that neither man, woman, or child fhould come at me, nor any of my family ftir out, fo much as for food, money or any other neceffaries whatfoever, infomuch as my friends who came to vifit me were forced to ftand in the ftreet, with foldiers at their heels, to hear what we faid, whiles I fpake out at the iron bars unto them. And in the night, when no one of my friends or acquaintance might hear a word thereof, he fent a meffenger, very late, to bid me be ready by fix in the morning, for I muft be carried on the other fide the water, this being the firft notice I had of their fecret defign, nor would he tell me whither, to whom, or for what, nor (as then) fhow me any order for it, nor would he fuffer any of my friends to know of it, but to my great aftonifhment I heard fome calling under my windows almoft all night and by day break very much, whom we thought our enemies, till the morning difcovered them to be our friends, who by a fpecial providence of God were raifed out of their beds and had heard a rumour that I was to be carried away that morning by day break, and waited at the prifon gates where I was to come out, with many tears, and prayers, and fupplies of my wants, but the ruffians, ftruck, fhoved, and pufhed them away what they could, and hurried me from them, and fo carried me to Windfor Caftle.

That day word was given before to the Governor of the

Caftle, and by orders the foldiers were fet on both fides, with their arms and matches light, to receive the prifoner coming ; but when they faw me come in, fome of the Officers told me, they were ready to fink down in the place where they ftood, they expecting fome Cavalier, or lewd perfon rather, and not me, as they faid, to be fo dealt with, fome of them knowing me both in this nation, and in Ireland, and looking upon one another with amazement, faw it an apparent perfecution, as they faid upon good men for their confcience and the Caufe of Chrift. After a longer attendance I was put into a little room, which had one little window, and which did fo exceffively fmoke, that the wind made it worfe than a prifon, if in that cold feafon we would keep a fire, the very coals thereof being blown into the room about, but I ran to the door to eafe my eyes a little, and to take fome air, thinking to have walked a little in the yard, but it was denied me, the fentinels ftanding at my door to keep me in, yet afterwards, for very fhame, and perhaps pity, I had more liberty, and the fentinels were taken off, which continued till the fixth of the third month enfuing.

With a tolerable modefty and humanity, they admitted me the liberty of the prifon, and accefs to my brother *Feakes'* chamber for one month, without interruption, where we worfhipped the Lord together. But on the 29th day of the fecond month [April], being the Lord's day, in the abfence of the Governor, two of the officers, viz. *Capt. Wefton*, and one *Pepper*, an enfign, the latter (being lately fetched out from a common foldier, and lifted up with fo fudden an exceffive pride, conceit, and ambition, zealous of higher promotion and therefore ftriving to exceed and fo to fupplant his fuperior in cruelty to us), falling out with the other for admitting us to meet in the worfhip of our God upon the Lord's days, although privately in our prifon chamber, and to amend fo great a miftake and foul a crime,

they forthwith forced a Sentinel upon the door to hinder
me going up to my fellow-prifoner's chamber, which, when
I faw, I was defired by the Lord's people prefent to begin
there, and fo I drew out my Bible; at the door, (feveral of
our friends, with my brother *Feake* being by), we began
in an Hymn and prayer, proceeded on with the text, but
was often interrupted by the foldiers, and the hearers
driven away with violence, at laft the aforefaid officers
admitted we fhould go into the Chamber as before, and took
off the Sentinels, and fo we continued together with much
comfort, a few of us, in praying, finging, and exhorting
one another, until late at night, according to the primitive
practice of the perfecuted Saints. But the Devil did not
like this, and therefore againft the next Lord's day following he had made ready his rage, the day before which the
Governor* himfelf, being come home, and inftructed with
the matter by his *Enfign Pepper*, fent for us two prifoners
with a peremptory fword power of *coram nobis*, who after
we had looked up to the hills, from whence our help comes,
went readily and cheerfully. The Governor affaulted us
fiercely with fome other of his officers like fell beafts,
charging my fellow prifoner with a foul fault in his child
of three or four years old, that he fhould call *O. C.* fool,
at which my Brother *F.* faid that he would affirm more,
viz. that he is a tyrant, which made them high in their rage
againft him, with whom I thought I was bound to bear
my witnefs modeftly, but the Governor brake out into fuch
bitter rage, that he was mere anger, without ears, or reafon,
threatening to lay me forthwith into the hole, if I preached
againft his mafter. At which I rejoiced, and faid, yea do,

---

* Colonel Whichcot who fix years before had " roughly and pofitively"
refufed to allow Charles the 1ft to be buried according to the rites of the
book of Common Prayer (Clarendon, vi. 242) was ftill Governor of Windfor Caftle. Feake mentions him by name.—*Thurloe*, v. 757.

Sir, with all my heart, I am as ready to suffer it for my Master, as you are to do it for yours; and I tell you, Sir, I fear not the worst you men can do, and, with the Grace of my God, I will preach for my Christ, against *Cromwell*, or any other that oppose Christ, though I die for it; if I have but a peeping hole, or a hole to breathe out at, I shall preach, if you do not suffer us to do it in our prison lodges privately, for my commission is not from man, but God, and my authority is greater from above than thy power. In the interim, be it known to thee, that I fear neither thee, nor thy sword, in these matters of our God.

The next day (being the Lord's) they began to put their hell-begotten plot into practice, for our friends that came to visit us from London they kept upon their guard, and would not admit them to us, which when my con-captive heard, unknown to me, he went into the chapel, and with the people's leave, he began prayer in the pulpit, which they were attentive unto, I, hearing thereof, whilst I was pleading with the Governor in the yard for our Christian liberty upon the Lord's day, to meet together in our chambers, to pray and worship (who was called from me to fetch soldiers) I went into the chapel, where he was praying, without the least touch of the times, or government, I stood at the pulpit door, but by and bye came up a file or two of soldiers armed, and ready as if they would have discharged presently upon us, led up first by the Governor and then by a Serjeant, one *Baker*, all very imperiously, and with their hats on. This *Baker* till then seemed unsatisfied with such unchristian proceedings, but upon his rise to preferment of an Ensign he became very rigorous like the rest, he came up to the pulpit door where I stood between him and my fellow-prisoner still praying, and, laying hands on me to pull me down and him out, I spake softly to him saying, 'O will you, a great professor and one who seemed smit in conscience for such cruelty, exercise it, and where too? when

H H

he is praying! let him but pray out, tarry but a little.'
'What,' fays he, 'will you juftify him?' 'Oh and alas,'
faid I, 'and fhould I not? Is he not ferving of a good
Mafter? Do not fight againft Chrift fo, oh, do it not, let
him but conclude his prayer.' 'Pull him down,' faith
the Governor. I faid, 'Sir, let him but pray out a
quarter of an hour, but till the Minifter comes.' But then
faid the rude foldiers to *Baker*, 'Do you not hear the
Governor, pull him down,' and up came the foldiers like
raging beafts, the Governor ftanding under the pulpit to
fee the execution. Then the firft foldier of the file with
his mufket ftruck at my brother *Feake*, while he was yet
praying, but I ftanding received the blow, the Governor
ftill purfuing his command, fo that *Baker*, (being prejudiced
as hath been gathered by his words againft brother *Feake*
for his judgment againft dipping, which this *Baker* was fo
rigid unto) and the foldiers pulled, and tore me, who held
the pulpit door, with fuch bitternefs, eagernefs, and roughnefs, that they therewith and the blows ftruck at us, that
fell upon the pulpit door, brake it in pieces, and fo pulled
me down, and laid violent hands on him, and carried us
away with very great abufes, both in word and deed,
Pepper with one party of foldiers fent with me, who did
drag, hale, punch and pufh me one way to my prifon lodge,
and another party of foldiers carrying him, another way, to his
prifon lodge. Our friends, who feeing us fo brutifhly handled
offered to intercede, or fpeak for us, were beaten, threatened
and put quite out, and not fuffered to vifit either of us. After a
little breathing being thus haled in and kept clofe with
Sentinels fet at our doors, my brother *Feake* began to
preach out of the prifon window, which I heard at my
prifon door, the day being very calm, where the Sentinels
ftood to keep me in, and when they beat up the drums to
drown his voice at that end, I at my end was ftirred up
upon the fame fubject and text to proceed until the drums

ceafed, and then he began again. In the afternoon, at the door, on the fame fubject, I proceeded, (fome few of our friends that came from London having gotten into fome holes and corners in the yard, where they were hid, to hear), but in my prayer was a Serjeant with foldiers fent up to drive me in and ftop my mouth, a little fierce man, who fell to it with great fury. As I was yet in prayer holding up on a brick in the wall, defiring with tears the Lord to open their eyes and confciences, fome two or three of the poor foldiers were ftruck in their confciences, and though commanded could not fall on in that duty, but with tears defired the reft of their fellows to let me alone, faying they would to prifon firft. But the little fierce Green Dragon, the Serjeant with fome others, fell on the more barbaroufly, laid hold on my throat as if to have ftrangled me, tore off my cloak and rent it, and me, my arms, and clothes, ftill I praying, and looking up to my God whiles they were beating, bouncing, tearing and thumping me. And then I faid, ‘ Yea, ftrike on, ftrike on, thus did the foldiers deal with Chrift my Mafter, him they beat, haled, thumped, fpit on, and the difciple is not better than his Mafter, beat on, beat on, firs, O, bleffed blows !’ But thus they caft me in, and fhut the doors upon me, and fet other Sentinels upon me. So after a little breathing, being fo cruelly handled, I continued out at my prifon window, preaching, finging, praying, and praifing my moft dear Lord and Father in Chrift who hath made me, fo poor a finful wretch, to be numbered and accounted among them that fuffer for Jefus, and his Kingdom’s fake. In this clofe imprifonment, though nothing fo clofe as now it is, I was, though very ill and fore in my body, ftirred up to exercife every morning, as I ufe to do in my family, at the window of the prifon for the benefit of the poor Sentinels who ftood under in the yard, expounding the Scriptures, and praying, and upon the third day of the week, which was the eighth of the third month, 1655, my brother

Feake with two foldiers at his heels paffing by ftood ftill to hear me pray, but an Irifh Enfign, then captain of the guard (formerly I hear a Cavalier) commanded them to bring him away, and not let him ftand, but he faid, Let me alone a little, I am much refrefhed, pray hear, fays he, &c. But that Enfign fent up more foldiers, who preffed much upon him, but he faid he was about a good work, and wifhed them alfo to hear the prayers, but C. *W.* faid it was forbidden fruit at that time, and defired one to come to me, and fpeak to me to be fo civil as to forbear praying, but the party refufed fo to do. The Enfign called upon them to bring him away without delay and to take him by head and heels, but a poor Serjeant, an officer fent up for that purpofe, refufed fo to do, and faid he had rather go to prifon, yet entreated B. *F.* to come away, and when he found his arguments of no more force with him in that duty the Serjeant was returning, but in the way this wicked Enfign, whofe feet were fwift to fhed blood, faluted him as an enemy, for not tearing him away by head and fhoulders at firft, with fword and fcabbard ftruck blows in fuch ftrength that the iron thereof cut through his fkull, and brake his brain-pan. So fadly gafhed, mangled, and wounded, the blood fpinning out a great diftance from him, he with much ado reeled to a feat, where he affayed to break his fword, and throw away his fcabbard, with a witnefs againft them to wear it no more in fuch fervice. But in the mean time this enraged monfter with his naked fword laid about the reft who now ran away with B. *F.* as with a light burden, and fo, like the dog in the fmith's forge, they that would not ftir at the many ftrokes upon God's anvil, whiles we were at our work, could run now at the fight of a wand, yea, with wind in their wings, lift up their Ephah (Zech.v. 9). Work, poor wretches! Such miferable flaves are they all. According to the Arabic adage (which for want of charaĉters the prefs omits) 'Men' la a-rifo-tchaira,

&c,' they that cannot difcriminate are company for beafts. The Serjeant was conveyed into a houfe, and as it was by the Chirurgeon himfelf fuppofed, mortally wounded, and a dead man, for after he had taken out two or three pieces of his fkull, he concluded him doubtful of recovery, if not beyond it, it being fo contiguous and ambiguous, for at laft he found it but a hair's breadth between him and death, being hewed to the caruncles and concavity of the head, and fhould have utterly defpaired but that the cerebran fkin was marvelloufly kept from the cuts. Thus blood was fhed in their rage againft religion and the worfhip of God, who formerly and when it was their intereft have with blood contended for it. But the Avenger of blood will purfue thefe fons of *Belial,* and woe unto them that build their city in blood, for when their plague comes the name of their place fhall be called Kibroth-hattaavah, the graves of luft, for whiles the flefh is between their teeth the Lord fhall fmite them. In the interim confider—

Firft, that we lie as yet among the pots in the hot kiln, the iron furnace of Egypt between the very hearths, where the fire is kindled in the hotteft urn among the tile-pots. I mean in thofe ovens of men's wrath—garrifons of foldiers.

Secondly, we may fee ' e polypragmofyne,' the pragma-tical proclivity and activity of the Cavalierifh fpirit to pro-fecute and execute the rage of the Beaft upon us under the Sword Sovereignty.

Thirdly, it appears a conviction of confcience is a capi-tal crime with them, and merits cutting, flafhing, and fhed-ding of blood without mercy, calling the touch of confcience contempt, melancholy, and madnefs, they themfelves being feared, and having made fhipwreck thereof.

Fourthly, it is evident we are under as barbarous a fpirit of the Beaft as at this day exercifed in any part of the world, and as miferable a fervitude as among the Turks, for in all places they will ufe their prifoners civilly, and not

multiply afflictions upon them every day as thefe men do,
and ftudy to, much lefs fo monftroufly and murderoufly
hack and hew men for making confcience in their unreafonable commands. But to make us in a yet more Turk-like
flavery, and that what is now our caufe may be quickly
the cafe of others, and of all, if need be, behold the
Bafhaws and Begler-Beys fent down to fettle their Divans
and Militia into every county,* with the Timariots alfo, and
Zamiacks, or Deputy Bafhaws, under them, befides the
Janizzaries, Gemoglanies, and Spahies, or Guards, about
their Grand S. at Whitehall. And in the army there are
alfo their Achingies (Hinds of the Country) or new Militia
troops, too, to forage up and down for prey, and to
keep the Lord's Lambs from meeting and feeding together
on Chrift's commons. Is not this a new Turkey, then?
Let them palliate all as they will with good words, yet as
the proverb is, 'Soltanon bila adalin kanakrin bila maa.'
'Their Sultan without juftice fhall be found like a
brook without water,' and neither his foldiers nor multitudes, can fave him when the time of his judgment is come,
'Iflah ho-rai, &c.'

Fifthly, it is certain, too, thefe red *Efaus* muft
have red meat, I mean blood, to feed on, and I eafily
forefee with what greedinefs and defign they do provoke
poor fimple plain *Jacobs*, honeft hearts, by exaggerating and
accumulating, to fome rifing or (untimely) action of defence, for them to have a full blow at them, the belly-ful's
of the Saints' blood, which they fo much threaten and thirft
after, that their Shebna himfelf faid he, could freely have
his arms up to his elbows in their blood.

---

* About this time the counties of England were diftributed into diftricts and with their militia placed under the government of "Major-
Generals." The arbitrary conduct of thefe military governors and their
fubftitutes caufed great diffatisfaction.

Sixthly, it is our comfort that all they can do unto us is but to drive us to our God and Father. For a teftimony whereof, I muft refer to that beam of light which led me into a moft lucid and facile fupputation, proved and illuf-trated in my forefaid treatife, having found very excellent food from the roots of the Hebrew (Chaldy, Samaritan, Syrian), Arabic, (Perfian), and Æthiopic tongues, which I daily con-verfe with, and reading the Scriptures by, I find Manna wrapped up in the Dews of Heaven.

But to proceed. Upon the 16th day of the third month, 1655, were Commiffioners fent from Whitehall, in a colour of juftice to be done for our diverfified injuries, which by this had made a loud noife in the ears of men, fo as the Courtiers were put to this policy for a fhift, and in pretence of wrongs done unto us, and to enquire after the matter of faft, we found the integral of their ne-gotiation to be againft us, that all the information they could fqueeze out of any forts of perfons, foldiers or ene-mies, might be modelled and formed up together againft us, and fo prefented to their *Lord Protettor.* The Com-miffioners that fat upon us were *Mr. H.* Mr. Wood, Mr. Creffet, Mr. Carter, Mr. Woodard, Mr. B., Mr. Oxen-bridge,* and *Angelo.* The firft day they fat I was interrupted in the duty of expounding and praying in the morning, and from my fweat out of that exercife taken away by the Marfhall in the company of my brother *F.* to be cooled in

* Mr. Cornelius Holland originally ferved the King, then fided againft him, and fat in the High Court of Juftice which condemned him to death. He was M.P. for Wendover in the Long Parliament, and his name, as well as that of Col. Whichcot, the Governor of Windfor Caftle, appears on the lift of many Berkfhire committees. Mr. Woodard was Vicar of Bray, near Windfor; and Oxenbridge was a fellow of Eton, and Woodard's fon-in-law.—*Athen. Oxon.* ii. 537.

the other. When we came before them in the Governor's lodgings they told us their errand by the mouth of *Mr. Holland*. We defired to fee their Commiffion and to hear it read, which their clerk did ; and as on the one fide it fignified fome wrongs we had received of the foldiers, fo on the other fide (and which was the main body of the bufi- nefs) upon complaint againft *Mr. Chriftopher Feake* and *Mr. John Rogers*, that they ftirred up the foldiers to fedition and mutiny againft their officers and the Government, thofe whofe names were underwritten by the forefaid Commiffion were authorized to examine and make report to him. Given under his feal manual, and in the head of it *O. P.* When we heard it, the defign was obvious unto us. Under the head of hearing a little of what we fhould fay, to hear all they could poffibly fcrape up, or that any could forge or find out againft us. Brother *Feake* firft fpake, and I feconded him. We both told them we were in the capacity of pri- foners, and that clofe, but if they had power to right us we required our due liberty, or at leaft to be in *ftatu quo* and to have the liberty of the Caftle as the Cavaliers and all prifoners but ourfelves had to breathe in ; but that denied, we demanded a copy of their Commiffion. We were bid to withdraw, and after a long debate called in again with this recufation—that we did not own the Government, and therefore they could not allow us a copy of their Commif- fion without we would own the Power that fent them. We told them that was not the point, nor was it now the matter in hand, yet we could affure them we fhould not own them as they were Commiffioners, for fo our lives would be in jeopardy and our liberties betrayed, for that what they were to do was as Juftices of the Quorum, to hear, exa- mine, prepare, and to give their prepared papers to their *Lord Protector*, whereby he may pretend we have had a trial, depofitions taken, and nothing refts to do but to hang or head us ; therefore we did not intend to be involved into fuch a fnare, nor to be thus treated with or tried in a hole. Anfwer was made us they had no fuch defign, but we told them they had not the intentions of their *Lord Protector* in their hands, however, and through our fimplicity, and it may be theirs too, he might make his game; but although as Commiffioners we would not meddle with them, yet as brethren or friends in an amicable way, we were ready to give them or any other an account of our faith, hopes, and fufferings. Anfwer was made us they were our friends and brethren too, but were fent for our good, and fat to hear what injuries we received. We told them, whether for our good or hurt, we excepted againft the matter, the form, the rule, and the end of their Commiffion, and could take no cognizance of them in the capacity of Commiffioners. For matter, I faid, for that fome men, as *Mr. Oxenbridge*, &c. were parties concerned; as to form, they were an illegal court, nor ought they to rake the prifons for informations againft poor prifoners; but to immure us fo long and barbaroufly, and now to ftir every ftinking puddle to find matter for it is not fair, but like the Tyrant that did firft hang the man and then hear his caufe, or the Conftable (as the *Protector* calls himfelf) that firft knocks the man down and then bids him ftand, &c. Befides, as they were incompetent judges, and no authentic court, fo the end for which they fat (let them fhape it as well as they can) was wicked and unchriftian, to rake up informations and declarations againft us in the matter of our faith and confciences. They told us they were to take report of matter of fact. We faw it incumbent to deal·plainly with them, and to tell them the utmoft our enemies had to impeach us was but for words in preaching and praying, or Chriftian conference with us. *Mr. Oxenbridge* anfwered that words were matter of fact. With that we knew their meaning, and *Mr. H.* faid he muft needs confefs the charge againft us was very high; yea, faid we, in your calendar or law

See p. 174

you make it Treafon to do fuch things as in your Commiffion feems charged upon us; but we valued not that, yet
infifted upon a copy of their Commiffion.

The next day thefe locomotive Commiffioners adjourned
to Frogmore, the Governor's houfe beyond the town, and
there fat to hear, receive, and examine all that would
come in with any accufation againft us, which we in clofe
prifon were kept in ignorance of.

The next day early *Mr. Br.* came to me (who had
preached the day before a little too reflecting upon us, but
being my worthy friend, I am tender of him and entirely
refpect him), he defired me to forbear my exercife, which
I did that morning, and we were haftened again before thefe
gentlemen, with a friend or two then with us. They
offered then to read the accufations and informations they
had taken up againft us if we would confent they fhould
report them to *O. P.* But we faid, as before, our minds
were the fame, and they were the fame, fo that as Commiffioners we would not fo much as hear them read to us or
reply a word to them, with which they were offended, and
we renewed our exception againft them, both grey and
black Miffionaries, the Minifters having no fuch rule from
Chrift left them to fit in Commiffion thus againft their brethren, nor had the other either law or confcience to commend them to this employment, and particularly in that
fome there prefent were conftituted members of the High
Court of Juftice for the punifhing them with death who
fhould declare *Charles Stuart* or *any other perfon* chief Magiftrate in the three nations, &c. and this they had folemnly
fworn to fo. I drew out the Act of Parliament to read it to
them, and offered reafons why we could not in confcience
take cognizance of them, but they were deaf and obtufe of
hearing; yea, two or three of them, viz. *Mr. Wood* and *Oxenbridge*, rent away from the reft in difcontent, and fo, after a little
difcourfe with fome of the other about the Fifth Kingdom,

they diffolved, and left us in our clofe prifons and cruel hands where they found us. They went home with a flea in their ears, it feems, but well fraught with informations againft us to their mafter, who hath doubtlefs laid them up with the reft for a timous and more terrible treatment, and whiles with *Joab* they fay brother with the one hand, they ftab us with the other hand under the fifth rib, and fhed out our bowels in the duft. But the Lord will raife the duft of Sion (Ps. 102), and in general we may note,—

Firft, that Apoftates are the worft and fubtileft fort of perfecutors, and of all people moft brutifhly bent on their own ways, &c.

Secondly, that more juftice is to be had from a downright heathen Government than from an apoftate intereft.

Thirdly, that the Juftice of God doth ever avenge with the fword upon an apoftate intereft (Lev. xxvi. 25), 'I will bring the fword upon you that fhall avenge the quarrel of my covenant.' So Exodus xxxii. 27. Now this Apoftafy is that which immediately precedes the rife of the Holy Camp or Sword in this our ftreet firft (Rev. xi. 3, Dan. vii. 22, 25, 27) at the end of the forty-two months.

This is the male child that Sion's travail will bring forth now immediately, and begin to move us ; yea, the found of the feven trumpets gives the alarm, and the third woe is now at hand. Only this caution love as your lives, as not to ftay behind at the Call, fo not to ftir untimely, left you fall before your enemies, like them (Numbers xiv. 40, 42, 44), and they be heightened againft you. But be firft united in the inner court and the outer. Yea, thefe called Fifth-Monarchy-Men and Commonwealth-Men muft unite too* upon the principle of Righteoufnefs to all men, which

---

* " That party of men called ' Levellers,' who call themfelves ' Commonwealth's-men.' "—O. Cromwell's fpeech, Jan. 22, 1655, in *Carlyle,*

may eafily be obtained, and then, March, for the figns are upon us, and the trumpets found, Horfe, horfe, and away! Fourthly. . . . . And note from hence, 1. . . 2. . . 3. . . 4. . . . 5. . . . 6. What eminent teftimony hath been borne from Heaven againft thefe practices of theirs. For at Lambeth the great accufer *Abdy** was ftabbed that day he fhould have been rewarded by them for his good fervice, and another, one *Porter*,† fpitting upon my head when I was preaching with my head out at the grates, killed one of their own officers, for which he lies in the Gatehoufe, if he be not executed : and here at Windfor, *Mr. Wood*, one of our bittereft enemies amongft the Commiffioners, pleading much for the Governor and foldiers in the wrongs they did us, hath not enjoyed himfelf fince, as it is reported, but was prefently after fnatched away by a fudden hand of God, fo that ' in the way of Thy judgments, O Lord, have we waited for Thee.' And as Judges v. 31, ' So let all Thine enemies perifh, O Lord,

---

ii. 330. "There have been endeavours—as there were endeavours to make a reconciliation between Herod and Pilate that Chrift might be put to death, fo there have been endeavours of reconciliation between the Fifth-Monarchy-Men and the Commonwealth-Men, that there might be union in order to an end—no end can be fo bad as that of Herod's was— but in order to end in blood and confufion."—O. Cromwell's fpeech, 17th Sept. 1656, in *Carlyle*, ii. 436. See alfo *Thurloe*, vi. 185.

* " Fleet Street, London, Jan. 18.—There was one hanged this day at Fetter Lane end named James Rawlins, who not long fince, in a mad ranting humour, took a refolution to kill the firft he fhould meet; and fo meeting in the ftreet one Mr. George Abdy, he without any more ado ran him through. He upon the gibbet acknowledged the faft that he killed him wilfully, and profeffed hearty repentance."—*Merc. Pol.* No. 241.

† " March 28.—Young Porter, fon of Endymion Porter, who lately carried away a young lady formerly mentioned, was brought before his Highnefs, he having yefterday run a foldier through in Covent Garden, who is fince dead. He was committed for it to the Gatehoufe."—*Perfeft Proceedings*, No. 286.

but let them that love thee be as the fun when he goeth forth in his ftrength.' Amen and Amen.

My imprifonment at Windfor continued until the fecond day of the eighth month. Upon the firft day of the eighth month, in the evening, a Cornet of horfe came to Windfor with orders from Whitehall (or hell, rather, as from men, but indeed as to us from Heaven) to carry us away with him to Sandown fort; and fo he gave us time to prepare till the next morning, and we muft not difpute it. My difficulty lay in the managing of this fo fudden news to my poor wife, who was very weak and in childbed, ready to fink upon any fudden motion, in fo dangerous a condition as fhe was, being but four days (not five full) out in childbed, after fo hard and fore a labour as gave her up in the judgment of them about her for a dead woman, or at leaft the child, but that the God of prayers, yea, our prifon God, almoft beyond expectation faved both, but yet fo as the leaft trouble, grief, or fudden fright would probably have endangered her as much or more than before. This made me look up to Him in whom I centre, who giveth wifdom and upbraideth not. Weighing her weaknefs, for a fpace of time I was treating with her upon the promifes efpecially to the perfecuted and fuffering ones for Chrift, and fo was I firft infinuating, preparing, warming and affecting her heart with the precious truths and promifes before I could break the matter unto her, who notwithftanding received it with tears and troubles of heart, not knowing whether they would banifh me to Barbados, or fuch like place, or elfe barbaroufly murder me before we fee the faces of one another more, and not having time to provide for wife or children, or the poor Prifonborn babe, I was the next morning, notwithftanding I wanted neceffaries, and had not riding coat, boots, or things fit for fuch a journey, yet with mufketeers and officers they fetched me out of my chamber by violence, and rent

[Oct. 1655.]

me from my weak wife in childbed and weeping babes and children about me. But I blefs the Lord that I had firft fome fealing refrefhment to my inward man. For in my fleep, before I waked in the morning, the Lord met me, at which I faid, 'Jehovah is on my fide; I will not fear what flefh can do unto me,' with which I awaked, fell to prayer, and arofe preparing my family with prayers and exhortation to all that were about me; and conveying a few of my papers into the bottom of my ftockings at the foles of my feet, to preferve them from their hands and fearches, I was brought away to my brother *Feake.* So by force we were brought to horfeback, and with the troopers led like the flock of thy flaughter, O Lord (Zech. xi. 4, 5), the poor people on both fides the ftreets, ftanding weeping, lifting up their eyes, blefling, pitying, and praying for us as we paffed through, to fee us fo carried and hurried into banifhment for the name of Chrift. I blefs my God I much rejoiced, though I was fo harfhly rent from my deareft relations and worldly commodities, not having one foot of land, houfe, or eftate in the world to live upon, but only the providence of my God. And yet I fang, I fay, in this blefled fuffering for joy, like the bird of the day or the nightingale at the thorn. Yea, 'Dum ova in gremio funt.'

The firft night we reached Farnham. The next morning was very cold, bluftering, ftormy, and bitter; yet before I was fully ready they had taken horfe and I was called away and ftayed for, fo I hafted and we rode through great rain, ftorm, winds, and very fore weather to Alton, I think they call it, where we about noon being foaked quite through our clothes, and I and fome others bitterly ill, feverifh, and weary, had leave to refrefh a little with fire and provifions for ourfelves and horfes. So we all tarried there a fmall time hoping it would hold up, the weather yet continuing as bad as before, and the way which we had to go being worfe, which made the Cornet and his company of troopers well content we fhould tarry until the next morn, and myfelf, being very violently afflicted with the headache and in a high, burning, feverifh diftemper, did much defire it, as alfo did our friend, C. D. (now Epaphras our fellow-prifoner), he being likewife fomewhat troubled with the pain in head, fo I laid me down upon the bed, brother *Feake* and his wife being both well, through the goodnefs of God. Yet fome of them would be going, although we were fo ill, and the weather and the ways fo exceeding bad, but then I did beg in that bitter diftemper to ftay but one hour upon the bed, only until I had took a little flumber, hoping to be a little better by it, but I could not obtain it, notwith-ftanding fome did entreat it for me, yet to no purpofe, for away they went, took horfe and left me behind with fome troopers to follow in that violent, bad weather, which I was but ill provided againft, which when I faw I was forced to arife, muffle my face about with a fcarf, and ride after a great pace not only to overtake them, which I foon did, but to get to fome inn as foon as I could poffibly, that I might lie down and eafe my afflicted head, the Cornet ftraightways appointing the place we fhould go unto that night, which was a little village three or four miles fhort of Portfmouth, whither, I blefs the Lord that enabled me! though with pain I reached, fome of the troopers and the Cornet himfelf being with me, late at night; I called for a chamber, which the hoft brought me into, a little poor pitiful room, and made a fire. I laid my head a little on a bed for eafe, yet I entreated the man to make a good fire and provide a room for my brother *Feake* and his wife, who were near, the which he did, and fix, yea fix, were forced to lie in my room all that night, and fome four or five the next day and night, when we came to Portfmouth, fo ill were we accommodated in lodgings.

The next day, being the fifth of the 8th month, 1655, we were in the morning called away with the tide to tranf-

port out of our native country into exile, which was fome
trial to our flefh, not knowing their further defign therein ;
but whiles I was committing it to our Heavenly Father, I
was called away and the friends that were with us, fo we
went to the waterfide ; and upon the fea-fhore I put my
brother *F.* in mind of our Lord and Mafter's practice upon
the feafhore to the people, and of Paul's practice at fuch
times to preach ; whereupon he agreed, and began fpeaking
until the tide came very near us, then I effayed to exhort
the people, which were gathered about and did affectionately
hear, out of Acts xxviii. 20, but the Cornet forbad me and
interrupted me often with the tides rifing upon us and the
people's increafing, fo I was broken off abruptly in the
midft of the application, at which the people fhowed abundance of affection by tears abundantly, prayers, and earneft
cries to the Lord for us, fome laying hold on my hands,
fome on my garments ; and fo we parted, the people looking
after us upon the fhore a long time, and fo we were carried
away to Ryde, toffing but a little on the feas, and there
horfed away, and conveyed to Sandown fort. A mile before
we came at it, the Enfign who was the keeper being at
Brading, and knowing who we were, rode galloping, and
overtook us, but gave no refpect at all ; he kept on before us
prifoners very full and fell, as it feems, againft us, at a venture
fpeaking fuch bitter and enraged words, as made us wonder,
and the Gaol being as black as the Gaoler and as threatening
an earth-hole, without fhelter, tree, or houfe about it, upon
the fea and bogs, it looked already as if it were the end of
the world to us, infomuch as the very troopers were
troubled and wept, fome of them, to fee it (a little defcription of the place I gave in my Poft-fcript of the Prifonborn
Treatife, and fo I fhall forbear here), but when we came to it,
we were carried into the fort, or rather dungeon, lately
made out of the earth, fo bad as the worft prifoner, or
Cavalier, that ever they had they never caft into it, though

Fifth-Monarchy-Man.

Fifth-Monarchy-Man.

Mr. Bull speaks of one C. _Kern_ put there, nor was ever any prifoner, as the Enfign himfelf faid it often, put there before, and for many nights, fix nights together after our weary journey, they made us lie in our clothes, notwithftanding they had bedding locked up in a room, allowing us neither bed nor ftraw, thus turning us into the hole like beafts. This continued until the noife thereof about the ifland ftirred up fome honeft people in Newport to fend us beds, which was a great refrefhment to us, bleffed be the Lord.

For other things alfo we were forely put to it: the bread we could get for money, which was not eafy, was very bad, of bad favour and of worfe tafte, but good enough for poor prifoners; and the water we drank was of a filthy ditch (without we catched fome rain now and then), brackifh, black, and very unwholefome, if not venomous.

Now to obviate this report of our hard ufage, which brake abroad about the ears of the Court, they cunningly caufed an order to be printed (which was cried about London ftreets, and the report thereof fpread about the nation, to ftop the other report of their inhuman Tyranny and bad ufage of us), that we were removed to a private houfe for better accommodation. The contents are as followeth of the two orders:—

'_Friday, the 28th of September_, 1655.

At the Council at Whitehall.

Ordered—By His Highnefs the _Lord Protector_ and the Council, that _Mr. Feake_ and _Mr. Rogers_, now Prifoners in Windfor Caftle, be forthwith removed to Sandown Caftle, under the command of _Captain Bourman_,* in the Ifle of

---

* Captain Bourman was one of the three officers to whom Colonel

K K

Wight, there to be fecured in fafe Cuftody, till further orders, to which purpofe warrants are to be iffued, and it is referred to our *Com. Gen. Whalley* to take order for appointing a guard to convey them accordingly.'

Upon this order and other warrants, as if we were felons or fearful villains and mifcreants, we were carried into this Banifhment. But that faying of our Saviour hath fweetly refrefhed me (Luke xxii. 52), ' Be ye come out as againft a thief with fwords and ftaves ? When I was daily with you teaching, ye ftretched forth no hands againft me ; but this is your hour, and the power of darknefs.' The other order follows :—

' *At the Council at Whitehall, Tuefday, 9th of Oฮober,*
1655.

Whereas His Highnefs and the Council are informed that Sandown Caftle, in the Ifle of Wight, where *Mr. Feake* and *Mr. Rogers* are at prefent fecured, doth not afford them convenient accommodations, Ordered by His Highnefs and the Council, that the faid *Mr. Feake* and *Mr. Rogers* be removed from the faid Caftle to fuch part of the Weft of the Ifle of Wight as *Maj. Bourman* fhall judge meet for accommodation of their health and with refpeฮ to their fecurity and privacy.'

The pretence of this order they alfo printed and fpread about that the *Cornet Str.* who brought us hither, upon his return made report of the badnefs of the place and the want of fitting conveniences (as if they knew it not before), and thereupon they printed it (Oฮ. 12, 1655) that order was immediately fent for our removal to fome private

---

Hammond entrufted the cuftody of Charles I. in the Ifle of Wight.— *Rufhworth's State Papers*, viii. 1351.

houſe, where we might be lodged, and have air and things fitting for our health. Now this counter-report pretending love and pity almoſt quaſhed the former of their cruelty to us, but for all this high noiſe there was no ſuch matter really effected, but people were deluded and gulled, and lulled with a good opinion of theſe Perſecutors for this pretence of their charity to us, and then the enemy could take a better blow in Cruelty at us, and with leſs noiſe than before, as he did indeed at me, as fully as foully, in my removal to this monſtrous Theatre of Tyranny, where I now am, under the rage of wild Beaſts rather than rational creatures, looking when to be torn a-pieces, trampled under foot, yea murdered by them ſhould the Lord, whom I ſerve, ſuffer them to be let looſe. For if ever there were ſuch a people as *Philaſtrius* tells us of (Lib. de Hær.) called Caiani, from *Cain*, whom they honoured for his fratricide, ſaying he had the greateſt power, but his brother *Abel* the leaſt, and they would ſerve the greateſt power, ſure theſe I am now amongſt, of all men I ever ſaw, are ſuch, and their Caſtle may be called not Cariſbrook ſo much as Cains-brook, for they ſerve his power and principle. But for all their pretences, there we continued at that worſe than *Bonner's* Coal Houſe until the 31ſt day of the 8th month, and notwithſtanding the Lord viſited me like a Father with a ſore and fierce fever in the hole, I was, with that on my back, carried away through ſad ſtorms, ways, and weather, by order from the Court, with ſoldiers and the Enſign from this fort further into Baniſhment to Afton Houſe of Freſhwater Iſland, an Iſle within an Iſle, an exile within exile, &c. 'ubi lateres duplicantur,' and about this time did ſome of the ſiſters of the Church ſociety go to Whitehall with a Demand of me, refuſing to petition or ſend in a prayer, but after long tarrying and much difficulty, word was brought them from *O. C.* with a great aſſeveration, that orders were ſent down to open the Priſon

[Oct. 31, 1655.]

doors to me, and let me out, but if I would not, then to
accommodate me with all conveniences in the prifon.   But
' pectus Satanæ mendaciis fœcundiffimum eft,' there was
never any fuch matter that ever I heard of, but this policy
was invented to pack them away by thofe that have made
lies their refuge.   They afked why the brethren came not,
and why my wife came not, but I had indeed fent letters to
her to keep off, left parleying with the ferpent fhe fhould
be enfnared.   With me I carried about my papers in my
clothes and other ways hiding them at Afton Houfe in
holes and walls, and pots and pans, to preferve them from
the enemy.   In this prifon alfo, being near the fea, I had
Nazianzen's fight of fad fhipwrecks (as they have done
with their faith and confcience that banifh us) and of the
fea working (like the wicked enemies, who foam nothing
but filth, mire and dirt).   In this houfe was I guarded with
a fierce company of Herodians (foldiers), for as they, who
handled my Lord Chrift fo cruelly, would fancy *Herod* to
be the Meffias (Epiph. Hær. xx.), fo they who handle us
fo hardly (fome of the beft) fancy their *Lord Protector C.*
to be the man on whofe fhoulders the Government of
Chrift lies, according to Ifaiah ix. 6 (and blafphemous
fpeech to his Parliament Jan. 22, 1654, p. 31, 32).   But
thefe fat up day and night to watch me, and yet indeed it
was a much better prifon than the other for air and other
accommodations, for diet, lodging, &c.   Thither came my
poor wife with two children unto me.   Upon the Lord's
days, becaufe I preached, were four foldiers, or fore biting
leopards, fet afrefh upon my bones, but upon other days
but two, who were renewed upon me day by day, and followed me fo clofe with their Herodian rudenefs that fome
of them would force within my room at unfeemly feafons,
and that with very irrational brutifhnefs indeed.   Two or
three gentlemen and my dear friends from London who
came to fee me were there affaulted, and more foldiers of

the fierceſt ſort were fetched from Yarmouth, a mile or
two off, to ſeize upon them and their horſes, carrying them
priſoners before the Deputy Governor for no other reaſon
but for viſiting me. I ſhall paſs over the daily wrongs
the people had in whoſe houſe I was kept priſoner, the
ſoldiers put upon it by officers. Some poor people of the
iſland that creeped in to hear me preach on the Lord's day
were wonderfully menaced by the ſoldiers, yea their names
taken and conveyed to the Deputy Governor to be ordered or
committed, yea ſome of theſe brutiſh bears were ſent abroad,
before the poor creatures that came to hear the Word were
at the houſe, to force them away left they ſhould hear me
preach. A Lieutenant came to tell me if I would not
preach nor meddle with *L. P.* in my ſermons I ſhould
have liberty to take the air a mile or two on the downs, a
ſoldier or two attending me, to whom I ſaid that liberty
was my right, but to take it on ſuch terms I would loſe my
right firſt. The worſt Churls they could pick were appointed to watch and ward me day and night; but this
priſon being too commodious where I might ſee friends in
the yard if they came to ſee me, it being a good air
and in itſelf well accommodated, I was removed from
thence with a company of ſoldiers upon the fifth day [Dec. 5, 1655.]
of the tenth month to Cariſbrook Caſtle, or rather Cains-
brook Caſtle, where I now am. And indeed they did
ſhow a moſt unchriſtian inhumanity in the manner of removal of me, the days being ſo ſhort, the ways ſo bad, and
the weather ſo bitter, and, to boot, by reaſon of ſo long
and lamentable an impriſonment, my body ſo unuſed to it,
and yet with poor little horſes at 2 o'clock in the afternoon,
ſo late, they called me out and away, which when I boggled
at (it being ſo unreaſonable an hour for ſuch a journey in a
dark cold night over bleak downs, dangerous ways, ſcarce
going by one houſe till Cariſbrook, for my wife and two
children), the Leopards conſulted together, and one of the

officers concluded to pull me out by the ears, and fo by
force and fury to fetch me away; but when I faw I muft
go, knowing their bloody difpofitions, and that by no means
I could be permitted to tarry until the morning, I required
of the chief officer, the Serjeant, a copy of his warrant;
who fhowed me his, although the other officers, as they
ufed to do, faid to fome others his fword was his warrant,
pointing to it by his fide, which when I heard I faid, ' In
good time is it come to that : and thus every thief in the
Highway fays.' But in this Ifle it is the conftant and
common anfwer of the foldiers, when we afk by what law
or order, to fay, ' By this,' drawing their fword or laying
hand on the hilt. The order was to convey me hither.
Within one hour or little more the night was come upon
us, the ways were exceeding glib and rough with ice and
frofts, the winds high and fharp, which blew the fnow out
of the clouds full upon our faces, the night was very black,
difmal and dark, without moonfhine or ftarlight, until we
came at Carifbrook town, the road being unbeaten and
over high mountainy downs up and down, fo that we did
alight often in the dark, and footed it as far and faft as we
could. My wife being weak, rode, but once was very ill
with the unufual black night air. I alfo was at laft overcome, and I fell down twice in the way, but with hot
waters I was refrefhed a little, and forced to trudge in the
dark again, until, with a very dangerous difficulty, contemplating the hard travels of Saints and Martyrs, after
feveral hours in the night we were brought into a poor
houfe in Carifbrook, and there lying upon a bed I was
pretty well refrefhed, after an hour or two, and then a
Serjeant came to me in the deep of the night with a copy
of the order for the keeper of the Caftle to receive me
his prifoner under *Scobell's* hand, Clerk of the Council in
Whitehall, not fignifying for what caufe or crime, nor
hath any order fo done to this day, that ever I could fee,

but only their will and pleafure. The orders are as followeth :—

'In purfuance of an order of the Council of the 28th
of November laft, you are hereby authorized and required
fafely to convey *Mr. Rogers* from the houfe of *Mr. Urry*
at Afton, and fo to deliver him to the Commander in Chief
at Carifbrook Caftle, to be there fecured till further orders
from His Highnefs or the Council. Given under my hand
at Brook this 4th day of December, 1655.

To *Serjeant Nollard* thefe.

THOMAS BOREMAN.'

'*Wednefday, the 28th day of November, 1655.*

At the Council at Whitehall.

Ordered—That *Mr. Rogers*, now reftrained to a private houfe in the Ifle of Wight, be removed to Carifbrook
Caftle, and there fecured till further order. And that the
Deputy Governor of the Ifle of Wight do take care that
he be removed accordingly.

HENRY SCOBELL,

Clerk of the Council.' *

---

* The removal of Rogers from a private houfe to the ftrifter confine-
ment of Carifbrook Caftle was owing probably to the intelligence which
the Government had received of a projefted infurreftion. On the 13th
of November, 1655, Thurloe wrote to Henry Cromwell, "It is certain
that the Fifth-Monarchy-Men (fome of them, I mean) have defigns of
putting us into blood, but I truft this will be prevented."—*Thurloe*, iv.
191.

Here is no crime nor caufe, I thank the Lord; which minds me of that in Jer. l. 20, ' Their iniquity fhall be fought for, and there fhall be none.' Nor could their juggle of accommodation be now pretended, it being becaufe of the accommodation rather in Afton Houfe, and becaufe of the incredible cruelty and tyranny of this Caftle that I was brought hither.

But to proceed. In this pitifully diftempered eftate of body I was fent for from that poor houfe, the Commiffary and fome others being ready, to convey me with the fore-faid Sergeant, Corporal, and Soldiers into the Caftle, and for my encouragement they told us the moon was up; but perceiving their refolution and importunity, I defired liberty to prayer, after which we were carried up into the Caftle; as I came in at the firft gate I made a ftand, refigning my-felf, foul and body, into the hands of my moft dear God and Father through Jefus Chrift, not knowing that ever I fhould come out alive. I faid aloud to them all, ' In the name of the Lord do I enter here, and for the fake of Jefus,' which they all witneffed unto, as well enemies as others. I was guarded through the Mufketeers, ftanding on both fides with mufkets, pieces, and matches light. I was with my wife and two children put up into a very little, poor, fmoking, cold garret, upon the top of all which was a common foldiers' room ; and although it was a little trial to my wife, not having a chair to fit on, and fo little that we could not readily turn or fet about bufinefs in it, the bedftead which was borrowed taking up the moft part, and the fmoke of the chimney turning all into the rooms at fome times, fo as we could fcarce fee one another ; yet did I much rejoice to be fo pent up.

The next morning came my dear con-captives for this moft noble and excellent caufe of the King of Saints, to fee me, *Maj. Gen. Harrifon* and *Mr. Courtney*, who were a long time kept up in this clofe Gaol where now I was brought to

be their companion. Some part of our time which was fpent
together was in praying, inftructing, and praifing our God,
not omitting this His merciful overruling fweet Providence,
which has brought us togetlier into one Gaol as well as one
exile, for one and the fame Mafter, and in one and the
fame Caufe, Teftimony, and Truth, and this too by thofe
very men that not long before would not let me come near
this Caftle, left I fhould once have feen thefe fervants of
the Lord upon the walls. Upon the Lord's days I preached
in my room, as I ufed to do, and who of the foldiers would
had liberty to hear me for two or three days. Yea *Bull*
himfelf, the grand keeper hereof. But this liberty at firft
was to find out matter againft me for a colour of their pre-
intended future Tragedy, Tyranny and Intrenchment. I
was alfo foon after removed into better rooms, which now
Mr. Bull brags of, where I now am, but the bedding we
had in the garret was taken from us, and we forced to fome
want therein, till fome at Newport fent fome in unto us,
for which, with what we hire, we blefs the Lord, notwithftanding I told *Bull* I was well contented to lie on ftraw,
or elfe, if they would not allow me ftraw, on bare boards,
only I pitied my poor wife being not well. Some honeft
people of the country did defire me to minifter to them
fome light of the Kingdom of Chrift and of His fecond
Coming, fo that we kept every fifth day in the afternoon
for that purpofe, and poor people came in apace many
miles about to hear me. Yea fome Prefbyterians who came
out of novelty, or with no good will, when they once came
brought others with them the next day, fo that the noife
was great about the Ifland, and the Priefts raged, it is reported, left their offices fhould be left unto them defolate ;
and fome Officers came to hear with a purpofe to catch
matter of accufation againft me, but went away with ap-
proval. Yet the enemy could not reft thus, but finding
nothing which they could fix upon againft me, and the

people increafing, upon the twenty-feventh day of the tenth month *Bull* went forth of feafting, and left men of moft brutifh fpirit to manage his new plot and orders in his abfence, fetting Sentinels upon my door, and driving away the people who came to hear the Gofpel. Some poor people got in and ftood under my prifon windows, the Herodian foldiers not fuffering them to come into the room. But fome poor fouls having got in did occafion a defire to hear me preach in the yard, out of the window, or anywhere, but for this once, but the rude leopards began to rave and roar at that motion, faying they would not fuffer it, and were forely incenfed, uttering as we fay ' Decempedalia ' and ' fefquipedalia verba,' or ' Uper-olcha.' But I, *Maj. Gen.* and *Mr. C.* withdrew into my lodge, and after a little fpace I began in prayer, and fell a little to preaching out of the window to the poor people who defired it, and becaufe fome few of the foldiers were touched in confcience and could not exercife their com-manded cruelty, they took certain lewd fellows of the bafer fort, and fo fet upon us and the poor people hearing under the windows, who weeped, cried, and prayed that for this once they might hear, but the brutifh foldiers haled and furioufly drove them away with their fwords (the law we are now under), men and women, fhutting and fhoving them out at the gates, yea threatening to put the poor hearts into their hole or dungeon. Although I did fo ply the rough brutes with Scriptures, entreaties, tears (as the Lord did melt me then exceedingly, that I think I might fay with *Aug.* ' Ad pedes prociderem et flerem quantum poffem '), to let the poor fheep alone for this once, yea but a little—a little, feeing they came fo far and fo many miles, about 8 or 9 miles afoot, poor hearts, many of them, yet thefe Soldiers would not hear me, only one or two who heard were weary of this work of the Devil, and others frefh and crank to it recruited them. They had

turned away that day, before this, many great companies
round the Ifland, and *Mr. S.* a godly minifter, told me at
leaft five hundred had come from about the Ifland, could
they have had liberty to hear the noife of the Gofpel of
the Kingdom. But by and by came *Bull* in to make a
thorough execution of this perfecution. He took fome of
the Soldiers to tafk, threatening them, and if any were refolved to hear me he required them immediately to lay
down their arms and begone. He told them they were
weak and were foon deluded, and whatever I faid of Chrift
I meant no fuch thing, and the Caftle would be in danger
to hear fuch a one as I was, and he would not fuffer it.
After a while the *Maj. Gen.*, *Mr. C.* and I did look up
unto our Maker, and proceeded from fuch an accefs to
fome difcourfe with *Bull*, who was worrying of the poor
foldiers that were not yet in full compliance with him.
When we came near he bruftled up fiercely through a
forced compliment which he hath learned the art of. The
Maj. Gen. firft fpake unto him, by whom we demanded
his grounds to deal fo injurioufly with us and the poor
people. But he in a quandary what to fay (though his
tongue is too voluble and violent with lying and flandering), he hammered out at laft that he did it to prevent inconveniences, faying the people had itching ears, and he
confeffed he had heard me preach very good things, but he
believed I had a defign in time to infinuate into the people
againft the Government, to throw down his *Lord Protector*,
and fet up *Maj. Gen.* ; notwithftanding I preached Chrift,
yet that was the thing he perceived I drove on, and with
words to that effect he fell on a very beftial fury of rage
and railing upon the *Maj. Gen.*, but yet as very grofsly
flattering me to my face as abufing me behind my back.
But we told him we drove on no defign but the pure
defign of God, nor had I the leaft word or thought
ever (I blefs God) of throwing down one man to fet up

another, much lefs *Maj. Gen. H.*; but this was his own device.

And thus this pitiful, ignorant, but, as he carries it, a moft proud, Sultan-like, infulting *Orbilius*, and indeed a moft conceited Wretch of Wrath, he now foully falls upon the poor miferable enflaved people of this Ifland, falling into moft foul, irritating, unfavoury, provoking language, with his wonted impudence, and open faculty of lying, flandering, bearding and abufing, for which he is fo notorioufly famous in this Ifle, that we went for fhame from him, ' furdis auribus fed oculis intentis in Chriftum,' and fo left him to that fpirit that poffeffed him. Upon the Lord's day after fome men of the Ifland came into the Caftle to hear, but the Sentinels at the door drove them off again and turned them into their own chapel. Yet I preaching near the window and my voice heard through, fome poor people would fteal under the wall and in holes to hear, but were foon difcovered and driven away. Yea *Bull* himfelf, when he came out of the Caftle, did beftir himfelf, and lay about him, and becaufe fome of the foldiers would ftand behind the guard door, or make as if they walked about bufinefs in the yard to hear (as they did at Windfor often make as if they lay on the grafs and flept), he drives his foldiers into the guard and there keeps them in himfelf till I had done (as the *Bifhop of L.* ufed to tell *K. James* a tale in the fermon time, when any good man preached againft the Hierarchy or ceremonies of their Church, left the King fhould overhear them, and fo receive the truth preached), talking to them of Cocks and Bulls as we fay, left any of them fhould hear a word of the Sermon. In the middle of the week he came to me, and threatened to deal with me and remove me out of thefe rooms if I let my voice be fo loud as to be heard out at the windows more, to their difturbance as he faid, but I told him I fhould obey God and not man in this matter ; then he bid

the bed I had to lie on to be taken away, which was done,
at which I demanded of him ftraw to lie on; but the good
people, efpecially *Mr. B.* a well affected honeft man, at
whofe houfe the godly people meet at Newport, kept me
from lying on the boards.

Upon the 21ft or 22nd day of the 11th month the [January, 1656.]
Protector's *Bull* began to roar and gore again more fiercely
than formerly, without any caufe fhown why, kept us
up clofe prifoners with incredible cruelty, fuffering none,
man, woman or child to come near us, nor our victuals or
neceffaries to come to us, or any of our families to fetch it
in unto us, but when we would have fent out for provifions
the fervant was ftayed by the Captain of the Guard and told
none fhould go, which he had orders for, nor any provifions
come to us, but by their hands, which when we heard we perceived clearly their defign, now began, to deftroy us, ftarve
us, murder us, or maffacre us for to make us comply with
their lufts, and thus they laid fiege againft us to conquer us
to their fide, i.e. to play the Hypocrites, Apoftates, perjured
Wretches and Beafts with them; and now behold what a
Providence of our Father, (who taketh care for the fpar-
rows and worms and clotheth the lilies, feedeth the birds),
did minifter unto us in this great ftrait, there was fent in to
the *Major-General* by a Knight of their own party (not of
their own make nor of the poft), peradventure in pity, it
being the firft and laft of that kind, a little lamb, and to
my poor wife bound up in brown papers, and fo undif-
covered, a neck of veal from Newport, yet, after all this was
gone, and we in want as before, we prevailed with a little
girl of one of the foldiers for a piece of money to fetch us
a little bread, we being without; but upon her return they
took her and carried her into *Bull's* hall, and there
examined, frighted, roughly handled and threatened her,
and kept her from coming into the Caftle any more.

This day did a godly minifter, *Mr. S.*, of Newport, get

in to a lodge of *C. F.* with exceeding defire to fee us, and
a friend of the faid town had fent us a cold pie ; but the
honeft man which brought it was carried before *Bull* with
his pie, with whom he had for a long time pleaded, near an
hour, for liberty to come into my lodge and bring the pie ;
but at laft and with much difficulty he obtained leave for a
quarter of an hour with a Corporal, at his elbow, to peep into
our prifon upon us. Who, poor man, with tears and troubles
did deliver it ; and left this with us before the Corporal's
face, that thefe cruel perfecutions, fo far exceeding them, in
this matter, that we read of in the book of martyrs, had by
all he could perceive fome bloody defign againft us, but he
prayed us to be cheerful in the Lord, for they could but
kill the body.   I hearing of the Minifter of Chrift ftepped
to the lodge where he was, with the foldier at my heels, but
they put him out again at the gate prefently and would not
fo much fuffer us, fo much as at the gate, to fee one another,
though at a diftance and a foldier between ; fo I was returning in again to my own prifon full of comfort in my fpirit
at all this, and prefently I heard feveral at once, the Serjeant, Corporal, and Soldiers falling upon the honeft man
who had brought the pie, with very vile and blafphemous
language ; for that it feems he, as he was going out at the
gate, with tears did exhort them to take heed of what they
did, and to beware of perfecuting and offending of Chrift's little
ones, &c. But they brake out many at once, ' What ! What !
Preaching !   We will have no preaching, no fermonizing,
none of the Spirit, begone about your bufinefs.   What ! you
turn preacher too.   All preachers now !' with much more of
fuch ungracious, unfavoury ftuff.   At which I confefs my
heart ached, and by a mere Providence hearing God and
his Ordinances fo blafphemed and mocked at, I could not but
turn me, contrary to my intention and purpofe, to them, and
particularly fpake to one *King*, faying, ' O, Sirs, I am forry
to hear fuch words, from you indeed I did hope better

things than ſo to ſcoff and mock at preaching at the
Word and Spirit, indeed I have ſcarce heard the
like or worſe from the worſt Cavaliers, and will you
imitate them in this alſo?' At which they were incenſed
and turned upon me bruſtling like wild boars whoſe tuſks
were whetted in their own foam, and ſo fell bitterly upon
me and told me I was their priſoner and I did not know it,
meaning, I ſuppoſe, for that I durſt be ſo bold as to reprove
them. I told them I was the Lord's priſoner for all that,
for whoſe ſake I was willing to ſuffer bonds. But ſaid *K.*, the
Serjeant, 'You are not in priſon for the Lord.' 'For
what then?' ſaid I, (for I am ſure none of their Orders or
Mittimuſes that ever I could ſee yet did ever ſignify any
cauſe why they committed me, and have kept me now in
ſeveral priſons nearly two years already and in baniſhment.)
'If we are tranſgreſſors and you have matter againſt us, why
do ye not try us? O ſearch into your conſciences, for you
never treated the Cavaliers ſo brutiſhly here.' (Nay, they
would let the Cavaliers that were there liberty to go abroad
and ride about to Newport, and up and down to ale-houſes,
drinking, feaſting, gaming, and committing ſin every day
and partake with them too in it, yet we muſt gnaw the
bit and be kept without bread.) 'Is this righteous in the
ſight of God?' *Corporal Haddaways* anſwered me that we
were worſe than Cavaliers therefore. Then I perceived
that their teeth were on edge to be upon me, and one bade
me begone in; but being warm in my ſpirit 'Quo magis
illi furunt eo amplius procedo,' as Luther ſaid, I told them
I was doing no harm, and prayed them to conſult with the
word of God about their preſent condition; but then came
out an old man and bid me go in; I told him I was about
the Lord's work and did no harm, nor was I ever forbid to
ſtand in that place where I ſtood, and I did think it as good
ground to ſtand on as that in my priſon; but now they
began fierce upon me, many at once, like ſo many wide-

mouthed wolves, to fall on, as if they would not have left
the bones until the morrow, and out came *Bull*, who immediately, without hearing me, gave them either the fign or the
word to fall upon me, notwithftanding I cried out to him,
' What have I done, only rebuked fin and blafphemy.'
But he was far more barbarous than the Heathen chief
captain of the band (Acts xxi. 31, 32), who, as foon as he
came, they left beating of Paul, and he refcued him ; but this
worfe than Heathen was hot in his gall, and greedy,
' furdis auribus fed plenis faucibus,' he commanded and
encouraged them, and looked on and directed them with
his cane to do it ; and as foon as he came the cruel Soldiers,
armed as for a combat, fell thick upon me with their bent
fifts, beating and fome haling, as if they had intended my
death forthwith (Acts xxi. 31), ' colaphis et verberibus
pluentes et grandientes.' After a while two or three of
them, efpecially *S. King*, the Captain of the Guard, then cried
out, ' Let us carry him to the Dungeon, to the Dungeon, to
the Dungeon with him !' at which I was by fome hauled and
turned about that way ; and then I faid, as they were thrufting, pulling, and ftriking me, ' Yea, yea, with all my heart,
with all my heart, I rejoice more therein, for I fhall find my
dear Chrift therein, I am fure, I fhall find my God there as
well as in my chamber, do what you can.' And indeed I
was refrefhed thereat. Thus in effect I faid and my fpirit
leaped ; but when they faw my comfort and courage in it
when they cried out to the Dungeon, to the Dungeon
with me, they were daunted at that, and then hauled me
up a pair of ftairs, at the foot of which came fome
frefh foldiers to help the reft, who were weary with haling
and abufing me. One *Robert Jenkins* particularly with
his fifts ready bent, firft held them to my face to fhow me
them, (to whom I faid, ' Ah, I know your weapons') and
then he fell upon me amain ; thefe greedy brutes learning
no other way of preferment and favour with the grand

gaoler *Bull*, before whofe eyes he fhowed his valour in violence, but by fuch exploits, as we fay, that when they cannot fhoot men they will fhoot pigeons, or anything, *Bull*
with others crying and following, as Aɛts xxi. 36, John
xix. 15, 'Away with him, away with him.' 'Ah,' faid I,
' fo did the foldiers deal with my Lord Jefus, and the fervant is not greater than his Lord. But O, thou hypocrite,
doft thou profefs the Word, and read it, and yet, contrary
to the Word of God, Law, or Reafon, biddeft thy men to
abufe me thus without any caufe ? the Lord will judge thee
for thy hypocrify and contempt. Doth not the Word fay
to foldiers, " Do violence to no man ? " ' But this renewed
their rage and roughnefs, and then this *Serjeant King*, as if
he had been at cuffs for his life, fell on afrefh with his fifts,
doubled his blows about my head, neck, and fhoulders, fo
unreafonably, that fome of their creatures cried out to him,
' Hold your hands—ftay your hands—hold your hands ! '
But I faid, ' Ah, Lord my God, look thou down !—but do
you ftrike on, Sirs—ftrike, ftrike, ftrike ! for my Lord
Jefus Chrift takes thefe blows, for His fake, well at my
hands, though I am fure not at yours.' But as they had
often done before, they mocked at Jefus. ' Pifh ! ' fays the
Corporal Haddaways, ' what talk you of Chrift ? ' But
they, fome hauling, fome thumping, and fome beating, had
gotten me up a wrong pair of ftairs, and when they knew
that, they never ftayed to let me come down, nor offered
it, but fome at my back, thrufting, fome at each fide, and
S. King at my hands, pulled me out at length with the
Corporal, and all at once pulled me down, at one pluck, the
ftairs, as if they had rent mine arm from my fhoulders ; but
falling upon other foldiers, by the gracious Providence of
my moft dear Father I was preferved, my poor wife being
by, and the maid fcreeching and crying, and then they
hauled me, almoft fpent out of breath, the other pair of
ftairs, and at the door of the room wherein they with fuch

cruelty carried me, and where I now am, they renewed
their violence with fuch redoubled ftrength and atrocity,
that feveral of them laying hold on me, fome at my back,
fome on fhoulders, and fome at fides, caft me headlong
(who not knowing their defign could not prevent it) with
fuch an united force, fiercenefs, fury and wrath, as if they
meant no longer to dally, but dafh me in pieces, fo that
the leaft they could have conceived therein was to have
broken my bones, or put them out of joint, imitating thofe
favage fpirits filled with wrath which carried my moft
blefled Saviour to the brow of the hill (Luke iv. 28, 29),
that they might caft him down headlong. But the fame
God that delivered him, delivered alfo me, a poor wretch
not worthy to be named, much lefs honoured thus, and
that by a very marvellous appearance, for in the fall my
head and face were preferved from the battery of the
ground by lighting upon the arms and fhoulders of the
maid and one of my children, the blow of which threw
both them alfo to the ground, but my face was fo preferved
though my body bruifed with the fall, which fall I perceived rejoiced the bloody fpectators at their hearts, and if
otherwife it was, I think, that I was not quite killed with
the fall, as Tully fays, ' Quia totum telum in corpore non
recepiflet,' to whom I turned with thefe words paffing
through tears unto them, ' Well, Sirs, now you have done
thus, O that I could entreat you to fearch into the Scripture, and fee if you find any warrant there for this practice.
If you do, then the Lord give you the blefling for it ; but
if not, then the moft righteous God convince you of it, and
judge you for it.' And this was all I faid to them, knowing they were hardened, and at thefe few words and tears
they fell a fcoffing, and there left me, where I now am at
the writing of this, with very great confolation and joy
through believing, forafmuch as thefe ' verbera ' were
' ubera,' full dugs for my foul to fuck out of.

And methinks I now may fay I begin to be the
Minifter of Chrift, and the fervant of Chrift Jefus, and
companion with Chrift in the world. As *Ignatius*, when
he came to the wild beafts to be devoured, his bones
broken, his blood fucked, and his whole body crufhed with
them, ' Now,' fays he, ' now I begin to be a Chriftian.'
Your dainty, mincing profeffors, who are afraid of fufferings
at this day, fhall be fhut out in that day when the Bride-
groom comes, for ' Chriftianus eft Crucianus' and ' Lu-
cianus,' faith *Luther*.

Obj. But we live not under fuch Perfecutors as the
former Saints did, who were headed, hanged, flayed, beaten,
broken on racks, toffed on bulls' horns, rent and torn of
wild beafts, broiled on gridirons, ftarved, ftoned, &c.

Anfw. 1. No! If you did, I do wonder where we
fhould find a Chriftian then, or them that would come running to the tortures as thofe Martyrs, wearying the Tyrants
with their faith, courage, and conftancy to their teeth as they
did, when indeed ye are afraid of and faint at a little plundering, prifonment, banifhment, foft beatings, and eafy
deaths, for the Teftimony of our dear Jefus, who now
fuffers.

2. Yet we have fuch perfecutors of Chrift and his Caufe
at this day as would not fpare us were we as high, as refolute, and of as noble a fpirit for Chrift as the former martyrs, who had not learned the State policy of profeffors
(now-a-days) to fpare themfelves and comply a little, and
not to run themfelves into fufferings, for fo they call it,
but they rather ran to them, accounting it their glory, challenged and provoked in a manner their Tyrants. Now, it
is not fo much becaufe our prefent Nimrods and Oppreffors are better than the former tyrants, as becaufe we poor-
fpirited Chriftians and white-livered milkfops are worfer,
and indeed a fhame to the Saints and Martyrs of former
days, that we fuffer fo little for Chrift our Lord. Ah,

alas! we love, indulge, eafe, and pamper the flefh more than the former Saints ever did or durft.

3. To anfwer this objection with *Mr. Burroughs* out of Salvian, I muft fay to them, then, the lefs they have to fhow of paffive obedience the more they are to fhow of active, and the greater faithfulnefs, conftancy, and courage in the prefent trials, for as there was fuch a magnanimity and fpirit in the fuffering Saints as made the whole world wonder amazed, and think them mad, defperate, and befide themfelves, fo is there to be in the acting Saints at thefe days, who are to make it a fport, play, and pleafure to them to run upon cannon-mouths, fword-points, and on thoufands for one, in the fervice of Chrift. Therefore let us look to it, that we may make amends that way, and that the world may fay of us alfo, for the active part, fuch men were never heard of.

4. I had my fingular confolation, too, that the Lord hath made it my lot to fall into this fierce *Bull's* hands, of any, becaufe he hath not his fellow in this dominion that I can hear of, for all manner of brutifh and barbarous tyranny, unreafonable and infatiable cruelty, fo that *Bonner* I believe had not a more apt gaoler for his turn in thofe times, if *Cluny* or *Alexander** came near him; wherefore let not my words be thought the complaints of a fqueamifh fpirit, for I affure you I do heartily digeft all he can do againft me, and if it were faid of *Luther* that ' pafcitur conviciis,' I may fay it with no little foul-folace that ' pafcor conviciis et verberibus.'

5. For that it is fo teaching a difpenfation. O, it is good, it is good to be beaten into more good rather than be without it, for thefe blows do make my head ring with the mufic of Heaven. It is faid that *Domitian* his mother, when fhe was of child of him, dreamed that fhe had a wolf

---

* Cluny and Alexander, gaolers mentioned in ·· Foxe's Book of Martyrs."

in her, flaming with fire out of his mouth. Such a flame
came out of thy mouth, O fierce *Bull*, as shall be sure to
burn thee up, like *Sampson's* foxes, in the field which thou
thyself haft set on fire, for thy wickednefs burneth as fire.
  6. Nor is it fit we fhould lofe fuch fruit as this by our
finful filence, for, as *Solomon* fays (Eccles. iii. 7), ' There is
a time to fpeak and a time to be filent,' as Is. lxii. 6, 'Ye that
make mention of the Lord keep not filence.' To be filent in
fuch day of rebuke and blafphemy as this is, is a crying fin.
  But I fay I have the feal of the Lord's acceptance, and
Jehovah Shammah is my company in this clofe bonds and
imprifonment, to whom I fay (as Ps. lxix. 19), ' Thou haft
known my reproach, and my fhame, and my difhonour;
mine adverfaries are all before thee.'
  But to proceed. In this condition, thus beaten and
bruifed, I was laid down, and fear being that my bruifes
were moft inward, which as yet I had but little felt, means
was ufed to have liberty but to fend out for a little Parmy
Citterne * and fnow water to drink for an inward bruife,
which they refufed to fuffer, with more barbarous tyranny
than the very enemies in war fhow to wounded prifoners,
and nothing near to the compaffion of that gaoler (Acts
xvi.) who wafhed *Paul* and *Silas'* wounds, nor to the kindnefs of the barbarians to *Paul* at Melita—the greater will
be their judgment. When I began to be cold and ftiff I
began to feel their blows fore indeed ; but by a good providence of the Lord's, the *Major-General* had a precious
ointment and falve for fuch purpofes, as to outward bruifes,
which I ufed. This horrible tyranny of theirs took report
round the Ifland and into England our own land quickly,
and this began by the means of a poor Barber then in the

---

  * " And telling me the fovereign'ft thing on earth
  Was Parmaceti for an inward bruife."
      —*Shakfpeare : K. Henry IV.* Act i. Sc. 3.

Caſtle, who carried the ſaid news of this ſad Tragedy to
Newport, where the next day, being market, it abounded,
and ſo ſpread of a ſudden ; but this poor Barber was brought
before *Bull* for it, and hardly eſcaped ; yet the truth, which
is always beſt to ſtand to, ſet him free from them.   Then
their work was to lay their heads together to kill this report
by denying that ever they abuſed, beat, or bruiſed me, notwithſtanding ſome days after, when I ſtirred forth again, I
offered to ſhow them the marks they had given me, both
myſelf, wife, and maid being black and blue in divers places
divers days after, on the one and thirtieth day of the eleventh
month.   But after this *Bull* ſent word with an engagement to them we might ſend out for things, which was the
firſt time they offered ſo much to me ; but I could not compound with them in a Cauſe which was none of my own to
compound in.   And in theſe ſtraits we had another ſeaſon-
able experience from our Father, for with the compaſſion
which Chriſtians about the Iſland and Newport had to hear
of our ſufferings and want of proviſions, they ſent a man,
and we deſired him to come to the priſon-gates with ſome
proviſions, as bread and meat, &c. every ſeventh day, and a
woman once a week with butter for us to buy ; and although they were threatened for coming, yet they made
conſcience thereof, and continued it to the praiſe of our
dear God in this our extremity ; ſo that we had ſome proviſion brought to us for our money at laſt, notwithſtanding
the vexation of the enemies (for ſo they have declared they
are) thereat, ſearching, handling, toſſing, and tumbling our
proviſions in their hands up and down, yea, throwing the
very butter in the dirt after we have bought it, and exa-
mining the very bones of the meat for letters, as they pretended, or ſome other ſecret deſigns ; ſuch are the dreads
of the Lord upon them.   This hath already continued upon
us above twelve weeks, and how long it may we know not.
Some may think us ſomewhat obſtinate not to engage or

subscribe unto them, rather than be starved or so used as we are to this day, but indeed it is a comfortable obstinacy then, and for my Christ only, whose Cause I cannot with a good conscience betray upon a composition with his enemies. What is this obstinacy but the same with the primitive Saints who would not cast one grain into the fire, to save their lives! and shall we? God forbid! But as *Nic. Shellenden* said, he that kept off the ban-dogs at stave's-end, not as thinking to escape them, ' but that I would see,' says he, ' these foxes leap high above ground for my blood, if they have it.' And shall not I for my most dear Lord make these gaping Leopards get it then, 'Saliendo, saliendo,' by sweat and leaping for it too, that all men may see they are greedy of it, whiles they give out they desire it not? Yes, surely!

Notwithstanding all this, their cruelty was yet greater to me in that they knew I had no estate, nothing to live upon, nor would they suffer one to minister unto me or mine, nor one to come in, and such as have sent in have hitherto miscarried. I have heard of some letters with tokens sent to me, and at one time five or six together, but I never received more than one, with six shillings and two cheeses, to this day, being above this twelve weeks now, the tokens not only causing the letters to miscarry, whether through the hands of these soldiers or no I am not sure, but *Bull* himself keeping some of them from me; and then they report about we are bloody men, bloody men, laying, *Athaliah*-like therein, guilt upon the Lord's poor innocent ones, saying they intercepted letters which show it. The maid went to this upper gaoler for some of my letters after he had done with them, read, and showed them to many with much scoffing, but he said they were not fit for such a fellow as I, but bid her tell me when I was sober and out of my frantic fits I should have them. She saying, ' Why, Sir, you have never seen him distempered yet,' he threatened to kick her down stairs if she held not her tongue, calling her mifnames, and afterwards bade her pack up and begone forthwith that day, for that none fhould live with us but of his choofing, my wife all this while being very ill.

The carriers of this Ifland are ftrictly warned, we hear, not to bring or receive our letters for us, but fhall bring them all to him. A letter which the *Major-General's* man wrote to fend out, after it had paffed his approbation, was returned back again, writ upon in the fides, and after fo fent out, with a moft ungracious, unfavoury fpirit, mocking and flouting me thereon by name, faying I was in one of thofe fits which I was in when I was tied to my bed; by which he meant my condition in the way which the Lord took to my converfion, which he had read in my book of Church Difcipline, among the experiences of the works of grace therein recorded; but this fo profane a foul-mouthed Ifhmaelite, this fo irreligious a railing Rabfhakeh, may be fo miferable in foul and body for want of fuch experiences and deliverances that he one day may (and fhall if he make not hafte for 'pœnitentia fera raro eft vera') feek them with tears, and find no place for repentance; to which judgment I muft leave him.

But for all this, and an incomparable abundance more from day to day of our fufferings which I might write, we are accounted no fufferers, nor this any perfecution, by the prefent Apoftates and timefervers. Yea, and notwithftanding all this tyranny and cruelty to us, my wife and children and all the family kept clofe prifoners with fuch heavy and unreafonable provocations every day, two officers of the army did profefs to us that in their hearing *Bull* is much blamed at Whitehall for not being more ftrict and rigid unto us, and fuffering us fo much as he does, which is but the very air to breathe in, and he doth what he can to difcontinue us in that. Therefore, O Lord God of Righteoufnefs, do thou declare whether this be a perfecution or no.

It was deemed ridiculous as well as moſt rigorous in the hotteſt of the wars upon the worſt enemies to have im-poſed what they do daily upon us, and yet they have the face to juſtify it, as if it were nothing. Wherein we ob-ſerve : 1. The exceeding, horrible height of their impu-dence and hypocriſy ; and,

2. Their cruel ſubtilty, whilſt they are whipping and beating us, they bid us be quiet and patient, like the tyran-nical ſtep-dame, that knocks, beats, and makes the poor child cry, and then whips him without mercy for crying, and ſays he may thank himſelf ; they call for patience, and bid us be patient in our ſufferings, whiles they are laying on upon us till they make us cry out, and then they ſay it is our impatience ; ſuch an unreaſonable generation of men are our gaolers, perſecutors and murderers ; yea they pretend plots, and do this leſt there ſhould be any riſings, when in-deed by their inſupportable oppreſſions, perſecutions, and provocations, they do all they can to ſtir us up, whether we will or no, unto it, for the neceſſary preſervation of our lives, liberties, relations, religion, and conſciences, from their ſo monſtrous inhumanity and perſecution in hypocriſy.

3. That they put us into the worſt priſons and hardeſt perſecutions, yea bait us with the wickedeſt and worſt per-ſons they can find out, men of the moſt notorious debauched principles, practices, ſcandals, impudence and atheiſm, and all this too in pretence of love to us, as appears in their Orders for removal from Sandown Fort ; and ſo they ſaid in my laſt removal from Afton Houſe, it was for my better accommodation, but indeed it was for my more bitter affliction in fleſh and worſe uſage, except my dear com-panions' company.

4. We ſee by this what it is to be ruled by the ſword, which hath neither eyes nor ears but ' pro ratione voluntas.'

5. The impudent practice of the lying ſlanderous reports of us breaks out either immediately before an intended

mifchief, or as foon as they have done it. Sometimes
they report us mad and frantic, as perfecutors have done,
and fo doth *Bull* and his mafters make as if we wanted
fenfes, when we are fulleft of the Holy Ghoft, witneffing
for our dear Chrift againft their rotten intereft and hypocrify, and fometimes, as we find before of *Bull*, like *Morgan*
to *Philpot* (Fox, vol. iii. 572), they fall a raving, and blafpheming of God and his tabernacle, and abufing us as if we
were not fober. So faid *Morgan*, ʻ I ween it to be the
fpirit of the buttery which your fellows have had that have
been burned before you, who were drunk the night before
they went to be burned, and, I ween, went drunken to it.ʼ
ʻ But it appeareth,ʼ faith *Philpot*, ʻ you are better acquainted
with the fpirit of the buttery than with the Spirit of
God. Wherefore I muft now tell thee,ʼ faith he (and
fo fay I to thee, thou raging *Bull*, with the very fame
fpirit and authority of the great Judge of Heaven and
Earth), ʻ thou painted wall and hypocrite, in the name of
the living God whofe truth I have told thee, that God fhall
rain fire and brimftone upon fuch fcorners of his Word and
blafphemers of his people as thou art. Thy foolifh blafphemies have compelled the Spirit of God which is in me to
fay thus unto thee, O thou enemy of all righteoufnefs ; and
I tell thee, thou Hypocrite, I pafs not this for thy fire and
fagots or what thy bloody heart can do unto me, neither, I
thank God my Lord, ftand I in fear of the fame, my faith
in Chrift fhall overcome them ; but Hell fire is thy portion
and is prepared for thee, except thou fpeedily repent, yea
the hotteft of Hell for fuch Hypocrites as thou art.ʼ

At other times we are reported fools, and that is a very
pleafant reproach too. Go on, fcorn, deride and flout us,
as long as you lift, for this our foolifhnefs profits us, and fo
for all your other reproaches which are chiefeft riches
wherein we rejoice and make a jeft of them and of all they
can do unto us.

6. It appeareth a plain defign to ftarve us or reduce us to fuch extremity as might make us to ftoop, and fo to betray our confciences and our Chrift in this Caufe, as appeared by their impofing of conditions upon us and the fervants for the meat we muft eat, if they went out to fetch us in any : befides as to my own particular, I confefs their conditions were moft hard to me and my family in the paffive part, they (knowing I lived by Providence, having no means, land, houfe, or eftate to live upon) kept back not only all people, but all letters, from coming or miniftering unto me, all this upon me being only becaufe I would not ' perdere fubftantiam propter accidentia,' lofe my Chrift for a crown, nor confcience for coin, which doubtlefs I might have had enough in my own country if I had fought or accepted of a defire to *O. C.* for his grace to remove me near to my acquaintance and friends at London (which my poverty in the world might call for more than any others), who would not have fuffered me to want, which notwithftanding the Lord of his mercy prevented (by the help of my honoured Con-captivated Coexiles and other ways), and of his great Grace, gave unto me in this difpenfation left I fhould feek a carnal kingdom. I remember *Lot's* wife lies at the entry of fuch temptations.

But befides thefe there be fome other particular experiences as teaching me,

1. In that I am all along fo clearly and conftantly under the Beaft's rage as if I were, I think, more than others more particularly aimed at, for their goring, gufhing, horning, worrying and grievous perfecuting from one prifon to another, both in my native country and in exile, efpecially fince I have been hurried about in this ifland, and put to *Bulls* and *Boremans* who obey the orders of the Beaft ; but efpecially in the firft's very brutifh and indeed barbarous, unreafonable, pufhing fharp horns, fo that it is evident I am thus ufed by the Beaft's dominion and fpirit. I remember

that *Purchas* in his Pilgrim tells us of one that did write of the firſt Creation of the Chaos, in which lived monſtrous Creatures, bulls that were headed like men, and dogs with divers bodies, but I leave ſuch fancies to the Adamites, only I dare affirm in this Chaos and confuſion, which precedes the new Creation, men are very monſtrous in their principles and actions, and wild *Bulls* do bear the faces of men to flatter with in this ſerpent eſtate of the old world, whoſe hired men are like bullocks (Jer. xlvi. 21); but (as Jer. l. 27), 'Slay all their Bulls, let them go down to the ſlaughter. Woe unto them, for their day is come, the time of their viſitation.' 'O Lord, rebuke the Company of ſpearmen, the multitude of the Bulls, with the calves of the people, till every one ſubmit himſelf.'

2. In that my moſt gracious over-ruling Father hath made the enemy to impriſon and perſecute me, not only in the ſame way and ſpirit, but in the very ſame places where the Martyrs of old were impriſoned and perſecuted, which did refreſh me indeed, as at Lambeth, that old Butcher's ſhop and ſhambles of the Saints, where ſo many, even *Wickliffe* himſelf, and all along ſince, have ſuffered, their rings whereto they were chained remaining in the walls to this day, which did affect me much to ſee. And after that at Windſor, where eminent martyrs, *Cranmer*, *Ridley*, and *Latimer*, were put, in their way to Oxford, in bloody *Queen Mary's* days.

3. In that I am alſo inſtructed how to want as well as to abound, having paſſed through priſons, reproaches, tumults, beatings and buffetings often, throwings headlong, baniſhment and ſpitting upon, yea ſpoiling of my goods, which hath been much (one letter hath ſignified to me the loſs of an hundred pounds at one time), and in plunderings often, and in perils of life, ſickneſs, fevers, ſtorms, cold, ſnow, and tempeſts, without bed, without bread, in ſore travels and ſeveral other trials. Yet all this for my moſt dear

Chrift againft *Cromwell* and the whole earth, bleffed be Jehovah. Therefore I wait but for Whitehall or the Prætorium hall.

4. In that the enemy though he hath fought it greedily, yet to this day hath not found any juft caufe or colour for my imprifonment and exile, nor fo much as fignified why in their Orders of Commitment, which is my great comfort and advantage. As Paul faith in his fourth complaint (Acts xxv. 7, 8, xxiv. 12, 13).

5. . . . .
6. . . . .

7. In that the Lord hath in this fchool inftructed me to preach in tumults and uproars (2 Cor. vi. 4, 5, 6), and in all things to prove myfelf the minifter of my God.

But before I finifh we find a frefh affault of Satan upon us, in this clofe prifon, perpetrated to make our bonds the more heavy. Upon the 20th of the firft month, 1656, came *Captain Floyd* and *Major Strange* with an order from Whitehall to remove *Maj. Gen. Harrifon* from us to Highgate to his own houfe, a prifoner, under pretence of the very defperate danger of death his father, the Colonel, was in, as alfo his dear yoke fellow fo near the time of her travail ; but our precious Con-captive thus furprifed was in great fears of the ferpent's fnares in this order, and would not give them any refolve what to do until he had acquainted us therewith, affured us of his jealoufies left his further liberty, company, and outward comforts fhould be any entanglement unto him or let to his inward joys and prifon experiences, fo that he did earneftly defire us to fet it before the Throne for a refolution, which we agreed to, and at the end of that day came in the two again who were to take him into cuftody, who, after we had given him our apprehenfions, dealt very roundly and plainly with them that he could not thank them for their pretended love, nor did he think his father or wife would be worfe by his continuance in this prifon, but

[20th March, 1656.]

rather the better, for he was perfuaded they fhould do well, and for a gaol he had rather have this than any for the cruelty thereof, and of *Bull* (who made fo little confcience of what he faid or did, and who had indeed played the very Beaft with us), fo that for fuffering it was the beft prifon we could be in, nor would he make his houfe a prifon ; to this effect he fpake, and told them that he could not declare his readinefs to go with them, but if they would carry him away he could not help it. They faid they did defire to ferve him with all civility and refpect, and were loath to ufe any violence, but could not go without him, and they were now to take cuftody of him, and fo defired him to prepare himfelf the next day and to give directions which way he would go. But he told them that he would have nothing to do with it, but he was a fufferer ; nor would he direct, nor bear any of the charges, for he was a prifoner; and fo that night they parted, and we prayed, as we ufed to do together every night. The next morning *Bull* delivered him up to the other two, who took poffeffion of him ; we had much difcourfe, and indeed the Lord gave him a very noble fpirit, though broken in himfelf, to deal plainly both with *Bull* and them, expreffing his unwillingnefs to leave us behind, or rather his defire to partake and tarry with us ftill in fo fore bonds. But when we faw he muft be gone, we parted with no little heavinefs for a feafon, and I faid to C. *Fl.* ' Sir, tell your Mafters or any that afk after us, that it were a little more mercy, if they had it, to put us into any Dungeon in London, our own land, than to leave us here in the hands of fuch Blafphemers and Brutes fo fkilful to deftroy, but ftill we blefs the Lord, for our Father makes it fweet to us.' We got upon a wall and looked after them till they came near to Newport, and then my dear fellow-prifoner, *Mr. Courtney* (who is left here) and I kept the reft of the day in prayer, eafing our hearts and emptying our tears into the bofom of heaven, being a little troubled for our lofs of fo precious a help, fo choice a companion as he was to us.

After this, we being like men out of mind in this iron grave, their cruelty increafed yet more upon us to tire us out. And *Bull's* brutifh modefty was to have impofed upon the maid fervant's father that his daughter muft tell him all the tales that fhe could ; if fhe heard us at table, bed, or board, but fpeak a word of *O. C.* or any of their cruelty, that fhe muft betray her mafter and bring him word of it, and would have bound her father to it in a bond. To me particularly was their malice monftrous ; they put another foldier and his wife and four children into our other room, where *Bull* himfelf had put us, threw our wood and things out of doors, brake open the locks, and nailed up the door from us, with reproachful words to boot, and this by *Bull's* command, but we let them patiently, in our own matters, ufe any tyranny without taking notice.

Strict orders were given that no one dare to fhow familiarity unto us, and the woman with her four children put into our room was charged when fhe came in to beware of us, for if any of them were found to be familiar, that is refpectful or civil to any of us, they fhould be turned out of the Caftle without remedy, or if any fhould but liften or ftand to hear me at prayer or in duty to God, except it be fuch as were or are fent to liften under the windows and into holes for that purpofe, to catch or fetch fome matter to make a crime of, which above thefe two years they have been raking for, fo good is my God who blinds them that they fee not where my infirmities lie moft—but where the Almighty hath armed me with His buckler of truth, His back-piece of innocency and breaft-plate of righteoufnefs, there they fhoot their arrows to hurt me.

As for their rigidnefs continued unto us in clofe prifon, wherein they keep me and my wife and family, not fuffering one of us to ftir out, nor man, woman, nor child to

come at us, the like cruelty was never inflicted upon the
worft of men of late years in thefe nations, neither among
Papifts, Prelates, nor to the Cavaliers, Scots or Irifh, nor
in the worft of wars.

Upon the 14th of the 2nd month were two brethren,
fent from the Church at London to vifit us, and particularly to minifter to me, not fuffered to come in, the gaoler
Bull and his complices being hard at bowls, yet had time
to forbid it, and more too, fo that before they returned
home to London again, I with my con-captive *Mr. C.* got
out at a hole upon the Caftle wall on high, and they two
were let into the Ramparts without the walls, and we fpake
to one another on the walls with tears and joys at their
defire (being their teacher and overfeer), but prefently
orders came from the bowlers to the foldiers to fall upon
the two Meffengers, which they did pretty greedily, and fo
pulled, tore, and thumped them, who were ftanding by
with nothing but Bibles in their hands, out of the Ramparts into the highway; but becaufe they could not well
beat them out of the highways (which was as far off from
the Caftle Wall as I could well be heard with my loudeft
voice), and for that I think twenty were by this time
gathered to hear me (and almoft all poor women), they did
no more then but threaten them, and fend foldiers to over-
fee and look whether any were foldiers' wives, that either
their hufbands might correct them, for that is an allowed
practice with foldiers here to beat their wives, or elfe their
hufbands be turned out upon it.

Within thefe few days it was reported as if there would
be fome ftirs in England, at which they rage againft the
Independent and Anabaptift rogues as they call them, and
particularly threaten what they will do with us upon it,
Corporal Had. faying to his other foldiers that if he knew
but one of themfelves that were any ways familiar, meaning
civil in refpect, with *Courtney* or *Rogers*, he would run his

fword into his guts prefently with his own hands. Their
daily breathing feems to be after our blood, for to name no
more the laft fecond day *Serj. King* with fome others took
my little child in coats, examined him about us, and with
flatteries tempted the child to tell what we faid, did, and
eat, or anything that he could get out. This *S. King* is
fuch another ambitious, covetous, pragmatical youth as was
Pepper at Windfor. The title this *King* gives to me is
fagot-maker, and fo reports I hear that I was a fagot-
maker up and down. But indeed I may live to make
fagots by the King of Heaven's appointment to bind up
fuch ftubble as they are for the day of wrath, if they repent
not. He does alfo rage exceedingly that Quartermafter
Gen. and I have our diftinct rooms.

Thus are they every day infulting over us at their pleafure; if they do but fee us their hearts fo rife againft us
that (as Acts vii. 54, 57) they do even gnafh, fome of
them, as I have faid, with their teeth, and look as if they
were ready to run upon us with one accord, notwithftanding we do endeavour when they do fall foully upon us to
convince them with foft and found words, miniftering as we
are able to their wives (whom they keep poor enough)
either in money, clothes, or food, though they dare not be
to know it, and fo returning good for evil; and if any of
them be feen by another to fhow any kind of refpect to us,
to do anything for us, or ftir his hat kindly, he is as I faid
before under a public check, if not in danger to be turned
out.

Thefe are I confefs but trifles to what might be mentioned, and to what we fee and fuffer every day; yea to
mention but yefterday, becaufe it was the laft day of all,
for every day affords us new matter, and fo I conclude with
this tragical hiftory at prefent."

[They ill-treat his maid, and throw her out at the gate of the
Caftle]

—" where the poor creature is even now, like *Lazarus,* and hath been many hours lying with her lame limbs and bundle for admittance if it may be, but there fhe may lie yet many a day, they that go by many of them fcoffing and abufing her bitterly, knowing all my family is ill, wife and children, and not a fervant that they fuffer to live with us and help us in this need. I afked indeed *King* by what rule he did this, and that on the Lord's day, faying if he were a Chriftian the rule was (Luke iii.), ' Soldiers, do violence to none,' but he made a fcoff at what I faid and turned away in great fury, and then I faid, ' Well, the Lord will look down and fee all thefe things,' at which he turned and faid, ' Pifh ! the Lord ! What do you tell us, the Lord ! Who is the Lord ? You are not the Lord, are you ?' and fo went on raging and blafpheming, and the reft fcoffing for company, as full of fury as they could hold, who indeed have not the patience to hear the Lord's name fo much as mentioned unlefs at Ale-houfes and in fin, fo fadly profane are they ! and indeed how can they be other- wife ? When men with wicked and idle courfes have fpent all their means and cannot, or will not, work, they get into thefe garrifons, to drink and guzzle their pay out before their pay-day comes, and, for other mifdemeanours deferv- ing too to be cafhiered, can find no way to fecure their places but by their brutifh, premeditated and barbarous cruelty to us, wherein they merit moft that are monftrous. And thefe things I declare, as in the fight of the God of truth, to be true, having read over again and again what I have written, and do not know one line I have written too large, the Lord knows.

I had thought long ere this to have been at an end, and that this perfecution would have added or impofed a Quietus eft to my body by death, out of the continuance of their cruelty, but it pleafes the Father that I fhould yet live as one always

dying under their immanity, and now, fince that of the poor
maid's fufferings before mentioned, I am entreated by friends
to enlarge this fad hiftory a little further, but I had rather a
thoufand times to fet it before the Lord my God than once
to make mention of it to any below, yet by reafon of
friends' importunity, to whom I muft not be ungrateful,
I fhall give you a fhort view of this new link added to my
chain fince.

Since the maid's fuch monftrous ufage without any
caufe, and being caft out at the gate with her clothes rent
and torn, where, befides that, fhe lay on the ground lame,
like *Lazarus* at the gate, fix or feven hours the next day
for admittance, and at laft was let in again with no little
ftir and threatening, I had liberty to go into my dear Co-
exile's chamber, not knowing of any defign they had upon
me, which it feems they watched for, and had orders from
Bull, as they fay, to obferve when I did fo, being now refolved to take their rage from the lame creature (having
little credit of their cruelty to her), and to wreak it upon
me and my poor weak wife, which they did at prefent thus,
(but O Lord, let the remainder of their wrath praife thee !)
upon a fudden, after my fellow-prifoner had invited me
into his chamber, four or fix mufketeers, with fwords, guns,
and light matches were fet upon me there, and foon after
more followed them, they fet alfo foldiers upon my weak
wife and family, yea, into the very room raging, which
frighted her for the fuddennefs of it, fhe being as ignorant
as I of the meaning of this new piece of tyranny, and fo
keeping us afunder that we could not come at one another,
fee or hear, fo as to know of each other's condition or what
the matter was, which made it look like a bad bufinefs, as
bad as if forthwith they had intended to murder me at leaft ;
my wife's ficknefs fubjecting her withal to very frightful
fancies, fears, and apprehenfions, wondering what would
become of me, ftill afking after me, and what was become

of me, or what they had done with me ; and befides, to
make it a thorough piece monftrous matter to her, they fet
within her chamber the moft uncivil, drunken, raging
wretches, ftamping, threatening, grinding their teeth, calling jade, quean, carrion, with many fuch obfcene names,
bending their fifts, ftriking, tearing, thumping, railing, with
their ftaggering, if any offered to go in the room, not fuffering them to ftir for neceffaries within the room, offering
and drawing the naked fword upon them with affeverations
feveral times, without any provocation given them in word
or deed ; and foon after followed ten or twelve more, as
they inform me, and filled the room with fuch rude creatures and doings, without any regard at all to fex, ficknefs,
or condition.   As they were at this inhuman fport, perfecuting my wife and family, thofe armed foldiers with me
were not wanting with great violence and fury to execute
their orders, as they called it, for I, offering to go to the
door with defire to fee my wife, being fearful of fome mifchief to her, though I knew not of this cruel ufage of her
in her fo weak and fickly condition, was forcibly beaten
and punched in again, although I defired I might but ftand
at the window to fee her, with as many armed foldiers to
grind me as they would, but it could not be obtained,
which did augment our mutual fears and troubles for one
another.   But thus were they infulting over us, laughing at
us, and abufing of us here, whiles others of them were
rending, tearing, and ranfacking in my prifon chamber with
great violence and threats, pulling the very fheets off the
bed fo immodeftly as fome Turks would abhor, that the
maid afking if they were not afhamed, they even fhouted at
her again, calling her limping carrion, jade, quean, and what
they pleafed.   At all which and infinite other taunts, inci-
vilities, threats, and abufes, my poor wife was, I may fay,
frighted almoft unto death, as hath appeared ever fince, and
for fome time days and nights her continual cry was ' they

would kill her, they would be her death, they will make
an end of her, fhe fhall never recover it,' &c. Within this
time the Commiffary came to me and told me I muft be
put into a little hole or the dark chamber at the end of my
fellow-prifoner's chamber, they would bring my things
thither, but the bed I had allowed me to lie upon they
would take away ; and fo, it may be, fuppofing they had
fufficiently affected my wife and me for once (if I do not
wrong them with charity), they brought what pleafed them
into this cave, where I am now left to feed upon, Heb.
xi. 38, ' of whom the world was not worthy ; they wan-
dered in deferts, mountains, in DENS and CAVES of the
earth,' and v. 36, ' others had trials of cruel mockings and
fcourgings, yea, moreover, of BONDS and IMPRISON-
MENT,' this being the 8th or 9th removal, 5th or 6th
PRISON, and the 2nd or 3rd year, all which is true,
though it may feem ftrange. Into this little dark, cold,
fmoky, ftinking, and unwholefome HOLE they put me,
my wife and family guarded hither to me. My family,
which are five of us, caft into this one little room, as if like
beafts we fhould be altogether day and night, and in a room
too that would not hold two beds, for one will take up the
greateft part, indeed, too little a cave for one body, the
foldiers many of them deriding and making fport to fee this
ufage, though fome had a little reluctancy and pitied us.
Yea, for all my wife was fo very ill they took away our
bedding, which a friend had lent us, and carried it into the
Lieutenant's chamber, who had been a bufybody in this
tragedy, as it proves to be, and there kept it, fome faying
the boards were too good for us to lie upon, and what
were we that we muft have beds, we were prifoners, indeed they would have us to the dungeon, and we fhould
live in that, and that we fhould know we were prifoners,
and the like, although moderate men that have pleaded for
them yet confefs where they have put us in is the very

next degree to a dungeon, and all they can fay is, others
have lived there; but then they confider not how it was
accommodated, hung, kept warm, and fitted for others, and
that never any family did or could live in this hole, but
had other rooms to live in that were lightfome, more wholefome, and tolerable, and but that my dear fellow-prifoner's
man left a little garret for the maid and child to lie in on
his bed, we muft have lain one upon another like horfes in
a litter; nay that they will not allow us neither for our
money which they allow to beafts. Yea, they took away
even curtains and valance, not allowing us a curtain to keep
out the wind or cold, which are known to be very bitter in
this place. All which and more too I truft I can take thank-
fully and joyfully for my deareft Jefus' fake. Only I muft
confefs, the prefent condition, weaknefs, and illnefs of my
dear yoke-fellow doth cut deep, and would deeper had not
the Moft High cut a covenant in Jefus Chrift with me,
which ftandeth fure and well-ordered in all things. (Gen.
xv. 18; 2 Sam. xxiii. 5).

The ground of this act of tyranny lies, as the reft does,
in their arbitrary breafts to weary, tire, or provoke, con-
fume, fpend us out, break our very hearts' ftrings with fuch
lingering tyranny, and fo to kill us if they can that way,
who feem weary with letting us live fo long, and fure the
fpring of this continued frefh-fprouting cruelty cannot arife
altogether out of WHITE-HELL. Nor can I conjecture
other fubordinate caufe as to this unhandfome force upon us
from that room, but that then we fhould fee their horrible
wickednefs every day, drinking, fmoking, profaning the
fabbath and name of God at the alehoufe, beating and
abufing the Saints or fuch as came to vifit us, and if friends
came to vifit us that they would not let in, at a back window I could fee them, which was an offence, but in this
hole we know not when any come, nor will they let them

fo much as with foldiers come to fee us, but turn them away
weeping and unknown to us, as two men, friends that
came from London, they have done fo to already, I hear;
and now one, a Gentlewoman from London, at this time
we by a Providence hear is at the gate, that they will not
let come to us, fo that I think thefe may be the reafons,
befides the threats of *Serjeant King,* who lufted for this
cruelty, and threatened it long.

And here alfo have I done nothing that they fhould put
me into this Dungeon, and that it is a Dungeon, yea, not
only beyond *Jofeph's,* but far exceeding fome felon's in
England, I fhall a little defcribe it to you. It is fome three
fteps long and three fteps broad, not fo long as one of
the little garrets they put us into firft, when they brought
me into this Caftle with a promife of two rooms, two beds,
and better accommodation till they have gotten me in, but
now they gripe me and perform not a tittle of their promifes ; but 'tis no wonder from men of fuch principles that
they make no more bones of breaking an oath than a foldier does of cracking a loufe. Nor is it fo large as any of
the rooms we had at Windfor. Underneath it is a deep
low vault, from whence arifes into the room day and night
unwholefome vapours, winds, and filthy, damp mifts, very
dangerous, the boards being broken and rotten. The
chimney is a little low thing, cafting fmoke fo unreafonably in fuch a little clofe room that it is uncomfortable, and
better to be bitten with cold than fmothered with fmoke.
All the light that comes in is a little dark window, which
for many hundred years I fuppofe never faw the fun, unlefs
a little at nights upon the long days of fummer, fo that it
looks at noon in the room as if it were night. Before the
window is a great hill which keeps off light and air, fo that
the air that comes in to us is either out of the vault, a
deep, damp, hollow cave underneath us, exceeding unwholefome, as we find by woful experience to the flefh day

and night, or elfe in at the door, and what that is let any one judge, for at the very door, within three fteps, is the filthy common fewer, &c. And I think when it is beft and fweeteft it is when there is lefs of the common fewer air and more of the other, that is, when it fmells but fufty and foggy, like a well, cave, or low cellar underground, with raw, cold, and aguifh humours. Now, if in thefe and other refpects it be not a Dungeon, and far exceeding many, yea, in many refpects the very dungeon of this Caftle, which they threaten me fo much with, I am much miftaken.

But now for fome fruits too of their tyranny, that we may tell you how it taftes, as from them, ever fince hath my poor wife been weak and fick, yea, fo by fits and through frights as I feared her diffolution before this, and that which made her yet the more dejected and down, as at death's door, was the want of means, they not fuffering help to come when fent for, but rather upbraiding and faying, Pifh! we could be fick and well when we would; the fenfe whereof made her complain deeply and look upon herfelf as a loft woman for fome days. Befides, the lame maid was now taken ill alfo, fhe feeling their cruel ufage, lying and complaining full of pain and torment for fix or feven days together, but they would not fuffer fo much as a woman fent for to help her, fhe keeping her bed, which one in pity lent her to lie on. But we fought the Lord for help, for compaffion, for remedy, we not being fuffered neither to fend out a letter to fignify a word of our condition or cruel ufage; fome feven or eight letters we have reckoned they have kept of late, though not a word in them, for the moft of them, that meddled with thefe matters or their government, only of my wife's ficknefs, fending for means, as alfo for a little money which one had of ours, but they neither let thofe letters go the right way, nor told us of their ftay, fo all loft it is like. All I hear they can fay is that I dated one of them from ' Carifbrook Caftle, a

Den of Cruelty,' which they pretend a high capital crime,
fo afraid are they the leaft truth of their tyranny fhould
come to light. But the Lord our God heard us gracioufly,
and gave us fome hope of their recovery, infomuch as my
wife began to grow a little cheerful, lively, and in hope to
outgrow her frights and fits; but ah! behold their barbarous
wickednefs, O thou God of righteoufnefs, O, how envious
are they at thy goodnefs, for this time they take (*Bull* and
a company of them being feafting, ranting, gaming, making
merry and bowling in a green they have for that purpofe,
and from this fport he orders his cruelty, commands a violent party of foldiers, not once regarding my wife's long
weaknefs and the maid's lamenefs) to fet upon us afrefh,
and fo tear away this bed alfo, that my wife now lay upon,
from under us; but it pleafed God to give a forefight
of it by feveral figns I had of a new trouble coming upon
us, *Bull* with the foldiers being fo exceeding crank, merry,
laughing, and like them in Amos vi. 'at eafe;' whereat
befides, feeing them caft their eye fo at my dung-hole
lodge, I did refolve they had a new defign, fo communicated my thoughts to my wife, wifhing her to be of good
cheer, and fo going into my Co-exile's chamber, which is
the help we have for air, we locked up our own chamber
door, and a while after came in thefe foldiers, like greedy
leopards, for the bed we lay on, and perceiving our door
locked, according to orders with hatchets, fwords, &c,
broke open the door, lock and all, notwithftanding that I
pleaded with them my wife's weak condition, how they had
already almoft killed her ; but they would not hear ; in they
went, tore all the things off the bed and carried away to the
very bolfter and pillow, where they now lie in the aforefaid
Lieutenant's chamber. And I was anfwered that in no
prifons were felons and murderers allowed a bed to lie upon,
ranking us with them. Yea, they had taken away the very
fheets. My poor wife was this while ready to faint, very

ill, and falling into her fits again, through frights, which for prefent were prevented by means, my fellow-prifoner alfo ufing all endeavours to comfort her, but afterwards fhe fell ill again as fhe ufed to be before this laft cruelty renewing her ficknefs, fo as all her flefh would fall a trembling, her whole body be as in an agony, but efpecially her head, which doth fwell fo that for want of the means here, and becaufe they feem refolved to give no reft, as we think, until they have murdered her or been her death, fhe muft now be forced to leave me in their clutches, and, if the Lord make her able, to get to London for the prefervation of her life, which the Lord in mercy grant me.

I fhall break off abruptly here, by reafon my poor weak wife is now leaving me and creeping out of this Caftle gaol, yet Rehoboth, where is room for me, and my foul is left at a frefh fpring. O bleffed be my God! but I muft confefs it is grievous to the flefh to be left in the hands of fuch as have threatened and feemed to thirft for my blood as greedily as the dog for the fheep's; but yet, by God's Grace, they fhall leap above ground for it, and not get it by gaping, (Ps. xxxvii. 32, 33, 34), 'The wicked watcheth the righteous and feeketh to flay him, but the Lord will not leave him in his hand; wait on the Lord, and keep his way, and he fhall exalt thee to inherit the land.' This is a fure word, and in feafon here where I hope to wait, and wait in hope that will never make me afhamed, notwithftanding the violence done to my flefh, the afflictions of my body and relations, and the danger of death in this Dungeon-like hole, which I hope in Chrift we dare fometimes look full face upon and meet; though many times I muft needs fay with *Bifhop Ridley*, martyr, I think I could creep into a moufe-hole, and that is when through thefe late outrageous exercifes I have fits of fudden fear and am fo fubject to frightings. But O pray! pray! pray for us inceffantly with faith, all ye that fhall hear thefe tidings, that He may always ftand by us, who ftood by *Paul* againft the Beafts of Ephefus, and before *Nero*, not knowing which way our moft dear deliverer will come, whether by life or death, to free us from fierce and unreafonable creatures, though for my own part I rather expect the latter in this place ere long, defiring to be found faithful unto death in this moft glorious Caufe of Chrift Jefus, my Lord, King and Mafter. Nor do I think if I die that you will hear the perioding paffages of their Tyranny or this Tragedy upon my body ; or that I fhall write more to get it out, my papers lying hid under ground, where I fear they will rot, but the Lord will raife up the truth from the dead, I do know affuredly.

Now to offer my thoughts a little further. From what I forefee and may eafily gather, I dare affirm—

1. That either extraordinary fufferings or extraordinary actings, in either of which we muft carry our lives in our hands to offer up, are at the door of England. But the laft rather I look for.

2. But if it break forth and continue in worfe fufferings by perfecution, &c, I expect it in *Julian* the Apoftate's way of policy, by returning the worft of the old Clergy and ejected fecular P. or fuch like people and fpirits into place again, ' ut bello inteftino expugnarent ecclefiam,' notwithftanding our perfecutors feem at prefent fo unmerciful to fome of the honefteft and beft of them, that they would not have them by fchool * or otherwife to earn bread for their families honeftly, which is monftrous tyranny even to the worft of men, and makes my heart

---

* By an Act of Parliament, paffed in 1654, and confirmed in 1656, "no minifter was permitted to teach fchool in the parifh from which he had been ejected."—*Collier*, viii. 375 ; *Scobell's Acts*, part ii. 346.

fometimes bleed within me. But fomewhat like to this
feems their reviving of the old orders, degrees, Popifh cuf-
toms, forked caps, hoods and tippets, and fuch antichriftian
trafh, which fo many martyrs have witneffed againft, befides
the famous burial of the Archbifhop of Ireland at *O. P.*
charges in England,* whiles we may rot in his prifons.

3. If in actings amongft the Saints, as I am moft inclined to think, then look for fuch a fpirit to be doing with,
as the Saints had in primitive times to be fuffering with,
like the woman of Valenciennes, who faid fhe would rather
burn her body than burn her Bible, and fo was burnt ; or
rather that woman which the martyr *Guy de Briz* mentions
in a letter to his mother. ' I remember,' fays he, ' I have
read how the poor Chriftians in primitive times were affembled together in great numbers to hear the Word, and a
great Commander was fent by the Emperor to put them all
to the fword, which a Chriftian woman hearing, hafted with
all the fpeed fhe could to be at this meeting, carrying her
little one in her arms. As fhe drew nigh to the troop of
horfemen fhe rufhed in to get through. The Governor,
feeing her make fuch hafte, called to her and examined her
whither fhe pofted fo faft. She gave him this fhort anfwer, " I am going," faith fhe, " to the affembly of Chriftians." "What to do?" fays he. "Haft thou not heard
that I am commanded to put them all to death?" "Yes,
yes," fays fhe, "I know it well, and therefore make I hafte
that I may not come too late, left I be not worthy to lofe
my life with them." "But what wilt thou do with the little
child?" fays he. "I will carry it with me," fays fhe, "that
it may alfo have the crown of martyrdom." '

I could tell you in primitive times of whole flocks that

---

* In April, 1656, James Ufher, Archbifhop of Armagh, " was buried
in Weftminfter Abbey, Cromwell allowing two hundred and fifty pounds
for the expenfe of the funeral."—*Collier,* viii. 378.

would run in voluntarily to be tormented when they heard
Chriſtians were to ſuffer. Now I ſay I do expect as high,
forward, and excellent a ſpirit to come down for action, that
will make nothing but ſport for Chriſt's ſake to run in
among multitudes of enemies in the name of the Lord, and
though men account them mad, deſperate, or ſuch as throw
away their lives, they will on upon ſwords and pikes, and
play as prettily, merrily and cheerfully with cannon-bullets,
as at ſtool-ball. And if the Roman, Trojan, and Perſian
ſpirit was ſo invincible and reſolute in the day of it, do we
think the Fifth-kingdom ſpirit ſhall not be ſo much rather ?
and what a ſhameful thing is it, as Jerome ſays, that faith
in Chriſt Jeſus ſhould not make us as courageous for Him
as ever infidels or carnal men were, or are, for their Maſter.

4. For that reſolution goes before action I find in my
proſpective that the Lord hath ripened his Saints at a high
rate already, eſpecially ſuch hidden ones of his as hang moſt
in the Sun of generation light. Methinks they begin to be
ſhod with Goſpel preparations (Ephes. vi.) and hoofs of
braſs to break in pieces many people (Micah iv.) Theſe
Levites, of the order of twenty-four (in Chron. xxiv. and
xxv. and xxvi. and xxvii.) who are to execute the judgment
thoroughly upon all that have run a whoring from the
Lord (Exod. xxxii. 27, 28, 29) with the ſword. In the
mean time, O Lord, look down on thy priſoners and behold
how greedy theſe beaſts are (as Micah iii. 2) to pluck off their
ſkin and fleſh from off their bones, yea to eat the fleſh of
thy people, to break their bones and chop them in pieces as
for the pot, and as fleſh within their chaldron ; yet (v. 4)
' They will cry unto the Lord.'

Now for concluſion, let my moſt dear and honoured
brethren, in bonds and out alſo, be of good cheer, full of
faith and expectation, unmoveable in the Lord, knowing
their labour, their love, and their bonds be accepted
(1 Cor. xv. 58) ; yea your infirmities, my friends, are over-

looked (Jer. l. 20) in the Covenant of Grace, and your Caufe of (Chrift) affifted and laboured after by the whole Creation. As Luther faid, upon Henry 8's letters againft him, ' Agant quicquid poffint Henrici, Epifcopi, atque adeo Turca, et ipfe Sathan, nos filii fumus regni." Pifh, let all the Harries, Bifhops, Turks, and Devils do their worft as long as Chrift is ours. And fo we are the children of the Kingdom, we care not, we fpare not, we fear not, though they kill us, fpit upon us, beat, bruife, imprifon, or crucify us to death for our Chrift. Therefore, O you, the Lord's prifoners and royal perfecuted ones, in Pathmos-ifle exiles, and in Pathmian prifons, my moft dear and honoured brethren indeed, and now more than ever, *Maj. Gen. Harrifon* and *Mr. Courtney, Mr. Carew, Col. Rich, Maj. Gen. Overton, Cornet Day, Brother Feake,* &c, and all the reft whom I falute in the Lord's name, and look towards from this top of Amana (for it is a nurfe as the word fignifies in the truth), this top of Shenir (where is the profperous teacher as the word fignifies), and this Hill of Hermon (Cant. iv. 8), full of dews dedicated to God, yea from thefe Lions' dens and mountains of Leopards, where I am now caft for a prey by man to be devoured, in Carif-brook Caftle, a clofe prifon and kennel of unclean creatures ; from hence, I fay, do I cry aloud and call upon you, (having no other way to fpeak unto you but this, where you be in the world) as men already forgotten by fome, and as dead men out of mind. And now, my brethren in bonds and banifhment, how reft you in your Arimathæan fepul-chres ? are you not fweetly embalmed in your fufferings ? and do not the affectionate Marys find you out with their fpices ? or is it a refurrection time with you firft, before they can do that ? will the Whale's belly vomit you out, and up again, amongft your brethren at liberty, after you have lain like dead carcafes your part of the three days ? What fay you, O you honourable ones of the earth that is to come,

to all thefe things? Do you not lie eafy and fweet in your
prifons and exiles? are not your beds bleffed and green for
your beloved and you to lie down in? O that I were with
you! O that I could vifit you! that I could hear what you
would tell me! how cheer you, how live you, how feed
you, how lodge you, what find you, what feel you, what
fee you, what fatisfies you, and what enjoy you of the day-
fprings from on high at hand? Doth not the moft High
Jehovah-Shammah ftand by you faying, Be of good cheer,
Harrifon, Rich, Carew, Courtney, Overton, &c, for even
to-day do I declare that I will render double unto thee,
when I have bent Judah for me, filled the bow with
Ephraim, and raifed up thy fons, O Sion, and made thee as
a fword of a mighty man? I am with you, I have oiled
your bonds and made them eafy and fweet unto you. Yea
I have muzzled of this mis-fhapen Court-Monfter, this
ugly Creature, this Baftard of Afhdod, this feed of the
Dragon, begotten in darknefs, brought forth in weaknefs,
and nourifhed with unreafonablenefs, growing up in wickednefs, to continue with fhortnefs and to be confounded with
the fiercenefs of the wrath of God which is at hand (Rev.
xiv. 10-20). Wherefore Up, Up, O Concaptives and Co-
exiles, if ever now with courage, Sirs, be ready and look
about you, for I tell you truly after our forty-two monthed
voyage, we may fee the land. Let us fing and fhout for
joy, for that our fails are filled, our tackling is good, our
motion is fwift, our compafs is true, and we are near the
haven; come then, tack about, Sirs, and to our bufinefs, to
our work with might and main, make hafte, keep ground,
prepare the cable and caft anchor, yea awake, awake all you
that be aboard, for the time is come to vifit the coafts and
fet afhore, yea, my beloved, the Sun of perfecution grows
now low and will fet foon, O therefore let us ftand to it
like Heart of Oak without warping in the leaft. O confider a little, is it comely for us to hang down our heads!

and fo near the Haven, or to droop at the end of the forty-
two months? What—Now!—now to yield or parley
about it, being this fort of Truth our ftronghold hath held
out fo long and valiantly too againft the Beaft and his image
by all the Saints and Martyrs and for fo many hundred
years; yea and all the Saints that have left us their fculls,
blood, afhes, and bones behind them for an encouragement,
yea the whole creation, yea God, Chrift, Angels, and men
do expect our conftancy and faithfulnefs to the end; and
fhall we now faint or fear the enemy, feeing we are fo well
accommodated with all neceffaries, yea much beyond our
blefled predeceffors for outward things? and upon fo poor
a flight fiege too of the enemy as this is—who is almoft
worfted without hand, and now too that fuch great relief is
raifing for us by the Spirit of Life, the Fifth-kingdom Spirit,
which we wait for every day, fuch as hath not been heard of
for above this thoufand years, and fhall not we ftand to it?
Shall not we hold it out, and die like Chrift's men? or
fhall we admit of any compofition, capitulation or terms
with them, or be routed in the rear for want of faith or
courage to carry it up? Oh, no, no, God forbid, but let us
rally by faith, and by the Grace of God keep our ground
like men, and make hafte with the main body, as they
began blefledly in that wing of honourable Wales,* to move
for the relief of the engaged forlorn. For the Lord's fake
make hafte and march up, yea fally out moft fiercely, O ye
men of courage, upon this Apoftate and perfidious enemy,
with fuch an undaunted, invincible, and impregnable refolution as may make them know they are not ordinary
prifoners whom they would bury alive in thefe iron graves,
for the moft blefled Caufe that ever was on foot in earth, or
that ever was betrayed by men. Come, come, Sirs, pre-

---

* The Fifth-Monarchy Men relied much on an infurrection which
Vavafor Powell was to have organized in Wales.

pare your companies, for King Jefus His Mount Sion
mufter-day is at hand; His Magazines and Artillery, yea
His moft excellent Mortar-pieces and batteries be ready; we
wait only for the word from on High to fall on, and faith
and prayer to do the Execution according to Rev. xviii. 6,
'Reward her as fhe hath rewarded you,' and then, by the
Grace of God, the proudeft of them all fhall know we are
engaged on life and death, to fink or fwim, ftand or fall
with the Lord Jefus our Captain General upon his Red
Horfe againft the Beaft's Government, fo as neither to give
nor take quarter, but according to his orders.

Therefore take the Alarum, my brethren, be up and
ready, for we are not our own, but Chrift's, nor are we re-
deemed to men, but to God; therefore, like champions
refrefhed with wine, let the fhout of a King be heard among
us. Are we not yet awakened and warmed? Is it not
high time for the two Witneffes to be uniting, ftirring and
rifing, yea ftanding upon their feet? and I hope we (you
of the magiftracy and we of the miniftry) are of the fame
fpirit with them. Befides, let us confider how eagerly
Shear-jafub, or the little Remnant, is making ready for your
rife; yea, Maher-fhalal-hafh-baz is ready to pitch his great
tent and to blow his great trump; yea, the man among
the myrtle-trees (Zech. i. 8) on his red horfe is already
mounted, if I miftake not, and ready to march, with his
fword to execute, and fire to plead with all nations; for
his bow he ufed upon his white horfe (Rev. vi. 2) hitherto,
but the next is his fword on his red horfe, and the flain of
the Lord fhall be many (Ifa. lxvi. 16). Yea, and after the
harveft (wherein I hope to be a reaper, a cutter down or a
gatherer in), the blood of the vintage will be up unto the
horfes' bridles (Rev. xiv. 20), viz. thofe horfes that are
to carry the 4th Chariot from between the two mountains
of brafs, wherein the Lord Jefus fits to give laws unto the
whole earth (Zech. vi. 1, 7, 8); and this I can eafily fore-

fee, for I have a moſt obvious undeniable proſpeſtive of it
from this cliff of the rock where my preſent lot is. But ah !
Lord, may I ſay, what meaneth this that men be ſo huſh
and ſtill then at this day ? yea, good men ſo aſleep, ſo
ſecure (Zech. i. 11). ʻ Behold, all the earth ſitteth ſtill and
is at reſt.ʼ Why, it is that they may be ſurpriſed as in the
days of *Noah* and *Lot*, and with the coming as a thief in
the night. Therefore, O my brethren, let us enter the
Ark, for no ſafety will be found but in the work, believe
it ; liſten, for the noiſe of his chariot wheels is in ſome
meaſure come upon us ; look about, and believe with boldneſs and with gladneſs ; yea, up, and make ready to run,
to run with theſe horſemen who are at hand ; prepare, prepare, put on the whole armour of God to ſtand, outſtand,
and withſtand, in this evil day.   Awake, awake, yea rouſe
up, O Saints, with moſt royal reſolution, and ſhake your-
ſelves from your priſon duſt, O captive daughter of Sion,
for it is high time ; yea, the time is now come to ſtart up
like Lions (too ſtout for ſufferings as before), putting off
your ſackcloth or captivity garments, and putting on your
beautiful Zion robes to follow the Lamb with (Iſa. lii. 1, 2).
And when you put on theſe robes you muſt put off all
thoſe Relations, though ever ſo dear, that may make you
ſtagger, yea even ſtamp upon them ; as Jerome ſaid, ʻ If
my father were weeping on his knees before me, and my
mother hanging on my neck behind me, and all my brethren, ſiſters, and kindred round about me, I'd run over
them all,ʼ and in this caſe we are bidden even to hate them
if we follow Chriſt. Wherefore, O my moſt honourable
Brethren, Con-captives and Co-exiles, yea moſt noble Fellow-
commoners at the King's charges, let us up together all at
once and fall in all at once (Numb. xiii. 30) with one
mind, as one man (Zeph. iii. 9). Appoint the day, appropriate the duty, and to it. Yea, do it with ſuch a ſhout
too (Jer. l. 14, 15 ; Amos. ii. 2) as may make the ears of

the enemies to ring; yea, begin the earthquake (Rev. xi. 13), and rend up by the very roots the foundations of thefe perfecuting Nimrods with their prifons (Acts xvi. 26), fo as one ftone be not left for a corner of them; yea, till there be fuch a trembling, fhaking, and confternation, yea a μετάθεσις, tranflation, over-turning, and total amotion of them, that the Beaft's government may never have a being more in England, neither in Civils, Ecclefiaftics, nor Militaries. For Jehovah Sabaoth will confound them and break them to pieces before us, yea this houfe of Saul rejected muft fall flat before the houfe of David, the little ftripling, and all this Apoftative intereft of Councils, Courts, Triers, Clergy, Academies, and Armies, whom the Lord is departed from. But our Caufe cannot mifcarry, my friends; it cannot fail us, who are heirs of the promife, becaufe every iota of it, as we contend for it, is founded in the new and everlafting covenant, bleffed be the Lord the Holy one of Ifrael, who hath already given us fo many gracious and fpecifying prifon prognoftics of the great day of Jezreel at hand.

I am prevented in my word to the little Remnant; I mean the Lamb's faithful followers, of the Woman's feed, that keep the commandments of God and teftimony of Jefus; but in my Banifhborn treatife (lib. laft) I write at large to them and of their work (if it ever come to light), though I confefs my *Bucer*-like hand, which writes but bad, may be fome let or at leaft delay therein; yet at prefent I am to bid them BEWARE and PREPARE: beware of running before orders come from Jehovah of Armies, and prepare for them when they come, yea to make all their arrows ready againft Babylon, for the time to vifit her is now come, and it is eafy to fee the figns of the times come upon us, yea the figns complete them, this little Horn, this laft B., this ὁ Ἄνθρωπος τῆς Ἀποστασίας (as the learned read ἁμαρτίας), this laft limb of the Beaft's go-

vernment and the man that maketh up his number fix
thoufand fix hundred and fix (as we have proved in Prifonborn), he is now come. O up! and be ready, then, like
Roaring Lions againft the end, the time, times and dividend,
to run and climb the wall like mighty men, and Jehovah fhall
utter his voice before you, his dread fhall be on your enemies who have infulted over you, but fhall fall before you
(Jofh. ii. 9; Rev. xi. 11); yea, they fhall tremble and
fear, and wax feeble as women (Jer. li. 30; Nahum iii. 13),
and become bread for your fwords to eat, becaufe their defence is departed from them (Numb. xiv. 9). Nor are the
moft godly among them that have apoftatized thefe times
any more to be reckoned amongft the Lamb's number than
Dan and *Ephraim*, becaufe of their Apoftafy (Judges xvii.
and xviii.), were reckoned among the fealed ones of the
144,000 (Rev. vii. 5, 6, 7, 8). Wherefore up, O my dear
Hearts, who are of that number that ftand before the
Throne (Rev. vii. 9), or with the Lamb in Mount Sion
(Rev. xiv. 1). Up and be ready with your Ahod weapon;
awake, arife, O Englifh Shear-jafub, for out of Judah,
Chrift with us Gentiles of the fea, comes forth the corner,
out of him the nail, out of him the battle bow, and they
fhall be as mighty men which tread down the enemies as
mire in the ftreets in the battle, and they fhall fight becaufe
the Lord is with them (Zech. x. 5).

Wherefore—1. Be fure you begin your mufter or to
mount your horfes (Zech. i. 8) upon a Mount Sion ground,
or in a new covenant principle: that is, purely for or rather
with Chrift and his Kingdom, and for no earthly perfons,
things or Interefts of men whatfoever. Such a war was
never yet in the Four Monarchies. And 2. Be fure that
you be fully feparate from the Beaft's dominion in all things
and in every miniftration, as well civil and military as eccle-
fiaftic. And furthermore, 3. Be fure you lofe not the leaft
opportunity or nick of time put into your hands to do the

work when the end comes. And 4. Be fure you fet not upon it with your own fpirits, nor pour out in it your own wrath and revenge, but God's only, and upon fuch fubjects too as the Word reveals. Yea, 5. Laftly, be fure that you in your actings, executings, and fufferings, be upon no other bottom or foundation but the Lord Jefus.

Therefore, Up, O ye Saints, to take the Kingdom (Dan. vii. 18) and to poffefs it for ever, for the Gentiles have poffeffed the outer Court this 42 months, and 'tis now time to arife—yea, high time to deliver thyfelf, O Sion (Ifa. lii. 1, 2), and fhake off thy duft to lay wafte the land of *Nimrod* with the fword (Mic. v. 6, 7). And the Remnant of *Jacob*, the worm, fhall be in the midft of many people as a Dew from the Lord, as the fhowers upon the grafs that tarrieth not for man, yea among the Gentiles as a Lion, who if he go through both treadeth down and teareth in pieces, and none can deliver (Num. xxiii. 24). The Holy City is the Holy Camp in the outward Court of the tabernacle that is to arife with the two Witneffes, and rout the Beaft that trod it under foot.

Therefore for the Lord's fake, Sirs, be Valiant, like *David's* worthies, yea *King Solomon's* men (Cant. iii. 7, 8), who all hold fwords, being expert in war. It is faid of *Sadeel* that with *Genes*, a citizen, he fought fo furioufly for the then Caufe of God that he himfelf put a thoufand Spaniards to flight, and fhall we fear? Regard not your lives for the work of Chrift when called to it. Bleffed Lord, when wilt thou raife us up with thy Spirit of life, or how long fhall all lie dead? O what cowards are we now to run into holes and corners for fear of fufferings! Surely, Lord Jefus, had all thy Difciples dealt thus with thee in their generations, there would have been but few Martyrs or followers of the Lamb. O I blufh for fhame when I behold them that are gone before with thefe that now follow. *Ignatius* faid he had rather be a Martyr than a

Monarch, but now men had rather be Monfters than Martyrs. When the Dragon Emperors gave orders to put all
to death that would confefs themfelves Chriftians, they
came in of themfelves by whole flocks, confeffing themfelves Chriftians, and defying the Heathen; they ran in
voluntarily to die and to be tormented. But ah, where be
they that run in flocks to Whitehall now, faying, we are
Fifth-Monarchy-Men, or for the Kingdom of Chrift, and
will live and die with our brethren together? (See 1 John
iii. 16), 'Hereby perceive we the love of God, becaufe he
laid down his life for us, and we ought to lay down our
lives for the Brethren.' Now I befeech the Lord awaken
you, if you be of that race, and roufe you up and fet you
all awork, as upon life and death, with all fpeed to overcome the Beaft and his followers, with as lively a fpirit, as
high a zeal, and readinefs to die in the fervice of Chrift, and
fo to overcome with the word of the Teftimony and blood
of the Lamb, not loving your lives. Bate me none of my
fufferings, fays *Gordius* to his tormentors, for it is my lofs
then, ' majora certamina, majora fequuntur prœmia.'

Wherefore becaufe I muft break off with thefe few
words to you as to Overcomers (for fo I truft you are, or
will be, in Chrift Jefus), and clofe followers of the Lamb,
I fhall leave you with that bleffed man *Mr. Holland's* legacy
bequeathed to his friends at his death againft Popery,
' Commendo vos dilectioni Dei et odio Papatus,' &c. So
againft this Apoftate generation I commend you, my brethren, to the deareft love of God and to the deadlieft hatred
of thefe Hypocrites and Apoftates. Amen. For (Heb.
x. 38) 'If any man draw back, my foul fhall have no pleafure in him.'

I would have had a word to this Baftard of Afhdod,
this illegitimate monfter, had he ears to hear, but his moft
irrational rage hath hindered me, and I muft be filent, with
a loud cry to thee, *O. P.*, out of this den, where thou haft

caft me fo inconfiderately, with fuch cruelty, and for fo long a time too, of whom I think I might have faid, as *Tacitus* of *Galba*, ' Digniffimus imperandi, nifi imperaffet.' How worthy hadft thou been of rule, if thou hadft not ruled. But as high as thou art, and as low as I am under thy foot, methinks when I am mounted and winged by the Holy Ghoft, thou art as much under me and my Chrift whom I ferve in thefe bonds and in this Caufe. Yea, as *Cirus Theodorus* faid to *Modeftus* about *Bafil* when he was under his tyranny, ' O *Modeftus*, why *Bafil* is above thee : thou art but a poor Pifmire to him, though thou roareft againft him like a Lion,' and be not offended at it, for I tell thee through thy cruelty I am fet upon a Mount fo high, as I fee thee and all the Kings of the Earth to boot, as proud as they be, but like Hoppimithumbs—I mean but like ants about a molehill, which I laugh at when I fee them moft bufy about their nefts, which in one crufh will be deftroyed, kicked down, and difperfed like the duft on the floor (Dan. ii. 35). Wherefore, Sir, that you had but once this fight, and if I fpeak not to a man moft defperately refolved and hardened up to irrecoverable deftruction, yea to one worfe than a ftone, yea guilty of the great fin againft the Holy Ghoft, let me be heard. And O that I might be heard in thy confcience, O thou ! O thou finful man ! before the decree come forth, and thy fentence be executed. How fore a ruin is running upon thee, though thou fee it not ! Wherefore either deliver us quickly quit of thefe dens (admiring our hitherto prefervation from on high, whofe Angel hath delivered us out of the mouths of thefe favage beafts), and give you glory to God as *Darius* did, if thou canft find in thy heart fo to do, forafmuch as innocence and truth is found on our fide, or elfe I fay unto thee by the AUTHORITY of the Lord committed to me, that thou fhalt DIE like a BEAST, yea more miferably than in a DEN or a DUNGEON. And as *Romanus* faid to the Tyrant, fo I tell thee and them about thee, that I appeal from this thy Tyranny, which hath no pity, to the Throne of Chrift, ' et cito vos omnes ' (as *Jerome* of Prague faid to his perfecutors), ' ut refpondeatis coram altiffimo et juftiffimo judice poft (45) annos '—I fummon you all that have a hand or heart in this perfecution to appear before my Chrift, His elect Angels and Saints, the moft fupreme power and righteous Judge, after the 1335 days, where We fhall judge you that now judge us, though this is your hour and the power of darknefs. So be it, as faith the faithful Witnefs, the Amen, for a little feafon, yea a very little while and He that fhall come will come, and will not tarry.

    Even fo, Amen, come quickly, Lord Jefus. Amos i. 11, ' For three tranfgreffions and for four I will not turn away the punifhment thereof, becaufe he did purfue his brother with the fword, and did caft off all pity, and his anger did tear perpetually, and he kept his wrath for ever.'

Finis in Imis, Ultimis et Noviffimis.

Amen.   Hallelujah."

" *A Poftfcript.*

    READER. Thou art defired to take notice, that in the forced abfence of the Author in banifhment, the Prefs lets many miftakes in printing pafs uncontrolled, and for want of due help and ability doth mifcarry of the Latin, Greek, and Hebrew which was intermingled in fome eminent paffages. Now the Lord blefs thee in thefe evil days, and give thee bowels to the fuffering Saints and truth, and help thee to follow that which is good, and which make for thy peace and comfort in the world to come. Amen."

MY CHRISTIAN FRIEND—

It is about a year ſince I had a perfunctory glance and peruſal of theſe papers in this piece called an Introduction, &c, to Priſon-born Morning beams, which I found, as you ſee, ſo infinitely mangled and miſhaped, that I was, and yet am, in ſuch a dreſs aſhamed to own them. Which deformity put upon them by others through want of ſkill, care, or love to the ſuffering author, ſhall be greedily multiplied by ſome men to abuſe me with, upon whoſe back the erratas of other men it ſeems muſt lie till truth and Innocency may come abroad and find juſtice.

But yet I muſt befeech you to a little charity and candidneſs towards me, and not to impute the many pitiful ſoleciſms of books, which iſſue in my name, to my pen, but to their pates and the preſs together intruſted. For ſome, I hear, ſince my long impriſonment have been glad of the opportunity of traducing me freely about my treatiſe of Church-diſcipline, but I for ever bleſs my God though the unreaſonable ſword hath given them leave to inſult over me and trample upon me, yet the Truth is above them and their malice. She may be blamed but never ſhamed by thoſe monſtrous reports, which be moſt made of her in her ſufferings and bonds, for ' chagor charbecha gnat-jarech' (wherein is written King of Kings and Lord of Lords, Rev. xix. 16), ' Gibbor hodecha ve hadarecha,' yea, ' tſelach rechab gnaldeberemet ve gnavah tſedeg' is ſome of my daily ſong to my King. Nor do I greatly fear the foiling of the hotteſt enemies I have, with the power of His truth, meekneſs, and righteouſneſs, whether they be the ' Rozenim' (lean ones as rulers are called, Ps. xxii), or the ' Abburim,' fat BULLS (as enemies are called, Ps. xxii. 12), and fierceſt

foes that now triumph over us, for it is their time. Nor
had that frothy rabble of airy ftuff, gathered up together into
a cloud of Vapour and exhaled from the dung hill of one
CRAFTON, a malignant Prieft of London, a little before
my imprifonment, efcaped the public fire, but the long lawlefs fword interpofed, took away my papers, and plundered
from me amongft them the reply to (what is fober in) his
ftage-play Treatife. Neverthelefs I do yet more abundantly
blefs the Lord for his light of the feven lamps of fire which
burn before the throne, only I muft entreat thee, my
reader and friend, to wait with patience and in hope with
us till deliverance and liberty to the truth be reftored, and
in the interim mend with thy pen the following erratas
before thou proceedeft in this part called the Introduction.*

.   .   .   .

.   .   .   .

What the other part called Jegar Sahadutha,† or a Heart
Appeal, &c, is for errata I am ignorant, nor have I feen
fheet of it, only I fear fo hard a travail, through fo many
obftructions in the birth and fo little help from the neighbourhood will at the leaft deform it, if not endanger the very
being of it, in my abfence and exile. Yea, and which is
worfe, I am informed thofe few feeming friends that do
affift the birth have agreed to cut off fome members of that
little Treatife to facilitate the Birth, but how can it then
live? or if it does, fo monftroufly mifhapen as they think, I
hear, to make it, I fhall want will and affection to own it as
mine, for I differ from their vote who had rather have it
born a cripple than not at all.

    My dear Reader,—A word more. It may be thou
wilt wonder to fee the Introduction to a year or two prifon

---

* The hiftory of his fufferings at Lambeth, p. 137-168.
† The hiftory of his fufferings at Windfor and in the Ifle of Wight,
p. 225-304.

travail of fpirit put in this place, and therein hear news of an enfuing treatife or two about the Two Britifh Witneffes, and of a more obvious fupputation of times according to the Danielian and Apocalyptic accounts; alfo of the 42 months period upon us, and of the flaughter of the two Witneffes in this Street for the fingle time, dual time, and a dividend, with the myftery of that number 666; alfo a fynopfis of the Lamb's Government, fhewing the difference between the Lamb's and the Beaft's G.; alfo a very lucid difcovery of the Kingdom of Chrift on earth, and the prefent work of Saints in England, the order, inftruments and matter of the vials, the thoufand years and firft Refurrection with the order thereof, and much more, but fee nothing. Alas! alas! (as Lam. iv. 3) it is becaufe this (Tannin) ferpent fea monfter hath fought to devour it, and the truth betrayers and murderers have purfued thefe males that they cannot come forth, none being fo hardy to help them, he that offers it makes himfelf a prey. But this poor mifcellany of general matter hath with much ado remained untaken to declare aloud their cruelty, who have hindered and ftifled the moft fpecial.

Much more might be added, in this Tragedy, of our hard trials to the flefh, both as to the prefent condition of my own body, fo much diftempered in this unwholefome hole of this Caftle whereinto I am caft, fo alfo my wife, whofe fufferings have been fo great in this gaol, that feveral Doctors of Phyfic in London have affirmed her ficknefs to have rifen from the rude handlings and frights with the unwholefomenefs of the pit we are put into together, to the evident hazard of her life. (This is known to him in Power). Yea and the reft of my family with me, fome or other or all, being continually ill and afflicted with diftempers, pains, ficknefs, lamenefs, and other fore trials of the flefh. But I had much rather affect to make my condition known to God than to men who have not the bowels

of men. Wherefore ' karenu Shemcha Jehovah mibbor,'
we have called upon thee, O God, from this grievous pit of
Caines-brook-Chaines.

To conclude ; forafmuch, loving reader, as I find no
faith, no truth, or conftancy in men, but (through the perfecution of undoubted foes and perfidioufnefs of dawbing
and doubtful friends, who promifed fair but perform foully),
all I do for the public is either betrayed, killed, fpoiled, or
obftructed in my abfence, and a true friend to one in prifon
being ' rara avis in terris,' I am forced now, in this third
year of my imprifonment and banifhment, to convert my
time more particularly than I had intended to my own ufe
and profit, by perfecting my fearch of and ftudies in the
Holy Scriptures through the Hebrew, Chaldaic, Syriac,
Arabic, and fo Perfian roots, which is my prefent and daily
work, and I do blefs my God for this great blefling upon
me in that little progrefs which through His Grace I have
made into the Pentateuch, Pfalms and Prophets. For by
the Hebrew, Chald., Samaritan (Rabbinic), Arabic (Perfian), Æthiopic, Armenian, and Coptic tongues, in all which,
except the two laft, I am now perufing the Scriptures of
holy infpiration, I have received a moft fweet light, tafte,
and fingular comfort to my own foul, and have yet a lively
hope that I fhall one day therein ferve the public again,
although for days, weeks, months, and years, I have now
lain among the tile-pots in the fiery furnace and burning
kiln, and by the walls like a Dead man out of mind.

Now, O all ye friends, fellow-citizens of Sion and fel-
low-waiters with us for the help of Ifrael, bear us a little in
your bowels and bofom before the Father, (me and my
deareft Concaptives and Co-exiles in this glorious Caufe of
Chrift). When you come before the King into his Prefence Chamber of grace and fupplication, be fure you forget
not *Jofeph*, and I befeech you in thofe open, bleeding,
yearning bowels, which hung upon the Crofs, to mind a poor

worm and prifoner of hope (and of a little faith) in this valley of Achor and Efhcol.

Now I commit you all to the Inner Court comforts and counfels, that ye may be meafured in thefe diforderly times by the Angel's cubit, the golden reed, and not by men's rotten rules, according to the which I am laid out and meafured in the Lord's tabernacle of Teftament, yea bound with thofe golden chains which faften the fhoulder-pieces to the Breaft-plate, wherein is put the Urim and Thummim by the finger of God, and thereby I have an anfwer of God to my great encouragement and rejoicing, who yet remain, in the faith, hope, and patience of the Kingdom,

THINE as a heave-offering to the Lord by
the hand of Chrift, in this fat foil,
wherein my foot is dipped in oil,

Jo. Ro."

CHAPTER VIII.

OGERS carries down the hiftory of his prifon fufferings to July or Auguft, 1656. In September of that year *Sir Henry Vane* became his fellow-prifoner at Carifbrook; an intimacy appears to have fprung up between them, and from this time *Vane* was fpoken of more and more as a leader of the Fifth-Monarchy-Men, and *Rogers* * became the ftaunch and zealous fupporter of *Vane*. Towards the end of the year *Cromwell* felt himfelf able to releafe many of his political prifoners. *Vane* and *Feake* were releafed on the 31ft of December, and *Rogers* a fortnight afterwards.†

In the winter of 1655, while *Rogers* was a prifoner in the Ifle of Wight, a confpiracy had been organized in London, which came to a crifis in April, 1657, about three months

Jan. 14, 1657.
Thurloe, iv. 191 ; vi. 163, 184.

---

* In one of his later publications he fpeaks of the great comfort he had received from hearing Sir Henry Vane open and apply the Scriptures "in Carifbrook Caftle and elfewhere."—Διαπολιτεία, p. 21.

† "Whitehall, Jan. 14, 1657. It hath been ordered by his Highnefs and the Council that Mr. Rogers, who was committed to the Ifle of Wight, and Mr. David Jenkins, commonly known by the name of Judge Jenkins, be fet at liberty."—*Mercurius Politicus*, No. 344. For an account of Judge Jenkins, fee " Forfter's Life of H. Martin," p. 258.

" Mr. Rogers, preacher, being releafed by order of his Highnefs and the Council from the Ifle of Wight, came this Wednefday, Jan. 21ft, about three of the clock in the afternoon, into London."—*Mercurius Politicus*, No. 345.

after his liberation. The ringleader was a wine cooper of the name of *Venner*, and his accomplices were chiefly from the lower ranks of the Fifth-Monarchy-Men. The more confiderable members of the party—*Harrifon, Rich, Carew, Rogers,* &c.— were founded, but refufed to act. Some of the defigns of the confpirators are explained in the following extracts from *Thurloe*.

April, 1657.

Thurloe, vi. 163.

"*Refolutions about fome defign of an infurrection.*

1. That the time with fubmiffion to the will and providence of God be the third day of the week, and the feventh day of the fecond month in the night.

2. . . . .

3. That . . . principally we endeavour and engage againft the army and principals of the army, the greateft and . . . . the general and officers, and that according to reafon and wifdom we do not feparate colours and engage againft many ftrong enemies at once, as the priefts and lawyers.

4. Our judgment is, that having a convenient place and providence we will feize upon a troop of horfe and execute their officers and any fentinel of guard of any and all proved foldiers that do oppofe us, and take their horfes and arms, and horfe our men withal, to take in with us thofe proved foldiers that fhall fubmit themfelves.

5. That fuch gain and fpoil as is due to the Lord and to the treafury and work of the Lord, according to the rule and practice of the Scripture, both of gold, filver, brafs, and precious things, &c, be brought into a common ftock and treafury, and that officers be appointed to that charge, to receive that account and . . . . it accordingly, and that that which is for the brothers for their particular encouragement be equally diftributed to the whole, thofe that engage and thofe that ftay with the ftuff; befides, refpect is to be had to all others with us in the work, over and above their wages and hire.

. . . . . .

24, 1ft *month.*

. . . . . .

The meeting of *Mr. Portman* and his brother with us, what they propounded . . . the anfwer we gave . . . the

Life and Opinions of a

three things he objected. That *Jones* affirms that we have no the fpirit of God, fhall be blafted, &c, and his two reafons—1. becaufe the ancient wife Chriftians are not with us, as *Mr. Carew,* *Mr. Rogers, Mr. Harrifon,* &c, and—2. becaufe the time is not come by two months." . . . .

The infurrection was a complete failure.

Thurloe, vi. 186.
"It pleafed God to give fome light into their actions all along," faid *Thurloe;* in fact, his fpies had given him from the beginning an exact account of the whole confpiracy, and when the proper time arrived "his Highnefs fent a party of horfe and feized upon twenty of them, who had with them twenty-five pair of piftols and holfters, powder, fhot, and match proportionable, their ftandard " [a red lion couchant, with the motto, 'Who fhall roufe him'], " and were booted and fpurred, ready to take horfe and begone." Afterwards fearch was made and more arms and ammunition were found. Other prifoners alfo were taken, and *Harrifon* was arrefted and fent to the Tower. *Rogers* was not molefted.

Thurloe defcribes *Venner* as a man "that had about two years fince a place in the Tower, from whence he was removed, being obferved to be a fellow of defperate and bloody fpirit, and was fufpected to have had defigns to blow up the Tower with powder, and would fay that the time would come that the hand-maids of the Lord would make no more of killing men, than . . . . He had alfo fpake at the fame time very defperate words concerning the murdering of his Highnefs. This bloody man was to be the ringleader of this bloody bufinefs." *Thurloe* adds that his accomplices " were mean fellows of no note, but fuch as had blown up one another by a weekly meeting they had at a

Thurloe, vi. 185.
place called Swan Alley, in Coleman Street."

The prifoners were fent to the Tower, but were never brought to trial.

Two months later the Government received intelligence of another Fifth-Monarchy confpiracy.

" *An information about Col. Harrifon, &c.*

June 15, 1657.
Col. Harrifon, Mr. Pheake, Mr. Can,* and Mr. Rogers,

---

* John Cann was one of the moft active preachers of the Fifth-Monarchy-Men. About this time (1657) he publifhed " The Time of the End," to which are prefixed two prefaces, one by Feake and the other by Rogers.

meet ordinarily at *Mr. Daforme's* houfe in Bartholomew Lane, near the Royal Exchange, where they profefs themfelves ready for an infurrection, the time being now come, as they fay, wherein the three years and half is at an end in which the witneffes have lien dead, and that there will be a refurrection of them. It is confidently believed that upon this delufion they will ground an attempt which may be attended with fome mifchief, they profeffing it to be their refolution to deftroy all that fhall oppofe them."—*June* 15, 1657.

Thurloe, vi. 349.

It does not appear that this information was acted upon.

In the beginning of the next year (1658) *Cromwell's* Houfe of Commons grew reftive under his government, they fcrupled to recognize his "other Houfe" as "the Houfe of Lords," and "fome fpake reproachfully in the Houfe of Commons of the other Houfe." "The Protector looked upon himfelf as aimed at by them . . . and he was the more incenfed becaufe at this time the Fifth-Monarchy-Men began again their enterprifes to overthrow him and his Government by force, . . . he therefore took a refolution fuddenly to diffolve this Parliament." He arranged his plans with his ufual promptitude and completenefs. Before five o'clock in the morning of Feb. 3, he had defpatched the following note to the Lieutenant of the Tower.

Whitelock, 672.

Feb. 1658.

"Feb. 3, 1658.

Sir,—I defire you to feize *Major-General Harrifon, Mr. Carew, Portman,* and fuch as are eminent Fifth-Monarchy-Men, efpecially *Feake* and *Rogers.* Do it fpeedily and you fhall have a warrant after you have done."

Somers' State Tracts, vi. 482. Burton's Diary, iii. 448, 494.

The formal warrant was forwarded in the afternoon, and the arrefts were made before night.

"Oliver P.

Whereas we are given to underftand that feveral perfons have been of late endeavouring, inafmuch as in them lay, to afperfe, reproach, withftand, and fubvert the governors and government of this commonwealth, as it is now eftablifhed; and have been at work and fought by all means to difturb the public peace, raife feditions and commotions, feeking to difaffect and exafperate the hearts and fpirits of the people, fo that thereby they might bring the nation again into blood : And whereas fome of the contrivers and actors are made known unto us to be *Hugh Courtney, John Rogers,* and *John Portman,* who obfcure themfelves in and about our City of London : Thefe are, therefore, to will and require you to make, or caufe to be made, ftrict and diligent fearch for the faid perfons, and them and every of them to apprehend, or caufe to be apprehended and brought into our Tower of London ; and that you keep them there in fafe cuftody until you fhall receive our further order therein concerning them, every or any of them refpectively. And we do alfo hereby authorize and require you to feize or caufe to be feized all books, writings, letters, and papers, as fhall by you be found requifite ; as alfo all fuch weapons, arms, or any dangerous things, to them or any of them belonging, or that are in their cuftody. And for the better execution whereof, you are hereby authorized to break open any doors, locks, boxes, or bolts, trunks, chefts, boxes, or other places. And herein all our officers, as well civil and military, are required to be aiding and affifting you ; and for which this fhall be your Warrant.

Given at Whitehall, this third day of
February, 1658.

To *Sir John Barkftead,* Knt, lieutenant of our
Tower of London."

Having thus provided againft thofe who were moft likely to be dangerous, *Cromwell,* the next day (Feb. 4) went to the Houfe of Lords, fummoned the Houfe of Commons, and diffolved Parliament, the laft Parliament he was deftined to meet.

The following account of the ftate of affairs in London, at this time, appeared in a foreign newfpaper :—

" *Extract out of the printed news at Amfterdam.*

De Londres, le 21*m. Febr.* 165$\frac{7}{8}$.

Sur quelque difficultez furvenues entre le parliament et le fieur *Protecteur Cromwell,* de quoy on nous efcrit, que le mefme Parliament f'eft feparée avec un grand mefcontentment, ce que voyant ledit fieur Protecteur, il f'eft tenu maiftre abfolu de la

Tour, dans laquelle on efcrit que *Monfieur Rogers* a efté mis prifonier depuis peu de jours de quoy on ne parle point du fujet, et depuis l'on a imprimé quantité de libelles ou lettres, que l'on a diftribués entre les foldats et le peuple, lefquels ne tendent qu'à fédition. . . . .

. . . .

From Prefident Downing [to Thurloe].

I thought fit by the above extract to let you fee what news is printed at Amfterdam, which is publifhed there by a brother of the Secretary of the Spanifh Ambaffador laft here."

Thurloe, vi. 795.

In the mean time the London Government newfpapers were bufy writing down the prifoners.

"Feb. 4, 1658.—It is obfervable that *Major-General Harrifon* and his wife, *Mr. John Carew*, and *Major Courtney*, though formerly fuppofed to be perfons a ftory or two above ordinances,* being defirous to enter into the way of the re-baptized, have all of them fometime fince the beginning of this frofty weather, been dipped, notwithftanding the bitternefs of the feafon, and it is further obfervable that when the faid *Major Courtney* was apprehended (who, with *Mr. Rogers*, the minifter, &c, now ftand committed to the Tower) there were found in his lodgings feveral dangerous printed pamphlets, divers of which were enclofed in letters directed to feveral perfons in the country, being the very fame pamphlets with thofe which have lately been fcattered up and down among the foldiery and elfewhere."

"Tower of London, Feb. 10.

Merc. Pol., No. 402. See alfo Burton's Diary, iii. 449.

"What endeavours have of late been ufed by fome to pervert the foldiery and others from their due obedience is now apparent,

* Sir Henry Vane is fpoken of by Clarendon as "a man not to be defcribed by any character of religion, in which he had fwallowed fome of the fancies and extravagancies of every fect or faction, and even became (which cannot be expreffed by any other language than was peculiar to that time) *a man above ordinances*, unlimited or unreftrained by any rules or bounds prefcribed to other men, by reafon of his perfection."— *Clarendon*, viii. 373.

the feditious books and pamphlets which were fcattered up and down among the army and elfewhere being many of them taken in the lodgings of *Major Courtney* and *Mr. Rogers*, the minifter, who both ftand committed to this place, and bundles of the fame books they were preparing to fend abroad to infect the people there. But befides thefe two there is a third who likewife ftands committed here, and that is one *Mr. Portman*, formerly a fecretary in the fleet under *General Blake*, of the fame party with *Rogers* and *Courtney*, and every whit as high and peremptory. . .

Merc. Pol., No. 402.

More there are abroad of this gang.''

But two days afterwards the " Mercurius Politicus" qualifies the charge fo far as *Rogers* is concerned.

" Tower, Feb. 12, 1658.

Left the account from hence lately printed fhould feem to reflect upon *Mr. Rogers*, the minifter, prifoner here, as if the feditious books and pamphlets then mentioned had been found with him as well as *Mr. Courtney*, the truth is none of them were found with him, but he ftands committed here by fpecial warrant for other caufes."

Merc. Pol., No. 403.

Merc. Pol., No. 411.

Rogers was not detained long in the Tower. He and *Feake* were releafed on the 16th of April.

There was a notorious Fifth-Monarchy meeting-houfe in Swan Alley, Coleman Street. In this had been contrived *Venner's* abortive infurrection of April, 1657, and from this the Fifth-Monarchy-Men iffued armed in the later infurrection of 1661. On the firft

1658.

of April, 1658, the Lord Mayor and one of the Sheriffs proceeded to this meeting, and while they fat on horfeback outfide, the City Marfhall broke open the door and arrefted all who were within. " Old *Brother Cann*" was in the pulpit. The prifoners were fent to the Counter in the Poultry, and fome of them, *Cornet Day* amongft the reft, were examined afterwards before the Lord Mayor. Nothing could be drawn from *Cornet Day* " till he told them he would give it under his hand to prove *Oliver Cromwell* a juggler by his own confeffion, and fo much did he leave with the Mayor in a piece of paper, which was the great charge he was afterwards arraigned for." After three weeks he was brought before the feffions at the Old Bailey, and came before them with his hat on, carefully explaining that he wore it, not becaufe he was a Quaker, but becaufe he did not acknowledge the authority of the Court. It was of courfe pulled off. He then refufed to plead. "I require," he faid, "that my accufers come face to face, and I will anfwer to my charge : that is, prove *Oliver Crom-well* a juggler by his own confeffion." But they preffed him to plead guilty or not guilty. On the third and laft day of the trial "*Brother Rogers*" (who had been releafed from the Tower juft eight days before) "went with him and ftood by him at the bar." *Day* ftill perfifted that he could prove *O. C.* a juggler, and offered to call witneffes. The jury "found not the prifoner guilty of the indictment; but for two or three words which he had fpoken, and brought Scripture for it, that they did not quit him of; for he had confeffed them and ftood to the juftification of them." On this, *Day* was fentenced to a fine of 200 marks and fix months' imprifonment, after which he was to find bail. This account is taken from a pamphlet publifhed at the time.* *Ludlow*, writing probably from memory, gives a flightly different verfion of the ftory :—" Some perfons that ufed to meet in Coleman Street to deplore the apoftafy of the times, and particularly that of Whitehall, were feized by the Lord Mayor's officers, purfuant to *Cromwell's* orders, as they were coming out from their meeting-place. Amongft thefe was a Cornet whofe name was *Day*, and who being charged with faying that *Cromwell* was a Rogue and a Traitor, confeffed the words, and to juftify himfelf faid that *Cromwell* had affirmed in the prefence of himfelf and divers other officers, that if he did opprefs the confcientious, or betray the liberties of the people, or not take away Tithes by a certain time now paft, they fhould then have liberty to fay he was a Rogue and a Traitor. He moved therefore that he might be permitted to produce his witneffes who were then prefent to the particulars before mentioned. But the matter was fo ordered that he and fome

---

* "A narrative wherein is faithfully fet forth the fufferings of John Cann, Wentworth Day, &c, called as their Newfbook faith ' Fifth-Mo-narchy-Men,' publifhed by a friend to the prifoners and the Good Old Caufe they fuffer for."—Lond. 1658.

Ludlow, ii.
604-5.
Sept. 3, 1658.

others were fined and imprifoned for their pretended mifdemeanours."

The third of September was in *Oliver Cromwell's* opinion his
fortunate day, for on that day he had won the battles of Dunbar
and Worcefter. On the third of September, 1658, he died.
Richard Cromwell fucceeded to the Protectorate, and fummoned
a Parliament, which met on January 27, 1659.

At this time the ftruggle for power lay between three parties.
Firft were the fupporters of *Richard Cromwell*, including *Baxter*
with fome of the more eminent Prefbyterians. Many of thefe
men fupported the protectorate not becaufe they loved it, but becaufe they thought it the neareft approach to a monarchy which
the nation would endure ; when *Richard* failed them they tranf-
ferred their allegiance more or lefs openly to the King.

Secondly were thofe Republicans, Independents, and Fifth-
Monarchy-Men who ranged themfelves under *Sir Henry Vane.*
Vane's republicanifm was fincere and uncompromifing, and in
fpite of a religious enthufiafm which bordered upon infanity, he
was one of the moft able politicians of the day.

The third party was compofed of officers, and was called the
Wallingford Houfe* party, from the quarters of *General Fleetwood*, where it met. Thefe men were noify Republicans, and
great fticklers for the " Good Old Caufe," but as politicians they
were felfifh and incapable. The two latter parties, under *Vane*
and *Fleetwood* refpectively, coalefced for the overthrow of *Richard
Cromwell.* They forced him firft to diffolve Parliament, and then
to abdicate.

Rogers contributed his affiftance in his own peculiar department. " *Richard Cromwell*," fays *Baxter*, " was not fo formidable as his father, and therefore every one boldly fpurned at him.
The Fifth-Monarchy-Men followed *Sir Henry Vane*, and raifed
a great and violent clamorous party againft him among the fectaries in the city. *Rogers* and *Feake* and fuch like firebrands
preach them into fury and blow the coals."

Reliquiæ
Baxterianæ,
part i. p. 101.

After the abdication of *Richard* the Wallingford Houfe party
were for a fhort time fupreme, and recalled to power on their
own authority the remnant of the old Long Parliament. This

---

* Wallingford Houfe ftood on the fite of the prefent Admiralty.

confifted of thofe forty or fifty* members of that Parliament who had acquiefced in the *King's* execution, had eftablifhed a republic, and had clung to their feats in fpite of purgings, profcriptions, and feclufions, until they were violently expelled by *Oliver Cromwell.* They refumed their feats on the 7th of May, 1659, and imme-diately appointed a Committee of Safety and a Council of State. *Sir Henry Vane* was a member of both. *Rogers* was quite as much elated when they were reinftated as he had been formerly when they were expelled, and for his fervices on their behalf he claimed now as much credit as he had claimed formerly for his zeal againft them. In an addrefs " to the Parliament of the Commonwealth now returned to the great exercife of fupreme truft," he fays : " You are brought together to do your laft works by the fame hand that bleffed you to do your firft, neither have we been wanting in our poor prayers to the Almighty, and incef-fant endeavours with the Mighty, particularly the Army, Council of Officers, and others, to effect your return and the late turn."

May, 1659.

But a Parliament of Republicans and Regicides, reftored by the Army, and fupported by Fifth-Monarchy-Men, was very dif-tafteful to the Country generally, and quickly became equally diftafteful to the Army itfelf. It was particularly odious to the citizens of London, who had been fufficiently frightened by the plots and infurrections of the Fifth-Monarchy-Men in the time of *Oliver Cromwell,* and were now panic-ftricken when they found the leaders and allies of thefe men fitting, not only in Parliament, but in the Council of State and Committee of Safety. The fol-lowing " broadfide " bears witnefs to the fears of the citizens and to the notoriety of that ill-feeling which already exifted between the Parliament and the Army :—

" *An Alarum to the City and Soldiery.*

God grant they may not neglect it.

Gentlemen and Fellow-Soldiers,

At this time, when our ruin and deftruction is upon us, this

---

* Oldmixon fays 65; Echard and Rapin 40; Prynne fays 42, and gives their names, " there being 300 members more of the old Parliament yet living, befides thofe who are dead."—*Prynne's True and Perfect Nar-rative,* 1659, p. 35.

is no place for many words. The Fifth-Monarchy-Men are armed, officered, and every way in readinefs, upon the word given them, to furprife and fupprefs the Army, to fire the City, and to maffacre all confiderable people of all forts whom they fuf-pect averfe to what they impioufly defigned. *Feake* hath lately given them the Alarum in print. *Sir Henry Vane* is chief in the defign, and lately faid in confidence to a friend, This Army was every way to be fuppreffed, for otherwife they fhould not be per-mitted to fit long. The Parliament's new Militia and their lift-ings in feveral counties is in order to no other defign. If God gives you not eyes to fee the deftruction that is even at your doors, or if you fee it, [and] want hearts and courage to prevent it, it then feems the decree is gone out againft you. You may have your warning, and we have done our duties. Beware Tuef-day next. We fay BEWARE."

In the mean time *Rogers* was bufy fupporting the new Govern-ment, with his pen. *William Prynne*, the barrifter, who had been twice fentenced to ftand in the pillory and lofe his ears for libel, and on whom the fentence had been twice, fo far as it was pof-fible, executed, who had written more feditious libels, and had been confined in more prifons, than perhaps any other man in England, was now the boldeft writer on the Prefbyterian Royalift fide. He and *Rogers* foon came into collifion ; they both profeffed the moft profound veneration for the "Good Old Caufe," but they could by no means agree what the "Good Old Caufe" was. *Prynne* publifhed "The true Good Old Caufe rightly ftated, and the falfe uncafed." *Rogers* anfwered with "*Mr. Prynne's* Good Old Caufe ftated and ftunted ten years ago." *Prynne* rejoined with "The Republicans' and others' fpurious Good Old Caufe briefly and truly Anatomized." *Rogers* with "Διαπολιτεία, a Chriftian Concertation with *Mr. Prynne, Mr. Baxter, Mr. Har-rington*,* or an anfwer to *Mr. Prynne's* Perditory Anatomy," &c. &c. *Prynne* wrote "A brief neceffary Vindication . . . from the falfe malicious calumnies of . . . *Mr. John Rogers* and *Mr. Needham*." *Harrington* anfwered with "A Parallel of the Spirit of the People with the Spirit of *Mr. Rogers*," and the

---

* James Harrington, the Author of " Oceana."

controverfy feems to have ended with " *Mr. Harrington's* parallel unparalleled," from the pen of *Rogers.**

Prynne reduces all material differences between himfelf on one fide, and *Rogers* and *Needham* on the other, into fix diftinct queftions, of which it will be fufficient here to give but one. " The firft queftion between *John Rogers* and *Mr. Prynne* . . . is but this, whether the defence, maintenance of the true Proteftant religion, the King's royal perfon, authority, government, pofterity, the privileges and rights of Parliament, confifting of King, Lords, and Commons, the laws, ftatutes of the land, the liberty, property of the fubject, and peace, fafety of the kingdom, were the only true 'Good Old Caufe,' for which the Long Parliament and their Armies firft took up arms in 1642, and continued them till the Treaty with the King, 1648 (as *Mr. Prynne* afferts and proves, like a Lawyer, by punctual evidences, witneffes, votes, declarations) . . . or whether the erecting of a new Commonwealth and Parliament without a King and Houfe of Lords, and majority of the Commons' Houfe, upon the ruins of the late King, Kingdom, Parliament, fince 1648 to 1653, and the reviving of it May 7, 1659, by fome fwaying Army Officers and the far minor part of the old Commons' Houfe confederating with them . . . [were the Good Old Caufe], which *Rogers* endeavours to prove, like a Logician, without any evidence, witnefs, but his own *ipfe fcripfit* . . . making that which was never in being but fince 1648 to be the Good Old Caufe for whofe defence they took up arms in 1642." In fhort, it feems that the " Good Old Caufe," as interpreted by *Prynne*, meant a limited Monarchy, and the " Good Old Caufe," as interpreted by *Rogers*, meant a Republic.

Prynne's "Brief Neceffary Vindication," p. 2.

Befides the pamphlets elicited by his controverfy with *Prynne*, *Rogers* wrote many others about this time without his name, which can only be identified as his by fome accidental reference to them in his own or his opponents' writings. Such were " The plain cafe of the Commonweal near the defperate gulf of Common-

---

* About this time was publifhed " A vindication of that prudent and honourable Knight Sir Henry Vane from the lies and calumnies of Richard Baxter." Anthony à Wood attributes the authorfhip to Henry Stubbes, Stubbes quotes it as the work of Mr. Rogers, and Rogers quotes it as the work of " a godly Minifter."

woe." " A reviving word from the Quick and Dead, &c." " The
fad fuffering cafe of *Major-General Robert Overton*, prifoner in the
Ifle of Jerfey, ftated and prefented to the ferious confideration of
thofe who are either of a pious or public fpirit "—with probably
many others.*

The Council of State nominated by this Parliament feem to
have been very willing to recompenfe *Rogers* for his zeal on their
behalf, but the preferments they offered him fuggeft the fufpicion
that they found it at leaft as expedient to remove him as to reward him. The following is from " the letter-book " of the

In the Public
Record Office.

Council of State.

" *To the Commiffioners for governing, ordering, and fettling the
affairs of Ireland.*

GENTLEMEN,

July, 1659.

Mr. John Rogers being willing to go for Ireland to the end he
may apply himfelf to the preaching of the Gofpel there, and the
council being willing to give him their countenance in fuch an
undertaking, they have furnifhed him with fifty pounds out of
their contingencies, and have thought fit in an efpecial manner to
recommend him (as they hereby do) to your care, defiring that he

" Dd. to him."

may have like encouragement as heretofore in that work.

[Signed] A. JOHNSTON,

Prefident.

Whitehall, 19 July, 1659."

This miffion to Ireland had fmall attractions for *Rogers*, but
he was quite aware that the tide which was then in his favour
might turn againft him, and clearly thought that he had under-
gone already a fufficiency of fuffering for the " Good Old Caufe."
" Seeing," he fays to the Council, " I am not worthy to live in
my own nation, I am glad that you are fo worthy as to fend me

---

* " What fcurrilous books have been contrived by Needham, Good-
win, Milton, Rogers, and fuch like Billingfgate authors is not unknown to
any."—*Hiftory of the Wicked Plots and Confpiracies of our Pretended
Saints.* By Henry Foulis. 1674. 2nd Ed. p. 24.

into another. I would fay with Chryfoftom, ' Well, the earth is the Lord's and the fulnefs thereof,' ' et nil nifi peccatum timeo.' Yea, I would anfwer too with Ariftotle, when afked why he left Athens, ' ὅτι οὐ βούλεται 'Αθηναίους δὶς ἐξαμαρτεῖν εἰς φιλοσοφίαν,' I would not have the Athenians to fin twice againft philofophy, nor would I that our honourable worthies fhould run the fecond time upon the fame rock or danger of ruin." He figns himfelf—

" Your fervant to my utmoft power,
 whether in this nation or any other, for
  the Caufe of Chrift and his Commonwealth,

        Jᴏʜɴ Rᴏɢᴇʀs ;"

and dates " from my houfe in Alderfgate Street, 14th of 5th month, called July, in the firft year of our fecond deliverance or return to the liberty of a free ftate."

But this exile to Ireland was not actually inflicted upon him. Before he had fet out news reached London of the Royalift infurrection in Chefhire, under *Sir George Booth.* The Council of State met inftantly and iffued orders for raifing troops, commiffioning officers, and defpatching an army to the fcene of action. Among the regiments then officered, was that of *Col. Charles Fairfax,* and among the names of its commiffioned officers appears that of " *John Rogers,* Chaplain." In fact, none were at this time more zealous for the Government, than the party to which *Rogers* was attached. The Prefbyterian gentry had contrived *Sir George Booth's* infurrection, and " the Prefbyterian minifters," fays *Whitelock,* " did labour to further it." On the other hand, " the Congregational Churches defired leave to raife three regiments for the Parliament, and had their willing confent thereto."

General Lambert was one of thofe who figned the Order by which *Rogers* was appointed to a regimental chaplaincy, and on the fame day (Auguft 6) he marched out of London at the head of the troops againft the enemy. In lefs than a fortnight the Royalifts were utterly routed and difperfed, and their leaders taken prifoners. *Rogers* probably joined his regiment, for fhortly afterwards he fpeaks of having been " called afide of a fudden " into another part of the harveft, and in September he pleads " the late rebellion " as an apology for a delay of five weeks in the publication of an anfwer to *Prynne.*

Auguft, 1659.

Minute Book of the Committee of Safety, in the Public Record Office.
Whitelock, p. 682.

A lampoon of this date, written by a Royalift in the ftyle of the Seven Champions of Chriftendom, defcribes how *Sir Lambert* marched againft the loyal knight as far as the foreft of Northimbria, and how before *Sir Lambert* departed out of the City of London, the Seer Feko and the Seer Rogero, high priefts of the temples of the idols, came unto him and declared unto him their vifions.

Sept. 1659.

On his return *Rogers* procured the following order from the Council of State,

"Monday, 19, September, 1659.

" Rogers difpenfed with." From " Fair Order Book of Council of State," in the Public Record Office. October, 1659.

Ordered—That *Mr. Rogers*, the minifter, be difpenfed with from going to Ireland this winter, according to his defire to that purpofe fignified to the Council."

And about three weeks afterwards he was appointed lecturer at Shrewfbury. The date of this appointment is remarkable.

The fuppreffion of *Sir George Booth's* infurrection by *General Lambert* led to increafed jealoufy between the Parliament and the officers of the army, the latter prefumed more and more upon their fervices, while the Parliament grew more and more jealous of interference, until a trial of ftrength became inevitable. On October the 12th (1659), Parliament ordered the difmiffal from their commands of *Lambert*, *Defborough*, and feven or eight others of the principal officers of the army. On the next day, October 13, thofe regiments upon which Parliament could rely, marched out of their quarters in Scotland Yard and took poffeffion of Weftminfter Hall, with the Palace Yard and avenues adjoining. On the other hand, *Lambert*, with the regiments on which he relied, marched out alfo and took poffeffion of Weftminfter Abbey and the fpace around it. During the whole day the foldiers of the oppofite factions ftood face to face in Weftminfter, " expecting orders to fall on." The fitting of Parliament was interrupted, and the fpeaker turned back in his coach, but the Council of State fat in Whitehall, and as the leaders of both factions were members a " long and fmart debate" enfued. It was finally arranged that the Parliament fhould be diffolved ; and the Council of officers undertook to provide for the prefervation of the peace, to frame a conftitution, to fummon a Parliament, and " fo to fettle all things." When this was agreed upon the foldiers were ordered to withdraw to their quarters, and as *Lambert* and his confederates had accomplifhed all that they had defired, the order was obeyed, and the foldiers withdrew accordingly.

The following minutes in the order book of the Council of State are the whole official records of what paffed there in the morning of this eventful day. It does not appear how *Rogers* fucceeded in fecuring for himfelf fuch an undue proportion of attention.

" Thurfday, 13 of October, 1659—morning.

Lord Whitelock, *Prefident.*

Sir James Harrington, Lord Lambert, Mr. Nevill, Major Salwey, Col. Downes, Col. Dixwell, Lord Warefton, Lord Fleetwood, Sir Henry Vane, Col. Thomfon, Mr. Reynolds, Major-General Difbrow, Mr. Challoner, Col. Berry.

Ordered—That the *Lord Whitelock* be Prefident of the council for the prefent, and that he be defired to take the chair accordingly.

That all the forces of the army which are now ftanding at their arms and all other forces raifed by authority of Parliament, and now upon their march, or in arms, be and are hereby required forthwith to repair to their feveral and refpective quarters until further orders from the Council.

Paffed nemine contradicente.

That this order of the Council be forthwith communicated to the commanders of the faid forces by the clerks or meffengers of the council, that the fame may be obferved accordingly.

That the Lord Prefident of the Council do fign the aforefaid orders.

That the Council do adjourn for one hour.

Ordered—upon the petition of divers well-affected perfons in and about Shrewfbury that *Mr. John Rogers* be and hereby is appointed a public preacher in Shrewfbury, and that for the exercife of his miniftry and conveniency of the auditory, he have the free ufe of the public meeting place called St. Julian, and other adjacent vacant places mentioned in the petition, as he fhall have opportunity. And for the encouragement of the faid *Mr. Rogers* it is further ordered that the augmentation with the arrears formerly granted to *Mr. Burnet* or any other lecturer or minifter in

St. Julian's, together with fo much more as will make it one hundred and fifty pounds by the year, being the allowance granted to the feveral lecturers in the city of Hereford, be paid unto the faid *Mr. John Rogers.* And the truftees for the maintenance of minifters, and augmentations are to take fpecial care that the fame be paid accordingly."

The Council of Officers nominated a committee of ten from the Council of State to carry on the Government. Afterwards they appointed a Committee of Safety, confifting of twenty-three perfons. *Sir Henry Vane* was a member of both.

But this Government fatisfied nobody. It was not even fupported by the army itfelf, and very foon fell to pieces. On the 26th of December the foldiers brought back with acclamations the very Parliament which they had diffolved ten weeks before.

In January, 1660, *Sir Henry Vane* was ordered to repair to his houfe at Raby and remain there ; and in February *Monk* reached London and reftored the fecluded members to their places in Parliament. This threw the majority into the hands of the Royalifts, and was the beginning of the end. Parliament was diffolved, and and on May 1 the new Parliament voted that the Government is and ought to be by King, Lords, and Commons, and at the fame time received letters from and voted humble addreffes to *Charles II.*

Whether *Rogers* ever reached Shrewfbury is uncertain. He can be traced for a few years after the Reftoration as a private perfon, but his public career as preacher and politician ended with the Commonwealth, and little now remains to be done but to record a few incidents of the life or of the death of thofe in whom, for various reafons and in different degrees, he had been chiefly interefted.

His father *Nehemiah*, to whom he never alludes without due reverence, lived long enough to fee the bonfires blazing for the Reftoration of Monarchy, and to preach once afterwards, but not long enough to fee the King return, or to be himfelf reftored to the rectory in London and the ftall at Ely, which he had forfeited for his loyalty eighteen years before. On his way home from morning fervice at Doddinghurft he fell fpeechlefs to the ground in the churchyard, and died before the hour of afternoon fervice. He was buried May 9th, 1660, the very day *Charles the Second* was publicly proclaimed in London.

The Reftoration, which drove *John Rogers* into obfcurity, fent his more eminent friends, patrons, and accomplices to the fcaffold. The chief leaders of the Fifth-Monarchy-Men among the laity were *Harrifon, Carew,* and latterly *Sir Henry Vane.* All three were executed. *Harrifon* was the firft to fuffer, as he had been alfo the firft arrefted. He was tried and convicted as a Regicide, and was executed at Charing Crofs with all the ufual barbarities. While he was being drawn to the gallows on a fledge, fome one in derifion called to him, "Where is your Good Old Caufe?" He with a cheerful fmile clapped his hand on his breaft, and faid, "Here it is, and I am going to feal it with my blood." *Carew* fuffered two days afterwards with equal courage. *Vane* was kept in prifon and fufpenfe for two years, and was then tried and executed.

State Trials, ii. 406.

The proceedings againft the Regicides and their accomplices difpofed alfo of *Colonel Jones* and *Miles Corbet,* who had befriended *Rogers* in Ireland, of *Colonel Okey,* his fellow-fufferer under *Cromwell,* and of *Colonel Barkftead,* his gaoler in the Tower. They were all executed. *Ludlow,* another of his patrons in Ireland, *Colonel Hewfon,* whofe experiences he records in "Bethfhemefh," *Mr. Holland,* the fpokefman of "the Locomotive" Commiffion at Windfor Caftle, and his unkind kinfman *Serjeant Dendy,* were attainted for their refpective fhares in the King's trial, but efcaped abroad and died peaceably in their beds.

The Fifth-Monarchy-Men's infurrection of 1661 clofed the career of many of his affociates of the humbler fort. This infurrection was concerted in the notorious old meeting-houfe of Coleman Street. The Government had received intelligence of its defigns and had arrefted moft of its ringleaders, including *Cornet Day, Quartermafter-General Courtney, Colonel Overton,* and *Major Allen.* But they omitted to arreft *Venner,* and on Sunday evening, January 6, 1661, he and about fixty of his followers fallied out of their meeting-houfe in open infurrection. They marched firft to *Rogers'* old quarters of St. Thomas Apoftle's "to call in more of their party, thence into Whitecrofs Street, coming into the City again at Cripplegate, and going out again at Alderfgate, declaring for King Jefus, and killing feveral people. *Sir Richard Brown,* then Lord Mayor, having notice of their defperate defign, got together fome files of the Train Bands, who were at firft repulfed by *Venner's* party, who fought with an incredible

Infurrection of the Fi.th-Monarchy-Men.

Their horrid enthufiafm.

impulfe of infatuation, as making themfelves to believe that one fhould chafe a thoufand and no weapon formed againft them fhould profper. But finding themfelves harder preffed, and being told the Life Guards were coming down upon them, they retired, and under cover of the dark evening got into Caen Wood, betwixt Highgate and Hampftead : and a party of horfe and foot being fent thither to hunt them out, on Wednefday morning very early this villanous crew returned again to London, dividing themfelves into two parties, one whereof appeared about Leadenhall, and from thence marched into Little Eaftcheap, where they fought obfti-nately, but were difperfed by the Train Bands. *Venner* with another party came to the Lord Mayor's houfe, thinking to have furprifed him, but miffing their aim they marched into Wood Street, where they were met by *Colonel Corbet* and about twenty horfe. *Corbet* and nine only of his horfemen charged through the rebels and broke them, and the Trained Band foot fell in and

Defeated.

purfued them. They fought with a courage more brutifh and devilifh than was ever feen in men, and if their numbers had been equal to their fpirits they would have overturned the city, and the nation, and the world. *Venner*, who was much wounded before he could be taken, was foon after, with about fixteen of his crew, arraigned at the Old Bailey, and being all found guilty, they were executed in feveral places in London, moft of them raving and threatening judgment, and calling down vengeance upon the King, the Judges, and the City." *Venner* himfelf was hanged oppofite the Coleman Street meeting-houfe.

Condemned
and executed.

Bifhop
Kennet's
Complete
Hiftory of
England, iii.
225.

The feverities exercifed on the Fifth-Monarchy-Men after this infurrection were fufficient to reprefs, but not to extinguifh them. For years their confpiracies were a continual fource of uneafinefs to the Government, and moft of thofe who confpired under *Cromwell* re-appear as confpirators under *Charles II*. Brother *Feake* clung to his old trade, and paffed his life either in hiding in and round London, in ftealthy journeys about the country, or in prifon. *Quartermafter-General Courtney*, after his arreft in January, 1661, was detained in the Gatehoufe until the following June, when he was releafed on giving fecurity in £1,000 that he would go abroad within fifteen days and not return. But five years afterwards, while the plague was raging in London, the Government received intelligence that a wide-fpread confpiracy was on foot, that the head of this ferpent lay between Edmonton and Ware, in retired

places in Epping Foreſt and Enfield Chaſe, and in London, that
" thoſe two pernicious fellows *Hugh Courtney* and *Walter Thim-
bleton*," had been ſeen lurking about the neighbourhood on foot,
and that unleſs they were inquired after ſerious miſchief would
enſue. *Courtney* ſeems to have eſcaped. If arreſted, he would
probably have ſhared the fate of another of *Rogers'* army friends,
Colonel Rathbone. In April, 1666, two or three months after
Courtney's viſit to England, *Colonel Rathbone* and ſeven others were
indicted at the Old Bailey for conſpiring the death of his Majeſty
and the overthrow of the Government, and "then to have declared for an equal diviſion of land, &c." It is ſaid "the evidence
againſt theſe perſons was very full and clear." At any rate, they
were found guilty of high treaſon on the 26th of April, and were
executed at Tyburn on the 30th.

    So far as the Reſtoration influenced their fortunes, *Rogers'* old
Preſbyterian antagoniſts, the lawyer *Maynard* and the preacher
Crofton, were to a certain extent repreſentative men in their re-
ſpective profeſſions, for the Reſtoration brought promotion to the
one and ruin to the other. *Maynard* was courted and honoured
by the Government of *Charles II*, and lived to compliment *William III.* on the Revolution. He was M.P. for Plymouth as late
as 1689, and died at the age of eighty-eight in the next year. On
the other hand, that "Jeſuitical Preſbyter," *Zachary Crofton*,
after having been ſent to the Tower ſhortly before the Reſtoration for preaching in favour of Monarchy, was ſent there again
ſhortly after the Reſtoration for preaching againſt Epiſcopacy.
In 1662 he was ejected from his living of St. Botolph, Aldgate,
"left preaching," and became a cheeſe factor in Cheſhire. But he
made himſelf ſo obnoxious to the authorities, civil and eccleſiaſtical, that he was arreſted again and impriſoned in Cheſter Caſtle.
On his releaſe he took a farm in Bedfordſhire, and afterwards a
ſchool in his old pariſh of St. Botolph, Aldgate. There he died
and was buried in 1672, the rector of the pariſh preaching at the
funeral.

    To return to *John Rogers.* After the Reſtoration the free
cities of Holland became cities of refuge for thoſe Republicans
whoſe names had become too notorious in England, and *Rogers*
emigrated with the reſt. In his early life, and in obedience to his
father, who had conſtantly oppoſed his inclination to the miniſtry, he had entered upon the ſtudy of medicine at Cambridge, but

In a letter
dated Jan. 8,
1666, now in
the Public
Record Office.

See page 81.

London
Gazette, April
26 and 30,
1666.

Calamy's
Memorial, i.
103.
" An Informa-
tion from Lord
Brereton," in
Record Office.

Smith's
Obituary, p. 97
(Camden
Society).

he was fwept away by the excitement of the times, and " fell to preaching" before he was nineteen. He was now thirty-three, with a wife and family, but without home, without property, without profeffional means of fubfiftence, and he returned to the calling for which he had been originally intended. The Univerfities of Leyden and Utrecht were famous then for their fchools of medicine ; he ftudied at both, and took the degree of Doctor of Medicine at Utrecht, in October, 1662, publifhing at the fame time fome inaugural differtations in Latin. There was the ufual colony of Englifh refugees in Utrecht, fome of whom appear to have fuffered by the Act againft non-conformity, which came into operation on " Black Bartholomew's-day," 1662. *Rogers* appended to his treatifes feveral of the congratulatory addreffes* he received from thefe men. He muft have returned to England fhortly after this time, for in the fame year (1662) he is defcribed as " *Rogers* of Bermondfey," in the Herald's vifitation of Surrey.

In the margin:
In the Herald's College.

In 1663 his exiftence is attefted to only by an entry in *Secretary Williamfon's* " Spy-book," a lift of difaffected and dangerous perfons who were watched by the Secretary's fpies. " —— *Rogers*, paftor of a church—dwells in St. Mary Madlen's parifh, practizeth phyfic, and meets often at his own houfe."

In the margin:
In the Public Record Office.

In 1664 he was admitted to an " ad eundem" degree of Doctor of Medicine at Oxford. *Anthony Wood* defcribes him only as the fon of *Nehemiah Rogers*, of Duddinghurft. Keen-eyed as *Wood* was where a Puritan or fectary was concerned, he failed apparently to identify the phyfician of Utrecht whofe " ad eundem " degree he regifters in his Fafti, with the " bufy," " pragmatical," " impudent," and " notorious Fifth-Monarchy-Man," whofe biography he had fketched in his Athenæ.

In the margin:
Fafti, ii. 159.

Athenæ, ii. 594, ed. 1721.

---

* Plaufus in honorem ac meritum inaugurale Doctiffimi, generis ac morum fplendore Ornatiffimi, Digniffimi D. Johannis Rogerfii, Anglo-Britanni, Cantabrigienfis, datus cum in celeberrimâ Trajecti juxta Rhenum Academia fummis fummo merito in Arte Medica titulis, honoribus, dignitatibus, auctus, ac Apollinari Choro confcriptus triumphabat, Oct. 17, 1662.

> Quis te Naturæ miris præfecerit aris,
> Qui modo de cælo fulmina facra dabas,
> Ecce alio nunc igne cales, Phœbique Sacerdos
> Non metuit pœnas, Bartholomæe, tuas, &c. &c.

In 1665 *Rogers* publifhed a fecond edition of his medical treatifes, which with amazing inconfiftency he dedicates to *Clarendon*.*
The great plague of London broke out in the fame year, and certain
advertifements, in the "Intelligencer" and "News," of "Alexi-
terial and Antipeftilential medicine, an admirable and experimented
prefervative from the plague," "made up by the order of *J. R.,
M.D.*," carry with them, in their phrafeology and pretenfions,
ftrong internal evidence of his pen. The faſt that one fo bent on
notoriety fhould have left behind him no trace even of his exiftence after that date, fuggefts the conjecture that he muft have
perifhed in 1665. But in truth the date of his death is abfolutely
uncertain.

July 31,
Auguft 3,1665.

The following extraſt is from the Vifitation of Surrey :—

"Rogers of Bermondsey.

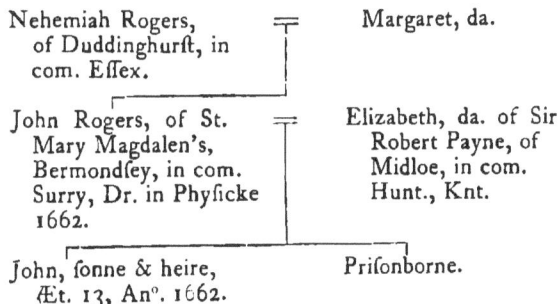

Nehemiah Rogers, ═══   Margaret, da.
of Duddinghurft, in
com. Effex.

John Rogers, of St. ═══ Elizabeth, da. of Sir
Mary Magdalen's,   Robert Payne, of
Bermondfey, in com.   Midloe, in com.
Surry, Dr. in Phyficke   Hunt., Knt.
1662.

John, fonne & heire,   Prifonborne.
Æt. 13, Anº. 1662.

[Signed]   John Rogers."

John, the eldeft fon, fettled at Plymouth, where he acquired
a large fortune as a merchant. He was elected M.P. for that
borough and created a Baronet in 1698, was High Sheriff of
Devon in 1701, and died in 1710.

Prifonborn, the younger fon, is faid by his nephew, the fecond
Sir John Rogers, to "have been chriftened by that name on

---

* This edition is dated "E Mufeolo meo in fuburb. Londinenfi atque
in Calend. Mart. anno τῆς Χριστογονίας, 1664," i. e. March 1, 1665.

account of his being born at Carifbrook Caftle, in the Ifle of
Wight, while his mother abode there with her hufband, then
confined a prifoner in the faid Caftle by *Oliver Cromwell*," " who,
the faid *Prifonborn*, after the Reftoration bore a commiffion
in his Majefty's army, and was killed in a duel in France."
Prifonborn was more probably " the poor prifonborn babe " born
at Windfor in 1655.

See page 245.

Two other children, *Peter* and *Paul*, died in Lambeth Prifon.

FINIS.

A Lift of Authorities quoted or referred to in this Book.

HE Works of John Rogers, viz.—
"To his Excellency the Lord General Cromwell: A few Propofals Relating to Civil Government," &c, a fingle fheet, folio, April 25, 1653.
"Ohel, or Bethfhemefh, a Tabernacle for the Sun," London, fmall quarto, 1653.
"Sagrir," 1653, fmall quarto.
"To his Highnefs Lord General Cromwell, the humble Cautionary Propofals of John Rogers," December 21, 1653, fingle fheet, folio.
"Mene, Tekel, Perez," 1654, 14 pages, fmall quarto.
. "Jegar Sahadutha," or "a Heart Appeal," with the Introduction to "Prifon-born Morning Beams," one vol. fmall quarto.
"Διαπολιτεία, a Chriftian Concertation with Mr. Prynne, Mr. Baxter, Mr. Harrington, for the True Caufe of the Commonwealth," &c. London, 1659.
"Difputatio Medica Inauguralis," Utrecht, 1662.
"Analecta Inauguralia, five Difceptationes Medicæ," London, 1663.
Works of Nehemiah Rogers—
"The Parable of the Prodigal Son," 1632.
"The Faft Friend," 1658.
"The Figlefs Fig-tree," 1659.
Contemporary Newfpapers, viz.—
"Mercurius Politicus," 1651-1658.
"Several Proceedings in State Affairs," 1654-1655.
"Perfect Proceedings," 1655.
"Perfect Diurnal," 1653.
"Weekly Intelligencer," 1653, 1665.
"London Gazette," 1666.
"Mercurius Rufticus, the Country's Complaint, recounting the fad events of this unparalleled war," 1647.

" Querela Cantabrigienfis," 1647.
Sprigge's " Anglia Rediviva," 1647.
" A Teftimony to the Truth of Jefus Chrift and to our Solemn League and Covenant . . . fubfcribed by the Minifters of Chrift within the province of London, Dec. 14, &c, 1647." London, 1648.
" Bethfhemefh Clouded," by Zachary Crofton, 1653.
" An exaft Relation of the Proceedings and Tranfaftions of the late Parliament, by a Member," 1654. Reprinted in Somers' Trafts.
" An Olive Branch, or fome Peaceable Confiderations to the Chriftian Meeting at Chrift Church in London, Jan. 9, 1654," by William Erberry.
" The Faithful Narrative of the late Teftimony and Demand made to Oliver Cromwell and his powers," &c, 1654.
" The Old Leaven purged out, or the Apoftafy of this day further opened," &c, 1658.
" A Narrative wherein is faithfully fet forth the Sufferings of John Cann, Wentworth Day, John Clark . . . and George Strange, called, as their Newfbook faith, Fifth-Monarchy-Men ; that is, how eight of them were taken in Coleman Street, month fecond (called April), day firft, 1658, as they were in the folemn worfhip of God, and by the Lord Mayor fent prifoners to the Counter in the Poultry ; alfo of the arraignment of Wentworth Day and John Clark in the Old Bailey . . . publifhed by a friend to the prifoners and the Good Old Caufe they fuffer for. Afts v. 38, 39. London, printed in the year 1658."
" An Alarum to the City and Soldiery," 1659.
" A brief neceffary Vindication of the Old and New fecluded Members from the falfe malicious Calumnies, and of the Fundamental Rights, Liberties, Privileges, Government, Interefts, of the Freemen, Parliaments, People of England, from the late avowed Subverfions—
     1. Of John Rogers, in his unchriftian Concertation with Mr. Prynne and others.
     2. Of M : Nedham, in his ' Intereft will not lie ' . . . by William Prynne, of Swainfwick, Efq., a Bencher of Lincoln's Inn."
Heath's " Flagellum, or the Life and Death, Birth and Burial of O. Cromwell, the late Ufurper . . . the fourth Edition," 1669.
Foulis' " Hiftory of the Wicked Plots and Confpiracies of our Pretended Saints," fecond Edition, 1674.
" A Colleftion of all the Public Orders, Ordinances, and Declarations of both Houfes of Parliament, from the 9th of March, 1642, until December, 1646." 1646.
Scobell's " Afts and Ordinances," 1658.
Thurloe's State Papers, 1742.
Somers' Trafts, 1809-1815.
Rufhworth's Hiftorical Colleftions, 1659-1701.
Whitelock's Memorials, 1732.
Clarendon's Hiftory of the Rebellion, 1826.
Wood's Athenæ Oxon. and Fafti, 1721.
Walker's Sufferings of the Clergy, 1714.
State Trials (folio), 1776.
Hiftory of England during the reigns of the Stuarts (Oldmixon), 1730.

Complete Hiftory of England (Bifhop Kennet), 1706.
Newcourt's Repertorium, 1708.
Reliquiæ Baxterianæ, by Sylvefter.
Calamy's Memorial, 1802-1803.
Ludlow's Memoirs, 1698.
Cleveland's Poems, 1687.
"The Hiftorian's Guide, or Britain's Remembrancer, being a Summary of all
   the actions, exploits, fieges, battles . . . and whatever elfe is worthy
   notice that hath happened in his Majefty's dominions from the year 1600
   to 1688, fhewing the year, month, and day of the month in which each
   action was done." London, 1688.
South's Sermons.
Laud's Works—Anglo-Catholic Library, 1847-1860.
Autobiography of Sir John Bramfton (Camden Society).
Smith's Obituary (Camden Society).
Burton's Diary, 1828.
Brooks' Lives of the Puritans, 1813.
Reid's Hiftory of the Prefbyterian Church in Ireland, 1834-1853.
Collier's Church Hiftory, 1845.
Godwin's Hiftory of the Commonwealth, 1828.
Mrs. Hutchinfon's Memoirs of the Life of Colonel Hutchinfon.   Eighth
   Edition, 1854.
Forfter's Life of Oliver Cromwell, 1839.
Carlyle's Oliver Cromwell.   Firft Edition, 1845.
Macaulay's Hiftory of England, 1858.

MANUSCRIPTS.

Entry, Order, and Letter Books of Councils of State and Committees of Safety,
   1655-1659, in the Public Record Office.
" Alphabet Book—names of perfons in England, what they are, their religion,
   politics, &c, or a kind of Spybook," 1663, in the Public Record Office.
" A Letter of — Eyton to Francis Manley, enclofed by him to Williamfon,"
   Jan. 8, 1666, in the Public Record Office.
An Information from Lord Brereton, Oct. 26, 1663, in the Public Record Office.
" Regifter of all the Church Livings in the Counties of . . . Effex . . .
   with an account of their actual Income, the names of the Patrons and In-
   cumbents, and the particular character of many of the latter."   Without
   date, but apparently made in the latter part of 1652 and the earlier part of
   1653.   Lanfdowne MSS. 459.
Herald's Vifitation of Surrey, 1662, in Herald's College.
Parochial Regifter of St. Thomas Apoftle's, London.

INDEX.

Index.

CHISWICK PRESS :—PRINTED BY WHITTINGHAM AND WILKINS, TOOKS COURT, CHANCERY LANE.